DATE DUE

DEMCO 38-296

Contemporary Empirical
Political Theory

Contemporary Empirical Political Theory

EDITED BY

Kristen Renwick Monroe

UNIVERSITY OF CALIFORNIA PRESS

Berkeley   Los Angeles   London

University of California Press
Berkeley and Los Angeles, California

University of California Press, Ltd.
London, England

© 1997 by
The Regents of the University of California

Library of Congress Cataloging-in-Publication Data

Contemporary empirical political theory / edited by Kristen Renwick
   Monroe
      p.   cm.
   Includes bibliographical references and index.
   ISBN 0-520-20725-4 (cloth : alk. paper). — ISBN 0-520-20726-2
(pbk. : alk. paper)
      1. Political science—History—19th century.   2. Political
science—History—20th century.   3. Political science.
4. Empiricism.   I. Monroe, Kristen R., 1946–   .
JA83.C6366   1998
320—dc21   97-1113
                                                                CIP

Printed in the United States of America
    9   8   7   6   5   4   3   2   1

The paper used in this publication meets the minimum requirements of American
National Standards for Information Sciences—Permanence of Paper for Printed Library
Materials, ANSI Z39.48–1984.

*It is a pleasure to dedicate this volume to David Easton,
a dear friend and colleague. This volume attempts, in a
small way, to honor David's contribution to political science
through an assessment of recent developments in empirical
political theory. I have chosen this format rather than the
more traditional collection of essays in praise of the
recipient's work for several reasons. First, David is a
remarkably modest individual, uncomfortable with effusive
praise. Second, David remains the consummate scholar, more
interested in future ideas than in past glories. Finally,
David's is a wide-ranging intellect, which enjoys dialogue
with opposing ideas. David loves the give and take of
intellectual exchange. He thrives on intense discussion with
no intellectual holds barred. And he cares deeply about the
state of political science as a discipline. How better to honor
him than to bring together scholars of vastly different
intellectual orientations to share their assessment of our
common enterprise?*

CONTENTS

INTRODUCTION

Empirical Political Theory
Different Perspectives on a Common Enterprise

Kristen Renwick Monroe

Is there a human nature on which we can construct scientific theories of
political life? What is the role of culture in shaping any such nature, in
molding our political potential? How objective and value-free can we be in
analyzing and constructing our political theories? When we disagree over
the content or universality of our political theories, in what language of
discourse do we construct our debates, and what methods do we utilize to
resolve our disagreements?

These are only some of the questions raised by the authors who contributed to this volume, which assesses recent developments in empirical political theory. By empirical political theory I mean theory that makes statements which ultimately can be tested by reference to the empirical world;
by contrast, in philosophical theory assumptions and, at times, conclusions
are warranted by arguments or formally adopted test criteria. The richness
of empirical political theory is illustrated by the contributors to this volume,
who represent different theoretical approaches and orientations to political
science, from cultural and rational choice theory to behavioralism and
postmodernism. They include four past presidents of the American Political Science Association and one past president of the International Political
Science Association. Some authors worked closely together to found movements and then parted ways as the particular approach developed and
changed in response to criticism. The discussions of their intellectual and
personal battles convey some of the excitement and intensity that have ani-
mated conversations about the future of political science as a discipline.
The chapters provide not just personal insights on the authors' own intellectual development but also their more reflective, mature assessments of
what lasting contributions the movements they helped pioneer have made

to a discipline still searching for its central core, its unifying theoretical framework, and a widely accepted methodological base.

The volume is intended as an introduction for the serious student of political science, an introduction that presents multiple views of the major debates and recent movements within the discipline. It fills an important gap in the literature by focusing on the point at which traditional political theory courses stop and courses that offer substantive discussions of politics begin. As such, it can be used in upper-division undergraduate courses on the scope and method of the discipline as well as in introductory courses for incoming graduate students. Because it provides both a history of the discipline and alternative views on recent trends in political science, it should prove an invaluable source for students preparing for doctoral qualifying examinations. The volume also should have general scholarly appeal, however, because of the diverse orientations of its contributors and the extent to which it weaves substantive discussions of particular theoretical approaches with a focus on our common enterprise. By assessing the most recent trends, where we have traveled intellectually as a discipline, and what remains of lasting significance in the various theoretical approaches that have engulfed the profession, the discussions in this volume should suggest fruitful paths to pursue in empirical political theory as the discipline of political science enters its second century.

ORGANIZATION AND OVERVIEW OF BOOK

The contributors were selected to reflect different perspectives in political science. Each author was asked to write a chapter assessing recent work in empirical political theory, suggesting which theories had made significant contributions and what major issues needed to be discussed.[1] Because of the general nature of the assignment and because the chapters touch on so many important aspects of political science, there are many different ways to organize and read these essays. Different readers will naturally find groupings other than the ones I propose. For example, the chapters by Easton, Almond, Riker, and Gunnell can be read as providing different historical perspectives on developments in political science. The chapters by Grofman, Edelman, Hartsock, and Laponce reflect quite disparate ways of thinking about political science as a discipline. When we ask whether we can develop a science of politics and construct a universal theory of political life, we can group Easton, Almond, Riker, and Hardin together as authors who respond affirmatively, whereas the Zuckerts and Euben argue against such an enterprise. My chapter and the chapter by Wendt and Shapiro can be read as leaning toward such a possibility but expressing some qualifications. When we sort the chapters by their assessments of the contributions of existing theories in political science we find multiple groupings. Riker and Hardin like rational choice theory. Monroe and Edelman emphasize the importance of psychological factors, and Almond stresses the role of culture. Lowi and Harpham offer a fresh view of state theory. Easton, Gunnell, and Wendt and Shapiro offer different perspectives on postbehavioralism. Hartsock presents the view from feminist theory, Laponce from political geography; the Zuckerts and Euben articulate some of the concerns of both the postmoderns and the ancients.

I encourage readers to group the chapters as best fits their needs. For purposes of presentation, however, I have grouped the chapters into the following four parts. The first part locates empirical political theory in the intellectual landscape of the discipline. Part 2 presents alternative views of political science as a discipline. Part 3 considers the possibility of constructing a value-free scientific theory of politics. And Part 4 assesses the contributions of some of the most important theories in political science: rational choice theory, state theory, cultural theory, feminist theory, and identity theory.

Historical Overview

Easton opens the volume by reviewing the various stages through which political science has passed since it became a distinguishable and separate discipline in the nineteenth century. His discussion essentially argues that each stage has solved certain problems and generated new ones of its own. Easton focuses on the postbehavioral phase of the last quarter-century. During this time, political scientists have begun to question whether our discipline has lost its central core and sense of purpose. The prevalent complaint, that we have become fragmented and no longer are able to speak meaningfully with each other, has been accompanied by the withdrawal of students of politics into highly specialized bailiwicks.[2] This has led to the exploration of many different kinds of methods, from the continuation of the rigid positivism that characterized the behavioral phase to certain postmodernist strands' virtual rejection of any objective methodology. But, Easton argues, we lack consensus about the methodologies that will succeed the original positivist view of scientific method.[3] General empirical theory, which once offered the hope of providing a unifying framework for the discipline as a whole, has been neglected in the face of pressing social issues and the narrowing focus of the disparate parts in a fragmented discipline. Will the discussions of the next decades bring the coherence and focus that the behavioral movement itself once provided? Easton argues in favor of this goal, and his chapter sketches an important route toward that end.

John G. Gunnell's chapter complements Easton's and provides critical intellectual history. Gunnell argues that the 1970s marked the end of the extreme polarization of the discipline of political science and ushered in the period of pluralization, or Balkanization, discussed by Easton. Gunnell argues that the pure tolerance that tends to govern relationships between enclaves at present is not conducive to dialectical exchange and the kind of criticism that might lead to the growth of knowledge. He then focuses on what has happened to the concept and practice of empirical political theory within the discipline of political science. He argues that the main-stream idea of theory was clear and unequivocal in the 1960s, when there existed a broad conceptual framework—illustrated by both systems and cultural analysis—somewhat comparable to that of natural science. Where has that idea gone? What, if anything, has taken its place? In addressing these questions, Gunnell discusses and evaluates the long-range significance of critical themes in the philosophy of science, the relation of political science to public policy, and the postbehavioral revolution.[4]

Alternative Views of Political Science

Bernard Grofman takes issue with the idea that empirical political theory faces a crisis resulting from want of a unifying paradigm, arguing that the field is at least as unified now as at any point in its past. He suggests that the real divisions are the same ones that have always been in existence, pointing to seven divisions of particular significance.

The first concerns the division between political scientists who see political science as a branch of moral philosophy and those who view it as a search for empirical understanding and explanation. The second division is between those who wish to immerse themselves in detailed description and an insider's knowledge of a delimited domain versus those whose first impulse is to look for comparative analysis to shed explanatory light on particular cases. Grofman's third division concerns political scientists who, in response to any question, begin by amassing data versus those who begin by thinking the question through from first principles. The fourth division concerns those who search for unequivocal answers to relatively small, manageable questions and those who would be willing to settle for not-so-certain answers as long as the questions were significant ones. The fifth division separates those who believe the important questions have already been answered by great minds of the past from those who think the process of knowledge gathering is ongoing.[5] Grofman then points to differences between those who think political science is the study of governmental institutions and those who see it as the study of power and outcomes, especially in terms of "who gets what, when and how."[6] Grofman's final division touches on the distinction between normative and positive theory, between political scientists who wish to understand the world and those who wish to change it.[7]

The discipline as a whole, and especially its scientific nature, is discussed in one of the most playful chapters in the book, in which Jean Laponce locates the current state of political science somewhere between psychology and economics, between philosophy and mathematics, between micro and macro, and between brute factism and intellectual disarmament. Laponce moves from the death of god to the death of man and the rise of structures to ask: what did we know twenty-five years ago that Aristotle did not know? What *should* we know that we do *not* know? His chapter provides a useful dose of humility to our scientific pretensions and reminds us of the connection between classical political theory and contemporary empirical theory.[8]

Murray Edelman provides an overview of the discipline quite different from those of Grofman and Laponce. His assessment of recent psychological literature in empirical theory demonstrates how political science still denies some of the most conspicuous current political trends, much as systems theory in the 1960s largely ignored the rampant conflicts and violence of that decade and as rational choice theory in the 1980s and 1990s overlooks the manifest irrationality of a great deal of public policy. Edelman then considers political science's links with other disciplines. The existence of such linkages blurs disciplinary boundaries, as structuralist and poststructuralist theories have promoted ties to the humanities, rational choice theory to economics, and functional theory to sociology. Edelman concludes with a consideration of the construction of substitute and disguised sites of contention over the existence and nature of such basic human potentialities as rationality, identity, equality, and the capacity to acquire secure knowledge.

The Construction of a Universal and Value-free Science of Politics

Edelman's analysis moves us into the more normative concerns of Part 3.[9] Here the basic premises of empirical political theory are challenged from the perspective of the ancients to postmodernism. This section begins with Peter Euben's creative and wide-ranging chapter. Euben begins with the riddle posed in Sophocles's "Oedipus": what creature walks on four feet, two feet, and three feet, all in a single day? The abstract, literally disembodied knowledge that enabled Sophocles's Oedipus to solve the Sphinx's riddle also prevented Oedipus from solving the riddle of Laius's death. In answering "man" to the first riddle, Oedipus thought he was defining human nature. He did not realize that the particular circumstances of his own life—the fact that he had to walk with a cane during adulthood— made him an exception to what he took to be a universal, and so he was unable to see that he was the answer to the second riddle. For Oedipus, and perhaps for all mortals, Euben argues, seeing is also blindness, knowledge a curse, delusion most powerful when we think ourselves most wise and in command. Euben weaves together insights from literature and from classical political theory and relates them directly to contemporary issues in social science and the philosophy of science.

Catherine and Michael Zuckert build on the themes developed by Euben to argue that the entire enterprise of constructing general theory, à la Easton and Almond, is bound to fail. They draw on arguments from postmodernists such as Rorty and from Straussian political theorists to suggest the misguided nature of attempts to discover regularities of political behavior that can then be built into general laws of science. Their views, though not popular among many empirical political theorists, reflect those of a growing number in the profession and must be taken seriously.

One answer to questioners about the scientific nature of politics is found in the intriguing chapter by Alexander Wendt and Ian Shapiro. This chapter reflects what is shaping up to be a major debate in current political science: can we have a science of politics that is not based on positivist assumptions? Wendt and Shapiro begin by discussing the emergence of the realist school in the philosophy of social sciences during the 1970s. This school is composed of social theorists who criticize positivism but reject the interpretivist worldview frequently offered in its stead.[10] Their first goal is to rescue an account of the possibility of social science that could withstand Kuhn's (1962) interpretive criticism of positivism. In this respect, the realist critique of positivism shared basic affinities with the critique of behavioralism propounded by Easton and the postbehavioralists. But many realists exhibit a loosely defined affinity with the Marxist tradition of social inquiry and seek to resuscitate the main insights of historical materialism from within the new realist view of science. Wendt and Shapiro explore these twin origins of the realist movement and examine the tensions between them, arguing that the realist account of social explanation is credible but raises difficulties concerning the parts of classical Marxism that realists have often wanted to save. Focusing on the Marxian commitment to the idea that there is a fundamental human interest in emancipation, Shapiro and Wendt argue that the existence of such an interest cannot be derived, as some realists have supposed it can, from a realist view of science. Marxists are correct in maintaining that Marx's claims about interests have often been rejected on spurious grounds, but they are incorrect in thinking that realism, by itself, proves those claims to be true.

Contributions of Recent Theories

What are the most important contemporary empirical political theories? Here, as might be expected, the authors offer quite different assessments.

Riker favors rational choice theory; Almond argues in favor of cultural theory; Hartsock endorses a feminist approach; Lowi and Harpham note the importance of state theory for public policy. And so on.

This section opens with a selection by one of the founders of rational choice theory, William Riker. In arguing that rational choice theory is the most significant empirical political theory in recent years, Riker constructs a two-stage argument.[11] He first suggests it is rational choice theory that effectively carries on and extends the traditional political science of Madison, Key, and Schattschneider. Riker then demonstrates how the current application of rational choice theory to political institutions is returning political science to the direction it traditionally and properly should follow, a direction from which it was deflected by behavioralism, which was essentially a psychological theory.[12]

Riker provides a valuable overview of the intellectual impetus for rational choice theory. He also discusses the most significant contributions made by rational choice theory and assesses the current criticisms of it. Riker concludes with a discussion of how rational choice theorists are now focusing on institutions, trying to construct the kinds of institutional analysis that traditional political science has tried to build from its inception in the 1890s but which traditional political science could not satisfactorily do because it lacked a solid basis of analysis and the rigorous methodological standards that rational choice theory now offers. Riker's chapter provides both an informative context in which to understand the growth and development of rational choice theory and a firsthand history of the growth of rational choice theory by its preeminent practitioner in political science. It is a fitting last statement by one of the intellectual giants of twentieth-century political science.

Russell Hardin extends the discussion of rational choice theory, focusing on the importance of economic reasoning in political science over the past few decades. Hardin argues that the best model of this kind of political economy is no longer the Arrow, Downs, and Olson literatures but rather work in law and economics. Much of this work is rather narrowly focused on issues of minor importance to political theorists, such as the effects of particular minor rules of trial procedure and evidence. But much of it is central to the effort to understand political institutions, some of the most important of which are those that promulgate, enforce, and adjudicate law. Of greatest interest to Hardin, however, are the actual arguments, especially the debates over value theory and institutional structures.

In his assessment of rational choice contributions to political science, Hardin touches on important arguments concerning both micro-macro distinctions[13] and issues of method and objectivity.[14] In his analysis of specific literatures in substantive areas of political science, Hardin contends that there are far too few substantive areas in which different theoretical approaches have been compared analytically and empirically. Hardin especially addresses the relationship of rational choice to normative theory, arguing that the vocabularies in these two areas should be more widely shared.

Gabriel Almond's chapter moves us from rational choice theory to cultural theory. Almond argues that Easton's concept of the political system was an intellectual innovation that made it possible for scholars working primarily from an institutional and process perspective to become genuinely abstract and theoretical. Easton's work was especially vital to those scholars working in the early years of comparative politics; in particular, it freed them from established historical frameworks and made it possible for them to think in strictly comparative ways, employing abstract models. Almond's discussion of the intellectual history surrounding the development of systems theory, socialization theory, and cultural theory will be of particular interest because of Almond's central role in developing and reorienting the field of comparative politics. His discussion of socialization theory and political culture traces the impact of systems theory on his own work and on that of his colleagues David Apter, Lucian Pye, and Sydney Verba. Almond steps back from his specific discussion of comparative politics, however, to assess the importance of socialization theory and cultural theory in contemporary political science. He offers an insightful and valuable appraisal of the contributions of these theories, one that will serve to orient future theoretical work in this area as political scientists grapple with the arrival in comparative politics of rational choice theory, deconstructionism, postmodernism, and interpretive theory. Almond's chapter will be invaluable for scholars concerned with the process by which we construct value-free comparisons, at both the individual and the macro level, that can move across cultures.

Nancy Hartsock also addresses the issue of bias in our analysis and further develops Euben's contention that there is no scientific objectivity in political science. Hartsock, however, argues primarily from a feminist perspective. She strikes deep at the foundations of political science, arguing that the traditional conceptualization and operationalization of "political" reflects gender bias that distorts reality. She reviews some important recent feminist literature to illustrate how feminist political science effectively seeks to redefine our understanding of the political and expand discourse to areas—such as the family—long considered the realm of the private and hence not subject to political analysis.

Theodore J. Lowi and Edward J. Harpham consider the important relations of the state and public policy, surveying the literature on the three major models of the relationship between the state and public policy: the neo-Marxist, the neo-Weberian, and the neoclassical, or public choice.

Their critique of these contemporary views of the relations between the individual and the state asks whether we can develop a republican theory of the state by bringing in public policy as the empirical base and jurisprudence as the normative base. This chapter is particularly important in relating work in policy studies to contemporary work in empirical political theory.

In the concluding chapter I attempt to draw together some of the general themes raised in the book, particularly those concerned with identity and the nature of the scientific enterprise in political science.[15] I consider human nature and ask whether we can use central tendencies in that nature to construct a science of politics. I argue that the assumption that there is a human nature, and that this nature can be discovered and analyzed, lies at the heart of social science. But what is human nature? Is it self-interested, as rational choice theorists and economists assume? Does it change over time and across cultures, as cultural theory suggests? Which political theories and methods are most helpful in revealing and explaining human nature? Systems theory? Cultural theory? Marxist theory? Behavioralism? I consider only two of these theories—identity and rational choice theory— and the arguments made in their favor, some by the other authors in this volume. A contrast of rational choice theory with work on identity suggests that cognitive theories stressing identity and perspective allow us to answer some of the postmodern concerns about objective reality yet still permit us to speak in terms of general theory. The chapter concludes with a discussion of the challenges in constructing general theory in politics.

NOTES

1. In describing the substance of the chapters in this book, I have relied heavily on the abstracts sent to me by the authors. I appreciate the authors' willingness to let me edit and reshape their prose.

2. Gunnell addresses this issue, as does Almond.

3. The chapter by Shapiro and Wendt attempts to answer this need. Euben also speaks directly to the issue of scientific knowledge, as does Hartsock in a slightly different vein.

4. In doing so, he touches on themes raised later by Shapiro and Wendt, by Lowi and Harpham, by Euben, and by Catherine and Michael Zuckert.

5. This anticipates arguments made in the chapters by Laponce, the Zuckerts, and Euben.

6. This anticipates arguments presented by Lowi and Harpham, by Hardin, and by Riker.

7. This topic also is addressed by Hartsock, Hardin, and the Zuckerts.

8. These are subjects also raised by the Zuckerts and by Euben.

9. Edelman's essay anticipates some of the arguments made by Hartsock, Lowi and Harpham, Hardin, and Monroe.

10. The realists reject the basic terms in which debates about knowledge in the social sciences have increasingly been cast since the 1962 publication of Kuhn's *The Structure of Scientific Revolutions*.

11. This piece was written shortly before Bill's death; I am grateful to Mrs. Riker for allowing us to print it here.

12. Riker's chapter also provides important intellectual history, beginning with the state of political science in the 1930s. Riker argues that the intellectual ferment in political science, centered at the University of Chicago in the 1920s, had been dampened by what was—for Riker—the satanic figure of Robert Hutchens. After the intellectual hiatus for political science created by World War II, the field was wide open and ripe for innovative theoretical work. This postwar void was soon filled by a variety of theoretical works, ranging from those of David Easton to behavioralist theory to rational choice theory, which grew out of John von Neumann's work in game theory and Duncan Black's work on social choice theory.

13. These issues are also discussed by Grofman and Laponce.

14. These issues are discussed by Euben and by the Zuckerts.

15. This is discussed by the Zuckerts, Hartsock, Euben, and by Wendt and Shapiro.

PART I

Historical Overview

1

The Future of the Postbehavioral
Phase in Political Science

David Easton

In my 1969 presidential address to the American Political Science Association, I characterized the changes that decade was witnessing as a postbehavioral revolution,[1] a term that seems to have stuck. I now wish to pose two questions: has this change in the direction of research achieved its declared purposes? And what kind of problems is political science likely to face in the immediate future? I shall conclude that we are undoubtedly in transition to a new phase in the development of political science, one to which it would be too hazardous at this moment to try to attach a label. Whatever its final configuration, however, what seems to be clear at the moment is that it will probably display what I shall call a high *neobehavioral* content.

For accounting purposes it has been useful to classify the historical development of American political science into the following more or less arbitrary stages: the formal-legal, governing most of the nineteenth century; the traditional or informal, probably dating from Walter Bagehot in England and Woodrow Wilson in the United States; the behavioral, beginning after World War II (although it had its origins in the preceding period); and the postbehavioral stage, which took root in the 1960s and has flourished since that time. Whether one agrees with this terminology (or, for that matter, with the underlying assumption about periodicity in the discipline) matters less than the fact that changes of this sort did occur, even if their meaning and consequences have been vigorously debated over the years.

As Thomas Kuhn has remarked about the natural sciences, every epoch

I would like to thank Professors Kristen Monroe and Mark Petracca of the University of California, Irvine for their helpful comments on this chapter.

in a discipline usually solves some problems but also inadvertently generates new and equally troublesome ones of its own.[2] Although what is true for the natural sciences need not be equally so for the social sciences, Kuhn's assertion seems to apply universally among the disciplines. Apparent solutions may indeed bear with them the seeds of, if not their own destruction, at least their own inherent difficulties. The postbehavioral stage of political science in the last quarter of a century is no different in this respect.

To understand the kinds of difficulties with which the postbehavioral movement has left us, we need to remind ourselves why it arose in the first place, something that is now easily forgotten or overlooked. It came into being during the 1960s and 1970s to address certain issues that, it was argued, behavioralism had generated but was unable to handle, given its assumptions, methods, and perspectives.

THE INDICTMENT

Most, if not all, behavioralists were positivistic in their inclinations. They did not question that there was a social reality "out there" that was accessible to scientific inquiry unencumbered by any preexisting beliefs. By their very nature, the methods of science could provide objective and impartial understanding. Within this basic positivistic conception, behavioralism in effect operated with the following credo, which I have described at greater length elsewhere:[3]

1. *Regularities*. There are discoverable uniformities in political behavior.
2. *Verification*. In principle the validity of generalizations must be testable by reference to relevant behavior.
3. *Techniques*. Means for acquiring and interpreting data cannot be taken for granted. They are problematic.
4. *Quantification*. Precision in the recording of data and the statement of findings requires measurement and quantification.
5. *Values*. Ethical evaluation and empirical explanation involve two different kinds of propositions that, for the sake of clarity, should be kept analytically distinct.
6. *Systematization*. Research ought to be systematic; that is, theory and research are to be seen as closely intertwined.
7. *Pure science*. The application of knowledge is as much a part of the scientific enterprise as is theoretical understanding. But the understanding and explanation of political behavior logically precede and provide the basis for efforts to utilize political knowledge in the solution of practical problems of society.

Behavioralism as presented here was accused of numerous shortcomings, of which the following are typical:

1. A tendency, where behavioralism pursued fundamental rather than applied knowledge, to divorce itself increasingly from immediate political reality, neglecting the special responsibility that, it was argued, the possession of knowledge imposes on the intellectual for its use.

2. A conception of scientific method that seemed to direct attention away from human actors and their choices and toward the conditions that influence and constrain action, resulting, it was claimed, in a subjectless, nonhumane discipline, one in which human intentions and purposes played little creative part.

3. The naive assumption that behavioral political science alone was free of ideological presuppositions that might shape its substantive concerns and its conception of its own methods of inquiry.

4. The uncritical acceptance of a pristine positivist interpretation of the nature of science, despite major criticisms that had already gained credibility even among many of those favorable to the continued use of scientific method in the pursuit of social understanding.

5. The entrapment in a degree of professionalization that increasingly hampered communication not only with the general public but even with other disciplines that were no less specialized.

6. An apparent indifference to the resulting fragmentation of knowledge, even in the face of the need for the use of this knowledge to solve whole social problems that, by their nature, are undifferentiated as to discipline.

7. An acknowledged inability to deal with value concerns, to describe the nature of the good society, with the denigration of values to a nonscientific and, therefore, nonconfirmable status.

Many of these and other criticisms were lodged by scholars who opposed behavioralism fundamentally and felt it was ill-conceived and flawed in its very conception. For them, human behavior simply was not subject to the kind of regularities found in inanimate matter and hence was not explainable through the use of the methods of science. Other opponents of behavioralism did not take so irreconcilable a position, however. Criticisms arose from within the fold of behavioralism itself, from those who firmly retained their commitment to scientific method but would revise and modernize our understanding of its nature. The result was that the apparently solid phalanx of behavioralism (and it is arguable as to whether such solidarity ever did exist except in the minds of a few diehard proponents and antagonists) was breached, as some within its ranks sought to identify and rectify its shortcomings without necessarily abandoning their belief in the scientific method's value in the search for reliable explanation and under-standing.[4]

In the end, the antagonists of behavioralism formed a motley crew: tra-ditional institutionalists, natural rightists, Weberian interpretivists, human-ists of various sorts, some Marxists, historical sociologists, and so on. Their grounds of opposition to behavioralism were, therefore, as varied as all these labels suggest. But what is often forgotten is that this body of critics also included scientific revisionists, students of politics who retained their initial commitment to scientific method but saw the need for a new under-standing of its assumptions and characteristics.

The postbehavioralists—and today these include most political scien-tists, excepting perhaps a few rigid, traditional positivists—sought to deal with the perceived shortcomings of behavioralism in their various ways. But in the process of solving some immediate problems to their satisfaction, I am suggesting, they have given birth to a whole generation of new issues that beg for solution and that are no less troubling than the difficulties behavioralism left behind. Our answers to these new problems will help shape political research over the next decade or more. It behooves us, there-fore, to look at some of these postbehavioral solutions, the nature of the difficulties they are leaving behind, and the possible directions in which political science may look in the immediate future as it seeks to cope with them.

THE POSTBEHAVIORAL RESPONSES

Loss of a Central Focus

As we know only too well today, dissatisfaction with the pristine positivism of behavioralism opened up the floodgates of proposed revisions in both methods and subject matter. These proposals ranged from complete rejec-tion of systematic methodology[5] in favor of the revival of interpretive un-derstanding and historical analysis, on the one side, to the introduction of formal modeling and rational actor deductivism, on the other. These new or revived methodological approaches were designed to bring the actor back into the picture of research. But they were also intended to compen-sate for the failure of the basic methods associated with behavioralism to deal satisfactorily with many of the pressing social issues of the day. As I have stated elsewhere, "The mainstream of U.S. political science moved off in a variety of [new] directions. The interests of the behavioral period in voting, judicial, legislative, administrative, and executive behavior as well as in interest groups, parties, developing areas and the like have continued. But during the postbehavioral period new topics of political research have arisen to satisfy the desire to understand the new concerns typical of this period—environmental pollution, ethnic, racial, social and sexual equality, feminism and nuclear war, for example."[6] And whole new areas outside the dominant traditions of the discipline, such as feminism, have been opened up.

With the decline in confidence in the subject matter and methods of behavioralism, the anchor for the discipline was unexpectedly lost. Political scientists were left free to move off in a multitude of new directions, to experiment with and advocate a great variety of methods and new subjects for research. The discipline shattered into a multitude of methodological and substantive pieces.[7]

The overriding consequence of this fragmentation has been a deep sense of loss of purpose and direction. As I noted recently, "[D]uring the 1950s and 1960s, in the behavioral phase, there was a messianic spirit and collective effort in the promotion and development of the methods of scientific inquiry even while there continued to be opposition to it. Today there is no longer a single, dominant point of view or one that unmistakably catches the imagination, especially of the younger members of the profession. Nor is there even a single defensive adversary."[8]

Not only have we lost our sense of a dynamic purpose concentrated, as it was, on the pursuit of scientific validity, but political science seems to have lost its core. At one time in the not-too-distant past we might have been able to agree that our subject matter consisted largely of the study of values or of the good life. When this became no longer acceptable as a focus for the discipline, we were left with numerous alternative conceptions. And even though it may seem self-serving for me to say so, if during the behavioral stage there was any single and widely accepted description of the subject matter of political science, it was probably to be found in the notion of the authoritative allocation of values for a society—an idea, of course, that I had put forward as early as 1953.[9] That concept, together with the term "political system" as the most general way to refer to the political aspects of society, became absorbed into the ordinary language of the discipline.

Today, however, students are no longer certain what politics is all about, at least at the conceptual level. For a short while, as the postbehavioral phase got under way, it seemed as though the state might be adopted as the central orienting concept, displacing the political system. In the United States the state concept, as part of state theories, was revived in the 1970s, partly as a by-product of Marxism's reemergence as a major mode of analysis but also partly as a way of reintroducing the actor as the focus of attention. With the dissolution of the USSR and the collapse of socialism in Eastern Europe, the viability of Marxism as a philosophy and analytic approach has come into more serious question than ever before. With Marxism's demise or temporary eclipse, as the case may be, the state as a central analytic concept has already lost some of its appeal. Yet we cannot write it off too quickly. Adoption of state terminology does not rest exclusively on its central place in Marxist theory. Scholars at all points on the ideological spectrum, even the most conservative,[10] have found the state a useful concept for focusing on the government as an actor and for importing moral criteria to assess its actions.

As matters stand, then, in the present, postbehavioral stage it would appear that there is no longer any general orienting concept, acceptable to most, that would be used either with the intention or consequence of providing some kind of substantive intellectual coherence for political research. A random element seems to have crept into the literature. Concepts such as the political system, the state, government, the authorities, elites, and the like are used without any real commitment to the intellectual consequences that should follow if the concepts are to be taken seriously as central theoretical guides.

The result is that the postbehavioral differs from the behavioral stage in its general tone. The behavioral stage was imbued with a deep sense of euphoria and dedication to a mission. There was little question about the nature of desired research products. The postbehavioral spirit is markedly different. There is little collective exhilaration left, and although there is much intellectual dedication, the discipline is noted more for the fragmentation of its overarching perspectives than for its unity, coherence, or sense of common purpose.

The Actor versus the Acted Upon

One of the main criticisms against behavioralism was that in the application of scientific method the individual subject, the real human being underlying all action, got lost. For those using the methods of science, the subject became an object for the intersection of various influences, to which he or she responded in one way or another. Through the individual, the consequences of social forces could be tracked. These forces might produce varying results, depending upon the attributes of the person they were influencing, but essentially the explanatory emphasis was upon the nature of the social factors. Thus, partisanship might represent a confluence of the effects of social class, religious affiliation, party identification, ideological orientation, and the like, with various personal predispositions shaping the way an individual responded. This represented largely a society-centered rather than an actor-centered approach, to use Theda Skocpol's popular and helpful conceptualization.

What was lost from sight, so the argument ran, was the individual person. Does the subject just react to social factors in accordance with his or her personality and experience; or does the subject actively intervene in some significant way so as to modify the situation in which the reaction takes place? Furthermore, does the consequent behavior represent some kind of blind or mindless response to social circumstances, or is there room for the reasoning capacity of the individual to express itself? In raising the issue of the place of the actor, the postbehavioralists were posing the fundamental question of the role of reason-guided behavior in social action. If all behavior is just a response to social and internal psychological influences, where, if at all, does the individual's capacity to think, assess, plan, strategize, gauge the moment of action, express intentions, develop new purposes or goals, or modify the very conditions of action themselves come into the picture?

From the very beginning of the application of scientific method to human behavior, in nineteenth-century Germany especially, reservations of this sort about the application of scientific method have been expressed. In fact, Weber's *verstehen* sociology, the method of empathic understanding, was itself based on the assumption that scientific method could address only certain kinds of collective behavior but was helpless in trying to take into account the intention of the actor—hence the need for the special kind of interpretive method he sought to articulate. Although there had always been major exponents of Weber's point of view and although Talcott Parsons had tried to integrate it in a systematic way into contemporary sociology through his early theory of voluntary action, it had always been a minor player in political science research during the dominant period of behavioralism.

For explainable social reasons, the role of the actor became particularly pressing during the countercultural revolution of the 1960s and 1970s.[11] Unlike the tenets of deterministic Marxism, the dominant themes of the period were voluntaristic in nature. Through individual and collective action, it was intuitively held, change could be brought about. And although Marxists and others might stress the barriers to change inherent in the structure of society, the enthusiasm and exuberance of the period, driven as it was by a demographic bulge of young people, seemed to say that all that was needed to effect change was the will. Sheer concentrated effort would be successful in bringing about fundamental social transformations. The emphasis was on the actor, on his or her intentions, on the human capacity to overcome all external social barriers once the will was there.

In one sense the countercultural movement achieved many of its goals. It brought about fundamental reorientations in worldwide perceptions of important issues. Environmental pollution, poverty, racial and sexual equality, feminist perspectives, freedom in forms of personal dress and appearance, the new so-called style or nonmaterial issues,[12] came to the political foreground. But in another sense, the revolution, if not a failure, was certainly not a success. It left unresolved the question as to why, with its tremendous strength of numbers, passion, and discontent, the movement managed to put new issues on the agenda but failed to bring about many of the actual changes for which it fought. A long struggle still lay ahead. The movement also left unanswered major methodological questions for the social sciences. Just what is the role of social forces (social determinants and constraints) as compared to individual reason and will in bringing about social change? This has been one of the major questions hidden in postbehavioralism, however little we may be aware of it.[13]

Answers came forth from both sides: that is, from those concerned about the role of the individual actor in social change and from those who continued to see social influences on the individual—the context or constraints within which the individual acts—as major elements to be taken into account. Let us look at the actor-oriented response first and leave constraints for later consideration.

The postbehavioral response that has sought to compensate for behavioralism's neglect of the actor has taken several forms: Weberian intentionalism; the rational actor model; and the state actor model. These are not usually seen as falling into the same category I am describing here. I shall suggest that it is not only helpful but necessary to view them as such if we are to understand their simultaneous presence in the current stage of political inquiry.

WEBERIAN INTENTIONALISM. I have already touched on what I am calling Weberian intentionalism. At the turn of the century, in seeking to mediate between, on the one side, the adherents of the *kulturwissenschaft* movement in Germany, who fought against the introduction of scientific method for the study of social and individual behavior, and, on the other, those who sought to use this method in the rapidly developing psychology and sociology of the day. Weber adopted an intermediate position. In his compromise, science is seen as useful for the study of certain forms of aggregate behavior, those hospitable to statistical analysis. But because science is presumed to be unable to take into account the goals, purposes, and intentions of individual actors, another method needed to be invented or discovered. Weber found it in empathic understanding. He thereby embedded what we have come to call interpretive analysis inextricably into the panoply of methods available for research, especially when he linked it to historical sociology as a way of isolating and validating the personal factors of purpose, motive, belief, and intention in social change.

Thousands of pages of commentary have been written on the meaning and usefulness of ideal types in historical research and on the explication and communicability of the *verstehen* approach. The debate continues over how well Weber succeeded in finding a compromise methodological position between scientific method and a special method for understanding and explaining cultural or human phenomena. The important thing for our purposes is that we view Weber's interpretive method as one of the alternatives offered by postbehavioralists for solving the problem of how to fit subjective behavior, defined as intentionality and purposes, into the analysis of society.

THE RATIONAL ACTOR MODEL. The rational actor model stands as a second major response. Although it is not usually seen as part of postbehavioralism, and although its deductive basis met the ideals of formal scientific method even better than the inductive emphasis of survey and opinion research. This should not be allowed to obscure the fact that in a fundamental way it was also part of the postbehavioral movement.

Even though the rational actor model had its beginnings in the 1960s, we still need to account for its acceptance and rapid diffusion in later years, when postbehavioralism began increasingly to assert itself. As I have already indicated, postbehavioralism included a motley crew of critics, from natural rightists to rigid positivists. We need to bear that in mind. It has not always been distrust of scientific method that has distinguished postbehavioralists.[14] Rather, some took objection to the substantive or theoretical assumptions about the nature of social causation even while retaining their commitment to science. For them the need was to shift the emphasis from the conditions of behavior to the subject—that is, to the role of the individual.[15]

For those critics who did not wish to give up their belief in science, a method that permitted the inclusion of a central role for the subject had strong appeal. Rational modeling did just that. It was science at its strongest because it was deductive. It not only brought the subject back into the causal equation but actually made it the centerpiece. Best of all, it provided a bridge, especially for younger members of the discipline, to the newer postbehavioral sentiments that were developing across all the social sciences. They, too, could share in the move toward a recognition of the significance of the subject in social action.

In part, then, the rational actor model gained sway because it inadvertently fit into the voluntarist tendencies of the countercultural sentiments of the time. Simultaneously, it was able to capitalize on the criticism that the primary methods of behavioralism—survey and public opinion research—stressed social forces and neglected the contribution of the individual as a reasoning subject engaged in making choices among alternatives.

The image of the individual was subtly changed by rational modeling. He or she was not just a subject reacting to external circumstances but was proactive—choosing, selecting, rejecting in terms of his or her own preferences or utility-maximizing behavior. The focus shifted decisively from the structure or constraints surrounding behavior (what became for rational modeling exogenous variables) to the actor and his or her strategies of choice in pursuit of individual utilities. The reasoning human being driven by intentions and goals was brought back into politics.

Whether or not we regard rational modeling as part of the postbehavioral movement depends on how we interpret postbehavioralism. If we see it as made up of only those tendencies that rejected scientific method for the study of human behavior, then it would be contradictory to describe rational modeling as part of that movement. But if we understand postbehavioralism to be a far more complex response to pristine behavioralism, then there should be little difficulty or hesitation in including rational modeling. What brings the rational actor model under the same umbrella as other parts of postbehavioralism is simply a shared dissatisfaction with the current practices of scientific method—in this case, dissatisfaction with the excessive reliance on induction and the underemphasis of the subjective factor in social action.

Rational modeling has spread into many areas of political studies. It breathed new life into such fields as voting behavior and legislative and judicial research. And it has helped to bring about a remarkable revival of moral inquiry; moral questions no longer seem to be beyond the pale of methods consistent with the scientific approach. Thus, not only empirically oriented research but also political philosophy has benefited in a major way from the adoption of the rational approach. During the behavioral period, moral research had all but died out.[16] Values were sometimes thought to be mere expressions of preferences, as in economics. Postbehavioralism, under the inspiration of rational modeling, has led to renewed efforts to demonstrate that there is a rational basis for moral argument and judgment. Most of the work in this area has been inspired by John Rawls's *A Theory of Justice*,[17] itself influenced by economic modeling and game theory. Rawls attempts to develop valid and demonstrable criteria of justice derivable from the assumption of rationality. Using a similar convention about rational behavior, others have turned to the task of developing moral theories about equality, freedom, international justice, legitimacy, and the like.[18] Not only has the approach succeeded in casting new light on the way one might go about establishing moral judgments, regardless for the moment of debates about the appropriateness of the method, it has done so in a way that makes moral inquiry interesting and credible to persons committed to scientific method. In the history of the discipline it serves arguably as a major systematic bridge between the empirical and philosophical fields in political inquiry.

In effect, rational modeling fulfilled Weber's project of bringing the human subject back into the scientific picture, but this time with an explicit and communicable methodology that depends not on intuition and empathy but on logic and on certain psychological assumptions. In this way rational modeling also met the argument of behavioralism's critics without having to sacrifice the methods and criteria normally associated with science. It captured the role of the subject but retained the objectivity of science, a masterly historical strategy in mediating between critics concerned about the loss of the subject and the scientific defenders of behavioralism. But, as is now well recognized, the approach did not present its own alternative without giving rise to a host of new problems, to which I shall turn shortly.

THE STATE ACTOR MODEL. The state actor model was yet another response to behavioralism's apparent preoccupation with the conditions influencing the actor as against the actor's own predispositions and capacities to intervene in and modify the situation. Like the rational actor model, the state model is not usually interpreted in quite this way. We usually view it as just an effort to introduce into domestic politics another major variable that needs to be taken into account. It does represent this, of course, but it also signifies dissatisfaction with the emphasis on the subject (in this case, the state) as behaving reactively rather than proactively.

The actor here is not the individual but what Weber would call a corporate actor, a collectivity. From the point of view of the condition of research, however, the movement to "bring the state back in" and to promote a "state-centered" as against a "society-centered" form of inquiry played precisely the same role as did the shift to the individual in the revival of *verstehen* sociology and actor-centered rational modeling.[19] Wittingly or otherwise, this research follows Nicholas Poulantzas. By conceiving of the state as "relatively autonomous," it seeks to highlight the contribution to social policy that the set of actors identified as the state makes as an active rather than reactive agency.[20] In precisely the same way as individuals, the state manifests purposes, intentions, strategies, and the like. As a result, state theory not only allows but seems to compel the incorporation of moral judgments in its analyses. The state is not just a passive product, as it were, of the intersection of social forces such as interest groups, social classes, ethnic and linguistic units, and the like, as society-centered analysis would have it. It has an autonomous and active role in formulating and implementing social policy.

Emphasis on the autonomy of the state rather than on specific institutional actors did more than draw attention to the significance of human agency in social change. It raised important questions about the nature of that agency and how we are to characterize it if we are to understand its place in the formulation and implementation of authoritative policy.[21] As we shall see in a moment, the state actor model generated serious new problems at the same time it sought to solve an old one.

Basic versus Applied Research: The Policy Analysis Movement

The trademark of postbehavioralism has been the growth of a widespread interest in the application of knowledge to the solution of urgent social issues. Whereas the dominant theme of behavioralism was the discovery of basic knowledge—although the study of applied problems was by no means neglected—postbehavioralism shifted the rhetorical balance in the direction of social solutions. The study of public policy emerged as a new growth industry in the social sciences as a whole. Literally hundreds of policy institutes have grown up around the world incorporating not only political science but all areas of knowledge, not excluding the natural sciences.

Essentially, these new centers of learning have moved in two directions, depending upon local inclinations. Some have become involved in the actual application of knowledge, from a variety of disciplines, for the solution of particular problems. The latter are fed to them by governmental or voluntary agencies or may be inspired by internal deliberations in the centers themselves. In effect, these centers often become surrogate policy makers, pursuing their own priorities and preferences for those that might be used by politicians or legislators. They offer applied solutions based on available knowledge and information.

Some students of public policy, however, have leaned in the direction of behavioralism. They have sought not possible solutions to known social issues but fundamental knowledge about the factors that must be involved in creating such solutions. They focus on the elements that shape political policies, that are and can be used to assess them, and that enable us to understand their consequences. Instead of concluding with propositions about what policies will be likely to cope with known social concerns and the effects they can be expected to have, these scholars offer analyses of how alternative strategies are undertaken and have their particular consequences. The division is between those who in effect choose to act like policy makers and those who only wish to understand policy making. In practice we often find a mix of both types in individual researchers and in policy institutes.

This shift in the focus of political inquiry has raised several important issues for the discipline itself. First, whereas behavioralists assumed that research would be guided by the theoretical development of political science, a policy orientation assumes that research may legitimately be driven by the social needs of the day as interpreted by the researcher. Second, foundations and government agencies providing support for research have little hesitation in defining areas of inquiry about public concerns that will likely receive funding. Control over the direction of research has subtly shifted toward the "public," to the extent it may be represented by grant-giving organizations. Third, fundamental research, defined as topics suggested by theoretical as against social needs, has found increasing difficulty in winning financial support and even moral encouragement.[22] Impressionistically, the net effect seems to be that basic research, driven by purely theoretical criteria, constitutes a smaller proportion of the total output of the discipline than in the behavioral period. Beyond these consequences, however, the large-scale shift to the application of knowledge raises theoretical concerns about the integration of knowledge. These I shall address shortly.

UNFINISHED BUSINESS FOR THE FUTURE

The response to behavioralism in the last couple of decades has been reasonably clear. The old behavioral consensus in the discipline has broken down in the face of widespread criticisms of positivism, of the kind of scientific method associated with it, of abstract theory, and of the loss of contact with the human subject and, hence, the real political world. But these critiques have not given the degree of satisfaction that their vigor, depth, and prevalence might seem to have promised. In the very process of searching for alternatives to the prevailing behavioral strategies and orientations to the discipline, postbehavioralism itself has given rise to a host of uncertainties, ambiguities, and opacities that are no less challenging for the future than those of behavioralism were in the past. To these new problems I shall now turn.

The Substantive Future: The Search for Theoretical Coherence

Whatever the destiny of state theory as an orienting or organizing conceptualization for the study of politics, the fact is that it has not been adopted by most of the discipline. It seems to remain in use, however unwittingly or uneasily, side by side with the concept of the political system. The handicaps of the state as a unifying concept are varied, a matter I have dealt with extensively elsewhere.[23] Suffice it to say here that a survey in 1931 discovered that the term already had 145 different meanings.[24] Since that time, one might guess, half as many again have been added. There seems little hope of achieving even a modest consensus on its meaning. Does "the state" refer to the complex set of institutions we normally designate as government, the political authorities, an elite, and the like? If so, these other terms are reasonably well understood, so the state concept is superfluous; and if they were not, the substitution of the state concept would scarcely relieve the ambiguity. It would simply mean the substitution of one unknown for another. The reintroduction of this nineteenth-century term (ideologically closely tied to the notion of sovereignty) into the contemporary research lexicon contradicts our frequently expressed desire to increase the clarity of our tools of analysis rather than to compound their obscurities.

This is not the place to pursue the search for a general orienting theoretical concept for the discipline. What is clear is that the state concept is doing little today to draw the discipline together theoretically and that the sense of fragmentation, of the lack of a core, is real. What is perhaps even more disturbing is that so little attention is being paid to the matter. At least during the behavioral period there was serious talk about and attention paid to the need for some orienting and integrative empirical theory, or even a conceptual framework for political analysis. Several frameworks, such as systems analysis, structural-functional theory, and decision theory, were offered and seriously debated. Today the sense that some underlying unity in the subject matter and theoretical parameters of the discipline might be developed lingers uneasily in the background or has been lost. The discipline seems to be more narrowly focused on a plethora of middle-range theories—rational actor models, schema theories, formal models of various sorts, regime approaches in international relations, and the like.

Postbehavioralism destroyed the central focus and sense of commitment provided by behavioralism. Political science is now divided by ideologies, methodologies, preferences, and theoretical orientations, not to mention the vast array of substantive interests that continue to proliferate. In fracturing the old sense of unity and identity, postbehavioralism has yet to come up with an alternative theoretical focus to reduce the discipline's sense of being left in a sort of theoretical limbo. The fact that this fragmentation of the discipline is still being widely discussed[25] suggests that it continues to be correct to say, as I did a decade ago, that "political science is still trying to develop a new sense of identity and a new drive or sense of purpose."[26] We are clearly in a transition phase. There is little evidence to indicate that we are moving toward a new consensus. We have not yet resolved our understanding of the shortcomings of our various ways of approaching the study of politics.

If we are pessimistic we might see this as an unhappy state of affairs for the discipline, bordering on intellectual chaos. If we are otherwise inclined, we may choose to interpret the matter differently. Our continued questioning of theories, methods, and perspectives so characteristic of the current postbehavioral period and our continued search for alternatives can be interpreted simply as proof that a process of fundamental change in the discipline has not yet run its course. The transition from behavioralism to some new central focus is still under way. We ought to bemoan this process less and welcome it more as offering a period for innovation and change.

My remarks suggest that perhaps we ought to view postbehavioralism as a bridging period rather than as a stopping point. If so, the task of the decade ahead is clear. At some point the discipline will need to reawaken an interest in general theoretical orientations or even general theory if it is to recover the momentum, drive, and coherence associated with behavioralism.[27]

The Methodological Future

THE RATIONALITY MODEL. From the standpoint of discovering a mode of analysis that is innovative, attracts the energies of talented people in the profession, and offers intriguing insights into traditional problems in political research, the methodological future would seem to look very bright. Formal modeling, especially the kind found in the rational actor approach, has gained significant adherents in a number of research areas and gives every indication of spreading even further. Not only has it been used in a variety of empirical fields, such as voting choice, party behavior, legislative and judicial decision making, and state action in the international sphere, but what seems to enhance its credentials further as a possible unifying methodological force for the discipline as a whole is its applicability even in the field of political philosophy, as I have already noted. It has thereby been able to cast a scientific net even more widely than had been possible for behavioralism.

However, as with other innovations of the postbehavioral period, rational modeling's very successes have brought with them their own critical problems, which continue to agitate the discipline. Whether and how these challenges can be handled will undoubtedly determine the future of this approach in political research.

One major unresolved issue goes to the heart of the rationality model: how valid is its basic postulate about human motivation? Does it approximate behavior in the empirical world? These questions are typically answered in one of two ways: the heuristic or instrumental response—rationality is only a postulate, and its validity has no relationship to its usefulness for research—and the realistic response—the model is an accurate description of the motive driving all human behavior and can be so demonstrated.

Instrumentalism follows Friedman's positive theory of motivations.[28] For him, the rational choice model is only a norm representing the way individuals would behave if they were indeed rational. They are only *presumed* to pursue their self-interest by rationally calculating the gains and losses from various courses of behavior and maximizing their utilities. If the outcomes predicted on this basis reflect reality, then we need not be concerned as to whether people are or are not motivated by self-interest. If individuals do indeed deviate in some way from this model, this represents no intrinsic flaw in the approach; the deviance just needs to be identified and built into the model, which is increasingly fine-tuned so as to approximate more closely behavior in the real world. This procedure is seen as sufficient for the job put to it. And in economics, so the argument runs, because self-interest in fact explains behavior better than any other assumption, it has demonstrated its usefulness. Nothing is to be gained by going any further, as in trying to validate the assumption.

To the critics of the assumption, however, this pragmatist position breaks down. They find that in actual research even those who claim to see the postulate as only an heuristic device speak as though individuals are in fact driven by the assumed motivation—namely, the maximization of self-interest. In that event, they argue, the claim is fair game for critical assessment, and the rational modeler becomes burdened with the need to demonstrate that people really do act rationally in this sense.

The proof becomes difficult. Like all major orienting concepts, the notion of rationality itself suffers from considerable ambiguity. The economic definition of the term seems at times to be so comprehensive that it includes all possible behavior. And if all behavior is motivated by self-interested, rational calculation of net benefits, we cannot use it to discriminate any one kind of behavior from another. Of what use, then, is the concept? Essentially any actor, by definition, if sane and uncoerced, will always behave in a way that he or she believes is in his or her own self-interest. In this interpretation altruism itself is just a form of selfishness or self-interested behavior; the subordination of one's own immediate welfare to that of another fulfills one's own interest.

Defining rationality in this way reduces the term almost to vacuity, inviting articles with such titles as "Why Self-Interest Is an Empty Concept."[29] Yet, despite its apparently excessive breadth, the rationality model has in fact been a powerful tool in economics and has shown some of the same qualities in political research.[30] This would seem to suggest that perhaps political scientists use it with a more restricted meaning than economists would allow. We can perhaps get at this meaning if we begin not by trying to define rationality but by identifying the kinds of behaviors in which we are interested and only then deciding whether we want to label them as rational or otherwise.

With this in mind, Jane Mansbridge proposes that we distinguish between two kinds of behavior.[31] In the first, the individual takes into account his or her own interests (however the culture may define them).[32] In the second, individuals act in such a way as to indicate that "the long-term welfare of others is important independent of its effect on their own welfare."[33] Thus, I give up my own immediate good for a perceived higher good for all. In fact, as Mansbridge points out, society develops rules of social conduct that are internalized and that lead people to want to help others even at a material cost to themselves, a present cost that is to be repaid by some expected future and imprecise benefit for all (as, for example, a free or a more humane society).[34] In addition, as Jon Elster has noted, in the real world many emotions motivate us without thought of self-interest: love, hate, joy, friendship, shame, fear, and so on. When possessed by them we are largely indifferent to whether we obtain a net benefit from our behavior.[35]

From this point of view, rational economic decision making includes both kinds of behavior, and both—behavior in which the individual considers only his or her own direct utilities and behavior in which the individual ignores or deliberately sacrifices that self interest for the greater benefit of others—are considered self-interested. In describing both kinds of behavior as the pursuit of self-interest, economics would seem to violate normal language use. We tend to think of the first kind of behavior as selfish or self-interested and the second kind as unselfish or altruistic.

The implication is that any conceptualization that fails to recognize and highlight the fundamental difference between the motivations for these two types of activities will misconstrue the nature of much social behavior. Whether we call the first kind of action "selfishness type 1" and the second "selfishness type 2" or the first "selfishness" and the second "altruism" is a matter of preference. However, because we already have perfectly satisfactory terms for these two kinds of actions (i.e., "selfishness" and "altruism"), there is some modest advantage, for ease and clarity of communication, to sticking with normal usage.

This sort of conceptual clarification has considerable consequences with regard to the usefulness of rational actor modeling as a possible broad framework for the study of major forms of actual political behavior. Its power, as borrowed from economics, derives from its ability to develop parsimonious abstract models of behavior that are driven by selfishness type 1, wherein the welfare of the actor is paramount. There are numerous situations in politics where this is indeed the case and, therefore, where the application of the model appears to be very promising—for example, where politicians seek victory in elections or votes in committee discussions or power in many other competitive areas. However, although the model has been applied to altruistic (selfishness type 2) actions, there the assumptions and circumlocutions become increasingly complex, Ptolemaic rather than Copernican, and prove increasingly difficult to sell as convincing explanations. For this reason, undoubtedly, this method runs into considerable difficulty in economics when used to try to derive a welfare function for a collectivity.

It would prove fruitful and more in harmony with the real world if political science models were built for situations in which the actor seeks to maximize the welfare of the community rather than his or her own self-interest, narrowly defined. Social behavior is governed by norms, to which individuals are socialized. Such norms regulate behavior and often make community-oriented (as against individual-oriented) action on behalf of social solidarity as likely a social preference as the atomistic self-interest of the economic marketplace. Community-oriented models would at least reflect a part of the social world currently tangential to the rational actor model of economics and enable us to make use of a powerful deductive tool. In this way we would be able to preserve the technical advantages of the optimizing rational model but put it to more effective use in understanding real-world political behavior.

For better or worse, economics has been founded on the assumption that what is best for the individual actor in the end turns out to be best for society. Even if this assumption were true for economic behavior, there is little evidence to demonstrate that it is equally true in politics. In fact, historically one of the fundamental assumptions of political life seems to be that there is a broader interest—designated as the common weal, the public interest, the common good, and so forth—that, although arguable as to its content, is less in doubt as to its intuitive reality. If rational modeling is to leave a permanent impact on political analysis (except for the few areas in which economic assumptions may well prevail, as where political success or victory is the primary goal), it will have to be able to deal with what we may call communal[36] as against self-defined individual welfare, with rational strategies for optimizing or maximizing this communal goal worked out deductively. If the rational actor model is able to do so, it will likely have a longer life in political research before it becomes, as all good theories in the end must, a celebrated headstone in the cemetery of discarded theoretical approaches.[37]

Even if problems with the meaning of rationality and with the model's capacity to search out a public or common welfare could be resolved, another major hurdle would need to be overcome. In the end the adequacy of any analytic tool depends on whether it is able to help us to unravel the intricacies of the world. Here rational modeling may be faulted on a number of counts. One of these is of particular importance, as it goes to the heart of the model—namely, the fact that members of a political system are rule-conforming as well as outcome-seeking actors.

The maximization of utilities involves empirical complexities that may not easily be included in formal models. Maximization of one's self-interest is not always the major motivation in political activity, as I have already noted. Actors do not enter a political system, as it were, unencumbered. As James March and Johan Olsen have reminded us, we need to recognize that actors are constrained in their behavior by their participation in various political institutions.[38] Institutions, for March and Olsen, consist of a structure of rules, formal and informal, to which actors feel compelled to conform either because of the fear of sanctions or because the rules have become internalized through socialization. Hence, behavior is often driven

not by a calculus designed to maximize one's utilities but by a socially determined need to conform to rules. Such rules "constrain the free flow of
rational action and competition in a rational actor model."[39]

For March and Olsen the rules that constitute political institutions are
of central significance in political life in another respect. They not only
bring order to political relationships but also give "meaning" to political
life by helping members of the system to define themselves, their purposes,
and their relationships with others. In this view, political actors are less concerned with outcome (policy outputs) than with creating, confirming, and
modifying their (often conflicting) interpretations of life, their identities,
their communities, and their views of the public good.[40] Accordingly, the
authors argue, without attention to institutions that establish orderly relationships and provide for a meaningful participation in political life, central phenomena of membership in a political system would be inaccessible to research. The rational actor model is unsuited for addressing such
institutional issues; it is concerned rather with the calculus of strategies for
the achievement of goals or outcomes.

In dealing with institutions as they do, however, the authors may not
have gone far enough in uncovering the inherent limitations of the rational
actor model. They have defined institutions narrowly, as structures of norms
or rules of behavior. In construing institutions so narrowly, however, they
miss another major factor limiting the applicability of the rational model.
The definition of institutions as sets of rules represents a cultural view of
institutions, which is satisfactory as far as it goes. But institutions consist of
behavior as well as rules, of activities as well as of norms. When we speak
of Congress or the courts as institutions, we refer not only to the rules
that govern the activity of their participants but also to their actual behavior. This behavior is also structured; the members of institutions engage in
regular patterns of activity, and these distinguish one institution from another.[41] Behavior is not always predictable from the rules because it does
not always faithfully reflect the rules. How members of Congress feel they
ought to behave, what the formal and informal rules specify, what the public expects from its representatives, and how the latter expect to be able to
respond may all deviate significantly from the actual behavior manifested.[42]

The fact is that through their activities members of a political system generate large structures of power that constrain the behavior of groups and
individuals. The actual distribution of resources in a political system among
various groups and the very way the system is organized—its electoral system, command over organizations with the capacity for violence, the disposition of its decision-making bodies, and the like—serve to limit, facilitate, and determine the actual capacities that individuals and groups may
have for action, regardless of the strategies that logic may dictate. If these
conditions are known and taken into account in any calculus of choices,

then the rational actor model works. But the fact is that the model offers no systematic way for bringing into the analysis the big political structures that reflect how power is organized in the system. As exogenous variables, these structures are entered only on an *ad hoc* basis, at the will and caprice of the modeler. The history of political relationships and the intricacies of broad patterns among power groups are taken as givens or ignored. Yet the outcomes of any strategies are dependent on the extent to which these structures of behavior limit, define, determine, and facilitate various possible decisions or strategies.[43]

Clearly a major question for empirical research is whether the rational decision model has within it the intellectual richness to assume the role of the major theoretical orientation of the discipline. On the plus side are its power as a deductive tool; its attractiveness, because of its stress on logic, to mathematically inclined bright young entrants into the profession; and economists' long experience with it, from which political scientists have been able to profit. If a consensus were to develop around this approach as occurred around scientific method itself during the behavioral phase, the discipline could conceivably recover its sense of direction and its coherence, with a concomitant renewal of energy and dedication.

Unfortunately, at this moment the shortcomings of the approach—its narrowness in adopting self-interest as a primary motive, even if only for heuristic purposes; its inability to cope adequately with the notion of a common welfare; and its difficulty in handling institutional constraints on a systematic basis—are only too apparent. There is little evidence that the method can transcend these limitations, although it may be too early to draw any final conclusion.

THE IDEOLOGICAL BASIS OF SCIENTIFIC INQUIRY. Postbehavioralism has been least successful, perhaps, in challenging the basic scientific methodology of behavioralism. The only real alternative it has offered has been Weber's *verstehen* approach, and despite extended argument within the social sciences no one has yet been able to put it on a systematic basis, one that is readily communicable as a method between practitioners and novitiates. For those who stress the need for reliable knowledge based upon replicability of findings and predictability in the form in which such knowledge is presented, the covering law, or nomothetic model, remains intact. The search remains for generalizations about human relationships that can be and are regularly confirmed empirically by a community of scientific observers.

However, positivism, the presumed initial basis of behavioralism, has not emerged intact out of the postbehavioralist confrontation. For one thing, there is no longer any doubt that the method we use does help to constitute the reality we see. Even if scientific method cannot in practice avoid adopting a realist position—that a real world exists—what part of that world we see, how we see it, and how we interpret what we do see are influenced by our ideological and other predispositions. If the argument were to stop at this point, as it often does, it would clearly have serious implications for the way we justify the scientific enterprise. It would leave the impression that the products of scientific efforts are irretrievably tainted. What remains to be resolved is this central problem raised by postbehavioralists in their attack on the ideological bias of scientific research.

If all research is inevitably biased by our predispositions, can objectivity and valid representation of reality ever be achieved? And we can pose this dilemma without raising the more difficult one as to why we should even accept this postbehavioralist critique, as it, too, by its own evidence, must be ideologically infected and, therefore, subject to doubt? But setting this familiar philosophical contradiction aside—the so-called liar's dilemma— postbehavioralism does leave political research with a question about the nature of objectivity and validity. It is a question that those actually engaged in scientific research seldom seriously address, despite the fact that philosophers of science have been debating the issue for years and are currently engaged in a vigorous conflict over the nature of foundationalism and realism as one form of the issue.[44]

An initial step out of this dilemma is to admit straight out that different theories represent different ways of reading or constituting the world. They cannot help but emphasize different aspects. The rational actor approach, for example, leaves the impression of a world made up of atomized actors interested only in their own well-being, a view that fits in well with free-market philosophies of the 1980s.[45] The existence, in theories, of ideological predispositions such as these should not be news to social scientists. Long ago Weber wrote extensively on how personal values influence the whole research process: the questions we choose to pose, the theories we offer, the methods we use, even the answers with which we sympathize, especially in ambiguous outcomes.[46] And social scientists are clever in the way they may mask the values that intrude on their professional work.

Does this relegate objectivity to the scrap heap? Not necessarily. Although the reception of a position may be hastened or retarded by its ideological compatibility with current opinion, even if concepts do constitute reality for us, science is constantly in the process of working out ways to overcome bias and thereby to retain objectivity. These ways will undoubtedly be just as effective with regard to utility-maximizing approaches, for example, as for any other theory. In the end, the test of any theory is not its ideological conformity or nonconformity but whether it predictably reflects the real world or, if one is a strict pragmatist, whether it permits us to cope with our social problems under the given circumstances (thereby avoiding any foundationalist assumptions, perhaps).[47]

Though I shall not pursue the argument here in full detail,[48] it is clear that competing theories about political relationships will undergo the various tests of confirmation by communities of scholars separated in space and time. Out of this, hopefully, will emerge minimal agreement on the degree to which a given theory or body of generalizations corresponds to political reality. In short, despite the fact that ideology does color scientific research, there is an escape from the possible distortions so incurred. Competition among theories across space and time and the evaluation of those theories by communities of scholars through complex, informal, and unending processes of adjustment and adjudication is the actual path through which theories historically have come to be accepted as confirmed by, or rejected as inconsistent with, the evidence. Thus, we do not need to fear the valid charge that values intrude on the whole scientific enterprise. Objectivity of the scientific enterprise as a whole need not be impaired as long as an open, uncoerced, and genuinely competitive community of scholars is able to maintain itself.[49] Objectivity is more a function of the social organization of the scientific enterprise and of the political and economic context[50] than of the bias or ideological predispositions of a given individual or set of scientists.

THE POSTMODERNIST CHALLENGE: BEYOND THE ACTOR. As I have already suggested, not all criticism of traditional positivism (as represented by many unreformed behavioralists) comes from those postbehavioralists who reject scientific method outright. Some has come from those behavioralists who join neopositivism in recognizing that earlier interpretations of scientific method have misled us about the nature of the scientific enterprise and that it is high time we brought our understanding of scientific method into accord with the way science is actually practiced. Elsewhere I have sought to show how misleading it would be to assume that our understanding of scientific method today must remain the same as it was during the behavioral period. I need not cover the same ground here to demonstrate that our conception of science has not stood still. It is itself undergoing change.[51]

Positivists cast in the image of the Vienna Circle of the 1920s, as so many empirical researchers still are, have resisted revised interpretations of scientific method as developed by recent advances in the philosophy of science. Such old-fashioned, unregenerate positivists may, however, have been looking at the wrong, and certainly not the worst, enemy. Postmodernism would seem to hold that position. Pauline Rosenau argues that postmodernism stands for the end of science, the death of history, the elimination of objectivity and the very idea of truth, the denial of the world of things and events, the end of cause and effect, the elimination of reason, the disappearance of the agent, the loss of contextuality and, if one can imagine it, much more that is antithetical to the assumptions, practices, and goals of scientific method.[52] The myopia of the pristine positivists, whom we still have among us, has prevented them from seeing activity in the rest of the intellectual community that truly threatens not only the way we do science but the very notion of a search for reliable knowledge and understanding.

Postmodernism comes in many different shapes and forms. For the most prominent kinds, meaning is to be found not in what is assumed to be an unknowable external object world but only in text, in language. And the meaning of the text is self-contained; through a reading of the text alone can we understand it. No appeal to the circumstances within which the text was written, its history, or the personality, knowledge, or intention of the author can illuminate the text. In fact, to clear away this kind of under-brush, which obscures the search for the meaning of the text, it has been proposed that, metaphorically, "The author should die once he has finished writing, so as not to trouble the path of the text."[53] Meaning inheres in the text alone, not in context, author, reader, or history.

If the text alone is of such overriding importance, and if no contextual circumstances can help to explain its meaning, how can we acquire an authentic reading? Although the question of who can offer an authoritative interpretation of the text is an arguable one (and the answer depends on the postmodernist to whom we turn), for many postmodernists this capacity seems to rest with the person doing the reading, certainly not with any scholarly consensus. Each reader of a text is the sole arbiter of its meaning. This formula would seem to introduce a very capricious element into interpretation, to such a degree that deconstructionists, the major proponents of this point of view, have often been accused of purveying a kind of nihilism.[54] This perspective eliminates all objectivity, subjectivity, and, in the end, communication; the text speaks for itself, not between persons—that is, not between an author and a reader.

Some postmodernists go even further. In arguing that all meaning lies within the text, they posit that there is no reality beyond language. There is nothing behind language, nothing that "grounds" it, nothing to which it corresponds.[55] Such postmodernism rejects all attempts to establish a foundation—a "transcendental signified," in Jacques Derrida's term—external to the subject on which valid knowledge might rest. Language is the only possible object of language: "[A]ll awareness of abstract entities—indeed, all awareness even of particulars—is a linguistic affair."[56]

Although this position would seem to apply only to language, for many postmodernists behavior itself also constitutes a text. We "read" behavior in the same way we read a sentence. Behavior contains meaning in and of itself. Here, too, the intention of the subject who acts is irrelevant to the meaning of the act, just as the intention of the author is irrelevant to a written text. And the circumstances surrounding the act, to which social scientists typically refer for understanding and explanation, are equally irrelevant. Thus disappears all reference to socioeconomic context, motivation, cultural orientation, social structure, and the like as explanatory variables. No less than for the written text, the meaning of behavior is wholly self-contained and needs to be read out of that action—which leaves the authentic reading of action no more possible than that of a written text.

Postmodernism has made significant inroads into a number of social sciences, such as anthropology, sociology, and history. It is nibbling at the boundaries of political science. It is already a matter of considerable contention within the areas of international relations and political theory.[57] We might expect that unless there is a sudden shift in the fortunes of this point of view it might one day move into the heart of empirical political research as well.

Postbehavioral critics of scientific method have served as a bridge to postmodernism. It was certainly appropriate and necessary to challenge the inflexible and misleading interpretation of the scientific method innocently accepted from the descendants of the Vienna Circle. But in addressing one problem, that of an excessively rigid conception of scientific method, postbehavioralism has now left us with a new problem of monumental proportions. In opening up the floodgates of criticism, postbehavioralism exposed science to a tidal wave, represented by certain postmodernists, that threatens the very foundations of all systematic knowledge. In the coming decades the proponents of a modernized understanding of scientific method have the clear responsibility for offering a systematic response to these postmodern critics if the scientific enterprise is to be protected from what looks like a nihilistic onslaught.[58]

The Application of Political Knowledge: Integration of the Disciplines

Postbehavioralism faulted behavioralism for its neglect of the urgent social issues of the day and, together with other forces, it has succeeded in sensitizing political science to these issues. It led to and reinforced the policy analysis movement, as I have already noted. But, as with other recent areas of change in political research, this solution has created its own inescapable problems that must be directly addressed in the coming decades.

One of these is clear and obvious. If, as I suggested earlier, the proportion of disciplinary resources going to basic research has decreased significantly because of the tendency to select topics on the basis of social urgency (rather than theoretical criteria), we may well wonder what will happen to our stock of research capital in future years. Basic knowledge may be viewed as capital accumulation in a discipline. It represents knowledge whose uses may not be apparent at the moment but that, on the basis of historical experience in science, may turn out to be of critical importance for the development of solutions to social problems yet to come. To some extent we are living off that capital now (although, because of the intertwined relationship between basic and applied research, it would be misleading to suggest that the latter makes no contribution to basic knowledge). It is likely that the rate of growth of new fundamental knowledge has declined significantly during the postbehavioral phase. At some point in the future this balance will certainly have to be corrected.

The policy analysis movement has left us with a second major concern. How can political science hope to provide answers to the various social issues it is called upon to deal with—poverty, environmental pollution, racial and sexual equality, global climatic changes, and the like—when, as a discipline in a highly specialized world, it deals with only one fragment of problems produced by and affecting whole societies? None of these issues is exclusively political in character. We take it for granted that they may involve economic, social structural, cultural, historical, psychological, and even biological dimensions. Yet if we look at the innumerable institutions that have arisen to deal with social problems—the various schools and departments of policy analysis or public affairs—with a few exceptions the emphasis is on political, economic, and sociological aspects, and even within this combination only one or another discipline may be emphasized.[59] This situation poses what is clearly one of the major problems confronting not only the social sciences but all knowledge in the coming decades: how are we to bring these various bodies of specialized disciplinary knowledge together for the solution of problems that are themselves undivided, undifferentiated social issues?

In the seventeenth century Descartes instructed us that analytic reasoning, the foundation of science, "requires us to divide each of the difficulties . . . encountered into as many parts as possible and as might be required for easier solution."[60] Adam Smith learned this lesson well, and we, his faithful descendants, scarcely need to be reminded of the virtues of specialization, whether in the production of goods and services or of knowledge. The search for understanding has driven Western scholarship to break nature, both physical and social, into increasingly smaller units, assuming that when we have understood the smallest unit—the elusive quark of the physical word is the archetype—we will then be able to reassemble our knowledge for a comprehensive understanding of the whole.[61]

We do not need to address here the issue of whether the Cartesian impulse to analytic decomposition, which is built into the very thought patterns of the Western intellect, can ever provide a satisfactory understanding of the whole or whether in the search for knowledge we may need to begin with the whole entity before we seek understanding of its parts. Whatever the reader's opinions on that score, in the very existence of our highly specialized disciplines lies one of the major crises of modern knowledge. It is what I have called the Humpty Dumpty problem.

To understand the world we have deemed it wise, if not necessary, to break it up into many components—the disciplines and their own subdivisions. But to act in the world, to address the issues for which understanding has presumably been sought in this highly specialized way, we need somehow to reassemble all the pieces of knowledge. And there is the rub. Try as we may, we have been no more successful than all the king's horses and all the king's men in putting the pieces together again. Understanding that has been acquired through the theoretical and methodological commitments of economics fits only tangentially with knowledge from political science; anthropological perspectives may fit uneasily with those from psychology; the newly conceived applied humanities seem to move in their own idiosyncratic directions; and so on. It is commonplace to point out that scholars find it difficult not only to talk to each other across disciplines but at times even to carry on a credible discourse with colleagues in subspecialties within their own disciplines, the level of development in many areas of inquiry having become so highly differentiated and technical.

A number of solutions to specialization have been offered. Interdisciplinary or multidisciplinary training has been tried; however, it is becoming increasingly difficult to gain proficiency in one discipline, let alone two, and three seems to be well beyond the pale.[62] Another attempted solution, teamwork among the disciplines, is common. But there, differing theoretical perspectives, concepts, notions of evidence, assessments of validity, and kinds of discourses place enormous barriers in the way of cooperative inquiry except in special cases.

General theories to provide a common base, at least for all the social sciences, have also been proposed and tried in recent years—for example, Parsons's structural perspectives (one hesitates to call them theories), general systems theory (another slight misnomer), and various other efforts to elicit general principles underlying all knowledge. Whether over time this approach will yield significant progress toward the solution of the problems of specialization is not clear, especially as the sentiment favorable to overarching theoretical analyses has, for the moment, at least, markedly declined.

In any event, multidisciplinary training, teamwork, and a general theory covering all social behavior have so far failed to ease the path for the application of our knowledge in the search for solutions to social problems. The Humpty Dumpty difficulty in reassembling the whole has seldom been directly confronted, much less overcome. We continue to train graduate students with the illusory hope that, after having been socialized into a specialized approach, when left to their own devices they will transcend their own beginnings and draw the disciplines together when required to apply them. In calling upon political science to increase its relevance to social issues, postbehavioralism generated a new order of difficulties such as these that cannot help but continue as a major concern for the future of all disciplines.

The Globalization of Knowledge

The immediate tasks for the future have been preordained by the problems the postbehavioral revolution created in its quest to solve old ones. But it would be shortsighted to presume that these efforts will be taking place in a vacuum. Political science is developing within an increasingly complex world, one that is continuing to shrink. A global intellectual community is slowly coming together. If the new units of the former Soviet Union succeed in establishing their political, cultural, and intellectual independence, we can expect a new burst of energy in the social sciences. Because this output will be based on close to a hundred years of experience at great variance from that in the West, we may expect to find new and different perspectives on issues already being dealt with in Western political science.

Other great surges of creativity can also be expected from the new intellectual communities that are emerging in East and South Asia. At the most general level, for example, we tend to think of Western logic as reflecting the way the human mind works; we assume we cannot escape this logic. On this we base our science, and as this science has proven itself through enormous epistemic and technological achievements, our interpretations bask in the credibility so derived. In the future social science will undoubtedly continue to reassert the power of scientific research and analysis to provide us with reliable understanding and explanation, even though we may need to adopt a broader and more tolerant interpretation of the nature of science.

What is not clear, however, is whether the logic of science as it has evolved in the West represents the way the mind must necessarily work. There is the possibility, one that ought not to be arbitrarily excluded from consideration, that our view of this logic may reflect only the way we in Western culture understand the workings of our mind, even as varied and conflicting as our knowledge in this area may be. It could be that as other cultures apply themselves at a sophisticated level to explanations of social phenomena, including the political, they may introduce a way of looking at social relations that will open up areas of inquiry and methods of research and analysis as yet concealed from us, blinded as we may be by a logic or way of conceptualizing that is intimately tied to our own culture.

For example, Confucianism stems from a tradition quite at odds with that of Descartes. The decompositional conception of reasoning which we, as descendants of Descartes, take for granted as the basis of good and adequate science stands in stark contrast to the holistic assumptions of Confucian thinking. Some Western scholars, though acknowledging the known strengths of Cartesian-inspired analytic reasoning, have already been exploring its limitations and have turned to a holistic perspective as a new starting point. System thinking already reflects that concern for seeing elements within a whole.[63] But what we find as exceptional—the turn to the whole as the starting point of research—many working in the Confucian tradition may well find as natural and normal. Just what effect this might have on the way a newly sophisticated social science might develop in the East is difficult to say. But the clash between cultures that differ so widely in their orientations to the acquisition of knowledge will surely bring new ideas to the surface, ideas that could well change the character of our own research procedures and even our conceptions of science as our own philosophy of science continues to grow and change.

Whether Confucianism does move the emerging world or global intellectual community in this direction is not the important point. I use it only to illustrate that as we look beyond this century to the emerging global context in which social science must continue to evolve, we ought to contemplate the future dynamically. Clashes of ancient cultures with their own ways of thought will force us to reconsider more insistently our own ways of looking at things.[64]

Neobehavioralism in Our Future

As I suggested at the outset, if we have learned little else from Kuhn's *The Structure of Scientific Revolutions,* each era in political research can be expected to solve some problems but, in the very process, give rise to new ones. I have tried to indicate some of the latter with respect to the rise of postbehavioralism in political science, and I have tried to indicate the direction in which responses might move. What is clear, however, is that postbehavioralism has been no more of a panacea for the ailments of behavioralism than the latter was for traditional research. Although behavioralism and postbehavioralism certainly advanced the discipline, their solutions bore with them the seeds of new difficulties. And if, to shift metaphors, our discipline looks fragmented and rudderless today, this may be evidence not of ineptness, irreconcilable differences, or incipient chaos but, more likely, of reorganization. We are scanning alternatives, putting them to use, and assessing their strengths and weaknesses. Struggles are still under way to shape the future of the discipline, if not of the social sciences as a whole, for it is difficult to understand fully what is happening in political science without taking into account similar conflicts in other major areas of knowledge. Unless the process of disciplinary transformation has changed radically, there is every reason to expect that in due course a new unifying theoretical focus with a dominant methodological strategy will arise.

The scientific method, as anyone familiar with it might have expected, has shown great resilience, despite the wholesale assault on its underlying assumptions. Few departments of political science around the world would now fail to provide students with basic training in rigorous techniques for acquiring, assembling, and analyzing data and for relating theories of various levels to such data. Rational and formal modeling's success in slowly suffusing throughout the discipline—even into philosophy, as I have already noted—testifies further to the fact that, far from being dead, scientific research continues to grow as one of the major strategies for improving the reliability of our knowledge about the political world.

Despite the hazards of peering into a crystal ball that is still cloudy, assuming the recognition and acceptance of a more relaxed and authentic understanding of the nature of science itself, the coming period in political inquiry is likely to retain behavioralism's fundamental scientific assumptions about how we ought to go about acquiring reliable understanding. It is true that various kinds of postmodernist philosophies are mounting a serious challenge to the very notion of systematic knowledge. However, it is highly unlikely that they will be able to bring the whole scientific edifice tumbling down.

The fundamental assumptions of behavioralism are being permanently modified and ameliorated by the perspectives and tools of postbehavioral critiques, by the newer ways of interpreting the methods of scientific inquiry, by the greater acceptance of a deductive methodology as a strategy for research, and by an increasing appreciation of how scientific inquiry itself helps to constitute reality. If we were looking around for a label to capture one major aspect of the changes already underway as we move to a new phase in the discipline, *neobehavioralism* might well serve that purpose.

NOTES

1. "The New Revolution in Political Science," in *American Political Science Review* 63 (1969): 1051–61. I could take the occasion of being honored by the publication of this *festschrift* volume to reflect on my experiences of more than half a century as a student of politics and on the nature of my association with others equally committed to its study. But I have already generated more than 500 manuscript pages of such reflections. They appear as part of the Pi Sigma Alpha Oral History Collection in political science located at the M.I.King Library of the University of Kentucky and were the product of several days of interviewing under the skillful guidance of Professor John Gunnell. (For a short history of this oral history program and for a few published fragments from my interviews see M. A. Baer, M. E. Jewell, and L. Sigelman [eds.], *Political Science in America: Oral Histories of a Discipline* [Lexington, KY: University of Kentucky Press], 1991, pp. 1–5, 195–214.

Hence I shall pass up the opportunity to look backwards once again. I shall instead accept the challenge issued by the organizer and editor of this book to all its contributors—namely, to confine ourselves to an appraisal of the state of political science from the time I was president of the APSA in 1968–1969 to the present and to contemplate possible future directions of our discipline.

2. T. S. Kuhn, *The Structure of Scientific Revolutions* (Chicago: University of Chicago Press, 1962). Compare with M. Weber, "Science as a Vocation," in H. H. Gerth and C. W. Mills, *From Max Weber: Essays in Sociology* (New York: Oxford University Press, 1946), at p. 138, where he also observes: "Every scientific 'fulfilment' raises new 'questions'; it *asks* to be 'surpassed' and outdated. Whoever wishes to serve science has to resign himself to this fact. . . . In principle, this progress goes on *ad infinitum*" (italics in original).

3. D. Easton, *A Framework for Political Analysis* (Englewood Cliffs, N.J.: Prentice-Hall, 1965; reissued, Chicago: University of Chicago Press, 1979), p. 7.

4. In "The New Revolution in Political Science," my presidential address to the American Political Science Association in 1969, I stood among the earliest internal critics. However, at the time, and even to the present day, some of my erstwhile behavioral colleagues, failing to read carefully what I was writing, seriously misconstrued my effort at constructive criticism and reform of the prevailing misconceptions about the nature of scientific method. Unfortunately and inappropriately they assumed I intended to reject the methodological basis of science and of its goals. Despite frequent reaffirmations of my convictions about the methods of science, some even to this day fail to realize that I sought to salvage and broaden the use of scientific method in political science by taking into account the revisions thought necessary by an increasing number of modern students of that method. The mistake of many behavioral critics has been to equate a search for improved principles on which to base our understanding of scientific inquiry for the rejection of the validity of such inquiry, an inexcusable error given the enormous attention in the philosophy of science literature to the weakness of early positivism (upon which behavioral self-perception and understanding still rested in the 1960s). To this day, unfortunately, many behavioral scientists seem to be stuck with the kind of antiquated view of science as fashioned by M. R. Cohen and E. Nagel, *An Introduction to Logic and Scientific Method* (New York: Harcourt, Brace, 1934). They fail to take into account the fact that, as with any discipline, knowledge about the philosophical bases of scientific method grows and changes over the years. It is not too much to ask, therefore, that those areas of our discipline that seek to found their inquiries on this scientific philosophy be aware of the changes and build them into an understanding of their own methods. See my comments along these lines in "Political Science in the United States: Past and Present," in D. Easton and C. S. Schelling (eds.), *Divided Knowledge: Across Disciplines, Across Cultures* (Newbury Park: Sage, 1991), pp. 37–59.

5. P. Feyerabend, *Against Method* (New York: Lowe and Brydone, 1976), 3rd. ed.

6. D. Easton, "Political Science in the United States: Past and Present," p. 49.

7. I first made this point in a talk delivered at the Chinese Academy of Social Sciences and at various universities in the People's Republic of China in 1982. It was later published in China and in the West as "Political Science in the United States: Past and Present." See, respectively, *Political Science and Law* (January, 1984), Shanghai Academy of Social Sciences, and *International Political Science Review* 6 (1982):

133–52. See the similar point in A. Finifter (ed.), *Political Science: the State of the Discipline* (Washington, D.C.: American Political Science Association, 1982) and later, again, in G. Almond, *A Discipline Divided* (Newbury Park, CA: Sage, 1990).

8. Easton and Schelling, *Divided Knowledge*, p. 48.

9. In *The Political System* (New York: Knopf, 1953, 2nd ed. 1971; reissued, Chicago: University of Chicago Press, 1981).

10. See specific references to this type in D. Easton, "The Political System Besieged by the State," in *Political Theory* 9 (1981): 303–25.

11. See my discussion of this point in "Political Science in the United States: Past and Present."

12. See R. Inglehart, *The Silent Revolution* (Princeton: Princeton University Press, 1977) and *Culture Shift in Advanced Industrial Society* (Princeton: Princeton University Press, 1990).

13. See D. Easton, *The Analysis of Political Structure* (New York: Routledge, 1990).

14. That was evident from the beginning, a point I made early on when I first tried to describe the tenets of postbehavioralism and to attach that name to it as a movement. See "The New Revolution in Political Science."

15. As I have already observed, the countercultural revolution had strong voluntarist elements in it: all one needed was the will and collectively the world could be transformed. In August 1969, the uplifting, orderly happening at Woodstock, involving some 400,000 participants, dramatized the conviction about reliance on sheer numbers and the power of personal commitment.

16. Here I use, without benefit of quotation marks, words that appear in Easton and Schelling, *Divided Knowledge: Across Disciplines, Across Cultures,* p. 51.

17. John Rawls, *A Theory of Justice* (Cambridge: Harvard University Press, 1971).

18. See for example, C. R. Beitz, *Political Theory and International Relations* (Princeton, NJ: Princeton University Press, 1979); J. Elster, *Rational Choice* (New York: New York University Press, 1986); J. S. Fishkin, *The Limits of Obligation* (New Haven: Yale University Press, 1982); K. Lehrer and C. Wagner, *Rational Consensus in Science and Society* (Dordrecht, Holland: Reidel, 1981).

19. This has been the genuinely creative thrust of Theda Skocpol's well-known and numerous writings in this area.

20. On the relative autonomy of the state see N. Poulantzas, *Political Power and Social Class* (London: NLB Press, 1968); E. A. Nordlinger, *On the Autonomy of the Democratic State* (Cambridge: Harvard University Press, 1981); and Easton, *The Analysis of Political Structure* and "The Political System Besieged by the State."

21. See Easton, "The Political System Besieged by the State."

22. For example, see the statement from the Annual Report (1990–1991) of the Social Science Research Council, p. 9, that "the future of social science also will depend upon the willingness of social scientists to attach research priority to topics such as persistent poverty, environmental degradation, and health pandemics—these and other issues that are of high public importance and concern not only in this country but elsewhere as well. It is toward this goal that 'mission-oriented basic research' plays a key role. Mission-oriented basic science is research in which practical concerns guide scientists' choice of topics."

23. See Easton, "The Political System Besieged by the State."

24. C. H. Titus, "A Nomenclature in Political Science," *American Political Science Review* 25 (1931): 45–60, at p. 45.

25. Among the latest comments on this, see G. A. Almond, *A Discipline Divided*.

26. See Easton, "Political Science in the United States: Past and Present," p. 48.

27. It has led one appraiser to conclude that the discipline "badly needs generalists" at this time (W. Crotty, *Looking to the Future,* vol. 1 in the Theory and Practice of Political Science Series [Evanston, IL: Northwestern University Press, 1991], p. 37. On reading an earlier version of this paper, Professor Mark Petracca of the University of California, Irvine, commented that "the discipline of political science reminds me of the 'big bang' theory of how the universe was created. Once the explosion took place, matter has been spinning off into an infinite number of directions with a seemingly endless variety of results. What incentive is there for anyone to put the 'universe' (discipline) back together again? Precious little." And, of course, that is the very point. There is little encouragement for political scientists to think about their subject at the most general level of analysis. The highest rewards go to the specialists. One can hope only that the intellectual tendency to try to make sense of details, to try to give a sense of unity and coherence to what we do, will assert itself as it has done periodically in our past. Even a casual reading of the history of various disciplines reveals a periodic pendular swing between emphasis on fact gathering and theory construction, each displacing the other as its fruitfulness is perceived to reach its limit at the time.

28. M. Friedman, *Essays in Positive Economics* (Chicago: University of Chicago Press, 1953).

29. A. Wildavsky, "Why Self-Interest Is an Empty Concept: Cultural Constraints on the Construction of 'Self' and 'Interest,' " an unpublished paper (September 1991). He argues that culture gives different content to both how we see ourselves as a self and how we define our interest. Hence, as Wildavsky sees it, there is no single self or self-interest in economics.

30. For the clear ideological implications of this tool, see my discussion below, especially the reference there to T. J. Lowi, "The State in Political Science: How We Become What We Study," in *American Political Science Review* 86 (1992): 1–7.

31. J. J. Mansbridge (ed.), *Beyond Self-Interest* (Chicago: University of Chicago Press, 1990), pp. 43–53.

32. See Wildavsky, "Why Self-Interest Is an Empty Concept," for the importance of culture in the definition of self and of interest.

33. Mansbridge, *Beyond Self-Interest,* p. 53.

34. Ibid.

35. J. Elster, *Nuts and Bolts for the Social Sciences* (New York: Cambridge University Press, 1989), pp. 61ff.

36. In economics, the welfare function?

37. As Max Weber put it, "In science, each of us knows that what he has accomplished will be antiquated in ten, twenty, fifty years. That is the fate to which science is subjected; it is the very meaning of scientific work." See Gerth and Mills, *From Max Weber: Essays in Sociology,* p. 138.

38. J. G. March and J. P. Olsen, *Rediscovering Institutions: The Organizational Basis of Life* (New York: Free Press, 1989).

39. Ibid., p. 53.

40. "The individual personality and will of political actors is less important; historical traditions as they are recorded and interpreted within a complex of rules are important. A calculus of political costs and benefits is less important; a calculus of identity and appropriateness is more important" (ibid., p. 38; see also p. 48). See also Elster, *Nuts and Bolts for the Social Sciences*, pp. 113ff, where the author makes the same point—namely, that rational action is concerned with outcomes, whereas action guided by social norms refers to shared standards of behavior sustained by approval or disapproval through external sanctions or internalized sentiments.

41. See Easton, *The Analysis of Political Structure*, especially chapter 3.

42. Hence, the structure of actual behavior needs to be compared to the normative structure or structure of rules. Understanding the deviations between the two sets of structures is vital if we are to understand how the institution operates in reality and the direction in which it may be changing if people try to bring rules and behavior into some kind concordance. Of course, actors often find it to their advantage to mask their actual patterns of behavior behind idealized norms.

43. For a full discussion of the importance of structures of behavior as against cultural or normative structures, see Easton, *The Analysis of Political Structure*, chapter 3.

44. See for example the alternative positions taken by the following: D. Herzog, *Without Foundations: Justification in Political Theory* (Ithaca: Cornell University Press, 1985); R. Rorty, *Consequences of Pragmatism (Essays: 1972–1980)* (Minneapolis: University of Minnesota Press, 1982); I. Shapiro, *Political Criticism* (Berkeley: University of California Press, 1990).

45. See T. J. Lowi's explanation, in "The State in Political Science: How We Become What We Study," for the spread of survey research and rational modeling as a function of receptive ideological communities.

46. E. A. Shils and H. A. Finch (eds. and trans.), *Max Weber on the Methodology of the Social Sciences* (Glencoe, IL.: Free Press, 1949), esp. chaps. 2 and 3; and Gerth and Mills, *From Max Weber: Essays in Sociology*, esp. chapter 5, "Science as a Vocation."

47. See Rorty, *Consequences of Pragmatism*.

48. See further comments on this question in Easton, "Systems Analysis and Its Classical Critics," in *The Political Science Reviewer* 3 (1973): 269–301.

49. Much more needs to be said here, of course. The conditions for the existence of such communities are not easy to sustain even in democratic societies, especially where sources of funding and control of scholarly media and institutions may themselves be at issue.

50. See Lowi, "The State in Political Science: How We Become What We Study."

51. See N. R. Hanson, *Perception and Discovery* (San Francisco: Freeman Cooper, 1969); D. Shapere, "Discovery, Rationality and Progress in Science," in K. Schaffner and P. Cohen (eds.), *PSA 1972: Proceedings of 1972 Biennial Meetings of Philosophy of Science Association* (Dordrecht, Holland: Reidel, 1974), pp. 407–19; F. Suppe, *The Structure of Scientific Theories* (Urbana: University of Illinois Press, 1977); S. Toulmin, *Human Understanding* (Princeton: Princeton University Press, 1972); R. Lane, "Positivism, Scientific Realism and Political Science: Recent Developments in the Philosophy of Science," in *Journal of Theoretical Politics* 8 (1996): 361–82.

52. See P. M. Rosenau, *Post-Modernism and Social Sciences* (Princeton: Princeton University Press, 1991) and the extensive bibliography cited there.

53. Umberto Eco, *Postscript to the Name of the Rose* (Orlando, FL: Harcourt, Brace and Jovanovich, 1983), p. 7, quoted in Rosenau, *Post-Modernism and Social Sciences,* p. 25.

54. See Rosenau, ibid.

55. Rorty, *Consequences of Pragmatism*, p. xx.

56. Ibid., as quoted from P. Sellars.

57. See Rosenau, *Post-Modernism and Social Sciences*, for a comprehensive examination of the impact of postmodernism on the social sciences, including political science.

58. See I. Shapiro, *Political Criticism*, for one attempt to rescue scientific foundationalism.

59. See R. D. Lambert, "Blurring the Disciplinary Boundaries: Area Studies in the United States," in Easton and Schelling, *Divided Knowledge,* pp. 171–94.

60. *Discourse on Method*, Part Two.

61. In this section I paraphrase what I have dealt with somewhat more extensively in "The Division, Integration, and Transfer of Knowledge," in Easton and Schelling, *Divided Knowledge,* pp. 7–36.

62. For a discussion of how the National Science Foundation has recently been seeking to deal with this problem through the establishment of its new Directorate for the Social, Behavioral and Economic (SBE) Sciences, see C. B. Marrett, "Shoring up the Mansion House," *Items* 46 (New York: Social Science Research Council, 1992), pp. 24–26. There the author says the directorate is organized to arrange "research funding around the knowledge that is to be created, rather than round the disciplines from which the knowledge emanate(s). Fundamentally, the model encourages disciplinary research but stresses its intellectual rather than its field-specific base" (p.25). In its essence this effort reminds one of the undergraduate program at the University of Chicago during the Hutchins era, wherein courses were organized around intellectual problems—liberty, personality development, peace and security, etc.,—not around disciplines. Theoretically, students were not even supposed to know the disciplines existed. One simply went after knowledge relevant to a problem wherever such knowledge was to be found. In time, however, the myth of a discipline-free world broke down, and specific disciplinary concentrations were reintroduced into the college curriculum. Specialization continues to exert a powerful, almost inescapable force in modern Western society.

63. See my discussion in *The Analysis of Political Structure*, esp. Part 3. For a recent bibliography on the vast literature dealing with the reductionism-holism debate (only in Western terms, however), see D. C. Phillips, *Holistic Thought in Social Science* (Stanford, CA: Stanford University Press, 1976) pp. 135ff. The author himself is not sympathetic to the holistic approach, however.

64. See my comments in this direction and references in Easton, "The Division, Integration, and Transfer of Knowledge."

2

Paradoxos Theoretikos

John G. Gunnell

As an undergraduate I was, for a time, a geology major. The introductory course in the department was taught by an illustrious and dramatic professor who began the semester by addressing a Mercator projection of the earth with all the continents displayed. He would note that children, and the scientifically naive, might believe that, like the dispersed parts of a jigsaw puzzle, these "islands" had once been contiguous. We were to learn, however, through an inductive study of geological fact, the scientific truth that the continents were fixed in place on the earth's crust.

In addition to suggesting how the truth for one scientific generation may become a travesty for the next, this anecdote indicates, albeit elliptically, three somewhat disparate but related points. First, theories and facts are logically symmetrical. Second, theories, and theories of theory, have a genealogy. Third, the remote continents of empirical and normative political theory, which today might only appear to have some complementarity, were in fact once joined. These points will emerge as I explore the history of empirical theory in American political science and the manner in which there has been a consistent tension between the cognitive and practical purposes of such theory.[1] The idea of an empirical theory of politics was always conceived of as part of a program for intervening in political life, but, paradoxically, the basis of that intervention was understood to be the epistemological independence of such a theory. This paradox involved a simultaneous search for practical authority and scientific purity that led political science at once to distance itself from politics and to conceive of theory in a manner that reflected its practical aspirations.

In the early 1980s, at the height of the postbehavioral policy turn in American political science, the American Political Science Association (APSA) undertook a survey of the "state of the discipline." This collection of essays on the contemporary practice of various subfields of political science was remarkable in the extent to which discussions of scientific accomplishment and procedure lacked a consideration of the public role of political science. It is difficult, for example, to find any substantial echo of what, shortly more than a decade earlier, David Easton had announced as a "new revolution" in political science that would return the discipline to its historic mission of joining empirical theory to normative goals and public purpose.[2] Yet the practical concerns of the discipline were latent in its image of theory.

From the beginning of disciplined political studies in the United States, every principal statement about an empirical science of politics suggested that the essential aim of such a science was to affect political life. However, the separation of political science and politics was, by the late nineteenth century, largely an institutional given. In the early part of that century, the study of politics in American colleges and universities may have served to convey moral values to social elites, but by the post–Civil War era, when the modern university emerged, the United States, compared to most European countries, already manifested a distinct absence of conventional institutional ties between the academy and the structure of political power. Although the notion of political action was originally very much part of the identity of the social sciences, it did not prevail, and the discipline of political science opted, early on, for "objectivity" over "advocacy."[3] And how was knowledge to reach the world of political action? The dominant and most persistent answer was that it must do so on the basis of its cognitive authority.

There were many factors involved in the emergence of the state as political science's object of inquiry.[4] The most obvious is the influence of the German *Staatslehre*, but another was fear and loathing with respect to everyday politics and the belief that it was necessary to find something both more sublime and less dangerous, something that could provide the discipline with a distinct and authoritative scientific identity. The loathing was shared by the general public, which was distrustful of people who called themselves students of politics. Even the title "political science" was viewed with suspicion; Woodrow Wilson broke new, and seldom reworked, ground when he named the department at Princeton "Politics."

The fear emanated in part from anxiety about retaliation, as a consistent goal of political science was to abolish its subject matter politics, or at least the corrupt and distorted form in which it was often manifest. But the fear went even deeper than concern about retribution. Francis Lieber, the founder of institutionalized political studies in the United States, believed that only religious fanaticism exceeded politics as a cause of the "alienation of the mind" in modern society.[5] From Lieber to at least Harold Lasswell, politics was understood as inherently "pathological" (a term they both employed), and the purpose of political science was deemed therapeutic, something to rationalize and dispel the fantasies and excessive enthusiasm of political life. The idea of science as a source of authoritative knowledge that, however circumspectly, might challenge, overcome, or direct political life remained constant. Yet it was believed that this goal required science to remain pure, as the only authority it, and the university, possessed was objectivity and truth. The problem became one of how to speak truth to power.

American social science developed from two distinct but converging tributaries. It was in part an extension of the moral sciences in the traditional university curriculum and in part an institutionalization of reform movements that gravitated toward the university as a source of scientific authority. Although some early social scientists, such as the economist Richard Ely, attempted to combine science with direct political action, neither the university nor society were tolerant of this strategy, which blurred the very independence and authority that the university promised. By the time political science was institutionally, theoretically, and methodologically distanced from politics, the question was how to bring the authority of science to bear on political authority.

THE QUEST FOR SCIENTIFIC AUTHORITY

The historico-philosophical approach to the study of the state in the nineteenth century—the paradigm constituted by the work of individuals such as Lieber, J. C. Bluntschli, Theodore Woolsey, John W. Burgess, and Herbert B. Adams—was an attempt to be scientific in the manner of natural science. This search for a science of politics was never disjoined from the practical concerns of political education and political reform. Though for some of the early theorists, such as Lieber, the membranes separating academic and public discourse may have seemed relatively permeable, the creation of the modern research university and the development of a graduate curriculum based in form and substance on the German model, which emerged under Burgess at Columbia and under Adams at Johns Hopkins, signaled new problems. These early theorists attempted to adapt their understanding of the German relationship between the university and the state to the American context.

What they hoped for was the establishment of schools of both civic education and scientific expertise that would command the attention of government—private schools with a public purpose. This strategy was born from their education in Europe and exposure to institutions such as the Ecole Libre des Sciences Politiques in France and from awe of what appeared to be the academic and political integration represented in the position of the late-nineteenth-century German Mandarins. They failed, however, to take account of the degree to which the American university was

congenitally estranged from politics and of the extent to which the European model was inapplicable to the pluralized character of both the university and politics in the United States.

However, Burgess, who more than anyone else of the era set the form
for American political science education, remained unequivocal in his belief that a scientific political science was the key to sounder public policy
and that the latter was the essential justification of the former. For Burgess,
historical investigation was science; he understood himself as applying the
methods of natural science to the study of law, politics, and the "political
system," as he termed it. His goal was, first, to create a science in which
logic brought theory and fact into proper conjunction and, second, to incorporate the wisdom so gained into the practice of politics.[6] Only in modern times, he believed, had philosophical reflection attained a level that
allowed for the formulation of a set of propositions that could be "arranged
into a body of science."[7]

For Westal Woodbury Willoughby at Hopkins, the other principal theorist of the late nineteenth and early twentieth century, Burgess's science
was still too political to gain the credibility it required in order to have
practical purchase. He urged a more distinct separation between "teleologi-
cal and ideal" theory, on the one hand, and "scientific and analytic" theory,
on the other, as well as between political science and politics. He disagreed
not only with Burgess's particular normative claims but also with the manner in which Burgess had stepped over into the realm of "politics and states-
manship" and out of the "proper field of pure political theory."[8] But Willoughby did not reject the practical purpose of political theory. His concern
was with maintaining its purity and thereby, in his view, its authority.

The motives behind the creation of the American Political Science Association in 1903 reflected what was becoming the paradox of science and
politics. The break with the American Historical Association and the
American Social Science Association was precipitated not only by a search
for professional autonomy. The former was insufficiently focused on practical objectives, and the latter was still largely a para-academic organization
with little scientific status. A central concern of the new association was the
administrative and legislative reform so prominent in the work of Frank
Goodnow, the first president of the APSA. The goal was to displace politics
as usual, which was regarded as marked by corruption, irrationality, and
inefficiency.

The APSA was predicated on several not easily reconcilable propositions.
It was devoted to "advancing the scientific study of politics," with the explicit
intention of establishing the discipline on an "objective basis" that reflected
the "reconstruction which the general body of science has undergone at
the hands of inductive philosophy" and of going beyond particularistic studies to arrive at laws and "universal principles." The application of such a

science was equally explicit: to provide a basis for the "guidance of state-craft" and to "bring political science to a position of authority as regards practical politics." Yet the charter of the APSA stated that it would not "assume a partisan position upon any question of practical politics."[9] Somehow the authority of science was to be translated into political authority, and the history of the first fifty years of the discipline was to a large extent a search for that Rosetta stone.

Willoughby, more than anyone else in the formative years of the profession, set out to establish the identity of political science and political theory in a "new period of scientific study." He did much to rehabilitate the idea of "speculation," deprecated by the early empirical realists, urging that it produced the sort of theoretical principles and generalizations underlying systematic empirical political inquiry. Political theory, he argued, performed two essential functions: it offered a critical scientific perspective on politics, and it provided the concepts, definitions, and terminology of systematic political inquiry.[10] He maintained that scholars must devote more attention to the scientific and analytical dimensions of political theory, to conduct the kind of "rigid political analysis" that would produce a "true and useful science of politics."[11] Although Willoughby, like Goodnow, found ways of articulating theory and practice in his own life, he offered little in the way of an institutional answer to the general problem of the relationship between political science and politics.

Burgess's concerns about political enlightenment through political science consciously informed the work of his students, who included Charles Beard and Charles Merriam.[12] Merriam's principal teacher, William Archibald Dunning, had the least energetic attitude among those at Columbia toward the practical implications of political study, yet his methodological teaching, in both form and substance, had a profound impact on the reconstitution of the image of scientific inquiry in Progressive and post-Progressive political science. Dunning emphasized, first, the unity of science and objectivity and, second, the manner in which the study of history provided a critical understanding of how ideas at once responded to and moved the forces in society.

Whereas Woodrow Wilson searched for ways to make social science applicable to politics and finally joined the world of political practice, Merriam, frustrated after a period of political action, returned to the task of enhancing the authority of social science. Wilson initially rejected the extremes of both advocacy and expertise in favor of what he perceived as the mediating role of the "literary politician," who would produce factual knowledge as a basis for rational politics.[13] But he was as unsuccessful as others of his generation in finding a vehicle for the articulation of academic and public discourse. The failure of Progressive political science, such as that pursued by Beard and Arthur Bentley, to awaken democratic consciousness by exposing the facts of political reality weighed heavily on Merriam. Merriam's pursuit of systematic political theory as a basis of political transformation was the historical zenith and paradigm case of the vision that overcoming "anarchy" in social theory was the key to eliminating "chaos" in politics. Merriam was inspired not only by the Columbia ambience but, like his teachers, by his image of the German academy where he wrote his dissertation. He remained constant in his belief that social control exercised through general civic education and intercourse between academic and political elites was the solution to the problem of how to bring knowledge to bear on politics.

After Willoughby's early work, political thinkers paid little attention to the idea of systematic empirical theory until Merriam picked up the discussion at the University of Chicago in the early 1920s. The rejection, during World War I, of German philosophy and the rise of pluralist accounts of politics precipitated the decline of the state as the object of inquiry.[14] This period began the distinct Americanization of political science and a new emphasis on political theory, which was advanced as the special province of those who *know* as opposed to those who *do*. Political theory, from Plato to modern times, had been consistently understood, by Dunning and others, as the key to change in politics, and it was now, as formulated within political science, perceived as the basis of intervention. It was not an accident that the focus on theory increased as the distance between knowledge and politics, both domestically and internationally, appeared to widen.

Only by explaining political behavior, Merriam argued, was it possible to change that behavior. He insisted that the foundation of a truly scientific study of politics had been established by individuals such as Burgess, Dunning, Wilson, Goodnow, and Willoughby and further developed in contemporary sociology and psychology. The problem was refinement and deployment. In his 1920 assessment of the state of political science, Merriam called for a fundamental change in the "theory of politics" and a "reconstruction of the methods of political study" in order to explain relevant "facts and forces." He sought not to reject the ideas of his teachers but rather to focus on what they had emphasized—"the comparatively recent doctrine that political ideas and systems . . . are the by-product of environment." Through the development of this trend, he believed, political theory could properly be applied to the world of "political prudence." Political theory was the medium for the collection and classification of new acquisitions of political fact, and this organization of research was the basis for the "cross-fertilization of politics with science."[15]

In Merriam's work there also crystallized an image of the cognitive character of theory that, in subsequent years, would be philosophically enhanced, reinforced, and codified. Merriam had some limited exposure to the work of individuals such as Karl Pearson (*The Grammar of Science*) and maybe some vague sense of the arguments of Ernst Mach and other precursors of positivism in the philosophy of science, but his notion of theory was more a product of what he understood, in terms of his own experience and education, as its internal and external functional role. He articulated an instrumentalist interpretation of social scientific theory, one that would have a decisive impact on the discursive evolution of the concept of theory in political science.

THE QUEST FOR SOCIAL RELEVANCE

The instrumentalist idea of theory reflected the image of political science as a means of social change. And political theory was the core of political science. How and why theory came to be regarded as internally or cognitively instrumental is a more complicated issue of intellectual history, even though in some respects this conception flowed naturally from the external perspective. Just as science was construed as a social instrument, theories were viewed as instruments of science. Instrumentalism assumes a fundamental distinction between theory, as an intellectual construct, and the realm of facts, which are in some fundamental sense epistemologically given or primitive and in some manner accessible to immediate experience. Theory is conceived as the product of science, whereas facts are the preconstituted subject and object of science. Theories are interpreted as devices or approaches for economically ordering and generalizing about facts and thereby explaining relations between them. Facts are problematical with respect to their causal and descriptive relationships, but they are prior in that they are the basis for judging theories, which are conceived as less intrinsically true or false than useful in varying degrees for explanation and prediction.

By the 1920s there were several factors that further disposed political science toward this perspective. Not the least of these was a deeply rooted late-nineteenth-century suspicion of speculation, a suspicion that was reflected in the nascent field of the philosophy of science and that was beginning to have an impact on social science. Science, whether historical or natural, was understood as an inductive enterprise, and theory was depreciated. This attitude was reinforced in social science by the Progressivist rejection of formalism and the emphasis on factual realism as social criticism. Theories, however, seemed an essential element of scientific inquiry and required rehabilitation. Instrumentalism provided an interpretation that reconciled the necessity of theory with what was understood as the primacy of fact. Finally, it was widely accepted that just as theories ordered facts in social science, they ordered perceptions in politics and society. This nexus seemed to intimate a basis for theoretical intervention, for a conjunction between scientific theories and theories of practice.

However archaic the nineteenth-century idea of the state may appear today, and however obsolete and alien it had begun to seem to many social scientists after the turn of the century, its formulation represented characteristics that, in light of contemporary postpositivist work in the philosophy of science, might today be attributed to theory. The state was understood as real, as representing a universal ontological domain that stood behind and explained appearances. When the state was transformed into a concept that referred to the institutions of government, more than a theory was changed: the very idea of theory underwent a transformation. The rejection of the state in favor of the facts of politics was accompanied by the rejection of theories in favor of facts as the basis and purpose of science.

Merriam explicitly equated political theories with methods of inquiry, regarding them as instruments for the "observation and description of actual processes of government."[16] He saw theories as tools with which to order conceptually a world of burgeoning facts and with which to make social science an effective instrument of social control. His interest in pure science was negligible, and he was drawn to psychology because of the promise of its manipulative power for organizing "public intelligence." He claimed that the social sciences were approaching a stage where they potentially could control "political nature" and supplant "the language of traditional authority, or custom, or group propaganda."[17] The study of politics had reached a point, he urged, where it was possible to "bridge the gap between art and science and bring us to more precise methods of political and social control than mankind has hitherto possessed"—and thereby, through devices ranging from eugenics to education, to transform "jungle politics" into "laboratory politics."[18]

Although Merriam was effusive about the practical purpose of empirical theory, it was G. E.G Catlin who first addressed the question of the cognitive and practical role of theory in an extended manner. Like Merriam, he stressed the psychological dimension of "human behavior characterized by the recurrence of specific behavior patterns" that could be quantitatively analyzed.[19] He was explicit about his view that the purpose of social science was social control—nothing less than the search for a "social Wassermann test" as part of the "profession of social medicine" devoted to the health of democracy. Although Catlin approved of the Progressive ideology, he, like Willoughby, was concerned that social scientists had failed to make an adequate distinction between science and politics and thereby had undercut the very authority they wished to achieve. Theory was, he argued, still an "ethical philosophy" with a "liberal" bias rather than a "dispassionate study of actual human behavior."

Ideally, the relationship between social science and political practice should parallel that between biology and medicine. Social scientists needed to discover some "basal principles of political method" and to establish "a behaviorist science of politics" that, through observation, generalization, and prediction, would allow a scientific diagnosis of political pathologies and provide the basis for administrative and legislative treatment.[20] Catlin, much more self-consciously than Merriam, and relying explicitly on Pearson and the field of economics, also adopted the instrumentalist conception of theory as "a logical structure superimposed upon the observation of a highly frequent occurrence." He recommended the construction of an abstract fiction called "political man" (the power seeker) and the "political situation" (competing wills), just as economists had invented the notion of economic man and rational choice.[21] Catlin also attempted to locate empirical theory in the tradition of political science.

Though he distinguished "political theory" in "professional political science" from the broader category of "political thought," which included "ethics" and other normative matters, and from the nineteenth- century tradition of *Staatslehre*, he claimed that the current search for a science of politics perpetuated the great tradition of political theory that began with the Greeks and that had always been concerned with more than "ideals." Catlin continued to insist that, as in the case of Aristotle, "the end in view is practice and not mere knowledge" and that the "positive science of politics" was "one of the most hopeful elements for the more intelligent and . . . purposive ordering of society." He argued that "a grounded judgment on the practical strength or weakness of institutions and conventions" must be predicated on the axioms and laws of a systematic explanatory and empirical science.[22]

Stuart Rice's *Quantitative Methods in Politics* (1928) emphasized similar themes. He stressed the difference between science and moral philosophy and, referring to Pearson and to Percy Bridgman's *Logic of Modern Physics* (1927), explicitly adopted the instrumentalist metatheory and the idea of the unity of scientific method. In 1927 the Social Science Research Council initiated a project, under Rice's direction, that was designed as an inventory and synthesis of the methods employed in the social sciences. In the course of this "inductive approach to the study of methods" it became clear that, although inventory was possible, synthesis was not. There was not even a clear agreement on what constituted a "method"; the authors understood them as those concepts within a field that determined the units and boundaries of analysis. Such concepts, however, were crucial, because in the social sciences, even more than in the natural sciences, the "raw material" or "facts," they believed, were so volatile and amorphous that only through conceptual stability could they be systematically isolated and subjected to causal analysis. If the facts "are to have any coherent meaning, they must be selected in accordance with some guiding point of view, some preconception," which would comprise *"instruments* as well as *frameworks* of investigation."[23] The council project to a large extent codified the instrumentalist image of theory or method that had been developing in political science, and it pointed toward the future, a future that was most immediately the work of Harold Lasswell.

In his early writings Lasswell did not address metatheoretical issues in any very direct manner, but he embraced both dimensions of instrumentalism—as a cognitive account of theory and as a therapeutic psychological social science devoted to understanding and remedying political pathologies. Lasswell also represented the fourth and last generation whose members took inspiration from their limited experience abroad and lamented what they took to be the American social scientist's comparative impotence with respect to wielding public authority. In his mind, a policy science demanded an ambitious role for the elite academic intelligentsia, wielders of a science that exposed the realities underlying ideologies and the search for power and that provided a basis for "preventive politics" through social manipulation and planning for democratic purposes.[24] Theory, for Lasswell, was simply the "invention of abstract conceptions."[25] Joining Merriam and others in the Chicago school's study of power, he defined political analysis as the "study of changes in the value pattern of society"—in effect, "the study of *who gets what, when, and how.*"[26] His goal was to find a conceptual framework for this endeavor.

THE RESURGENCE OF PURE SCIENCE

Beginning in the 1940s, the basic values of American political science were fundamentally challenged by an ideologically diverse group of emigré scholars who coalesced around the project of initiating the first root-and-branch critique of the discipline.[27] Whatever other internal and external factors contributed to the behavioral revolution in the early 1950s, the intellectual core was a vindication and propagation of the content and purpose of the vision of a liberal science of politics that had been under siege for a decade. The defense of this scientific identity brought the discipline, and individuals such as Lasswell, into direct contact with the philosophy of logical positivism.

This philosophy—as represented in the work of Rudolf Carnap and other philosophers of science who were associated with the Vienna and Berlin schools and who emigrated to the United States—provided, first of all, a coherent image of scientific explanation and the unity of scientific method, an image that had been lacking in American philosophy. Second, though it stressed the role of theory in science and equated scientific ex-

planation with the subsumption of particulars under laws or lawlike generalizations, its account of the nature of scientific theory and of the relationship between theories and facts reinforced, and offered a more systematic
rendition of, the rudimentary cognitive instrumentalism that already attached to the notion of theory in political science. Finally, positivism emphasized a logical distinction between facts and values, between empirical
science and normative claims, that helped to underwrite further the discipline's commitment to scientific objectivity as a basis of practical authority.

Even if the connection with positivist philosophy was often secondary or
tertiary and rhetorically inspired, the new philosophical dimension in the
discussion of science was distinctive. It exacerbated the inherent tension
between the dual, but often paradoxical, commitments to science and politics, as well as empirical and normative theory, that through the 1940s were
still very much part of the vision of the authors of the behavioral revolution, such as Gabriel Almond. Numerous contextual factors, such as the
cold war, have been adduced to explain how science, between the late 1940s
and mid-1960s, increasingly came to be perceived as an end rather than a
means, but an emphasis on these external factors obscures the powerful
internal conceptual dynamics within the discipline that propelled it in this
direction. First, there was a growing, if hardly novel, sense that political
science lagged behind other fields, even in the social sciences, in terms of
its progress as an authentic science. Second, although there was increasing acceptance of the idea that science was more a theoretical than a fact-
gathering activity, the concept of theory and its relationship to facts had
been, at best, crudely elaborated in the field. Third, the assumption persisted that the potential practical authority of social science rested on its
methodological and institutional distance from politics, on its status as an
"objective" institution. Finally, there was the unprecedented need to secure
and defend the discipline's scientific identity in the face of a critique of
science from within political theory itself.

The increased tension between the scientific and practical goals of the
discipline was apparent in the circumstances and content of Lasswell's 1950
collaboration with the philosopher Abraham Kaplan, who had been a student of Carnap's, in developing a general "conceptual framework" for political inquiry. Not since the charter of the APSA had the ambivalence been
more singularly manifest. The original manuscript of *Power and Society*
(1950) had been written during the war and inspired by Merriam's and
Lasswell's fascination with propaganda techniques as a means of molding
opinion for "good" as well as "evil" purposes. The work had been commis-
sioned and funded by the Rockefeller Foundation as part of a project on
mass communication designed to recruit and train people in propaganda
deployment. After the war, however, the authors advertised their endeavor
as the creation of a value-free operational language of political inquiry and

as an exercise in scientific "political theory." They stressed that it had been prompted by political issues such as the dangers created by "war, famine, and atomic destruction" as well as the developing confrontation between the "liberal-democratic and the Bolshevist" ideologies. But they insisted that, although their ultimate concerns were practical, their goal was neither "to provide a guide for political action" nor to develop "techniques of political practice." They maintained that their aim was, through the development of a systematic language for "inquiry into the political process" and the phenomenon of power, "to bring the languages of political theory and of practical politics into closer harmony."[28]

One purpose of the book was to legislate the meaning of "political theory" as part of empirical science and to reject explicitly what the authors believed was the emerging tendency to identify the term with both "metaphysical speculation" ("abstractions hopelessly removed from empirical observation and control") and the history of political thought. The latter, they claimed, had been concerned not with "political inquiry" and the formulation of "concepts and hypotheses of political science" but rather with what "ought to be" and with the justification of "political doctrines." The authors noted that "in recent decades a thoroughgoing empiricist philosophy of science has been elaborated in a number of approaches—logical positivism, operationalism, instrumentalism—concurring in an insistence on the importance of relating scientific ideas to materials ultimately accessible to direct observation." This was the basis of their account of theory. Yet they again stressed that their scientific interest did "not exclude a political interest in its outcome and applications"—science and public policy were "intertranslatable" and "complementary," and "both manipulative and contemplative standpoints may be adopted."[29]

The simultaneous embrace of these standpoints was based on what the authors referred to as the *"principle of configurative analysis,"* in which the "functions of the scientist overlap and interact with those of the policy maker." The policy sciences, they claimed, stood in "the grand tradition of political thought," but in that tradition ethics and politics had been fused. Advances in social science, they claimed, required "giving full recognition to the existence of two distinct components in political theory—the empirical propositions of political science and the value judgments of political doctrine." They emphasized once more that they were not "unconcerned with political policy" nor with the "justification of democratic values" and "their derivation from some metaphysical and moral base"; their values were "those of the citizen of a society that aspires toward freedom," and their aim was to further the democratic ideal and thereby achieve "human dignity and the realization of human capacities." However, such goals were matters of political doctrine and should not be confused with an empirical science devoted to constructing an analytical framework for developing hypotheses that would provide the basis for a "naturalistic" treatment of "*ho-mocentric politics*."[30]

When David Easton arrived at Chicago in 1947, he quite explicitly embraced the spirit and substance of the Merriam/Catlin/Lasswell tradition, but he also inherited the paradoxes inherent in that tradition. The focus of Easton's earliest work was the widespread concern in the 1930s and 1940s about the "eclipse of liberalism." Much of the emigré literature, ranging from the work of Leo Strauss and Eric Voegelin to that of Herbert Marcuse and the Frankfurt school, consisted of a critique of liberalism. Easton's opinion about the fragility of liberalism was, however, considerably different. The problem of contemporary liberalism was, he claimed, its general "failure to put its theories to the test of social reality." He found hope for revision in the idea, advocated by late-nineteenth-century thinkers such as Bagehot, Mosca, and Pareto, of "political positivism," or the "use of scientific method to discover social facts about the source of political power" and empirically to test values in actual social contexts. Realism also led to the recognition of the creative role of the elite in society. Easton concluded that the "liberal must turn to the laborious task of rigorous empirical study of society" and incorporate the findings "into the body of active liberal thought."[31] He pursued this theme further in his analysis of Lasswell's search for a link between science and democracy.

Easton addressed the contemporary "attack" on scientism and on the idea of a "science of man" by arguing that Lasswell had suggested an answer to the problem of the relationship between science and values. Although Lasswell sometimes seemed to imply that social science could not break out of the Weberian impasse regarding the distance between the vocations of science and politics, he also implied that there might be a "scientific validation of values." If certain human values and goals were scientifically and demonstrably rooted in universal basic impulses, then it might be demonstrated that only certain institutional arrangements would satisfy these needs. This in turn suggested the possibility of "transcending the insecurities of relativism for the greater certainty of a science of values" oriented toward the needs of a democratic community. This had also led Lasswell to move from a narrow theory of elitism and power to a more general theory of decision making. The latter opened new avenues for "the development of a systematic theory of political science" that was "immediately relevant" to democratic goals rather than simply searching for "pure truth."[32]

The context of Easton's famous and influential 1951 article on the "decline of political theory" was a symposium "on the relation of political theory to research." Although the general spirit of the symposium reflected the increased disposition to separate empirical political theory from normative and practical concerns, Easton's contribution was primarily an extended argument about how the preoccupation with "historical interpretation" had led to the demise of creative value theory and undermined "the task of building systematic theory about political behavior and the operation of political institutions." It also had inhibited the joining of the "two major orders of knowledge," facts and values, in their proper relationship. The underlying problem, however, was the consensus and complacency that had marked the late nineteenth and early twentieth centuries. This situation had been profoundly changed by the "end of the first World War and the subsequent spread of totalitarianism," which demonstrated that "guidance for our conduct in practical affairs" required a rebirth of theory. An approach that urged the exclusion of values from empirical analysis was, as Robert Lynd had argued, detrimental to social research and, as Mannheim had demonstrated, impossible. Such an approach obscured the fact that "social science lives in order to meet human needs," deflected research away from relevant issues, and perpetuated the "feeling today that social science lives in an isolated ivory tower."

The age was one in which serious and sophisticated "political guidance" was necessary for both "the politician as well as the humble citizen." Although this task could conceivably be left to the "statesman," it was more properly within the "competence" of "those social scientists who are most closely associated with analyzing the content of past value systems" and who are "in a strategic position for contributing to a reformulation of contemporary theory." Easton claimed that the "task of the social scientist has been too sharply and artificially divorced from that of the politician." The well-rounded political theorist who understood both contemporary "empirical relations" and "human goals," who had grasped the art of value theory by studying traditional political theory rather than simply talking about that art, potentially possessed a perspective with which "neither the politician nor the citizen is normally as well-equipped." Creative value theory would make empirical research meaningful and relevant and "provide once again a bridge between the needs of society and the knowledge of the social sciences" by providing "the grounds of political action."

It was evident, however, that Easton believed social science could make a claim on practice only by validating its claim to scientific knowledge. Although his principal emphasis was on the reconstitution of value theory, the decline of political theory also involved "indifference to causal theory," or "systematic empirically oriented theory about political behavior." A systematic approach would "permit the construction of a meaningful applied science" that went beyond "the rank of exceptional common sense" provided by the journalist or statesman. Easton claimed that there were uniformities in political behavior but that to discover them social scientists must move beyond "crude empiricism" and low-level generalization. Rather, they must construct a "broad-gauge theory or the conceptual framework within which a whole discipline is cast" and which eventually and incrementally "might reach the stage of maturity of theory in physics."[33]

In *The Political System*, Easton markedly changed emphasis.[34] Although the concern with the reconstitution of value theory remained, most of the book was devoted to criticizing past empirical and theoretical work in political science. The basic goal, as expressed in the prefatory quote from Beard, remained that of developing a general causal theory that would serve as a basis for bringing politics under rational control. But the very idea of a science of politics, more than its application, was in need of defense; the scientific identity of the discipline was in danger. Political science research had, Easton claimed, been characterized by "hyperfactualism" and a failure to marry empiricism and theory. Although the focus on concepts such as power and the state had yielded some results, it had failed to provide a basis for formulating a "conceptual framework for the whole field." Here Easton proposed what would become his influential definition of politics as "the authoritative allocation of values" and laid down the rudiments of his systems analysis. This would be the focus of his extensive and detailed theoretical endeavors during the next decade and would substantially shape the general theoretical development in the field.

Given the dominant trends in political theory at the time, it is not surprising that the book began with the claim that it was "increasingly difficult to appreciate why political theory should continue to be included as a central part of political science." It was essential, Easton believed, to "win back for theory its proper and necessary place." The greatest problem was the "mood of the age," characterized by a "dissent against scientific method" and a "growing disillusionment about the whole of scientific reasoning as a way of helping us understand social problems." People had given up the idea that "progress is inevitable" and embraced the "humanistic feeling that scientific development, either social or physical, does not always lead to desirable moral results." The search for social laws like those in natural science, represented by the work of individuals such as Lasswell, Catlin, and Herbert Simon, had been treated with hostility. Instead, "in political science criticism rather than approval of scientific method and its cognitive objects is almost imperceptibly becoming the criterion of judgment."

To understand Easton's subsequent work and the initiation of the theoretical program of behavioralism, it is necessary to grasp the degree to which it represented less a break with the traditional values, motives, and motifs of American political science than an attempt to rearticulate them ever more forcefully in an era in which they were, for the first time, being fundamentally attacked. In large part behavioralism entailed a reassertion and defense of the authority of a science of politics. Many factors in the professional and political context may have contributed to the search for "pure" science in the 1960s, but a crucial element was the persistent assumption that distance and purity were the conditions of practical authority and efficacy. Ironically, what began to recede were the general focus on the articulation of normative and empirical theory and any specific consideration of strategies for joining academic and public discourse. These trends were evident in Easton's own work, both in his elaboration of the theory of the political system and his commentaries on the discipline. He still claimed that "a general theory of human behavior would provide a secure foundation upon which moral speculation could be elaborated" and that the two might be "woven" together in the manner of an earlier "premodern" era but with a "postmodern" sensibility.[35] However, the essence of behavioralism, he suggested in the early 1960s, was the quest for a "science of politics modeled after the methodological assumptions of the natural sciences."

Although a behavioralist was "not prohibited" from "ethical evaluation"—as long as the propositions were distinct from those of "empirical explanation"—and although the "the application of knowledge is as much a part of the scientific enterprise as theoretical understanding," Easton argued, "pure science" logically preceded "efforts to utilize political knowledge in the solution of urgent practical problems of society." Behavioralism, he argued, signified that political science had joined the interdisciplinary quest for a "common underlying social theory" in the explanation of human behavior. It was a theoretical transformation exemplified in a variety of "conceptual approaches," such as functionalism, decision theory, and systems analysis, which together represented the "coming of age of theory in the social sciences" and the transcendence of the substantive and ethical orientation of "traditional theories of past political thought."[36] Easton's strongest statement of this position was published, ironically, in 1968, on the eve of his proclamation of a "new revolution" in political science. He claimed that "by the 1960s the methods of modern science had made deep inroads into political research, under the rubric of the study of political behavior." This "full reception of scientific method" had brought about a sharp break with former modes of theorizing and involved "casting aside the last remnants of the classical heritage." Empiricism in political science had produced a wealth of data, which required a "new theoretical coherence" that was "forced upon the field with a sense of self-preservation." This development "tended to drive political science away from a prescriptive, problem-directed discipline" and toward a "growing acceptance of the difference between factual and evaluative statements."[37]

When Easton, in his 1969 presidential address to the American Political Science Association, spoke of a "new revolution," he implied not a rejection of the essence of behavioralism but rather a change in the distribution of emphasis. This new, or postbehavioral, revolution sprung from "a deep dis-

satisfaction with political research and teaching, especially of the kind that
is striving to convert the study of politics into a more rigorously scientific
discipline modeled on the methodology of the natural sciences." The new
"Credo of Relevance" would "reverse" earlier priorities regarding the relationship between basic theoretical empirical science and problem-oriented
research and "put whatever knowledge we have to immediate use" in order
"to respond to the abnormal urgency of the present crises." Although the
long-term goal of basic research and the "discovery of demonstrable basic
truths about politics" would not be abandoned, it was necessary to address
the "problems of the day to obtain quick, short-run answers with the tools
and generalizations currently available." It was also morally necessary, as
recognized in the "venerable tradition inherited from such diverse sources
as Greek classical philosophy, Karl Marx, John Dewey, and modern existen-
tialism," for knowledge once again to bear the "responsibility for acting."
The new revolution would recognize that despite all the past concern with
objectivity and value-freedom, social research always "rests on certain value
assumptions." Finally, like "the great political theorists of the past," it would
begin once more the task of "speculative theorizing" and "construct new
and often radically different conceptions of future possible kinds of political relationships."[38]

Given the history of both the discipline and Easton's own work, this statement could not, despite the rhetorical context, be construed as merely a
product of circumstance, a response to the mounting divisions within and
internal criticisms of the discipline during the 1960s. It was true to the
spirit of the past as well as responsive to the concerns of the present. But
although Easton recommended the creation of a federation of social scientists to focus on public policy, the long-standing problem of the relationship
between political science and politics seemed as intractable as ever. During
the next decade political scientists would enthusiastically seek to give meaning to the image that Easton had evoked, reclaim the heritage of the past,
and redefine the discipline as a policy science; however, the diverse notions
of what this effort might entail did not coalesce in either a theoretical or
practical manner.[39]

THE ERA OF FRAGMENTATION

One consequence of the winding down of the debate about behavioralism
was the pluralization, if not Balkanization, of political theory.[40] The redefinition of political science as a policy science largely muted charges of
political irrelevance and unconcern, and the methodological and professional triumph of behavioralism made possible an ecumenical spirit of pure
tolerance as the discipline extended its hand to all interests and intellectual

persuasions.[41] But, in an important sense, it was too late. A large portion of the subcontinent of political theory had broken off and drifted toward nether poles. Just as the larger territory of political theory, including the normative dimension, severed its ties to political science and fractured internally, the universe of empirical theory became less coherent. Despite some generally shared notions, principally the idea of the political system (most vigorously elaborated by Easton), behavioralism was not a paradigm in Thomas Kuhn's sense. Notwithstanding certain commonalities of mood, concern, and even method, it already most consistently defined itself in terms of a plurality of theories, research approaches, frameworks, conceptual schemes, and strategies. Continued differentiation was in large part a function of professional specialization, but it also represented the eruption of a suppressed and repressed problem inherent in the very idea of theory that had governed most of the history of the discipline and that found its fullest expression in the 1960s.

The search for theory in political science had culminated not only in Easton's "framework" for a "systems analysis of political life" but also in numerous conceptual schemes and forms of analysis, such as structural-functionalism.[42] Sometimes these were offered as prototheories, of the type characteristic of natural science, with the hope that they would converge in one general theory or that one would emerge as definitive of the field. But increasingly these were advanced as complementary perspectives that were deemed more or less useful depending on the data confronted and the research problem posed. The latent instrumentalist interpretation of theory came into full bloom, and what fertilized it was the growing dominance and popular assimilation of logical positivism and logical empiricism that propagated the instrumentalist epistemology. The appropriation of this philosophical construction was part of the process of articulating and legitimating images of empirical theory, but it also began to inform the practice of theory. This vision, reflected in some depth in the work of Lasswell, Talcott Parsons, Easton, Karl Deutsch, William Riker, and others, was by the 1960s no longer simply a justification of scientific identity but something that actively informed what was taken to be the task of "theory building" and "construction."[43] Instrumentalism became a validation of theoretical pluralism and even an impetus for the proliferation of "theory."

As long as instrumentalism as a theory of theory was tied to instrumentalism as a statement of the purpose of social science, its difficulties as a cognitive account of science were not so apparent. With the growing gap, after 1950, between the contemplative and manipulative perspectives and the renewed emphasis on justifying theory as part of a pure science prior to and apart from practice, instrumentalism increasingly required a defense on philosophical grounds. But it also became hostage to the fate of the transformation in the philosophy of science. Postpositivism involved a fundamental challenge to the instrumentalist account of theory and a turn to various faces of theoretical realism that could not be easily squared with either the idea or practice of theory in political science. The conceptual collapse of the orders of theory and fact undermined both the logic of the covering-law model of explanation and the instrumentalist epistemology. Theories were not instruments for carving out, ordering, or exploring domains of facticity but rather were reality claims, incommensurable constitutions of such domains. They were not simply the form in which facts were described and explained but the conceptual determinants of facts. But if conceptual frameworks were not theories comparable, in form and function, to those in natural science, then where did theory reside in political science—if it resided anywhere at all? John Wahlke suggested as late as 1979 that political science was still characterized by "a paucity of theoretical concerns."[44]

If, during the postbehavioral era, there has been any element of the eclectic world of mainstream political science research programs that has aspired to paradigm status, or to which such status has been attributed, it is the set of conceptual schemes dealing with rational, public, and social choice. It has even been suggested that this transfer of the economic approach to other areas of social inquiry represents a kind of theoretical "imperialism."[45] A great deal of criticism has been heaped on formal choice theory, but what has not received much attention is the question of whether it fulfills the dream of emulating theory in natural science. The question is whether there is some kind of logical equivalence between formal choice theory and its propositions, on the one hand, and what might be understood as the theories of natural science, on the other.

What is called economic theory has been distinctively instrumental in character and, metatheoretically, interpreted and defended instrumentally. There are, as in the case of political science, historical explanations for this fact related to the manipulative attitudes attending its origin, but in classical economic theory, with its image of rational action, theories serve as instruments. Although it is reasonable to argue that in the practice of science theories function in various ways instrumentally, this is something quite different from the claim that they are cognitively instrumental. The locus classicus is the rendition of Milton Friedman. It is necessary to tease out the instrumental assumptions in much of social science, but Friedman laid it on the line and took the language directly from positivist philosophy. For him, the goal of theories and hypotheses in science is prediction. The language of theory, he claims, has "no substantive content" and functions as an abstract "filing system for organizing empirical material and facilitating our understanding of it." When the system seems to fit the world or indicate the existence of a "material counterpart" and is useful for prediction, it is accepted as explanatory. A theory need not be descriptively "realistic"; those that are often fall more into the category of a Weberian ideal typification and have limited applicability. Consequently, theories are often descriptively false or distortive. They are somewhat arbitrary instrumental constructs, neither validated nor invalidated by their genesis, devised for parsimoniously perceiving the relations in a separate realm of observable facts that, however existentially related and embedded, are incorporated into a "conceptual world" or model deployed according to certain operational rules for "specifying the correspondence between the variables or entities in the model and observable phenomena."[46]

This basic image of theory, in both principle and practice, is still quite consistently accepted in contemporary political science and continues to inform variations of contemporary formal choice theory. The construct of the rational actor is, as in economics (from which it is derived), largely approached from an instrumentalist perspective. Jon Elster, for example, notes that "*social choice theory* is a useful tool for stating the problem of how to arrive at socially optimal outcomes on the basis of given individual preferences."[47] Anthony Downs, one of the founders of social choice analysis, explicitly embraces Friedman's antirealist account of theory.[48] Instrumentalist approaches such as formal choice analysis are less theories than models of human action that only imply a theory in their conceptual language and their observations. Theories in science (or in common sense or religion, for that matter) are ontologies. They are realistic claims about what exists and the manner of its existence. Theories are embedded or exemplified in singular or factual claims, which are in turn particularistic theoretical claims. If accounts of plate tectonics in geology or the structure of DNA in biology can be construed as what we mean by theory in science, it is impossible to render them as somewhat useful instrumental models for thinking about an observational given world. They tell us what kind of stuff constitutes the world. If, for either cognitive or practical reasons, political science wishes to emulate natural science, it must come to grips, in the principles and practice of inquiry, with what theories are and in a manner that transcends the instrumentalist interpretation.

Is it the case, then, that political science lacks genuine theories? The answer to that question is not easy, but the most accurate reply might be that although it possesses such theories, they have not for the most part been objects of critical reflection and elaboration. One of the major criticisms leveled against the conceptual frameworks that marked the high point of the behavioral movement was that no matter how abstract they became, they were to some degree self-defeating, because these models contained structural biases that contradicted the very objectivity to which they aspired and obscured the very phenomena they were intended to explain. But in addition to these normative and selective biases, there was a deeper inherent prejudice.

By assuming the givenness of a world of observed fact upon which models were imposed and against which they were judged as useful, instrumentalism served, on three ascending levels, to idolize the theoretical assumptions embedded in the framework of observation. First, it often underwrote the ideologies inherent in political facts. Second, it gave them an undeserved transconventional status that belied the extent to which human action and its products were open to radical change. Third, it insulated these "facts" from theoretical challenge and in effect theoretically privileged them. The irony is that if we are to look for the theories of political science, we might do well to look less at its "theories" than at its facts—and for the theories concealed in its "theories." Here is where its real theoretical assumptions are embedded and from which they must be extracted and examined—assumptions about such matters as the nature of human action and its relationship to its environment and about how the conventional historical forms of political life are related to these matters.

If—as Lasswell, for example, had hoped—social science was in the service of benign, consensually grounded democratic authority and deployed as social engineering and reform, then we might be able to settle for instrumental theory that could be judged pragmatically, much as we use exit polls to predict election results. But if we return to the ultimate paradox of political science—the fact that intervention in politics depends on the distance engendered by pure theory—instrumentalism ultimately deconstructs itself as a theoretical attitude. Max Weber and American political science may have been quite correct. Only by keeping science pure can it hope to be practical. But this also means that only by being theoretically noninstrumental can it be practically instrumental.

NOTES

1. Some aspects of the history of political theory in political science discussed here are more fully elaborated in John G. Gunnell, *The Descent of Political Theory: The Genealogy of an American Vocation* (Chicago: University of Chicago Press, 1993).

2. Ada Finifter (ed.), *Political Science: The State of the Discipline* (Washington, D.C.: American Political Science Association, 1983).

3. See, for example, Mary Furner, *Advocacy and Objectivity: A Crisis in the Professionalization of Social Science, 1865–1905* (Lexington: University of Kentucky Press, 1975).

4. For a full discussion, see John G. Gunnell, "In Search of the State," in P. Wagner, B. Wittrock, and R. Whitley (eds.), *Discourses on Society*, vol. XV (Netherlands: Kluwer Academic Publishers, 1990).

5. Francis Lieber, *The Stranger in America* (Philadelphia: Lea and Blanchard, 1835), p. 197.

6. See John Burgess, "The Study of the Political Sciences in Columbia College," *International Review* 12 (1882).

7. John Burgess, "Political Science and History," *American Historical Review* 2 (1897): 404.

8. W. W. Willoughby, "The Political Theory of John W. Burgess," *Yale Review* 17 (1908).

9. See W. W. Willoughby, "The American Political Science Association," *Political Science Quarterly* 19 (1904); Henry Jones Ford, "The Scope of Political Science," *Proceedings of the American Political Science Association* (1906).

10. See, for example, W. W. Willoughby, "The Value of Political Philosophy," *Political Science Quarterly* 15 (1900).

11. See W. W. Willoughby, "Political Philosophy," *South Atlantic Quarterly* 5 (1906).

12. See John G. Gunnell, "Continuity and Innovation in Political Science: The Case of Charles Merriam," *Journal of the History of the Behavioral Sciences* 28 (1992).

13. Woodrow Wilson, "A Literary Politician," in *Mere Literature and Other Essays* (Boston: Houghton-Mifflin, 1897); "The Law and the Facts," *American Political Science Review* 9 (1911).

14. See John G. Gunnell, "The Declination of the 'State' and the Origins of American 'Pluralism,'" in John Dryzek, James Farr, and Stephen Leonard (eds.), *Political Science and Its History: Research Programs and Political Traditions* (New York: Cambridge University Press, 1995).

15. Charles Merriam, "The Present State of the Study of Politics," *American Political Science Review* 15 (1921).

16. Charles Merriam, "Progress Report of the Committee on Political Research," *American Political Science Review* 17 (1923).

17. Charles Merriam, "Recent Tendencies in Political Thought," in Charles Merriam and Harry Elmer Barnes (eds.), *A History of Political Theories: Recent Times* (New York: Macmillan, 1924), pp. 20–21.

18. Charles E. Merriam, *New Aspects of Politics* (Chicago: University of Chicago Press, 1925), pp. 237, 330.

19. G. E. G. Catlin, "The Delimitation and Measurability of Political Phenomena," *American Political Science Review* 21 (1927): 255.

20. G. E. G. Catlin, *The Science and Method of Politics* (New York: Knopf, 1927), pp. x–xi, 284, 295.

21. Ibid., pp. 93, 200–205.

22. G. E. G. Catlin, *A Study of the Principles of Politics* (New York: Russell and Russell, 1930), pp. 22–24, 38, 51, 54, 119, 132.

23. Stuart Rice (ed.), *Methods in Social Science: A Case Book* (Chicago: University of Chicago Press, 1931), pp. 731–36, 7–10.

24. See Harold Lasswell, *Psychopathology and Politics* (Chicago: University of Chicago Press, 1930).

25. Ibid., pp. 45–46.

26. Harold Lasswell, *World Politics and Personal Insecurity* (New York: McGraw-Hill, 1934), p. 2.

27. See John G. Gunnell, "American Political Science, Liberalism, and the Invention of Political Theory," *American Political Science Review* 82 (1988).

28. Harold D. Lasswell and Abraham Kaplan, *Power and Society: A Framework for Political Inquiry* (New Haven: Yale University Press, 1950), pp. ix–x.

29. Ibid., pp. xi–xiii.

30. Ibid., pp. xiv, xxiv. For a similar argument, see Harold Lasswell, "The Immediate Future of Research Policy and Method in Political Science," *American Political Science Review* 45 (1951).

31. David Easton, "Walter Bagehot and Liberal Realism," *American Political Science Review* 43 (1949).

32. David Easton, "Harold Lasswell: Policy Scientist for a Democratic Society," *Journal of Politics* 13 (1951).

33. David Easton, "The Decline of Political Theory," *Journal of Politics* 13 (1951).

34. David Easton, *The Political System* (Chicago: University of Chicago Press, 1953).

35. David Easton, "Shifting Images of Social Science and Values," *The Antioch Review* pp. 17–18.

36. David Easton, "The Current Meaning of Behavioralism," in James C. Charlesworth (ed.), *The Limits of Behavioralism* (Philadelphia: Academy of Political and Social Science, 1962), pp. 8–25.

37. David Easton, "Political Science, Method and Theory," in David Sills (ed.), *International Encyclopedia of the Social Sciences,* vol. 12 (New York: Macmillan, 1968), pp. 295–7.

38. David Easton, "The New Revolution in Political Science," *American Political Science Review* 62 (1969).

39. See John G. Gunnell, "Social Scientific Knowledge and Policy Decisions: A Critique of the Intellectualist Model," in Philip Gregg (ed.), *Problems of Theory in Policy Analysis* (Lexington: D. C. Heath, 1976), and "Policy Analysis and the Paradox of Academic and Public Discourse," in William N. Dunn and Rita Mae Kelly (eds.), *Advances in Policy Studies Since 1950* (New Brunswick: Transaction, 1992).

40. See John G. Gunnell, "Political Theory: The Evolution of a Sub-Field," in Ada Finifter (ed.), *Political Science: The State of the Discipline* (Washington, D.C.: American Political Science Association, 1983).

41. See, for example, Karl Deutsch, "On Political Theory and Political Action," *American Political Science Review* 65 (1971).

42. David Easton, *A Framework for Political Analysis* (Englewood Cliffs: Prentice-Hall, 1965); Easton, *A Systems Analysis of Political Life* (New York: Wiley, 1965); Easton (ed.), *Varieties of Political Theory* (Englewood Cliffs: Prentice-Hall, 1966); and Karl Deutsch, *The Nerves of Government* (New York: Free Press, 1963).

43. For an extended critical discussion of instrumentalism and the deductive model of explanation in the philosophy of science and its exemplification in political theory, see John G. Gunnell, *Philosophy, Science, and Political Inquiry* (Morristown: General Learning Press, 1975) and *Between Philosophy and Politics: The Alienation of Political Theory* (Amherst, MA: University of Massachusetts Press, 1986), chapter 2.

44. John C. Wahlke, "Pre-havioralism in Political Theory," *American Political Science Review* 73 (1979).

45. See Gerald Radnitzsky and Peter Bernholz (eds.), *Economic Imperialism: The Economic Approach Applied Outside the Field of Economics* (New York: Paragon House, 1987) and Jon Elster (ed.), *Rational Choice* (New York: New York University Press, 1986).

46. Milton Friedman, *Essays in Positive Economics* (Chicago: University of Chicago Press, 1953), pp. 7, 24.

47. Jon Elster, *Sour Grapes: Studies in the Subversion of Rationality* (New York: Cambridge University Press, 1983), p. 30.

48. Anthony Downs, *An Economic Theory of Democracy* (New York: Harper, 1957).

PART II

Alternative Views of the Discipline

3

Seven Durable Axes of Cleavage in Political Science

Bernard Grofman

Like my colleague, A Wuffle, I call myself a "reasonable choice" modeler and am a member in good standing of the California Drive-in Church of the Incorrigibly Eclectic.[1] I have relatively little interest in extended abstract discussions of meta-issues in political science—about, e.g., the nature of human nature; or whether explanations of political phenomena should focus on individual preferences, institutional constraints, political culture, or norms; or the extent to which the discipline can aspire to being scientific; or exactly what such aspirations entail. I believe that, by and large, the proof is in the pudding; if you claim to have something useful to say about some aspect of political life, then you ought to say it, and let other people decide whether or not what you say makes sense and helps them understand politics.[2] I have no tolerance for obscurantism, whether it be couched in words[3] or in mathematical symbols.[4]

The aims of this essay are twofold: first, to identify seven axes of choice by which political scientists decide what to study and how to study it;[5] second, to argue against the claim (Almond, 1990) that political scientists are presently sitting at "separate tables."

My perspective is basically optimistic. I find that political scientists of all stripes usually have far more in common with one another than with just about anybody else. Though they may argue a lot with one another, by and large they are arguing about the same kinds of questions—and brandishing many of the same sacred texts. Moreover, comparing what we know today with what is discussed in, say, Charles Hyneman's 1959 overview of American political science, I see real progress on a number of fronts.[6] Also, I see the discipline moving away from 1960s-style "if you don't do it my way, then what you're doing must be either trivial or wrong" confrontations between behavioralists and antibehavioralists. Even the cleavage line between ra-

tional choice theorists and everybody else is far less rigid than it is sometimes made out to be. In my view, we are in a period of convergence of
approaches rather than one of growing separation—especially between
Michigan-style data analysis and rational choice modeling, but also between
rational choice and political culture approaches.

APPROACHES TO RESEARCH IN POLITICAL SCIENCE

In this section I will review David Easton's famous distinction between behavioral and postbehavioral approaches to political science, argue that this
distinction is more misleading then helpful, and then introduce a typology
of my own that reflects a set of differences that crosscuts Easton's dichotomy.

What Is Postbehavioralism?

In his presidential address on the theme of a postbehavioral political science, Easton identified seven basic characteristics of the scientific approach
(Easton, 1969).[7] He then suggested that most if not all of the basic elements
of this approach were being rejected by a substantial set of political scientists, whom he labeled "postbehavioralists." I find Easton's list of basic characteristics to be an apt and fair summary of the methodology ascribed to
the natural sciences, and I did not doubt in 1969, nor do I doubt now, that
a substantial number of political scientists find these prescriptions too narrow for what they want to do. Where I part company with Easton is a) in
my dislike of labeling those who reject a substantial number of features of
scientific method as "*post*behavioralists", and b) in rejecting Easton's lumping (in this volume) of rational choice theorists into the postbehavioral
camp.

The "post" label, as in "postmodern" or "postbehavioral," has one direct
meaning: those who are "post" come later in chronological order. However,
labeling something as "post" often clearly implies that "later is better." For
example, those who identify with postmodernism can claim the cachet of
being "with it," attuned to the most up-to-date intellectual currents, not
fuddy-duddies still using antiquated models and methods.[8] Thus, Easton's
use of the label "postbehavioralist" for views he appears to favor[9] can be
seen as a rhetorical ploy to give those views greater legitimacy,[10] especially
as many of the antibehavioral beliefs that Easton ascribes to the postbehavioralists can best be thought of as *pre*scientific.[11]

But my objection to the postbehavioral label is not merely based on its
apparent use as a rhetorical ploy. My chief complaint is that the various
groups of folks whom Professor Easton puts into the postbehavioral box

are an ill-matched lot who generally find each other's work irrelevant, incomprehensible, and/or distasteful, assuming they bother to read it at all. Using a common label for this range of groups is obfuscatory of useful classification. The term "postbehavioralists" includes scholars with views akin to the those of the romantics, who rebelled against both the precision of science and its disregard of human values, as well as postmodernist obscurantists and exponents of formal modeling (including me), who believe game theory is becoming to political science what calculus is to physics. There is a real problem here of lumping apples, oranges, and cucumbers into the same category.

In particular, if we treat rational choice modeling as a species of postbehavioralism (as Easton does in his chapter in this volume), then it is hard to know what, other than chronology, provides the defining characteristics of postbehavioralist thought; it is ludicrous to regard rational choice theorists as rejecting the seven basic tenets of scientific method identified in Easton (1969). A political scientist trained at Cal Tech or Rochester in the mysteries of positive political theory has far more in common with that apotheosis of behavioralism, the Michigan Ph.D. trained in the intricacies of survey research, than either has in common with the various deconstructionists, postmodern feminists, neo-Marxist state theorists, policy analysts, and even Straussians who, according to Easton, all share with rational choice modelers postbehavioral concerns.

Because even the author of the term "postbehavioralism" does not use it consistently, switching between chronological and content-oriented definitions, I will not use it in the remainder of this essay. Similarly, I will eschew use of the term "behavioralism" in the way that Easton defines it, because I do not find it the best term for distinguishing what many Michigan-trained scholars do from what many Rochester-trained scholars do; both sets of scholars make use of the scientific method, and both are concerned with behavior such as voting choices.[12] Instead, I will distinguish among political scientists in terms of seven (mostly) orthogonal axes:

1. normative versus empirical
2. description versus explanation
3. induction versus deduction
4. scope versus certainty
5. exegesis versus exploration
6. governmental orientation versus policy orientation
7. understanding versus change

1. NORMATIVE VERSUS EMPIRICAL. Here the distinction is simply between those who see political science as a branch of moral philosophy and those

who see it as a search for empirical understanding/explanation. The former often see "is" and "ought" as inextricably intertwined; the latter almost invariably seek to disentangle them.

2. DESCRIPTION VERSUS EXPLANATION This distinction, which applies to empirically oriented political scientists, is between those who wish to immerse themselves in insider's knowledge of a delimited domain (e.g., a particular country or region) and believe that little or nothing that is useful can be said about politics without such deep knowledge, and those whose first reaction is to look for comparative analysis to shed explanatory light on particular cases, with those cases often simplified in terms of "stylized facts." I believe there is merit to both sides of this argument, which is why I regard it as mostly a silly one between two straw men.[13] My own students are encouraged to do comparative analysis but also to know a great deal about at least one case so as to have a "reality check," not just on theoretical propositions that may seek to encompass that case but also on the ways in which variables that purportedly apply to that case get (mis)coded.[14]

3. INDUCTION VERSUS DEDUCTION. The distinction here is between those whose first recourse to any question posed is to go about amassing data and those whose first recourse is to think the question through from first principles. Of course, these are ideal types.[15] It is unlikely that any contemporary social scientists would argue in favor of a naive form of hyperempiricism. "Just the facts, ma'am," is an injunction that makes sense only if we have an a priori notion of which of the infinitude of facts are, in a given context, relevant ones. Nonetheless, data-oriented political scientists often act as if almost any sort of regression represents progress, as long as it has lots of variables in it and a high enough R^2. On the other hand, political scientists with a positive theory orientation often emulate economic theorists by seeking to model a phenomenon in terms of deductions from some limited set of postulates.

However, deductive reasoning that lacks connection to real-world phenomena is a branch of mathematics, not of the social sciences. The work of some positive theorists supports the old saw that "it's not what we don't know that hurts us, it's the things we think we know that really aren't so."[16] Sometimes, math modeling is like an absolutely stupendous basketball slam-dunk—except that somebody forgot the ball.

An exclusive focus on purely inductive or purely deductive approaches will ultimately prove counterproductive. But even if we get a reasonable balance between theory and data, there are other issues of division.

4. SCOPE VERSUS CERTAINTY. The distinction here is between those who search for certain answers to relatively small and manageable questions and

those who are willing to settle for not-so-certain answers as long as the questions are big ones. Some scholars relish being able to say with confidence that their answer is the right one, even if the question they are asking is not particularly momentous. Others are delighted with any kind of real insight, no matter how imperfect or incomplete, into "bigger" questions. These are matters of temperament and provide one of the permanent divisions among political scientists.

5. EXEGESIS VERSUS EXPLORATION. Even among those who are primarily empirical in orientation, there is an important distinction between those who think the important answers/insights have already been written down by the great minds of the past and those who believe the process of knowledge gathering is ongoing and cumulative. If political science is a conversation about great ideas, the basic elements of which were laid down anywhere from 200 to 2,000-plus years ago, then most of what modern political scientists do is a waste of time. One would be better off reading Plato, Aristotle, Machiavelli, or Hobbes than studying the budgetary reconciliation process in Congress or the effects of proportional representation on the city council of Ashtabula, Ohio, or reading the works of those who do. How much Aristotle versus how much Ashtabula is an ongoing basis of cleavage within the profession.[17]

6. GOVERNMENTAL ORIENTATION VERSUS POLICY ORIENTATION. The distinction here is between those who think of political science as simply the study of government and those who think it ought to be the study of policies and power, especially of "who gets what, when and how," regardless of the domain in which value allocations take place. If we exclude international relations, issues that dominate newspaper front pages—e.g., health care, immigration, crime, unemployment—are conspicuously absent from the *American Political Science Review* or are discussed only in the context of public opinion research. Also, articles in the *APSR* and similar journals are generally "bloodless"—i.e., they do not convey a sense that politics is an activity engaged in by real people and having real consequences. Often the focus is on puzzles—"Why do incumbents get reelected so often?" "Why does the in-party lose seats in midterm elections?" "Why is divided party control of state governments so common?"—or on measurement questions—"Is the increased issue orientation found in voters in recent presidential elections real or is it an artifact of questionnaire wording?"—or on purely abstract modeling.

There are at least three reasons why the subjects discussed in the leading general-purpose political science journals seem largely divorced from the issues that make up such a large part of ordinary citizens' understanding of what politics is all about.

First, the articles in the discipline's most prestigious general-purpose journals are primarily about government and its institutions: e.g., elections, congressional committees, Supreme Court voting patterns. Because of this focus on government and its institutions per se, we find very few articles that *directly* deal with "who gets what, when, and how." Many political scientists have tacitly accepted a division of labor with other social science disciplines, leaving to sociologists issues of race, class, and social inequality and to economists macroeconomic issues and broad questions of public policy but retaining primacy when it comes to Congress and the presidency. Such a division of labor is reflected in the courses taught by political scientists about American politics—courses that focus on institutions and public opinion.

Second, political scientists for reasons of pride wish to distinguish themselves from mere journalists. We do this in part by distancing ourselves from the day-to-day issues of political debate that are the stuff of journalistic commentary in order to take more "scholarly perspectives."

Third, with the exception of a few distinguished political scientists (e.g., Aaron Wildavsky), who have prided themselves on their ability to "speak truth to power," students of policy have generally not enjoyed great prestige. Moreover, to the extent that Bill Clinton's advisers were right that "It's the economy, stupid," political scientists are superfluous; they have very limited training or tools with which to contest claims by economists and so must leave such matters in the hands of others lest they be revealed as the ignoramuses they are.[18] Also, with a few notable exceptions, such as faculty at the Kennedy School (who view Washington as a suburb of Cambridge), U.S. political scientists in academic posts do not usually hold government posts (as their counterparts in other countries often do), and those who hold such positions are not thereby held in greater prestige.[19]

The extent to which political science should encompass topics such as power relations inside the family or allocative policies of all types regardless of locus remains one of the dividing cleavages of the discipline. I find it unfortunate that political science has been so preoccupied with government that it has lost sight of politics as the study of power or of authority relations in general (cf. Eckstein, 1969).[20]

7. UNDERSTANDING VERSUS CHANGE. The distinction here is between those who wish to understand the world and those who wish to change it. Some social scientists may pick topics for research in the hope that their work may, in some small fashion, change the world; others simply pick puzzles they find interesting or work on whatever topic seems convenient because of, say, data accessibility. Some academics pursue a topic to advance a particular political agenda; others have declared various areas of research off-limits on the grounds that the results might tend to reinforce racism, or

sexism, or whatever. Few political scientists see themselves as having to choose between espousing truth, on the one hand, or social justice, on the other; yet if certain truths are unpleasant, politically destabilizing, or potentially harmful to the short-term interests of the weak and disenfranchised, that conflict can arise.[21] Also, to the extent that certain topics are avoided because results might be controversial (and controversy may limit a researcher's ability to get future funding), then the insights offered by the discipline as a whole can be skewed. In any case, differences in personal preference on the understanding-versus-change dimension provide another one of the long-standing cleavages in political science—as in other social science disciplines.

TOWARD CONVERGENCE

Political science has been characterized as being in crisis for want of a unifying paradigm, having moved from raw empiricism to legalism to behavioralism to splintered postbehavioralism. We are presently seeing a strong reaction in political science to the hegemonic claims of rational choice modeling, on the one hand,[22] and to the older, survey-data focused approach of the Michigan school, on the other. Rational choice theory is commonly critiqued as being a) wrongheaded in its insistence on positivist canons of scientific inquiry, b) highly limited in its ability to account successfully for key features of political life, such as collective action or non-self-interested behavior, c) foolish in making the elegance of its mathematical modeling an end unto itself, and d) politically incorrect because of an allegedly inseparable association with right-wing views.[23] Michigan-style behavioralism comes under a different but equally strong attack: it is accused of being little more than a reporting of survey data that is about as enlightening as a reading of tea leaves in terms of its ability to account for patterns of change in public opinion or for phenomena such as, say, the rise of Ross Perot.[24]

I do not believe in a lost Eden, a time before the tower of Babel, when all political scientists spoke a common tongue and prayed to the same god. When I look at the body of research that appears in mainstream journals, political science to me appears at least as unified today as at any point in its past (i.e., not very); and the real divisions that are present are the same ones that have characterized the discipline for at least the last seventy years—namely, those along the seven axes discussed in the previous section.

In Search of a New Metaphor for the State of the Discipline

As an alternative to Gabriel Almond's powerful metaphor of political scientists sitting at "separate tables," I suggest the "Chinese dim sum brunch."

In a dim sum restaurant many trays with different items go by, and you take what you like (by pointing at the dish). Customarily, if you come alone (or with a small group), you are seated at a large table with a bunch of other people. Interaction is possible but not compulsory. And although everyone might have a unique combination of dishes, there is almost always some overlap between any two diners' meals, because there are only so many dishes on the menu and because almost all diners consume multiple items. Moreover, diners can see what other people are eating, ask them about it, and then either sample it for themselves or refrain in disgust—duck feet, for example, are an acquired taste.

I am not arguing that the differences among political scientists about methodological and epistemological predilections are trivial. However, I believe the "separate tables" metaphor overstates the case by implying that two political scientists of ostensibly different orientations have less in common with one another than they do with scholars outside of political science who share their epistemological perspective—recall the jape that "two parliamentarians, one a socialist, one not, have more in common with one another than two socialists, one a parliamentarian and the other not." All political scientists, regardless of persuasion, share a great deal—in terms of early socialization and the received litany of "names to conjure with"— that distinguishes them from other social scientists. This fact becomes apparent when one engages in conversations across disciplinary lines. In fact, I would argue that virtually any two political scientists of even a vaguely realist persuasion can rather quickly find common interests,[25] though the commonalities need not be the same between different pairs.

I want to say more than that things merely aren't quite as bad as recently painted. I want to argue that there are a number of signs of a "coming together" of rival approaches. One of these signs is the increasing number of technically well-trained younger scholars who are more interested in empirically testable formal models than in either purely inductive or purely deductive approaches; another is the growth of "soft" rational choice and pervasive use of metaphors derived from game theory.

THE GROWTH OF SOFT RATIONAL CHOICE. Game theory is one of the most powerful tools available to social scientists; I believe it will become for political science and economics what calculus is to physics.[26] Game theory models are becoming common in many different subfields of the political science discipline; even more important, in my view, game theory metaphors (e.g., zero-sum game, dilemma of the commons, security dilemma) are becoming ubiquitous, as are ideas borrowed from economics, such as increasing returns to scale and transaction costs.

Unlike some hard-core rational choice modelers, who appear to believe that if it isn't a theorem it cannot be a valuable contribution to human knowledge, I welcome so-called "soft" rational choice approaches.[27] I welcome, too, work that seeks to bridge the gap between rational choice and other approaches—e.g., the work by Robert Putnam and others that builds on James Coleman's notion of "social capital" (Coleman, 1990) or on Jon Elster's work on social norms (Elster, 1989). This work blurs the line between cultural and rational choice approaches in ways that I, as an incorrigible eclectic, heartily welcome.[28]

COMBINING MICHIGAN-STYLE AND ROCHESTER-STYLE APPROACHES. The political science departments at the University of Michigan and Rochester University have received the greatest recognition a discipline can award, that of becoming synonymous with a particular way to do research, of having provided a paradigm that has affected an entire discipline,[29] for which the Chicago School of Sociology was famous in the 1920s and 1930s and the Chicago School of Economics is famous today.

The principal fault laid at the door of Michigan-trained Ph.D.s is that they're great with data and don't have much in the way of theory; the principal fault laid at the door of Rochester-trained Ph.D.s is that they're great with theory and don't do much (or do nothing at all) with data. But who says you can't have it all? A set of younger positive theorists—some trained at Rochester (Keith Krehbiel), some at Cal Tech (Matthew McCubbins, Arthur Lupia), some at Washington University (George Tsebelis), some from elsewhere (Thomas Hammond, U.C. Berkeley)—and a number of younger scholars whose principal training is in data analysis—from Michigan (e.g., Dave King and Elizabeth Gerber) as well as from a host of other schools (e.g. Gary King, a University of Wisconsin Ph.D.)—are doing a superb job of integrating sophisticated modeling with empirical research.[30] Evidence of this new rapprochement between empirical and modeling orientations[31] is also found in the special edition of *Public Choice* celebrating the twenty-fifth anniversary of the Public Choice Society, wherein empirically testable theory is hailed by James Enelow and Rebecca Morton (1993) as the wave of the future[32] for Public Choice.[33]

If ever there was a time for optimism about the revitalization of political science called for in Easton's 1953 classic *The Political System*, that time, I believe, is now.

NOTES

1. See Wuffle (1992).

2. If this be pragmatism, then make the most of it (cf. the last several pages of Wendt and Shapiro, this volume).

3. For example, I have no doubt that deconstructionists have a lot to say, but by and large it's only about what other deconstuctionists have said—a circularity

that is not helpful unless your principal interest is in understanding the behavior of university professors or unless you think that pompous gibberish translated from French or German is inherently more enlightening than pompous gibberish available only in English. (My colleague, A Wuffle, has whimsically characterized deconstructionism as the belief that "what I think is more important than what you said or did.")

4. I am not saying that the use of mathematical symbolism per se is obsurantist; rather, for work that appears in journals intended for a general political science audience, what I find reprehensible is the failure to provide nontechnical readers the courtesy of an English-language translation of the key results and at least some clue as to why any political scientist might find them of interest.

5. I am not arguing that any of us has one and only one position on each of these axes. We each have tendencies, reflected to a greater or lesser degree in particular pieces of research, but some of us are more eclectic than others (i.e., have higher variance).

6. Cf. Laponce (this volume).

7. The same list is found in Easton's chapter in this volume.

8. Cf. "Progress is our most important product."

9. Exactly to what extent Easton ca. 1969 subscribed to the views he labels "postbehavioralist" remains a matter of some dispute. Heinz Eulau puts forward the view that Easton (1969) renounced the views he espoused in Easton (1953)—a charge that Easton (this volume) denies, asserting that in Easton (1969) he was more describing than endorsing. Having read both early Easton (pre-1969) and later Easton (post-1969) I can only say that I had no trouble figuring out where the "old Easton" stood—he was a "young Turk" who sounded the charge against a "great books" notion of the discipline and urged political scientists to do empirically and theoretically grounded research—whereas I find it much harder to figure out the "new Easton."

10. Recall that the Bolsheviks took for themselves a label connoting that they, not the Mensheviks, were the majority; Nixon claimed for his supporters the title of "silent majority"; Madison and other supporters succeeded in attaching the popular term "Federalist" to the constitution of 1787, forcing its opponents to become anti-Federalists, despite the fact that their confederal approach had at least as good a claim to the label "federalist" as did advocates of what William Riker has called "centralized federalism."

11. Much nonsense has been written by social scientists about how the scientific method ain't what it used to be—e.g., claims that positivist notions of science have been shown to be falsified by the work of Thomas Kuhn on paradigm shifts or by other recent work in the philosophy of science that demonstrates, i.a., that the link between scientific findings and empirical reality is problematic in that observations are inherently theory-laden. Space does not permit a discussion of philosophy of science issues here. Suffice it to say that I believe that political scientists should not allow such misleading claims to get in the way of their aspiring to do political science à la the seven tenets identified in Easton 1969. Of course, I also recognize that the seven tenets are an idealized portrait of science, because the day-to-day research of scientists does not look like the philosophers' vision of same.

12. However, I also argue below that we are moving toward convergences in political science research methods in which Michigan versus Rochester distinctions no longer have clear meaning (see below).

13. In ongoing work with Arend Lijphart, including a joint course on "The United States in Comparative Perspective," he and I are developing the argument that we can often best understand the peculiarities of particular countries—e.g., so-called "U.S. exceptionalism" (with respect to, say, low levels of voter turnout, or low levels of descriptive representation for women in Congress and state legislatures, or low levels of unionization)—by seeking to explain outcomes in that country in terms of variables drawn from crossnational analyses.

14. My colleague Rein Taagepera, a specialist on the Baltic states, tells a revealing story (personal communication, March 19, 1996) about some crossnational data analysis he did on the consequences of electoral laws. The Estonia data from pre–World War II were an outlier from his theoretical predictions, and he couldn't understand why. He just wasn't satisfied. Eventually he managed to track down an alternative source that reported raw data, and he recalculated the values of interest—to discover that his previous source (and several other sources that had taken that source to be definitive) were simply wrong, and wrong in a big way. Knowing Estonia, he knew that something just didn't seem right.

15. Nonetheless, the reader can undoubtedly fill in examples of scholars whose work falls far more clearly on one end of this continuum than the other, and similarly for the other axes of cleavage discussed here.

16. A particularly humorous example of this comes from a recent article in the *American Political Science Review* by two top-notch positive theorists, David Austen-Smith and Jeffrey Banks. They prove an elegant mathematical result to the effect that, when voters are free to be strategic in their voting choices, three-party competition under proportional representation leads to an equilibrium in which the party with the highest seat share and the party with the lowest vote share will form the government. They then contrast this result with that under two-party winner-take-all elections where it is taken to be true that "the party with the most votes has monotonic control of the legislature. . . . [and] (i)n equilibrium, both parties adopt the median voter's position, and this is surely the final policy outcome." Based on their modeling they conclude that "the popular conception that, in contrast with simple plurality schemes, proportional representation leads to legislatures—and hence to final policy outcomes—that reflect the variety of interests in the electorate seems mistaken" (Austen-Smith and Banks, 1988: 417).

Unfortunately, Austen-Smith and Banks, like some of the economists they emulate, don't appear to understand that the truth of an empirical proposition does not necessarily follow from a mathematical model from which it can be logically deduced, even if that model is an incredibly elegant one.

When we look at real politics: 1) there is no evidence that their model of three-party competition under PR is an accurate characterization of coalitional choices in three-party systems; and 2) there is a great deal of evidence that, in two-party plurality elections, party policy positions do not converge (Grofman, 1993a).

Of course, the work of Austen-Smith and Banks is only preliminary, as they are the first to acknowledge, and, because the assumptions of their model are so clearly spelled out, it is easier for us to figure out how we can improve on their model to develop one whose implications are better in line with what we observe. Still, it is bothersome to see an article that purports to tell us something about politics that is so utterly unconnected to empirical evidence. (In fairness, I've written plenty of such articles myself. I just try not to make that the only kind of article I write.)

17. Although I was an undergraduate at the University of Chicago well after the heyday of Robert Maynard Hutchins and the Great Books program, key elements of that program remained alive when I was there, albeit in watered-down form. My knowledge of the classics of political theory comes more from my undergraduate than from my graduate education. When I was informed by Joseph Cropsey at the beginning of his graduate course on Aristotle's *Politics* that Aristotle had asserted that the soul was divided into three parts (named, as I recall, something like the appetitive, the vegetative, and the dormative), I decided that I was not a political theorist, at least in the sense that Cropsey would have in mind, and dropped the course.

18. Of course, a few political scientists are also well-trained in economics, but they tend to respond to policy questions in the same fashion as an economist without bringing "something special" to the analysis as a result of their background in political science.

19. See discussion of politics as a "policy science" in Lowi and Harpham (this volume).

20. In this context, an important contribution of feminist writers has been to remind us that "the personal is the political" and that politics is not merely what happens when Congress makes a law or the Supreme Court decides a case. For example, feminist scholars have called attention to the real "gender gap"—i.e., gender-rooted differences in power.

21. On a personal note, as someone who has frequently served as an expert witness on behalf of racial minorities in voting rights lawsuits, my own primary commitment to truth rather than to social justice has gotten me into trouble with one or two of the attorneys for whom I have worked. They would have preferred that I downplay (if not suppress entirely) results that were uncomfortable for their side. Luckily, almost all the civil rights attorneys with whom I have worked are well aware of the pragmatic point that the credibility of an expert witness, once damaged, is hard to repair.

22. The greatest tribute to the success of rational choice modeling in political science is the number of people who now feel compelled to attack it (see Grofman, 1993b, 1996 forthcoming).

23. I am somewhat sympathetic to the second and third critiques, but I believe critiques one and four to be almost totally misguided (see Grofman, 1993b, 1996 forthcoming).

24. Moreover, it is sometimes asserted that neither rational choice models nor survey research have much to contribute to our understanding of the bloody events in Bosnia or Rwanda. This charge, too, I regard as quite misguided, but space does not permit an elaboration of my views here (on the application of rational choice modeling to the disintegration of Yugoslavia see, e.g., Posen, 1993).

25. Here by "realist" persuasion I mean what Wendt and Shapiro (this volume) mean by that term.

26. Of course, just as most applications of calculus cannot be viewed as contributions to physics, so not every application of game theory is a contribution to political science.

27. Harry Eckstein (personal communication, 1995) has made the intriguing point that the labels for "hard" rational choice and "soft" rational choice have been foolishly inverted. Only work that offers empirically testable (and falsifiable) hypotheses deserves the name of "hard science," and soft rational choice has at least as much of that as the largely theorematic contributions of the "hard-core" modelers.

28. As I have argued elsewhere (Grofman, 1993b, 1996 forthcoming), rational choice models need not posit that actors are driven solely by narrow egoistic perspectives.

29. Some would say "infected."

30. The scholars I mention are almost entirely from American politics simply because this is the disciplinary subfield I know best. Similar rapprochements of formal modeling and data analysis are taking place in subfields such as international relations and comparative politics. Names of scholars from these subfields are omitted simply due to my ignorance of their work, not from a belief that they don't exist or that what they do isn't first-rate.

31. In fairness, political scientists able to combine sophisticated modeling with sophisticated data analysis have been around for a while, as witness the work of relatively senior folk such as Kenneth Shepsle (committee assignments, legislative procedures, cabinet portfolios), Norman Schofield (cabinet coalitions), and John Ferejohn (budgetary rules, pork-barrel politics), to name but three. What is new is how many younger political scientists now possess an impressive combination of technical skills and substantive concerns.

32. Enelow and Morton (1993) also cite the works of several of the younger scholars I named above as especially promising in this regard.

33. Indeed, as evidenced by the 200-plus members of the Society for Experimental Economics, even some economists are recognizing the need to demonstrate, rather than merely assert, that various economic "truths" are self-evident.

REFERENCES

Almond, Gabriel. 1990. *A Discipline Divided: Schools and Sects in Political Science*. Newbury Park: Sage Publications.

Austen-Smith, David, and Jeffrey Banks. 1988. "Elections, Coalitions, and Legislative Outcomes." *American Political Science Review* 88 (June): 405–22.

Coleman, James. 1990. *Foundations of Social Theory*. Cambridge, MA.: Harvard University Press.

Easton, David. 1953. *The Political System: An Inquiry into the State of Political Science*. New York: Knopf, 2nd ed. 1971.

———. 1969. "The New Revolution in Political Science." *American Political Science Review* 63: 1051–61.

Eckstein, Harry. 1969. "Authority Relations and Government Performance." *Comparative Political Studies* 2 (October): 269–326.

Elster, Jon. 1989. *The Cement of Society: A Study of Social Order*. New York: Cambridge University Press.

Enelow, James. M., and Rebecca B. Morton. 1993. "Promising Directions in Public Choice." *Public Choice* 77, 1: 85–95.

Grofman, Bernard. 1993a. "Toward an Institution-Rich Theory of Political Competition, with a Supply-Side Component." In Bernard Grofman (ed.), *Information, Participation, and Choice: "An Economic Theory of Democracy" in Perspective*. Ann Arbor, MI: University of Michigan Press, 179–93.

——. 1993b. "On the Gentle Art of Rational Choice Bashing." In Bernard Grofman (ed.), *Information, Participation, and Choice: "An Economic Theory of Democracy" in Perspective*. Ann Arbor MI: University of Michigan Press, 239–42.

Grofman, Bernard. 1996 forthcoming. "Downsian Political Economy." In Robert Goodin and Hans-Dieter Klingemann (eds.), *New Handbook of Political Science*. Oxford, England: Oxford University Press.

Hyneman, Charles. 1959. *The Study of Politics: The Present State of American Political Science*. Urbana, IL: University of Illinois Press.

Posen, Barry R. 1993. "The Security Dilemma and Ethnic Conflict." *Survival* 35, 1 (Spring): 27–47.

Wuffle, A. 1992. "Credo of a 'Reasonable Choice' Modeler." Presented at the National Science Foundation Confrence on Rational Choice Approaches to Comparative Politics, UCI. May.

4

Political Science

Drunken Walk or Functional Evolution?

J. A. Laponce

An observation of Henri Poincaré, the nineteenth-century mathematician, may apply to political science as well as to mathematics. Poincaré classifies his colleagues as either "algebra" or "geometry"; some prefer abstract relations, whereas others need figures and visual representations. Both David Easton and I belong to the second of these two families, so, in homage to my colleague, I shall use arrowlike and boxlike archetypes to organize my reflections on the evolution and on the state of the discipline. Specifically, I shall use the imagery of the box and the cross.

THE BOX AND THE CROSS

There are two types of political scientists, as there are two types of social scientists: the cross people and the people of the box.* They lack overt signs of recognition. They often alternate teaching the same courses and cannot be reduced to any of the schools by which we normally classify our colleagues—neither the legal, the institutional, the behavioral, the comparative, the system theoretical, nor any other of the movements or chapels that have attempted, for the past two generations, to discipline the discipline. Admittedly, there are strong correlations. The cross people are more likely to look for models in economics and psychology; the box people are more

---

*The reader will have noted my inclination to dichotomize. A content analysis of the textbooks of the French private and public schools I attended would undoubtedly measure considerable differences between the two systems, notably in their recording of history. But these differences are less prominent in my recollections than the insistence of the lay schools of my childhood that we write our essays in two parts whereas the Catholic schools I attended were partial to the number three. I write this essay in a secular mode. A sociology of the number of categories used in political analysis has yet to be done.

likely to favor history and anthropology. The cross people are more likely
to be functionalists and more likely to quantify; the box people are more
likely to be philosophers and institutionalists. But these correlations are far
from perfect.

The two basic types are motivated by very different kinds of curiosity.
The primordial lure for the people of the box is the treasure chest of pirate
stories, an image that forces one to proceed from container to content. We
open the box, we rummage through it, and—impatiently or carefully—we
sort out the precious from the trivial. That type of curiosity leads one to
focus first on an institution or a concept—for example, the office of president, legitimacy, NATO, the House of Commons, Germany, the American
elector, the Supreme Court, local governments, or schoolchildren. At the
very least, this approach leads one to separate the finds according to type
and leads one to note recurring linkages. The exercise may well stop at the
creation of some kind of order, but that order may also put the analyst on
the road that ascends from brute facts toward models, theories, and laws.

The cross people proceed from the notion of an encounter. They wonder: what if x meets y? They do not start their quest from the notion of an
enclosing social, institutional, or physical boundary; they are led to it by
questions relating factors such as religion and politics, class and ethnicity,
jokes and party preference. The primordial experience at the root of this
type of curiosity may well be the toy one used to throw over the crib. Will
it or will it not come back? And, if it comes back, under what circumstances?

It would be wrong to say that the first approach is inductive and that the
other is hypothetico-deductive. The students of elections who present their
findings in the hypothetico-deductive mode are in many cases, as indicated
by the very questionnaires they devise, motivated by the treasure-chest psychology. They are often primarily interested in explaining a national elector
such as the French or the American.

Some researchers are firmly box or firmly cross; others shift from one
mode to the other. What motivated Easton (1969) to study schoolchildren?
The treasure chest, or the toy over the crib? An interest in American politics, or the encounter between socialization and legitimacy? The latter, I
think, but I am not sure. When I studied the Canadian elector (1969), I
was of the box; when I studied left and right (1981), I was of the cross.

In the 1930s, the bulk of the articles of the *American Political Science Review* (*APSR*) had a box approach. The proportion declined after World War
II, but this type of article still plays a role it has lost in psychology and
economics. The history of my department, at the University of British Columbia, records such an evolution. From a small group of colleagues who
could all be categorized by the nation-state or philosopher they studied, it
has become a department where the model of the cross has gained importance but where the national government specialists still have a determin-

ing influence on curriculum and recruitment by means of slots that describe nation-states, specific institutions, or specific policy areas.

Having detached itself from law, political science has—in the past generation—often sought guidance from psychology and economics, two disciplines that are most definitely of the cross. Why, then, should it be so resistant to becoming more fully cross-minded? What keeps it so strongly attached to the treasure chest? The answer is likely to be in one factor: the *state*.

The national state has remained the sun at the core of our discipline. We are supposed to have forgotten, then to have rediscovered it (Skocpol, 1979; Cassese, 1986). But did we really ever lose sight of it? Did we ever cease gravitating around it? I think not. Society wants us not to turn away from it. Political science can flourish only in democratic systems, and in such systems the polity needs political science as a checking mechanism. Such checking imposes on the practitioners a great deal of holistic descriptive analysis of national institutions. Psychology and economics do not operate under similar constraints; they have a more universalistic outlook. Being cast in the role of critical servant of the state made political science reluctant to follow the Eastonian prescription (1953) and study the "authoritative allocation of values" in contexts other than those defined narrowly by political institutions. Our attention has remained focused on one particular allocator, the not-so-cold Nietszchean monster that continues to fascinate us—a fascination that makes us reluctant to disaggregate the beast into simplified sets of factors, such as the stimulus-organism-response paradigm of psychology, or the cost-benefit analysis of economics. We do not want to cut to pieces the object of our fascination; we want to look at it whole.

THE TREE AND THE BRAIN

The archetypes that headline this section distinguish two types of growth, that of the tree and that of the brain. The tree grows by putting more and more tree stuff around its core, whereas the brain grows not so much by weight as by increasing the number of its synapses.

How has political science grown and by how much?

Its treelike growth is relatively easy to document. At the end of the nineteenth century, if one had wanted to convene a worldwide congress of political scientists, it would have been sufficient to pass the word to a few colleagues, notably the director of the Ecole Libre des Sciences Politiques, founded in Paris in 1871; the head of the Scola di Scienze Sociale of Florence, founded in 1875; the chairman of the Columbia University Department of Political Science, created in 1886; the director of the London

School of Economics, founded in 1895; and a few German professors, notably at Heidelberg. It would have been a remarkable congress that might have brought together von Stein, Tönnies, Jellinek, Weber, Mosca, Pareto, Siegfried, Brice, Pollock, Goodnow, Burgess, Wilson, Willoughby, Posada, Le Bon, Novicow, Fouillé, Boutemy, Durkheim, and Leroy Beaulieu, among others; a congress remarkable for the quality of the participants but remarkable also for their small number.

In the immediate post–World War II period, it was still possible to write a state of the art of political science, in a country such as Canada, by reading a dozen or so books and less than a hundred articles. That is no longer possible, neither in Canada, France, the United Kingdom, Germany, nor Scandinavia, not to mention the United States, where the annual meetings of the American Political Science Association (APSA) attract more than 5,000 participants.

Burdeau's *Traité de science politique*, published in 1980, may well be the last one-man attempt at a comprehensive overview of the field. Interesting as a personal statement, that work could never be taken, even at the time of its publication, as a guide to the discipline. Greenstein and Polsby, by contrast, farmed out their 1975 *Handbook of Political Science* to fifty collaborators. Ada Finifter's far less ambitious *State of the Discipline*, published in 1978, has twenty authors; Madeleine Grawitz and Jean Leca's 1985 *Traité de science politique* has fifty contributors, and the *Encyclopedia of Government and Politics,* edited by Hawkesworth and Kogan in 1992, contains eighty-four chapters written by eighty-nine authors. The *International Political Science Abstracts,* selective as they have to be, index more than 5,000 articles each year; and the *International Bibliography of Political Science,* which lists books as well as articles, has more than 7,000 entries annually. We are very far behind the 400,000-odd articles published each year in the field of chemistry and will remain far from that number in the foreseeable future, even if political science output in the newly democratic states of Eastern Europe catches up with that of the West. But even if it stays under 10,000 indexed publications per year, the field has reached considerable dimensions.

Has that growth been for the good? Rather than a contemporary world congress, would we not prefer attending our imaginary roundtable of the turn of the last century? That choice is tempting if we take the present for granted. But had the late-nineteenth-century founders been offered the reverse choice, it is almost certain that they would have preferred the kind of congress that the International Political Science Association held in 1994 in Berlin. Would they be impressed? My guess is that they would. Durkheim would be awed by our handling of statistics. Siegfried would marvel at the predictive capacity of our election surveys. Pareto would regret our shifts from nonrational to rational explanations but would understand them and would be pleased, I assume, by the wealth of data collected along our tortuous ways. The lawyers, the philosophers, and the historians would note the care we take to be objective and systematic. Few might understand our graphs, equations, simulations, and games, but most would take them as the logical outcome of a scientific evolution. Those in the grand sociological tradition would be distressed by our reductionism, and Durkheim would wonder whether the division of labor that enabled us to diversify our efforts has been balanced by the appropriate increase in internal communication.

Let us consider this Durkhemian concern. Political science has grown as a tree should grow. It has covered more and more ground. But has it also developed as a brain should evolve? Has it increased the number of its synapses? If so, do the synapses connect what should be connected? I cannot provide more than a very partial answer, and to do so will have to be outrageously reductionist.

INSIDE AND OUTSIDE CONNECTIONS

Let us distinguish two types of connections, those that link political science to other disciplines and those that link subfields within the discipline. The first will be easier to study than the second.

To measure the frequency of interdisciplinary connections, let us consider, very simply, the footnotes of selected journals and ask ourselves which journals quote which other journals. To make the search manageable, let us consider the "footnote trade" among the following disciplines—political science, sociology, history, psychology, economics, geography, and anthropology—and let us represent each discipline by two of its leading journals—one American, one British. For each article in our corpus, let us record the scientific periodicals they quoted at least once. Each discipline is represented by forty articles, twenty American and twenty British. Let us classify, by field, following Ulrich's system (1989), all the journals that appeared in those forty articles. If, for example, the forty articles representing political science on Table 4.1 (twenty from the *American Political Science Review*, twenty from *Political Studies*) had each quoted at least one sociology journal, we would give political science imports from sociology the maximum score of 100; if no import had taken place, the score would be nil (Laponce, 1980).

The major trade patterns highlighted by Table 4.1 are quite clear. They contrast political science and sociology on the one hand, psychology and economics on the other. The first two depend heavily on imports; the other two are close to autarky.

Is it chance that the only social science to be awarded a Nobel Prize is also the least dependent on other social sciences? Is awarding a prize easier

TABLE 4.1   Linkages among disciplines as
measured by the footnotes of selected publications*

	Political Science	Anthro- pology	Geog- raphy	Economics	Psy- chology	History	Sociology
Political Science	80	8	8		5	10	33
Anthropology		95	8		5	10	15
Geography	3	13	83			3	
Economics	18	5	18	95		18	25
Psychology	20	20	10	5	98		28
History	18	20	13	3		90	15
Sociology	40	23	13	3	8	18	90

From/To

*Based on Laponce (1980). In every cell the maximum is 100 percent. Zero is represented by a blank. Each discipline is characterized by a sample of ten articles from each of two of its leading publications, one American, the other British. Political science: *American Political Science Review, Political Studies;* Psychology: *British Journal of Psychology, Journal of Personality and Social Psychology;* Anthropology: *Man, American Anthropologist;* Geography: *Annals of the American Association of Geographers, Geographical Journal;* Economics: *Economic Journal, American Economic Review;* History: *American Historical Review, History.* The sample covers the years 1975–1980.

when the research boundaries are well defined, thus facilitating comparison and assessment? Has economics achieved higher scientific standing because of its intellectual independence? Whatever the cause, the correlation leads us to expect that psychology, rather than political science or anthropology, is next in line for a Nobel distinction and that political science may well never be given one.

If a heavy reliance on the outside is not good for a Nobel Prize, is it at least good for political research? Having taken great pleasure at crisscrossing disciplines, I am inclined to answer in the affirmative.

The evolution of the discipline has clearly been toward more diversified interdisciplinarity (Dogan and Pahre, 1990). That trend appears in Table 4.2, which plots the pattern of imports (as measured by footnotes) of two of the oldest political science journals, the *American Political Science Review* and the *Canadian Journal of Political Science* (formerly the *Canadian Journal of Economics and Political Science*). In the 1930s the *APSR* was tied almost exclusively to law, the CJEPS almost exclusively to law and economics. Since then, the import pattern has become more and more diversified, with the exception of the 1970s in Canada, when imports from economics declined sharply for a while. In little more than one generation the *APSR* has supplemented its traditional imports from law, adding imports from history, sociology, philosophy, psychology, economics, and mathematics. The CJPS

TABLE 4.2 Evolution of the imports of the *APSR* and *CJEPS/CJPS*
Percentage of articles quoting journals from other disciplines*

	CEJPS/CJPS					APSR				
	1935	1955	1975	1989	1991	1935	1955	1975	1989	1991
Law	10	10	7	23	30	33	17	7	13	23
Economics	20	13		19	23			10	60	30
History		13	10	23	23		13	17	23	
Sociology			18	37	35		30	43	43	27
Philosophy			10	17	10		7	20	10	37
Psychology			7					13	23	20
Math/Statistics			7					7	10	20
Geography				7						
Anthropology				7						

*Thirty articles in each year (and the year following when there were less than thirty articles in the year considered). Only the disciplines appearing in at least two articles are recorded here. Ten at the top of the table indicated that then percent of the CEJPS articles (N=30) quoted at least on law journal in 1935. When in doublt I followed Ulrich's classification. The 1935 to 1989 data are taken from Laponce (1980).

has, by and large, followed the same evolution. A different measure of interdisciplinarity—the number of journals linking at least two disciplines—would give us a similar picture and would lead us to identify linkages that do not appear in Table 4.2, notably the link with geography thanks to *Political Geography* and the link with biology through *Politics and the Life Sciences*.

Has this increase in dependence on the outside been accompanied by an increase in internal linkages among subfields? My impression is that it has not. The discipline's travels abroad may well have come at the expense of internal journeys. Indeed, there has been no great debate, at least no great academic debate, since the behavioral "revolution." Our recent confrontations have been over issues originating in society at large—political correctness, for example—originating outside rather than inside the discipline. They are debates over boundary maintenance rather than over scientific goals.

A simple, and for that reason very tentative, measure of our isolation and fragmentation into sects and chapels is rendered possible by the *Encyclopedia of Political Science* of 1992. This volume contains eighty-four chapters, each written by a different author. The chapters are grouped under the following nine headings: Political Theory (six chapters); Contemporary Ideologies (five chapters); Contemporary Political Systems (four chapters); Political Institutions (six chapters); Political Forces and Processes (eight chapters); Centripetal and Centrifugal Forces in the Nation-state (eight chapters); Policy Making and Policies (thirteen chapters); International Relations (sixteen chapters); and Major Issues in Contemporary World Politics (seventeen chapters). The author index to the *Encyclopedia* contains 750 names, excluding those of nonacademics. Because each chapter has its own bibliography, we can get a rough measure of convergence of attention across chapters by listing the authors whose names appear in more than one chapter. Setting the hurdle at 10 percent (i.e., at least nine of the eighty-four chapters) results in the retrieval of only two names: Max Weber (14 percent) and Thomas Hobbes (11 percent). Lowering the floor to 8 percent (seven chapters) adds the names of Lenin, Locke, and Kant; lowering it to 7 percent (six chapters) adds Aristotle, Hume, and Adam Smith.

I lack a benchmark by which to evaluate these percentages. To my eyes, the overall level of convergence appears low. I applaud Max Weber's scoring at the top of the list, but I find that list lacking in contemporary theorists. Is that a bias of a particular encyclopedia, or does the bias favoring the classics give a good measure of a discipline whose subfields appear linked by its past rather than its present? The latter, I think.

Using the same corpus, let us change the measure and take subfields instead of chapters as our units of analysis. By so doing we reduce the number of cases from eighty-four to nine. The question then becomes: what authors, and how many, link what fields?

Table 4.3 shows that some of the nine fields do not share a single author—for example, the two fields that Hawkesworth and Kogan labeled "Contemporary Ideologies" and "Policy Making." The highest levels of common sources are registered between "Political Theory" and "Political Forces" (nineteen authors in common) and between "Centripetal and Centrifugal Forces" and "Political Forces" (eighteen authors in common). These last two fields are analytically close; they could have been subsumed under the heading of "Cleavages and Processes." That these closely related fields have only eighteen authors in common (out of 148, hence only 12 percent) serves as a first indication of a low level of convergence of attention. That impression is reinforced by the even lower scores recorded between "International Relations" and "Major Issues" and between "Contemporary Political Systems" and "Political Institutions." International relations has developed independently of comparative government, possibly as a result of its moving away from the state while the rest of the discipline is returning to it.

The list of contemporaries quoted in more than one of the nine *Encyclopedia* fields is only in the neighborhood of sixty. Contemporary theorists who did not appear in our previous count are among the sixty (they include Talcott Parsons, David Easton, Karl Deutsch, John Rawls, and William Riker), but the classics continue to be the major focus of attention. The most often "shared" contemporary (G. Allison) covers four fields, whereas

Hobbes covers five and Weber appears in six. (The *Handbook of General Psychology,* by comparison, shows a higher level of commonality of both classics such as Pavlov and contemporaries such as G. Allport, R. C. Atkinson, and B. F. Skinner.) I find it disappointing that Laswell—who appears in three of the nine sections of the *Encyclopedia*—is less of a subdisciplinary glue than Kant, who appears in five. Quoting the one should not have prevented quoting the other.

Admittedly, these statistics lend themselves to more than one interpretation. Not being cited may actually be a measure of success (one no longer needs to quote Einstein), but, at the risk of being very wrong, I take the low level of communication through common references as reinforcing my personal impression of a low level of communication across subfields.

CONCLUSION

Plato wanted his ideal city to be located at the very center of an island in order that the shores be used not to conduct commerce with the outside world but to isolate the polity. Alexander the Great, by contrast, when asked where he wanted to locate the capital of his empire, is supposed to have pointed in all directions; he would not have one capital but a network of capitals. Economics has grown according to Plato's model; political science has followed Alexander. So did sociology, but political science did retain what sociology never had, a central core of attention—the state that we watch and that we hope to guide. We are thus led, in summary, to a final archetype, that of a floral pattern in which the core is the nation state and the petals are the subfields.

That is lovely. But is it good? My first, immediate reaction was negative. It was derived from the assumption that the core should not simply define the object of the study but also should include common analytical frameworks, common models, common theories. On further reflection, I wondered whether the floral metaphor had not led me to assume that what mattered was the flower rather than the petals.

If the petals are the essential, then why look at the flower as a whole? If we consider the petals one by one, then we see political philosophy joining in lively debates classics such as Plato or Hobbes and contemporaries such as Rawls and Michel Foucault; we see international relations abounding in theories—some of them, admittedly, theories only in name—that challenge and refine the balance-of-power models; we see a field of comparative government that does not compare much but covers an increasing number of countries and offers increasingly detailed information; we see survey research refining its techniques of sampling and questioning and becoming better than meteorology at predicting the near future; and so on. So maybe

TABLE 4.3 Number of Links among Subfields,
Measured by the Authors They Quote

	Contemporary Ideologies	Political Systems	Political Institutions	Political Forces and Processes	Centripetal and Centrifugal Forces	Policy Making	International Relations	Major Issues in World Politics
Political Theory	6	5	3	19	13	3	6	5
Contemporary Ideologies		1		6	3		3	3
Contemporary Political Systems			2	6	4	4	1	5
Political Institutions				6	9	6	1	2
Political Forces and Processes					18	3	5	8
Centripetal and Centrifugal Forces						3	7	6
Policy Making and Policies							2	2
International Relations								9

	Political Theory	Contemporary Ideologies	Contemporary Political Systems	Political Institutions	Political Forces and Processes	Centripetal and Centrifugal Forces	Policy Making and Policies
Political Theory	15						
Contemporary Ideologies	14 / 3						
Contemporary Political Systems	4	6					
Political Institutions	24 / 15	17 / 8					
Political Forces and Processes	16 / 8	11 / 11	11 / 11				
Centripetal and Centrifugal Forces	4	11 / 8	3 / 1	3			
Policy Making and Policies	3	3	5	6			
International Relations	8 / 8	3 / 1	5	6	2	2 / 8	6 / 8

*Source Hawkesworks and Kogan (1992). The number 6 in the top left cell indicated that six different authors appear in the references of the 2 sections of the *Encyclopedia of Government and Politics* identified in the rows and columns. The lower half of this table transforms that number into a percentage, the base (100%) being the number of authors quoted in the subfield with the lower number. Political Theory has 79 entries, Contemporary Ideologies has only 39; when comparing the two fields the base is 39.

political science does rather well because of, rather than notwithstanding, its fragmentation.

And thus, I find myself tempted to change my mind and—dropping boxes, trees, and flowers—to use an altogether different analogy. When an organism, such as the human body, has to produce the enzymes that will control a foreign germ, hence meet a challenge from the environment, and when its memory lacks the appropriate answer, it starts, apparently, to produce responses at random. Problem solving in the absence of known solutions is a disorderly affair; at least, it looks disorderly. If political science, having given itself the task of understanding the state—or, more generally, of understanding power relations—seems to be running in all kinds of directions, the apparent indirection may in fact be a very directed form of problem solving. *May* be.

I continue to wonder however, as did Easton (1953, 1965), whether the discipline, while continuing to fragment and shift from micro to macro, from psychological to rational choice explanations, would not do well to study—more than it does—power relations in general, political and nonpolitical. By so doing it might arrive at general explanations of the making and unmaking of human, and possibly even animal, hierarchies.

REFERENCES

Burdeau, G. 1980. *Traité de science politique* Paris: PUF.

Cassese, S. 1986. "The Rise and Decline of the State" *International Political Science Review* 7, 2: 120–419.

Dogan, Mattei, and Robert Pahre. 1990. *Creative Marginality: Innovation at the Intersections of the Social Sciences*. Boulder: Westview.

Easton, David. 1953. *The Political System*. New York: Knopf.

———. 1969. *Childen in the Political System: Origins of Political Legitimacy*. Chicago: University of Chicago Press.

Finifter, Ada (ed.). 1983. *Political Science: The State of the Discipline*. Washington: APSA.

Grawitz, M. et J. Leca. *Traité de science politique*, 2 vol. Paris: PUF.

Greenstein F., and N. Polsby (ed.). 1975. *Handbook of Political Science*. New York: Knopf.

Hawkesworth, M., and M. Kogan. 1992. *Encyclopedia of Government and Politics*, 2 vol. London: Routledge.

International Political Science Abstracts (since 1954). Paris: Fondation nationale des sciences politiques.

International Political Science Documentation (since 1954). London: London School of Economics

Laponce, J. A. 1969. *People vs. Politics: A Study of Opinions, Attitudes and Perceptions in Vancouver Burrard*. Toronto: Toronto University Press.

———. 1980. "Political Science: An Import-Export Analysis," *Political Studies* 4: 401–19.

———. 1981. *Left and Right: The Topography of Political Perceptions*. Toronto: Toronto University Press.

Poincaré, Henri. 1963. *Mathematics and Science*. New York: Dover.

Skopol, T. 1985. "Bringing the State Back in." In P.Evans et al. (ed.), *Bringing the State Back in*. Cambridge: Cambridge University Press.

Ulrich's International Periodicals Directory. 1989. New York: Bowker.

5

Veiled Uses of Empirical Theories

Murray Edelman

Until approximately the last half of the twentieth century, political science teaching and research were, for the most part, not self-conscious about the theories that guided the choice of topics, the generation of hypotheses, the procedures for examining them, or the interpretation of findings. There was an esteemed subfield of political science named "political theory," but a wall too often separated those concerned with it from those who analyzed current political institutions and processes. Political theory dealt largely with the classics and with traditional normative issues; political science dealt with empirical allocations of values through government.

Political scientists who analyzed these allocations were guided by theories, though often unwittingly. They had to use some criteria for selecting data and interpreting them in order to do systematic work, but most were inclined to take their theoretical orientations for granted or regarded them as self-evidently valid; they did not see these orientations as problematic or as representing deliberate choices among alternatives. This unselfconscious kind of theorizing meant that accepted and conventional ideas were likely to remain unchallenged.

In the 1960s many political scientists grew self-conscious about the fundamental sense in which political analysis and contemporary political theories shape each other. They began examining the uses and inadequacies of research based deliberately on specific theories. I believe it is that intimate link between conceptualization and research operations to which the term "empirical theory" should refer, rather than to any new focus on empiricism growing out of recent theories. Systems theory, for example, is considerably less empirical in orientation than the writings of Machiavelli. This definition of empirical theory dispels the notion that the concept is an oxymoron, as some claim it is. Still, the expression may not be a felicitous one, both because of its ambiguity and because it would be hard to find any theory that is not empirical in some significant sense.

If we consider the set of empirical theories that political scientists have employed widely in recent decades, revealing generalizations become evident. Perhaps the most obvious is that fashions in empirical theories change fairly rapidly, but the theories that are no longer the most popular do not fade away; each one leaves an influential legacy, and each continues to be deployed in some measure.

Every theory assumes a particular kind of social world and a particular kind of human nature. Those assumptions explain why theories can remain influential in spite of a momentary (or permanent) decline in popularity, for they are rarely alternatives that exclude others. Instead, each encourages a focus that the others ignore or fail to develop adequately: on popular influence or on exclusion; on rationality or on irrationality; on self-evident meanings or on deep structures; on conflict or on social equilibrium; on the individual or on collectivities.

Because all of these recent perspectives are relevant to our understanding of the social world, all continue to make their contributions. Perhaps the most striking and the most encouraging development in the last several decades is the greater sophistication available to scholars who have the benefit of all these perspectives. It remains far from clear how to integrate them or best use them, and most research relies heavily on one of them; but the set of extant theories reminds us, explicitly or subtly, that there are alternatives, supplements, and modifications. The devotee of psychological approaches who is bemused by the irrational and the nonrational, for example, forgets the rational capabilities of the mind at his or her peril.

Because of their constrained scope, empirical theories serve purposes other than assistance in explanation, and it is chiefly these aspects that I will address here. In a sense these are the political uses of empirical theories, as distinct from their scientific uses; they are powerful precisely because a scientific aura enhances and veils their political thrust. These applications of political theories serve the interests of some groups and hurt others.

All political theories—probably all theories of any kind—serve political purposes as well as explanatory ones. The two functions need not be incompatible, and they are bound to influence each other. Thomas Kuhn has shown that the adoption of paradigms depends upon agreements among communities of scholars rather than upon any inherent logic in scientific progress or the accumulation either of data or of anomalies.[1] Understanding why theories appeal to scholars in a particular social and political setting is, then, a necessary foundation for understanding why they are adopted and what scientific functions they serve, even when the bases of their appeal are subliminal or repressed. The veiled uses of the empirical theories influential in recent decades are, not surprisingly, closely tied to the political and ideological issues and passions that have been prominent in those years. Let me list and analyze some of the most conspicuous such uses.

EXCLUSION OF DISTURBING CURRENT DEVELOPMENTS

It is striking and paradoxical that some empirical theories that have gained especially strong favor ignore or deny the most obvious aspects of current public policy. Their popularity apparently stems in large part from precisely this exclusion.

Consider rational choice theory, which has dominated a great deal of the work of political scientists and economists in recent years. It is hard to avoid the conclusion that the focus on rationality is largely a reaction of policy makers and academics who identify with them to conspicuous evidence that major public policies in the twentieth century have too often been notably *irrational*. These policies have brought disastrous results in the form of, inter alia, needless wars, the Holocaust and other genocidal operations, and domestic policies that increase poverty, crime, homelessness, and drug abuse and ruin educational institutions and other aspects of the infrastructure. For those with a stake in the status quo, a comforting response to these disturbing trends is to persuade themselves and a wider public that policy choice is a rational process and can or should be evaluated by criteria based on that premise.

Much of the rational choice literature therefore impedes fundamental change in policy or in institutions, for it deters critics and policy makers from addressing the irrational features of politics and administration with which social psychology is chiefly concerned. In this way the words that succeed and the policies that fail help create each other.

Although rational choice theory, sometimes under other names (such as "formal models"), has been influential in the social sciences for at least three decades, it has become especially fashionable and widely deployed in the 1980s and 1990s, the years in which the outcomes of many federal foreign and domestic policies have most conspicuously failed to mirror their rational justifications. That failure, I believe, explains the intensified need of those responsible for such policy to assert and assume its rationality.

Another empirical theory that teaches the same lesson is systems theory. Influenced in its basic principles by physics and engineering, systems theory assumes that each of the components of the public policy "system" contributes to the continued functioning of the whole—which, in turn, adapts to changes in those components. There is accordingly a tendency toward equilibrium among demands on the system, supports for it, policy forming institutions, policy outcomes, and feedback from outcomes to demands and supports.

Systems theory was the most popular empirical theory among political scientists in the 1960s, the decade in which harmony and equilibrium were most conspicuously absent from the political scene—the decade of urban riots, escalating demands for increased status and influence from minority populations and women, and bitter domestic conflict over the Vietnam War. Yet systems theory ignored political conflict and violence or explained them away as evanescent trends. Here, too, it is hard to avoid the conclusion that an empirical theory helped the public and many social scientists to minimize or divert attention from the obvious and disturbing developments of the time. That observation applies not to the *formulation* of systems theory, which took place in the 1950s, but rather to popularization among political scientists in the 1960s.

Theories that have exercised continuing influence over many decades and still do so illustrate the point as well. Pluralism has been strongly influential since the early twentieth century, the formative years of political science as an organized profession. Its appeal arises from its reassuring premise that all groups with interests in public policy wield the influence that their support justifies, at least roughly. Pluralism was especially potent in the profession in the 1950s, bolstered at that time by renewed interest in the group theory of Arthur Bentley.[2] But the 1950s witnessed McCarthyism, the inauguration of the cold war, and a high measure of insensitivity to the plight of the poor, women, and minorities. Pluralism certainly eased the consciences of public officials and academics, who could justify the exercise of power as a response to the concerns and enthusiasms of political, military, and industrial elites. Though it was somewhat muted in the 1960s, it reemerged as a strong current in American ideology through the Reagan and Bush administrations, which were even more conspicuously responsive to the ruling elites than the leaders of the 1950s were. Pluralism would very likely fade away if its premises and promises were realized in practice rather than in textbook claims and patriotic oratory; it would then serve no function as an ideology.

Not all empirical theories compensate in this way for political practices that refute their assumptions and their assurances. It would be ridiculous to maintain that psychological theories are responsive in any sense to the rigorous rationality of public policy or that Marxist or other conflict theories can be explained even in part as a reaction to the harmony and cooperation that mark public life. But there is a plain distinction between the theories that serve such veiled functions and those that do not. The former are optimistic in outlook, and all the optimistic theories play this role. They tell us that governmental decisions are rational, that they reflect the demands of the general public, that they promote equitable influence in policy by all affected groups. People of good will want to hear these messages precisely because there is so much reason to suspect that they are not valid.

The history of Marxist theory offers a revealing lesson and caveat in this respect. In the late nineteenth and early twentieth centuries, the Marxist promise of an end to the exploitation and alienation promoted by capitalism, of a state that would wither away, did exemplify an optimistic theory that was offering reassurance about deplorable current conditions. But as more and more time passed without any revolution nor any utopian aftermath, that aspect of the Marxist promise, rather than the state, has seemed to wither away; both Marxists and their opponents are inclined to ignore it. At the same time, however, the Marxist critique of capitalism remains a lively domain of research and theorizing, perhaps more spirited than it has ever been, influencing virtually all contemporary social theory and continuously spawning modifications, refinements, and criticisms of Marx.

The optimistic promises a theory offers apparently must remain credible short- or long-term outcomes. Neither the advocates nor critics of Marxism can any longer find credibility in the rather cursory aspects of Marx's writings that foretell a socialist-anarchist future, though the more substantial Marxist writings that analyze the dynamics and evils of capitalism continue to energize scholars and social critics.

VEILED PROMOTION OF AN IDEOLOGY

Every empirical theory serves the interests of one or more social groups and works against the objectives and well-being of others. As far as its epistemological contribution is concerned, this is, of course, not the theory's paramount function, but it is likely to be a potent consequence, all the more so when it is unrecognized or veiled. Marxist theory promotes the interests of the working class by analyzing the range of ways in which that class is exploited in a capitalist economy. That ideological bent makes some cautious about accepting the premises and reasoning of this kind of theory, but it impresses and energizes others. It probably influences everyone in some measure, if only because Marxist ideas have often been incorporated into other theories and into some widely accepted beliefs of our time.

But it is less evident that most psychological theories subtly justify the status quo and therefore serve the interests of those who benefit from established social institutions. They do so in several ways. First, psychological theories that focus on individual behavior and thought, as most of them do, define normality and abnormality, success and failure, according to how well the individual copes, behaves, and adjusts within the existing social framework. These theories tend to label those who do not adjust as in some sense pathological. This orientation is therefore a powerful bulwark of that social framework and a politically formidable weapon against people who deliberately or involuntarily fail to adapt to the world as it is.

Second, the focus on the individual sees him or her as the site of key decisions and fundamental responsibility for the course of events, whereas the alternative orientation, on economic and social institutions, would attribute that role to these institutions and therefore raise directly the question of whether they should be changed to bring about more desirable results. Both these attributes of psychological theories exert exceptionally strong influences, subtly shaping the structure and scope of thought.

For a different and more evident reason, systems theory also helps sanctify the status quo. It postulates public demands and supports as the "inputs" of the political system and traces their conversion into "outputs" that correspond directly to the inputs. This is a highly reassuring schema; it tells us that governmental actions flow systematically from what the public wants. There is a built-in immunization here against political critics who suggest that administrative, legislative, or judicial actions may be disproportionately responsive to the interests of those who already command the largest resources. In this key sense systems theory can be recognized as an offspring of a pluralist political philosophy.

Formal models or rational choice theories are still another type of empirical theory that subtly reflects and promotes a status quo ideology. These approaches embrace the view that rational premises and calculation drive public policy, which can best be evaluated by how well it conforms to this criterion. But such assumptions ignore or minimize the central premise of most psychological theories: that irrational or unconscious motives significantly influence policy decisions. The concentration on rationality manifestly blesses public policy decisions and deters critics and policy makers from addressing the irrational aspects of politics and administration.

The concept of rationality is a construction of capitalist, bureaucratized, industrialized countries. More often than not it reflects the values upon which those institutions are built, notably the assumptions that human beings, natural resources, and planning are instruments for the production of profits and that everyone benefits in the measure that that goal is realized. The "rational" course of action therefore turns out to be the one that benefits those who already command most of what there is to get.

Rational choice theory has become popular with a considerable number of Marxists in recent years, a development that would seem to run counter to my analysis of its ideological thrust.[3] But these writings tend to conclude that the optimum strategy, and therefore the rational course, for Marxist parties in the late twentieth century is to compromise with bourgeois parties. Even here, therefore, rational choice theory has exerted a conservative influence.

Structuralism and poststructuralism are often characterized as instruments of the status quo as well, though the case here is certainly less clear than it is for the empirical theories just reviewed; in fact, these theories can also have the opposite effect.[4] Their focus on current, synchronic relations rather than on long-term change very likely does serve a conservative function most of the time, as does their erasure of subjects (and, in the case of structuralism, of objects as well). The poststructuralist penchant for play with words to exemplify verbal associations and "difference," "differance," and "traces" as sources of meaning can divert attention, moreover, from economic and social inequalities and exploitation. Clever games seem to displace social concerns and strategies for economic and social transformation. This tendency is based largely on the work of Jacques Derrida, though it appears in the writings of his devotees rather than in the work of Derrida himself.

However, some of the most searching radical theory of the twentieth century has taken its inspiration from structuralism, notably the work of Louis Althusser,[5] Maurice Godelier,[6] and other exponents of structuralist Marxism. The strategy of this form of theory is to unmask the hidden logic by which capitalist exploitation operates and justifies itself politically. Poststructuralism, too, has radical ramifications. The Derridean emphasis upon the multiple, proliferating, and contradictory connotations of texts amounts to a telling refutation of the concepts of rationality, instrumentality, logic, and other forms of "logocentrism" upon which extant economies and societies are based and by which they are justified. Derrida's work also lends itself to inversion of the values and meanings that are privileged in everyday discourse. Michel Foucault revealed the subtle and powerful processes by which knowledge buttresses power and power constructs what we accept as knowledge, and he published brilliant analyses of the roles of mental institutions, prisons, hospitals, and sexuality in bolstering established power as well. Jean Baudrillard probed the devices by which recent technologies, such as television and opinion polling, construct the realities that dominate late-twentieth-century politics.

It is evident that structuralism and poststructuralism, influential empirical theories of the late twentieth century, have served a range of social classes and ideologies, as has the whole corpus of empirical theories of that era. Such theories serve ideologies, then, and do so in especially potent ways when their ideological function is not explicit. But this veiled function need not detract from their usefulness as aids to explanation. Explanation is never value-free. The ideological bent of a theory is an integral part of its explanatory utility, not a diversion or an obstacle.

LINKS TO OTHER DISCIPLINES

Virtually all the empirical theories political scientists have employed in the late twentieth century originated in another academic discipline. This curious development can very likely be traced to the long-established theoretical posture of political scientists who did not define themselves as political theorists; to their recognition, approximately after the middle of the century, that this stance severely handicapped their efforts at explanation; and to the integral role of theory in other disciplines.

One of the few empirical theories (perhaps the only one) that has played a large role in political science but not in other social sciences is systems theory, and its emergence and influence are traceable to the initiative and intellectual resourcefulness of David Easton. Easton found some of the basic framework for systems theory in engineering and the hard sciences. The Society for the Advancement of General Systems Research was founded in 1956 to encourage the use of interdisciplinary models. But Easton's application of systems theory to government was really quite unique, and for a time it was enormously influential in virtually every area of political science.

Rational choice theory is a transplant from economics, and its early applications to politics and government in the 1960s appeared largely in the work of economists such as Anthony Downs, Mancur Olson, Thomas Schelling, Gordon Tullock, and James Buchanan. Indeed, a major change in the deployment of this form of theory in recent years has been the striking increase in its appeal and use by political scientists of many different varieties, often with considerable ingenuity. Its influence has extended as well to research that does not explicitly adopt the rational choice strategy, with wider resort in political science to such devices common in economics as ideal types, ceteris paribus assumptions, and comparative advantage.

Political psychology has manifestly adopted most of its premises and procedures from the discipline of psychology's various schools, which are themselves sometimes in conflict with one another. Freudian psychology has contributed influential concepts, has helped shape the work of political scientists who use depth interviews, and has been especially useful to political scientists who shrink biography. Learning theory has been applied fruitfully to election campaigns and other political phenomena. Cognitive psychology has exerted a major influence on studies of political attitude formation, and some psychologists have undertaken essentially political studies, so the two disciplines have enriched each other in some measure.

Structuralism and poststructuralism have provided a bridge between some political scientists and the humanities in recent decades. These forms of theory have been the dominant influences on scholarship in the humanities in the 1960s, 1970s, and 1980s. More recently, and in a more tempered way, they have helped shape political science studies, especially in electoral behavior, international relations, and political communication. Some of their specific emphases are listed above.

Though these two forms of theory create a close link to the humanities, they emphatically do not make political science more humanistic in the sense of a focus upon individual human subjects. On the contrary, both structuralists and poststructuralists define themselves as antihumanist and see the subject as a creation of the text rather than the initiator of action or the proper center of attention. The author disappears along with the subject, and so does God, who is the ultimate subject and a blatant form of logocentrism.

We should note in passing that structural-functional theory, conspicuous in political science in earlier decades, derived from sociology and forged a close link with that discipline, but recent decades have witnessed the fading of structural-functionalism as a major form of empirical theory. Like other theories that once occupied center stage, however, it has left a strong and probably permanent residue of ideas that continue to show themselves in political science research.

The conscious regard for empirical theories in recent decades has certainly made political scientists more interdisciplinary. It has exerted some of the same influence on other social sciences; however, the effect has been smaller for them, perhaps because these other disciplines, unlike political science, are built around a core theory or set of theories.

DISGUISED VIEWS OF HUMAN ATTRIBUTES

Each empirical theory presumes a particular conception of the nature and importance of at least one human attribute, the most prominent being rationality, identity, inequality, and the capacity to acquire secure knowledge. But unlike the philosophical discussions and empirical research, empirical theories do not address these crucial concepts directly but rather presuppose a particular view of them. This veiled approach may well be more compelling in winning assent to a specific orientation than an explicit argument that takes account of diverse evidence, as a brief survey of the implications of some widely used empirical theories illustrates. As if to underline the ease with which the veiled approach can support any view at all with minimal rebuttal, different empirical theories typically reach contradictory conclusions.

Rational choice theory is based upon the premise that rational considerations explain policy decisions; by contrast, most psychological theories are based upon the premise that decisions stem from a range of needs, desires, and impulses, most of them nonrational or irrational, that involve cognitive confusions, many of them unconscious. When a scholar engaged in research chooses to employ either of these theories, he or she presupposes one or the other of these conflicting assumptions without addressing the validity of the assumption, which would call for an entirely different conceptual framework.

Theories postulating fixed stages of ego development and psychoanalytic theories see the self, ego, or identity as a central and largely stable attribute of the individual. Social psychological theories, by contrast, define the self in terms of interactions with others and therefore see it as changing with alterations in reference groups or other social phenomena. Poststructuralist theory sees it as an epiphenomenon, a by-product of language. It is likely that all these views are valid in some sense, but the theories emphasize their differences and discourage research that would begin to synthesize them. In Chapter 14 of this volume, Kristen Monroe explores further the contributions of empirical theories to beliefs about human nature.

There are also strong differences among the theories in their views about the prevalence of inequality in contemporary democracies. Pluralist theory postulates that all interested groups have an equitable chance to influence policy; it assumes an impressive measure of equality, both as to opportunity and as to accomplishment. Marxist theory, by contrast, assumes there are built-in reasons why inequality and exploitation prevail, and the psychological theories that emphasize irrationality typically imply inequality as well. The conflicting premises by which these theories encourage divergent beliefs about a central issue in democratic theory probably cannot be confirmed or falsified conclusively, so adherence to one or another very likely hinges on ideological inclination.

Perhaps the most widely debated issue involving empirical theories concerns the ability to acquire secure or verified knowledge. This, of course, was the question addressed initially by logical positivism in the nineteenth century, and it continues to influence research at the end of the twentieth. The view that empirical verification and logical calculation are the only methods by which to produce secure knowledge continues to be challenged by a range of twentieth-century arguments that focus on the inevitability of interpretation in all observation and reasoning and try to examine interpretation systematically. From this perspective, objectivity in the positivist sense is impossible. Such modern approaches to knowledge include critical theory, phenomenology, the dialectic, and hermeneutics. Here again, contrasting assumptions about appropriate forms of theory yield divergent conclusions. It is to David Easton's great credit that his 1969 presidential address to the American Political Science Association reflected thoughtful sensitivity to the forms of theory that emphasize interpretation, marking a rather striking departure from his earlier contributions to behaviorism.

It is hardly surprising that different empirical theories should incorporate alternative implications about the qualities that are regarded as central to human nature. Like ideologies, these are issues that cannot be resolved by research itself; and, as with ideologies, our conceptual frameworks for coping with them implicitly incorporate conclusions that attract or repel scholars.

CHANGES OVER THE PAST TWENTY-FIVE YEARS

The major changes in the most widely deployed empirical theories over the last two and a half decades involve the fading from frequent use of some theories and the emergence of new ones, a process that characterizes science at all times.[7] Though theories do go out of fashion, they leave a residue of understanding that continues to influence research.

Fluctuations in the popularity of particular empirical theories have probably been related less to their ability to aid in explanation than to their links with public policy, social, economic developments. The Vietnam War and the urban turmoil of the 1960s, for example, brought with them widespread popularity for systems theory, which seemed to reassure social scientists that the political system was fundamentally responsive to popular sentiment, despite the claims of antiwar and urban activists that it was responsive only to a disproportionately powerful elite. The events of that stormy decade also brought increased interest in psychological theories, for they seemed to explain actions that, in the view of many people, were not rational. Conservatives also used psychological theories to label protesters and rioters as pathological.

Another set of dramatic developments, popularized by the term "Watergate" in the 1970s, coincided with increased interest in structuralism and in poststructuralism. It is a reasonable surmise that structuralism's emphases on epistemological breaks, as in the work of Michel Foucault,[8] and on "deep structures" underlying surface events[9] were seen as helpful in understanding and finding meaning in the era's spectacular divergences from traditional governmental practice.

Ronald Reagan's apparent effectiveness as a communicator and the striking success in the 1988 presidential campaign of sound bites and TV spots that played to underlying fears and biases certainly contributed to an interest in poststructuralism, especially Jean Baudrillard's work on opinion, hyperreality, polls, and television[10] and Jacques Derrida's writings[11] on the associations of linguistic terms. At the same time, the surge in the use and abuse of drugs, the persistence of poverty, and the neglect of the country's infrastructure helps explain the strong interest among social scientists in Michel Foucault's skeptical studies about the social institutions designed to deal with social pathologies. And, as suggested earlier, the escalation in the popularity of rational choice theory in the late 1980s and 1990s can reasonably be linked to growing sensitivity over the failure of government to deal effectively with the most serious social problems.

It would seem that empirical theories, though vital instruments of explanation for scholars, are integrally linked as well to current economic, social, and political problems and policies. They have origins and consequences that go well beyond either pure theory or objective empirical research and are closely involved with subjective impulses, peer constraints and pressures, and ideologies. That is true in some measure of all theories, including those used in the hard sciences; but it need not diminish their explanatory potential and typically expands that potential.

NOTES

1. Thomas Kuhn, *The Structure of Scientific Revolutions*, (Chicago: University of Chicago Press, 1962); *The Essential Tension* (Chicago: University of Chicago Press, 1977).

2. Bentley's 1908 book, *The Process of Government* (Cambridge: Harvard University Press), which had long been out of print, was reissued in 1949, and David Truman's 1951 book, *The Governmental Process* (New York: Knopf, 1951), awakened wide interest in group theory as well. Though Bentley's seminal work did not logically require the assumption that government is pluralistic, it was, and still is, widely misunderstood to do so.

3. See, for example, Jon Elster (ed.), *Rational Choice* (New York: New York University Press, 1986) and Adam Przeworsky, *Capitalism and Social Democracy* (New York: Cambridge University Press, 1985).

4. Michael Ryan, *Marxism and Deconstruction* (Baltimore: Johns Hopkins University Press, 1982).

5. Louis Althusser, *For Marx* (London: Allen Lane, 1969).

6. Maurice Godelier, *Rationality and Irrationality in Economics* (New York: Monthly Review Press, 1973).

7. Cf. Kuhn, *The Structure of Scientific Revolutions* and *The Essential Tension*.

8. Michel Foucault, *The Order of Things* (New York: Vintage Books, 1973) and *The Archeology of Knowledge* (London: Irvington Press, 1972).

9. Claude Levi-Strauss, *Structuralist Anthropology* (New York: Basic Books, 1973).

10. Jean Baudrillard, *Simulations* (New York: Semiotext, 1981), and *In the Shadow of the Silent Majorities* (New York: Semiotext, 1983).

11. Jacques Derrida, *Of Grammatology* (Baltimore: Johns Hopkins University Press, 1976).

SUGGESTED READINGS

Bernstein, Richard. 1976. *The Restructuring of Social and Political Theory*. New York: Harcourt, Brace Jovanovich.

Dallmayr, Fred R., and Thomas A. McCarthy. 1977. *Understanding and Social Inquiry*. Notre Dame: University of Notre Dame Press.

Easton, David. 1965. *A Systems Analysis of Political Life*. New York: Wiley.

Kuhn, Thomas. 1962. *The Structure of Scientific Revolutions*. Chicago: University of Chicago Press.

———. 1976. *The Essential Tension*. Chicago: University of Chicago Press.

Skinner, Quentin. 1985. *The Return of Grand Theory in the Human Sciences*. New York: Cambridge University Press.

PART III

Construction of a General and Value-Free Science of Politics

6

Oedipean Complexities
and Political Science

Tragedy and the Search for Knowledge

J. Peter Euben

If oxen and horses and lions had hands or could draw with hands and create works of art like those made by men, horses would draw pictures of gods like horses, and oxen gods like oxen, and they would make the bodies (of their gods) in accordance with the form that each species itself possesses.

Xenophanes (quoted in Kathleen Freeman,
Ancilla to the Pre-Socratics, Oxford: Basil Blackwell, 1948), p. 22.

The dead haunt the living. The past: it "re-bites" (il remord). History is "cannibalistic," and memory becomes the closed arena of conflict between two contradictory operations: forgetting, which is . . . an action directed against the past; and the mnemic trace, the return of what was forgotten. . . . (A)n autonomous order is founded upon what it eliminates; it produces a "residue condemned to be forgotten." But what was excluded . . . re-infiltrates the place of its origin. It resurfaces, it troubles, it turns the present's feeling of being "at home" into an illusion, it lurks— this "wild," this "ob-scene," this "filth," this "resistance," of "superstition"—within the walls of the residence, and behind the back of the owner (the ego), or over its objections, it inscribes there the law of the other.

Michel de Certeau, *Heterologies*, trans. Brian Massumi
(Minneapolis: University of Minnesota Press, 1986), pp. 3–4.

In this chapter I will use Sophocles's *Oedipus Tyrannos* as an occasion to reflect on some of the epistemological and methodological claims made by political scientists in general and rational actor theorists in particular about their object of study and about themselves as studiers.[1] I shall suggest that the play's themes of incest and patricide can illuminate the interplay between the analytic, rigorous, scientific objective and parsimonious[2] method rational actor theory embraces and the goal-directed, utility-maximizing (or "satisficing")[3] individual, or rational actor,[4] the method constitutes for study. Furthermore, I will suggest that the admirable traits found in Oedipus are also those posited by many political scientists (most vigorously by rational actor theorists) about political actors and themselves and that, as a result, the king's myopia parallels their own. Oedipus proclaims himself an independent agent free of fate and history, self-made and self-generated, and so able to see the world rationally. But in fact his knowledge comes with ignorance, and so the meaning of his acts remains bifurcated in a way he only comes to understand in the scene where, significantly enough, he blinds himself. Penultimately, I will offer an interpretation of the play and its conditions of performance as a way of proposing a balance between proximity and distance that political scientists might emulate if they wish to avoid using a method that simply mimics the culture they are studying and to avoid ignoring the cultural specificity of their claims to universality. Most rational choice theorists read a particular historical and ideological configuration into "nature," a construct which then becomes the premise for an historical narrative that justifies rational choice theory as either the telos of human development or the unacknowledged assumption of all previous (and subsequent) human behavior. As a certain stage of liberal capitalism becomes elaborated into a social ontology, rational choice theory becomes the thought within which all other thought must take place. It functions both as a postulate and a projection, a description and a prescription.[5] When its advocates acknowledge its circularity and limited empirical successes, opt for "thin" rather than "thick" rational accounts, accept multiple equilibria and segmented rationality, conclude that rational choice explanations are more likely to hold where the options agents confront are relatively fixed and the decisions are not urgent, and accept the need for other theoretical perspectives, their admirable modesty compromises the claims made for the power and promise of this approach.

Finally I will argue that the role of a spectator in the theater is as fruitful a model for political theory and political science as one based on economics or the physical sciences and that a tragic sensibility provides a needed antidote to the hubris of rational choice theory.[6] Here is the French classicist Jean-Pierre Vernant:

> In the tragic perspective, acting, being an agent, has a double character. On the one side, it consists in taking council with oneself, weighing the for and against and doing the best one can to foresee the order of means and ends. On the other hand, it is to make a bet on the unknown and the incomprehensible and to take a risk on a terrain that remains impenetrable to you. It involves entering the play of supernatural forces . . . where one does not know whether they are preparing success or disaster.[7]

OEDIPEAN COMPLEXITIES

Alone among mortals, Oedipus was able to solve the Sphinx's riddle and so to save the city of Thebes. The riddle was, "What creature walks on four feet, two feet, and three feet all in a single day?" The answer, "man,"[8] required a kind of abstract knowledge available to Oedipus because he was ignorant of the concrete circumstances of his birth.[9] The intellectual achievement that enabled him to see the changing nature of man and to discern what was continuous and similar amidst change and diversity disabled him from solving the riddle of Laius's death and saving Thebes from a second plague. He did not see that the particular circumstances of his own life made him an exception to what he took to be a universal statement.

Having had a child despite an oracle's warning that he would be killed by his son, Laius bound his infant's feet and exposed him to die. Thus, whereas most people progress from crawling baby to walking adult to cane-using elder, Oedipus never walked "normally," never moved through any of the stages of life; he was an unnatural unity who married his mother and sired his sisters.[10] Walking on three feet as an adult, he used that third foot, his staff, to kill his father. Thus did he unknowingly fulfill the oracle he thought to escape and take revenge on the man who had sought his death.

Ignorant of what was closest and nearest, Oedipus did not know that he was the answer to the second riddle, who killed Laius and so "caused" the plague.[11] Not only was he ignorant of the conditions of his birth, of who his father, mother, and people were, he did not even know his own name, a series of puns on *oida* (meaning "know") and *pous* (meaning "foot"). For Oedipus, and perhaps for all mortals, seeing is also blindness, success hides terrible failure, strength is a source of defeat, and delusion is most pervasive when we think ourselves most wise and in command. Oedipus's triumph in solving the first riddle was short-lived, because his solution unraveled into a riddle. "Between the certainty I have of my existence and the content I try to give to that assurance," Camus wrote, "the gap will never be filled. Forever I shall be a stranger to myself."[12] The unstable shifting identities of men and women make "man" suspect as an answer and the hidden subject of future riddles. Even worse, what escapes every construct and structure is violation and violence barely hidden by the surface calm of normal life, common sense, and established identity.[13] For some reason the civilizing hero cannot banish the savagery in himself. And to the degree the characteristics of Oedipus also characterize the Athenians watching the play, this violence and savagery mark "civilized" politics as well.

What makes the dilemmas of the play so relevant and disturbing for political scientists is that the characteristics that define Oedipus and make his triumph a tragedy are those traits political scientists find admirable in political leaders—and in themselves. Oedipus is an astute politician and a beneficent and responsible leader. He is solicitous of the views of others and of the people, confident in his abilities and decisive in action, yet concerned for the view of the gods. His pride in his achievement—prominent in the opening lines and tableau, where he is supplicated by his afflicted people as if he were a god—is balanced by his piety. Moreover, he is an acute problem solver, an enlightened man who promises to reveal what is hidden, bring all to light, dissipate confusion and uncertainty, and dispel superstition and ignorance. Thus, critics describe him as "a questioner, researcher and discoverer," a "calculator" who brings a quantitative sensibility to the empirical world, who demonstrates, investigates, examines, questions, infers, knows, finds, reveals, makes clear, learns, and teaches.[14]

But the logic of noncontradiction does not apply to this man, who is one and many and in whom opposites coexist.[15] For all his insight, he is utterly blind to the reality of his life (or lives) and identity (or identities) and so to the meaning(s) of his actions. He thinks he is escaping his past, fate, and history and boasts of being a self-made, self-generated, freely acting individual even as he fulfills it. Having been told by a drunken companion that he is a bastard and then dishonored by Apollo when he seeks to confirm what he has heard—the priestess tells him he will kill his father and marry his mother—Oedipus flees Corinth and his "parents," who have in fact adopted him, to Thebes, which "adopts" him, though it is his original home. Later, hearing that his Corinthian "parents" have died, he boasts of being a self-made man and a child of fortune and the gods—all this just prior to his discovering exactly who his parents are and what he has done to them.

By marrying his mother, Oedipus becomes an unnatural unity, too much one and singular, too close to home, too implicated in his past: by killing his father he becomes too much alone and too isolated, too divorced from his past. The crimes of incest and patricide can stand for, first, the "unnaturally" intimate connection between the way political scientists in general and rational actor theorists in particular constitute their field of study, the method they use to study it, and the political culture they are studying; and, second, their tendency to reject precisely those shaping features of the past that provide a justification for their rejection of the past.

"A social theory that adopts the same means-end individualistic rationality that the modern economy imposes," Michael Shapiro writes, "helps that structure operate rather than effect a theoretical distance from it."[16] Using the entrenched language of power and authority to study democratic politics reifies that authority and power and mutes the very possibility of radical critique. As this argument implies, there is no morally neutral language, if only because as accounts of social phenomena are accepted by social actors they become part of the social world itself, unpredictably altering the very institutions and practices that are being described.[17] One could even say that we become the language we use insofar as "the languages we speak and the cultural practices they at once reflect and make possible, mark or form our minds by habituating them to certain forms of attention, certain ways of seeing and conceiving of oneself in the world."[18] Every language encourages speakers to think and act in some ways rather than others, creates and sustains different kinds of characters with different understandings of human agency and action.[19]

Such theoretical incest may explain the often tautological nature of rational actor (or choice) theory[20] and—appropriately, given my choices of Sophocles—lend a certain irony to William Riker's preference for "the simplicity" of the rationality assumption that people or things "behave in regular ways." The rationality model allows one "to arrive at the regularity necessary for generalization," whereas "simple observation" or induction is too "inefficient" an alternative. What matters is "the easy generation of hypotheses" and a "single efficient parsimonious explanation of behavior" that allows "much of the complexity to disappear."[21] But this seems nothing less than a prescription for ignorance premised on the contradictory assumptions that the choice of method is arbitrary in the sense of being indifferent to the subject matter[22] but, nonetheless, can reveal nature and human nature. More than that, the preoccupation with regularity and clarity easily leads one to regard what is irregular and opaque as a threat. There is too much diffidence for desperation here, yet there is a Hobbesian attachment to method because it can maintain political as well as epistemic order.

Given Oedipus's generation, his unnatural singularity, his imposition of order and simplicity, and the fact that he puts out his eyes when he finally recognizes how wrongly he has read the meaning of his life, Riker's statement of preferences becomes deeply problematic.

Such theoretical patricide focuses on how the traits rational actor theorists attribute to individuals (the same traits they claim for their theory) presuppose a rejection of the past, the salience of traditional wisdom, and a minimizing of (if not complete disregard for) the shaping hand of culture. To be rational, actors and theorists must (or do) disregard what has fathered them, even as the unacknowledged background of history and sentiment give texture and concreteness to the lives of the former and the claims of the latter.[23]

For instance, the aim of objectivity is to escape those ties to place and people that compromise the neutrality of one's findings. Marx thought that such claims are almost always ideological; Nietzsche and Foucault that they are self-serving, self-defeating, and in bad faith; Tocqueville that they are distinctively American. Being antitraditional *was* our tradition, he argued, an observation that perhaps explains the extraordinary deracination present in the casual but confident insistence that "*no* goals that are pursued with tolerable consistency can be called irrational."[24]

Given the challenge the play presents to rational actor and rational choice theories (even when they are modified by numerous "side assumptions," which make them more modest but less what their advocates would like them to be), as well as to the scientific aspirations of political scientists as a whole, it may be time, if not to renounce the Sisyphean quest for methods and theories that ape those of natural science, then to "deprivilege" their status. It is true that Oedipus solved the Sphinx's riddle, and to the extent that the knowledge political scientists seek is analogous to that solution, their work is clearly worthwhile. But what is one to do about the ignorance of that knowledge?

One could begin by recognizing the "literary" dimensions of political science texts, the fact that how one writes, the texture of the prose—the use of equations, models, and/or metaphors, the rhetorical structure of an argument—is itself a claim about how one can know and represent the world. Form and style express a sense of life and value, of what matters and doesn't, of what learning and communication and knowledge are, just as *how* one teaches may be as "substantive" as *what* one teaches. Life is never simply presented by a text, whether that text be Plato's *Republic,* Anthony Downs's *An Economic Theory of Democracy,* Jon Elster's *Ulysses and the Sirens,* or *Oedipus Tyrannos*. It is always represented *as* something; there is always a choice involved, however constrained it may be by canons of academic professionalism.[25] More to the point, it may be that a work of "literature" such as *Oedipus Tyrannos* is more alert to the moral complexities of action and actors, more alive to the variety, allusiveness, and flawed beauty of the world, than is the hyperanalytic prose that characterizes writings on rational actor theory and the fetishism of method that characterizes political science as a whole.[26] It is at least worth asking what a style "so remarkably flat and lacking in wonder" does to the world it studies and the students it teaches. It is at least worth asking what is lost when the tale of Ulysses becomes an analysis of calculation and measurement by an individual mentality trying to reduce risk and achieve end states in complete detachment from social and institutional forms of valuing or when mythic time is transformed into the logical grammar and temporality of t_1 t_2 t_3.[27]

Measuring and counting time is one of Oedipus's talents. He, too, organizes time into logical patterns. But the patterns collapse in the terrible uncertainty of his life. "Go inside and reckon these things up," Tiresias taunts Oedipus after being provoked by the king to tell him who he really is. But anger prevents Oedipus from hearing. "And if you catch me as one who's false," the prophet adds, "then say that my intelligence in prophecy is nil" (461–62). Analysis, reason, logic, the penchant for precise speech, and the passion for method are as much biography as conscious choice. Whether we know it or not, we write our lives into a world that has already inscribed itself in our souls.

But my criticism is ungenerous and overstated: ungenerous because Elster's use of a literary text to dramatize the substance and limits (or costs and benefits) of rational actor and choice theory has stimulated my obverse strategy; overstated because political science, like Oedipus, does provide important knowledge. Still, I want to insist that a work such as *Oedipus Tyrannos* can help us see where political science in general and rational actor theory in particular are blind, bring clarity and depth where they are obtuse, and be winged and moving where they are dull and heavy. Such a work can indicate the need for methods to maintain a balance of proximity and distance toward the subject matter they are constituting and studying.

In crucial respects, Greek drama was a political institution analogous to the assembly council and courts.[28] During the Festival of Dionysus, playwrights competed for prizes before an audience of the entire citizenry. What that audience saw on stage were plays that dramatized the decisions (about democratization or empire) it had taken in other forums and the cultural accommodations (concerning sexuality, public and private life, and the relations between generations) by which it had defined itself. The mythical settings in which these decisions and accommodations were set provided both distance from the urgency of immediate decision necessary in the assembly council and law courts and proximity to the sufferings of the characters on stage, which resembled the audience's own sufferings. In this way theater provided an experience through which democratic citizens could reflect on the significance of their everyday lives and particular decisions in an arc of understanding more comprehensive and theoretical than was otherwise possible. In it they could see the problematic aspects of cultural hierarchies and distinctions that defined their lives. The qualities Oedipus displays on stage are the talents and temperament Athenians most prized in their democratic leaders, such as Pericles, and idealized in themselves.[29] "To attend a tragic drama," Martha Nussbaum writes, in language that echoes Bernard Knox's description of Oedipus, "was to engage in a communal process of inquiry, reflection and feeling with respect to important civic and personal ends."[30] From what we can tell, that engagement provoked extraordinarily powerful emotional responses and intense critical reflection that influenced the audience's real-world political judgments; the audience would bring the experience of the theater to the assembly courts and council, just as it had brought the experience of active citizenry to the theater. This is a representation of democratic deliberation that is almost unintelligible within the individualistic premises of rational actor theory.

What is clear from this perspective and from Knox's argument about Oedipus and Athens is that the talents of the king and audience were both political and intellectual. It was this combination that the Athenians came to identify as unique to their own democratic culture. No play dramatizes the greatness and limits of this combination more provocatively than the *Oedipus Tyrannos*. It does so in the context of what is often called the fifth-century enlightenment, during which the sophists challenged the "natural" status they saw in conventional notions of education, law, religion, justice, and the polis and suggested that man, not god, is the measure of all things. (A similar debate about the legacy of the eighteenth-century enlightenment has engaged political theorists such as Foucault and Habermas.)[31]

Given this viewpoint, the idea of being a spectator in the theater is as rich and generative a model for political theory and science as one based on economics and the physical sciences. At a minimum, it compensates for the limits of what Sheldon Wolin has called "methodism" and provides a way to democratize political wisdom against the presumptions of professional expertise, political economism, and technical jargon.

The actors on a Greek stage were, by definition, bound to play the parts assigned them, but a spectator could see what they couldn't: how those parts form a whole. Whereas the actor was, and enacted, his part, the spectator put the parts together; he or she (it is probable that women attended the theater) was literally less part-ial and part-isan. But the truth attained by the spectator was inaccessible and invisible to the actors on stage only as a matter of position, not of nature. By extension and analogy, ordinary citizens were limited in their capacity to judge not because they were incapable of what Hannah Arendt calls "representative thinking"—the ability to see the world from another's point of view—but by circumstance.[32] Figuratively, there was nothing to stop the actors on stage from being spectators at a different play. And, of course, when the audience members left the play, they exchanged the near-omniscience of spectators for their roles as actors in public life.[33] Having seen what Oedipus did not see, knowing all along the shaping hand of circumstance where he thought himself a self-made, independent agent, they knew that they might, individually or collectively, be like him, not because they might commit his horrendous crimes but because they may too confidently have assumed they could master the empirical world and define human nature, which only a god could do. Impartiality, in the sense of an ability to see more than one part and from many standpoints, is one thing; objectivity, in the sense that one is outside or above all parts, is another. The spectator in the theater (unlike the philosopher in *The Republic* or Parmenides) does not withdraw to some higher region but remains a member of the audience, at once disengaged from the particular characters on stage yet deeply affected by the sufferings they bear and the ignorance that plagues their lives.

But could they (can we) learn from the play so as to avoid living through the experience depicted in it? It is clear that the tragedians were the political educators of Athens. (The Greek word for producing plays is the same as the word for educating.) It is also clear that the wisdom shared by the audience in the theater helped justify participatory democracy, which relied on the deliberative capacity of ordinary men. But did Sophocles think, or does the play suggest, that the audience could be spared the experience of Oedipus because they had seen *Oedipus Tyrannos*? Could the same be said of rational actor theory and methodism? To put it in a thoroughly unliterary way, if Oedipus had seen *Oedipus Tyrannos,* would he have acted differently? Could he have "escaped" his fate and achieved the freedom of which he wrongly boasts?

What makes answering these questions so difficult (though I will attempt to do so briefly in my concluding section) is that the play provides no single vantage point on itself, no resting place where one can confidently say, "Here I stand, I can see no other." Instead, it dramatizes the questions in ways that leave us with a deeper sense of the problems rather than with solutions to them. I offer three examples.

The first concerns the play's dramatization of the theatrical experience itself. In its preoccupation with sight, insight, and blindness, *Oedipus Tyrannos* makes spectators self-conscious about the experience they are having. Yet the play itself presents important events (such as Jocasta's death and Oedipus's self-blinding) as outside the field of vision, accessible only in verbal fragments that the audience must make coherent, just as Oedipus must do with the pieces of his life. In calling attention to its withholding of visual experience in favor of verbal description, the play evidences a consciousness of the theatrical spectacle as a narrative mediating between what is inside and outside, between internal and external vision, between physical acts and the emotional world they reveal.[34] But in the agon between Oedipus and the blind Tiresias, the mediation breaks out into a conflict between the analytical, empirical knowledge possessed by the king and the prophetic knowledge of the seer.

Second, the play suggests that the careful seeing and hearing it demands of the audience is too much and not enough. There are things no man should see, boundaries no man should cross, truths about oneself that are unbearable to hear, times when anger, fear, or confidence prevent listening. And there are times when understanding the world requires the use of all the senses, not just the intellectual ones. Near the end of the play, in a scene of excruciating poignancy, Oedipus, now blind and equal to nothing, calls for his daughters so he can touch them in a gesture of love and loss, care and contrition.

Third, though the play warns us about our penchant for coherence, order, and logic, it has what Bernard Knox calls "a ferociously logical plot." But then how does the knowledge Sophocles or the play possesses fit the dramatization of knowledge in the play? Does it resolve the tensions it portrays between the ways of knowing represented by Oedipus and Tiresias? Or does it leave us (as I think it does) with a framework within which various interpretive communities recast the resolutions it provokes in their own context of performance?

Of course, this discussion is very "literary," probably abstract, and no doubt frustrating if one is concerned with the real world of political decision and policy. Yet I am not so sure contemporary political science approaches such as rational actor theory are any less abstract or, for that matter, any more forthcoming with solutions. And the frustration of having problems deepened rather than solved may be precisely the right antidote to policy analysts who have more solutions than a chemistry lab, rational actor theorists with their preference for parsimony, and political scientists preoccupied with methods and methodism.

In the following pages I shall look at four moments in the play to dramatize my claims about the significance of *Oedipus Tyrannos* for political scientists in general and rational actor theorists in particular. As I do, I will invoke David Easton as a reluctant ally. Though his language and starting point are quite different from my own, I think the radical conclusions of some of his arguments about the discipline and its relation to the world are similar in spirit to the ones in this essay.[35]

Easton has argued in ways very different from mine. He has, for instance, insisted that the problems of industrial society make old ways of thought (such as political theory, which he originally identified with natural law theory) irrelevant and that imitating the natural sciences' reliance on rigorous methods of data collection and analysis is essential. In place of the old theoretical paradigms that "forfeited [their] fitness by rejecting the possibility of a science of man,"[36] Easton embraced "positive" or "empirical" political theory. The problem is that such theory reduces the generative paradox embedded in the very conjunction of politics and theory, a paradox dramatized in Sophocles's play and useful for a self-critique that would make aspirations for a science of politics (whether deductively or inductively arrived at) seem less naive.

Let me begin with Aristotle. Aristotle regarded the realm of politics as an arena of action, choice, and decision, as it was "man"-made and so could be remade. Theory, by contrast, though also an activity, involved contemplation of what was eternal. Here the point was not to change what could not, in any event, be changed but to wonder at things as they were, to absorb the order and harmony of the universe. Thus, there was something oxymoronic about the notion of "political theory." The words necessarily posed the question of whether one could even have a "theory" of politics or whether all theories were somehow political and, thus, untheoretical.

The paradox of "political theory" was not merely one of subject matter; it was also one of presentation and language. This aspect is most obvious in a dialogue such as *The Republic,* with its particular tensions between analysis and parable, reason and myth, philosophy and rhetoric, truth and politics, rigor and poetry, and, more generally, dramatic structure and explicit argument.[37] Thus, although Plato was bluntly critical of the poets and tragedians, his own work displayed significant continuities with what he criticized, hardly surprising given how much the structure, preoccupations, and aims of classical political theory emerged out of a democratic tradition of self-critique, which drama helped define and constitute.[38]

Easton sometimes exemplifies and even recognizes the paradox obscured by his commitment to a science of politics and rigorous analyses. It was Easton who, in his American Political Science Association address of 1969, acknowledged that, for all its claimed explanatory and predictive power, behavioralism (and political science generally) was unable to predict the new forces that had shattered its truisms and reshaped the nation. It was Easton who insisted on historicizing methodologies by inviting political scientists to pay more attention to the sociology of knowledge and who saw that for every riddle a methodology might solve, there were others outside its purview. And it was Easton who argued that there was no such thing as a value-neutral political science and considered the possibility that the discipline was American both in its implicit normative commitment to American institutions and as a cultural artifact. Yet he remained committed to a science of politics even if there was (and is) something desperate about the commitment.[39] No one, he argued, could possibly deny that technical adequacy is vital, as without it "the whole evolution of empirical science in all fields of knowledge in the last two thousand years would have been in vain."[40]

The same tension is present in his most recent work. Though the expansion of political science has led to "depth and diversity," the fragmentation, communicative overload, and multiple approaches it has fostered symptomize and signify that "the field has lost its core and its dynamism."[41] We no longer know what politics is or what political science should be.[42] The growth of knowledge has not been unambiguously beneficial because it has "left Western scholarship with a host of intractable problems." The foremost of them is specialization, which leaves us master of less and less and powerless before the whole. In 1969 Easton endorsed the need for political science to analyze reality "by chopping the world up into manageable units" in order to achieve the precise measurements necessary to meet the "continuing need of a complex postindustrial society for the most reliable knowledge."[43] Analysis now is part of the problem. Though we can only understand the world by breaking it into pieces to "act and address the issues for which the understanding of highly specialized knowledge is presumably sought, we need somehow to reassemble all the pieces." Yet we can't, any more than all the king's horses and all the king's men could put Humpty Dumpty together again.[44] Given that Easton sees no prospect of integrating knowledge in a way that allows us to cope with "real-world problems," his continued adherence to a science of politics (though it is a "more relaxed" notion of science); praise of reliable knowledge based on rigorous methods of data collection; insistence that political science is invaluable because it permits the development of precise skills, concepts, and theories; and obeisance before the "epistemic success" of the natural sciences (even as he acknowledges the absence of any comparable success in the social sciences) seem nothing more or less than acts of faith. If, as Easton documents, political science has so often failed us, and if, as he also suggests, whatever successes it has had have led to intractable problems, and if few believe that science is neutral, and if there are good reasons to suppose that concepts are value laden and that "our very methods of inquiry reflect our own unique historical experience," then the continued search for objective knowledge based on a scientific method that can be "articulated, formulated and communicated to succeeding generations" seems quixotic. Perhaps it is time to demystify science and loosen the hold of disciplines (in all senses of that word). It is not so much that the emperor has no clothes as that the clothes he has are too threadbare to ward off the elements.

In his 1969 *APSR* essay, Easton rejected traditional political theory because of its disinclination or inability to formulate speculative alternatives to the present order so we could "better understand the deficiencies of our own political system." He identified this ability with science. Whatever the legitimacy of his rejection and hope then, it is unpersuasive now. Recall Shapiro's argument that a theory that mimics the dominant cultural forms and uses the entrenched language of power is unlikely to yield radical critiques and alternatives. Or recall Easton's own recognition of how far behavioralism was implicated in the political society it was studying, a recognition that could be extended to the entire enterprise of creating a science of politics. Why not give up the search for the Holy Grail, or at least recognize the search as the act of faith it is?

EXAMPLES/SCENES

Beginnings

The Oedipus we see in the opening scene is a man of generosity and intelligence. Compassionate toward his suffering people, who appear as suppliants before him, open and collegial in the exercise of his kingly power, he is quick to analyze a situation and take appropriate action. He is proud of his achievements, comfortable commanding others, and confident of his ability to control events. He is, after all, the man whose intellectual prowess saved Thebes from the death-dealing Sphinx and enabled him, a stranger, to become king.[45] Others saw only discontinuity, difference, and plurality in the riddle about what walks on four feet, two feet, and three feet in a single day; but he perceived unity in difference, identity in discontinuity, singularity in plurality, coherence rather than fragmentation. They saw the parts, not the whole; but Oedipus's abstract, analytical, generalizing intelligence enabled him to pierce the veil of illusion and uncover the solid ground of truth. Or so it seemed.

The legitimacy of his rule and the health of his city depend on his superior intelligence;[46] thus, in meeting the threats posed by the plague and new riddle ("Who is the murderer of Laius?"), he must exhibit anew the qualities of mind by which he sustains his authority. The plague is a particularly complex challenge, at once a reminder of the unpredictability of events, the limits of reason, and the connection of mind to body and of politics to nature. In Thucydides, the plague at Athens (which is contemporaneous with the play's performance) follows and is juxtaposed with the Funeral Oration of Pericles. Whereas the latter is a paean less to the fallen dead than to Athenian power—the city is represented as a collective Achilles, able to make the sea and land the highway of its daring—the plague destroys mind and body, city and family. Appearing out of nowhere, it kills with a randomness that mocks any assumption that nature is an inert object to be mastered by human intelligence and design. The plague reminds us that humans are part of an organically connected network of animate beings whose delicately balanced, mutually responsible interrelations are violated at the risk of disaster.[47]

Not only do the play's opening lines mention the plague, the very first phrase—"Oh children, sons and daughters of Cadmus' line"—is cause for unease, because it addresses the assembled citizenry as if they were children. The phrase represents a collapsing of generations, which enabled Oedipus to solve the Sphinx's riddle but also recapitulates his committing of incest. Apparently Oedipus's admirable qualities of mind are plagued by the unnatural acts that have so far defined his life without his knowledge. At the heart of his rationalism, animating his confident assertion of self and order, is his biography, paradoxically played out in the deracinated intelligence that allowed him to solve one riddle but that prevents him from solving the new one.

Thus, the first four lines of the play, with their reference to plague and incest, introduce a theme that will be elaborated in the symbolism of Oedipus's self-blinding: political meaning and order, as well as the construction of character and self, are neither rational nor irrational processes. They derive neither from the purposive decisions of self-conscious individual actors seeking efficient means for recognized goals nor from the incomprehensible actions of passive actors, victims of external forces and other agents. Oedipus moves within a preconstituted reality that constitutes the terms of his identity. He acts within a script that provides meaning and structure for decisions that are nonetheless his own. When the chorus asks what spirit drove him to put out his eyes, Oedipus answers: "It was

Apollo, friends, Apollo that brought this bitter bitterness, my sorrows to completion. But the hand that struck me was none but my own" (1329–33).

Oedipus and Tiresias

To aid him in solving the new riddle, Oedipus summons the blind seer, Apollo's prophet, Tiresias. He greets the old man with great deference as a savior who knows what only the gods know. For reasons obvious to the audience, Tiresias does not want to be there and at first refuses to talk. For Oedipus such recalcitrance seems to represent ungratefulness toward Thebes, but when the old man speaks the truth—which Oedipus, in his anger and certainty, cannot hear—the king accuses the prophet of being part of the conspiracy that murdered Laius and would now murder him. Provoked by Oedipus's false accusations, Tiresias proclaims Oedipus the city's pollution and the murderer of Laius. "You have eyes but see not where you are, in sin, nor where you live, nor whom you live with. Do you know who your parents are?" (414–15). As his fury mounts, Oedipus heaps abuse on the man he believes is abusing him and boasts of his brilliance in solving the Sphinx's riddle, reminding Tiresias of his failure to do so.

Tiresias's second mention of Oedipus's parents stops the king in his tracks. To the question, "What parents? Stop! Who are they of all the world?" the prophet answers with his own dark riddle: "This day will show your birth and will destroy you" (436–37).

From this moment on the play turns away from the city's pollution and toward the king's origins. All of Oedipus's energies and intellect are turned toward the riddle of his own life. It is a riddle that will disclose the grounds for his reason and will, in fact, reveal the murderer of Laius. From now on every step forward in the discovery of who Oedipus is will be a step backward, as present facts and distant memory forge inexorably toward a narrative of horrific violation.

The contest between Oedipus and Tiresias is a contest over ways of knowing and ways of presenting knowledge in language. Oedipus is impatient with Tiresias's riddling answers to his cross-examination. He wants clear, unambiguous answers to direct questions, not allusive evasions that "darken" rather than enlighten. He wants language to embody meaning appropriate to a notion of truth and enlightenment as something one is conscious of having achieved, uncovered, and disclosed. Oedipean meaning comes from what he can see, from things subject to his will and captured by his categories. Yet despite his insistence on clear speech, his emotions—anger, suspicion, pride, and fear—prevent him from hearing even when Tiresias does speak clearly. Apparently, hearing and speaking are as much matters of subtext as of text, as much matters of the dynamics between speakers as of what is said (as discussions in the classroom often reveal). Even the simplest exchanges are less and more than they appear to be. Because truth is embedded in the disturbances of language and passion, it retains an opacity and is subject to contests shaped as much by the will to power as by the will to truth. If so, the "vague" phrases, oracular pronouncements, and poetic transcriptions that capture this dynamic may more fully represent "the" world and our exchanges about it than the more precise language Oedipus—and political science—demand.

Insistence on precision, rigor, and analysis presumes that the world yields its deepest secrets to those who speak and think that way. It presumes, too, that with the right language as part of the right method, mortals can pierce the veil of illusion. But this may itself be part of the myth of rationality that is so much part of Oedipus's story. The one character who speaks reasonably and lucidly throughout is Creon, and he "has no drives except those which he can consciously control, and no relationships except those which bring an advantage, no qualities except those which can be calculated and entered on a balance sheet." But if he, rather than Oedipus, is taken to be the rational actor and theorist; if a man who is capable neither of receiving nor needing further self-knowledge through suffering becomes the ideal; if one who shrinks from every risk and danger, is satisfied with profit rather than power, and is reasonable in an utterly mediocre way becomes the standard; then we are truly lost. Better it be Oedipus.[48]

But what attitude does the play take toward the two kinds of knowledge it dramatizes—the empirical, analytic, "academic" knowledge of an Oedipus and the inspired prophetic reading of signs of Tiresias? Obviously, the play respects both enough to provide a stage for their agon. Less obviously, it speaks in both voices, manifests both kinds of knowledge, and refuses to make any final judgment as to their ultimate value, except perhaps to suggest that no final answer is possible for men and women living human lives. Thus, the play shares the deciphering knowledge of prophets who speak in the poetry of parables. In this it respects the gods in whose honor drama was performed and acknowledges the depth of a world that will not yield to the identities and categories humans impose on it. But the play also shares the logical, analytic, investigative spirit that defined Athenian democracy, as well as the enlightenment project of arriving at clear truths and firm answers. For all the suffering his trials bring, Oedipus perseveres in his search for truth and does solve the riddle of Laius's death and his own birth. And, though the oracles prove true and the gods stand vindicated against presumptuous men who suppose they may escape the forces that shape their destiny and character, the man we see at the play's end returns to something like the sense of command and power he showed at the beginning. Human knowledge, despite its propensity to take the part it sees for the whole it cannot, retains its majesty.

Oedipus, Jocasta, and Apollo

To reassure her "husband" that Tiresias is indeed lying, Jocasta tells Oedipus of an earlier prophecy that proved false: the prophecy that Laius would die at the hands of his son. But the reassurance she thinks to render by detailing the circumstances of Laius's death and the "killing" of the boy has the opposite effect on Oedipus. As the truth rises slowly out of its dark confines, so does madness. But there is still one thread of hope, and to it the king clings for his very life: Laius was killed by robbers, but Oedipus was alone when he murdered the man on the road. But before the sent-for shepherd can arrive to corroborate the plurality of the murderers, another messenger arrives from Corinth bringing news he expects to cause much pleasure and a little pain. Polybius, Oedipus's "father," has died of old age, and Oedipus has been chosen king of Corinth. (Oedipus supposes Polybius to be his natural father, which is why, when Apollo responded to his questions about his parentage with a prophecy of incest and patricide, Oedipus fled Corinth.) Jocasta, who hears the news first, exults in the pain, for it confirms her belief that oracles are of no account for the living of a human life. Hearing the news himself, Oedipus joins her in trumpeting their triumph over prophets and, by implication, Apollo, the god of prophecy.

From the "fact" that the oracles are false and the gods do not exist, Jocasta draws the "existential" conclusion that all is chance and opportunity. Men can do as they like without worry about the future, for it is all random, unstructured by history, institutions, or meaning beyond whatever we choose to provide for the occasion. Best then to live for the moment and at ease, discarding dire thoughts and fearful prophecies that disturb sleep to no purpose. But it is also Jocasta who first recognizes that their belief in the falsity of oracles may itself be false. The Corinthian messenger assures Oedipus that he need not fear killing his father because Polybius was not his real parent, then goes on to detail how he saved Laius's son by receiving the doomed child from the Theban shepherd, who could not bear to carry out his master's orders and let the boy die. As the tale unfolds, Jocasta pleads with the man who she now knows is her son as well as her husband to desist from his investigation. But Oedipus is constitutionally unable to stop his relentless pursuit of the truth about his origins, even to save his sanity. And so his mother/wife ends with what, given his character, she knows to be a futile prayer: "God keep you from the knowledge of who you are." Oedipus does not listen. Given the kind of man he is, he cannot listen. He presses forward, and the queen, in despair, goes inside the palace to commit suicide.

So intent is Oedipus on solving the mystery of his birth and "bringing all to light," so adamant is he about "finding out the whole thing clearly," that he completely misreads what Jocasta says and why she says it. He thinks her ashamed of his lowly birth and, in a final fantasy of escape, imagines himself Fortune's (Tuchēs') child, self-made and self-generated, unencumbered by past or culture, a free individual agent who lives by his wits and mind.

This fantasy was not the king's alone, for the sophistic enlightenment whose beginnings coincide with the play's performance emphasized the power of reason to confront and resolve the problems of existence without recourse to supernatural or mysterious forces. In this shift,[49] abstract and conceptual modes of thought largely replaced mythical and symbolic forms; the world was now seen as operating through impersonal processes that followed "scientific" laws. Where the earth had been an all-giving mother, it was now a measurable surface that could be mapped. Where the sun had been a god driving a blazing chariot across the heavens, it was now a huge molten rock. And although the gods were not wholly dismissed, they were increasingly understood as psychological forces within man or as allegorical expressions of nature. Finally, the laws of cities came not from the gods but from the deliberations of human assemblies and councils, whereas the cities themselves were human institutions, not seats of divine power rooted in a sacred landscape.

However, Oedipus is the child not of chance but of Laius and Jocasta. He is not a self-made, self-generated individual who produces meaning and decides his own fate but a man whose identity and character have been subject to meaning and forces spatially and temporally beyond him. We might say that humans are partly in life what Oedipus is fully as a character in a play: scripted figures whose freely chosen action manifests an at best half-glimpsed character. Even that glimpse will elude anyone who stubbornly adheres to the myth that one's behavior springs from individual self-interest and conscious choice, that one possesses extensive and clear knowledge of the environment and a well-ordered, stable system of preferences and computational skills that allow one to calculate the best choice (given individual preferences) among the alternatives available.[50]

Human beings are not the disembodied creatures that Oedipus wrongly supposes himself to be; they can recognize their mortality (i.e., that they are born, live, and die), but they cannot know their own nature. Possessing such knowledge would be like jumping over one's own shadow. Even the distinctive condition of being human is ambiguous, changing, and historical. Because thought cannot fix the essential meaning of our condition, it cannot define human nature. Only a god who left the theater entirely could do so. For Sophocles, the nature of man is as much a theological problem as is the nature of the gods.[51]

When Oedipus sees the truth, he puts out his eyes. The self-blinding is an act of compensation and recognition. It acknowledges that the pride he took in his far-seeing intelligence was unfounded; all his life he was blind to the realities that plagued his identity and action. It also reconciles him to Tiresias, whom he had ridiculed for his ignorance and obscure speech but whom he now joins as a blind prophet in a shared vision of the truth. And it honors Apollo, the god he had scorned, and the existence of an oracular structure of significance that remains opaque for even the most discerning eyes of the most enlightened human.

But the self-blinding is also an act by someone we recognize as Oedipus, someone we have known through the description of his acts by others as well as by what we have seen before us. In its forcefulness and excess, it is typical of the man who killed another in anger, impetuously left his "native" Corinth when he wrongly presumed to know the meaning of Apollo's oracle, was quick to find hostile conspiracies among men who wished him no harm, who physically tortured the shepherd into talking, and who called down such fierce imprecations upon the killer of Laius (who happens to be himself) at the beginning of the play. Here is a fitting son for Laius, who would not yield either to the oracle (who said that if he had children his son would kill him) or to the man on the road (who turns out to be his murderous son), and for a mother who commits suicide.

Whereas Jocasta's suicide takes place in the palace and so remains a private act,[52] Oedipus insists that he be made what the play as a whole is: a public spectacle. When he appears, the chorus asks him what madness (mania) has come upon him, what diabolical spirit has leaped so savagely upon his life that he should come to this. But they shudder at the sight of him and at the prospect of an answer to their question, not only because of their love for Oedipus but also because of their love for themselves. If a man of such consummate intelligence and courage, if the savior of their city, can be so wrong, what about the rest of us?

Oedipus answers that he and Apollo are the joint authors of his life. Apollo may have set the course, but he, Oedipus, took the actions that realized that fate. He may have acted in ignorance, but everything he did was his, in the sense that it belonged to him and expressed his character. This discovery about himself "is scarcely less crucial than the discovery of his identity."[53] In fact, the action of the play is not about the deeds he was fated to perform but about his discovery that he has already fulfilled them, and this discovery is due entirely to his own actions.[54]

The play dramatizes the darkness inside enlightenment, a darkness whose exposure leaves men blind to the world they thought they knew so well and in which they felt comfortable and in control. The most far-seeing of men and women, those deemed most rational and most empirically grounded, live with an ignorance proportional to the certainties of their theories and the stable identities they impose on others and themselves.

Endings

Though the paths of Oedipus's life have come together, his double identity is now one; the tension between the surface and deeper meaning of his deeds has been resolved, the ambiguities of his life are recast in the play's final "vision" of its chief protagonist.

On the one hand, the man who thought himself to be (and was thought to be by others) the equal of the gods, the supreme calculator, is now equal to nothing. The proud king, once confident in speech and clear of vision, expostulates in a series of monosyllabic cries and scarcely coherent exclamations.[55] The rational man who prided himself on being an independent agent is now, like Tiresias, a blind beggar dependent on everyone for everything. "To the extent to which a man's fate is dependent on other men," Simone Weil has written, "his life escapes not only out of his hands but also out of the control of his intelligence; judgment and resolution no longer have anything to which to apply themselves. Instead of contributing and acting, one has to stoop to pleading or threatening; and the soul is plunged into a bottomless abyss of desire and fear, for there are no bounds to the satisfaction and sufferings that a man can receive at the hands of other men."[56] At the heart of the play, the classicist Karl Reinhardt believes, is "illusion and truth as the opposing forces between which man is bound, in which he is entangled, and in whose shackles as he strives towards the highest he can hope for, he is worn down and destroyed."[57]

But that is only on one hand; there is another. It is suggested by Oedipus's exchange with Creon, now king of Thebes, with which the play concludes. He begs the man he had "used most vilely" to drive him into exile so he may never hear another human voice. But a moment and few lines later, referring to the burial of his dead mother/wife, he commands (*episkēpto*)[58] and begs (*prostrepsomai*) Creon to do the deed and he continues issuing orders until Creon has to remind this man, who should need no such reminder, that he must not "seek to be master in everything, for the things you mastered did not follow you throughout your life" (1522–23). This sense of command is consistent with the way Oedipus not only takes responsibility for fate but seizes it, proclaiming that the deeds done are his alone. Chastened, blind, and dependent he may be, but the old Oedipus is not dead. His search for the truth and the knowledge he now has, however dearly bought, give him the strength and courage to persevere amidst his misery.

And this is perhaps the most important thing about him: Oedipus did solve the riddle of his birth and Laius's death; he remained committed, single-mindedly so, to the hunt for the truth, even when he had premonitions of the disaster that awaited its capture. If no man has suffered as he has, which is the boast he makes now, then no man has learned so well the lessons of mortal life. Knowledge not borne of suffering, that does not touch the soul as well as the mind, that does not emerge out of, refer back to, and remain in the company of passion, is abstract, uneventful, sterile, intellectualized—perhaps not knowledge at all. A recent critic of rational actor theory's dependence on the economic approach to the analysis of political behavior argues that a "great deal of human conduct occurs under circumstances that are insufficiently similar to those postulated by the rational actor approach for that method to be of great use for the purpose of explanation. The highly touted virtues of elegance and simplicity are very attractive in the abstract. They are less so when their application to real world explanation is achieved at the price of implausibility."[59] Just so with Oedipus or Sophocles.

CONCLUSIONS

There is no conclusion to the *Oedipus Tyrannos*, if by conclusion one means a final scene that sets all things in place and in which some irrevocable synthesis of opposing views is achieved. Though it is true that in some respects Oedipus becomes Tiresias, the opposed views of knowing they represent and literally embody remain, in Mikhail Bakhtin's terms, "a plurality of independent and unmerged voices and consciousnesses, a genuine polyphony of fully valid voices," where each is a rejoinder in a continuing dialogue about enlightenment.[60]

Given the play's stance toward the riddles it dramatizes and the way it itself becomes riddling, this ambiguous ending is hardly surprising. Indeed, it would be strange if there were one integrating conclusion that answered all the questions raised by the play. If we are, as the play suggests, caught in a web of local meanings that necessarily leave us riddles to ourselves, if not to others, then reducing the play to a single term would endorse what it seems to warn against.[61] By the same reasoning, the aim of producing lawlike statements about measurable phenomena adhering to the virtues of a coherent parsimonious deductive theory or, more generally, anxiously purging contradiction seems naive and self-defeating.

Any obvious conclusion in *Oedipus* would diminish the play's capacity to disturb the alliance of reason, science, method, and progress that continues to flourish as the dominant conceit in political science—and does so despite the tragic sensibility of one of its most distinguished practitioners, who acknowledges that every success of political science has contained a failure. But Easton is also right not to give up the faith, even if he has reasons to become polytheistic. For political science can provide essential, perhaps even saving, knowledge. But it can do so only if it honors what it cannot do, if it recognizes that every way of seeing is a way of not seeing, if it avoids both incest—i.e., cozy accommodation with dominant discourses and structures of power—and patricide—i.e., a deracination that denies the shaping hand of the past in the name of rapid change, that discards inherited habits, beliefs, and institutions as mere obstacles to progress and regards memory as an irritant.[62]

Drama and poetry do not make arguments or offer logically consistent truths informed by a rigorous collection of data. Their power lies in surprise and disruption, in shocking excess and in provocations that push us to deeper and wider understanding than we wish to have of who we are, what we know, and how these are related. It teaches by ellipsis and by revealing the stake we have in our ignorance, which we count as knowledge.

It would be a foolish exaggeration to claim that this way of knowing and teaching is the only one, or even the most important, for understanding our political life. There are too many historical differences between then and now, between them and us. There are too many transformations of scale and sensibility between ancient Athens and contemporary America, too many disjunctions between theater and university, stage and classroom, drama and political science to suppose that some Greek play can retain its distinctive power to disturb and "enlighten."

Yet the premise of this chapter is that it can and does; that if we wish to avoid drawing our political and methodological gods too much in our own likeness or wrapping ourselves in them as a form of mental prothesis, we could do worse than make *Oedipus Tyrannos* companion reading for political science books, methodological primers, and treatises about rational actors and theory.

Perhaps there are political and moral standards that exist somewhere in the mind of God or in the totality of the universe. Perhaps we need to believe as much if we are not to lose something of value (however it is we came to value it). Yet we live not in the mind of God nor in the totality of the universe but in "specific places demarcated in their configurations and in their possibilities for action . . . by transient, partial, shifting, and contingent understandings of what is and what should be."[63] This is not to deny that some understandings are less partial and transient than others, that we can give reasons for our political judgments, nor that some visions of the future and constructions of the past are better or more accurate than others. It is simply to acknowledge that some have come to believe—and more have come to fear and rage against—the apparent fact that the world is not made for us, nor we for the world; that our history tells no purposive story and reveals no teleology and that there is no Archemedian point outside history from which we can confirm or authenticate our activities. There is no redemptive Hegelian history or universal Leibnizian cost-benefit analysis to show that it will all turn out well in the end. What does exist is evidence that our fondest achievements, including reason, critical intelligence, and the capacity for reflection, come at a high cost. Every step forward was and is an act of transgression. We are, in Bernard Williams's view, "like those who, from the fifth century and earlier, have left us traces of a consciousness that had not yet been touched by Plato and Aristotle's attempts to make our ethical [and political] relations to the world fully intelligible."[64] We are more like Oedipus than we suppose—or, better still, in a position analogous to that of the Athenian audience for whom his life was a warning.

NOTES

1. I do not distinguish rational actor theory from rational choice theory, public choice theory, and social choice theory. On the common assumptions of these theories and the disagreements within and among them, see Donald P. Green and Ian Shapiro, *Pathologies of Rational Choice Theory: A Critique of Applications in Political Science* (New Haven and London: Yale University Press, 1994).

2. The enthusiasm for "parsimony" might be less if the authors celebrating it knew its original Latin and Middle English meanings.

3. The issue of maximizing one's material advantage is raised in the play by the Greek word *kerdos,* which means a search for material advantage. (It can also mean crafty or shrewd.) Oedipus accuses Tiresias of being out for his own material gain when the seer tells him the truth.

4. See the discussion by Kristen Renwick Monroe in her foreword and "The Theory of Rational Action: Its Origins and Usefulness for Political Science" in *The Economic Approach to Politics* (New York: Harper Collins, 1991) and Jon Elster's discussion of the ideal rational choice explanation in his introduction to *Rational Choice* (New York: New York University Press, 1986), p. 16f.

5. Rousseau argued that Hobbes read seventeenth-century England into nature, thus freezing history and possibility within a conception of human nature. It has been such a powerful framework that to think outside it has often seemed insane, as Hobbes hoped it would. Marx makes a similar argument in his critique of the Rights of Man in *On the Jewish Question.* Here again "man" becomes a frozen concept, the necessary beginning and end of all thought, instead of a historically transitory figment of a social imagination.

6. In Greek, "hubris" suggests the unlimited violence that comes from passion and pride. It is licentiousness as well as insolence, legally a gross personal insult and assault.

7. Jean-Pierre Vernant, *Tragedy and Myth in Ancient Greece* (Atlantic Highlands, NJ: Humanities Press, 1972), p. 37.

8. "Long afterward, Oedipus, old and blinded, walked the roads. He smelled a familiar smell. It was the sphinx. Oedipus said, 'I want to ask one question. Why didn't I recognize my mother?' 'You gave the wrong answer,' said the sphinx. 'But that was what made everything possible,' said Oedipus. 'No,' she said. 'When I

asked, what walks on four legs in the morning, two at noon, and three in the evening, you answered Man. You didn't say anything about Woman.' 'When you say Man,' said Oedipus, 'you include women too. Everyone knows that.' She said, 'That's what you think.' " Muriel Rukeyser, "Myth," in the *Norton Anthology of Literature by Women: The Tradition in English,* ed. Sandra Gilbert and Susan Gubar (New York: W. W. Norton, 1985), pp. 1787–88.

9. The earliest form of the riddle was: "There is on earth a being two footed, four footed and three footed that has one name (literally one voice); and it alone changes its form. But when it goes propelled on most feet, then is the swiftness of its limbs weakest." This version is given by Charles Segal in his *Oedipus Tyrannus: Tragic Heroism and the Limits of Knowledge* (New York: Twayne, 1993), p. 56. See also the version and discussion in Thomas Gould's translation and commentary on *Oedipus the King* (Englewood Cliffs, NJ: Prentice-Hall, 1970), pp. 18–20, and Hugh Lloyd Jones in *The Justice of Zeus* (Berkeley and Los Angeles: University of California Press, 1971).

10. Segal, *Oedipus Tyrannus,* p. 87.

11. When Creon returns from asking the oracle (who has said that the plague afflicting Thebes is due to the city's harboring the murderer of Laius), the problem-solver king instantly starts the search: "Where is it to be found this obscure trace of an age old crime?" (*pou tod' heurethesetai/ ichnos palais dustemarton aitis?*). As Bernard Williams points out, though *aitias* refers to a crime, it belongs to the language of diagnosis and rational inquiry. "Oedipus plans to conquer the problem by the same means he used in overcoming the sphinx, by gnome, rational intelligence." *Shame and Necessity* (Berkeley and Los Angeles: University of California Press, 1993), p. 58.

12. *The Myth of Sisyphus and Other Essays,* translated by Justin O'Brien (New York: Knopf, 1955), p. 14. See the discussion of the point in Jeffrey C. Isaac, *Arendt, Camus and Modern Rebellion* (New Haven and London: Yale University Press, 1992), 110–25.

13. In a recent essay, William Connolly argues that Foucault both challenges conventional morality in the pursuit of a higher ethical sensibility and is aware of the danger inscribed in the effort to shift the terms and bases of moral doctrines. Foucault (along with Nietzsche, Arendt, and Todorov) sees that "systemic cruelty flows regularly from the thoughtlessness of aggressive conventionality, the transcendentalization of contingent identities, and the treatment of good/evil as a duality wired into the intrinsic order of things" ("Beyond Good and Evil: The Ethical Sensibility of Michel Foucault," *Political Theory* 21, 3 (August 1993): 365–66). Each one of these themes is dramatized in the play. I am not suggesting that Sophocles comes down on the same side as Foucault; however, I think such an argument could be made on the ground that though Sophocles believed there is a natural order of things and boundaries that had to be observed to avoid pollution (*miasma*), humans are, as historical beings, unable to fully fathom that order or adhere to it if known. For Sophocles, good and evil lurk in the heart and on the margins of their opposite, just as reason and passion or rationality and irrationality do, which is why such polarities are evasions as well as inscriptions and are, in the end, desperate attempts to categorize under the rubric of normal.

14. See especially Bernard Knox, *Oedipus at Thebes* (New Haven: Yale University Press, 1957), chapter 1, and Alister Cameron, *The Identity of Oedipus the King* (New York: New York University Press, 1968).

15. See Segal's discussion of this point in *Oedipus Tyrannos*, p. 118.

16. "Politicizing Ulysses: Rationalistic, Critical and Genealogical Commentaries," in *Reading the Postmodern Polity: Political Theory as Textual Practice* (Minneapolis: University of Minnesota Press), p. 29. I have suggested something similar in the introduction to *Greek Tragedy and Political Theory* (Berkeley and Los Angeles: University of California Press, 1986) by suggesting homologies between analytic argument, the bureaucratic state (as analyzed by Weber), and the technological society as portrayed by Jacques Ellul.

17. J. Donald Moon, "Political Science and Political Choice: Opacity, Freedom, and Knowledge," in *Idioms of Inquiry: Critique and Renewal in Political Science*, ed. Terence Ball (Albany, NY: State University of New York Press, 1987), p. 239.

18. Quoted in Terence Ball, "Educative vs Economic Theories of Democracy," in *Democracy, State, and Justice: Critical Perspectives and New Interpretations*, ed. Diane Sansbury (Stockholm: Almqvist and Wiksell International, 1988), p. 19.

19. Ibid.

20. See Gabriel A. Almond, "Rational Choice, Theory and the Social Sciences"; Harry Eckstein, "Rationality and Frustration in Political Behavior"; and Mark P. Petracca, "The Rational Actor Approach to Politics: Science, Self-Interest and Normative Democratic Theory," all in Monroe, *The Economic Approach to Politics*.

21. W. H. Riker and P. C. Ordeshook, *An Introduction to Positive Political Theory* (Englewood Cliffs, NJ: Prentice Hall, 1973), chapter 1, especially pp. 11–13.

22. In the *Nichomachean Ethics*, Aristotle argues that it is the mark of a well-educated man that he brings no more precision to a subject matter than the subject matter warrants, which suggests that some ways of studying politics are simply inappropriate given the kind of activity politics is. To put it another way, political knowledge is not just knowledge about politics, it is knowledge that is political in a deeper way. For him rational actor theory is such an inappropriate way of studying politics for the same reason that "political economy" is a contradiction in terms.

23. See Petracca, "Rational.Actor Approach."

24. (Emphasis supplied.) I am quoting Ronald Rogowski, "Rationalist Theories of Politics: A Midterm Report," in *World Politics* 20 (October 1977–July 1978): 299. See also Downs's seminal *An Economic Theory of Democracy* (New York: Harper and Row, 1957). For a powerful argument as to why the substance of the goals must count as much as the preference for them, see Hanna Pitkin's discussion of consent as a ground for legitimacy in "Obligation and Consent II," *American Political Science Review* 60, 1 (March 1966): 39–52. For an argument that no human community can or could live with such stricture, see Part III (on Aristotle) of Martha Nussbaum's *The Fragility of Goodness* (Cambridge: Harvard University Press, 1986). Tocqueville's argument is most explicit in Volume II, Part I, Chapter I of *Democracy in America*.

25. See Martha Nussbaum, "Form and Content: Philosophy and Literature," in *Love's Knowledge* (New York and Oxford: Oxford University Press, 1990), especially pp. 3–5. In the same way rational choice and actor theorists tend to present choices

of agents as the product of mentalistic acts by free-floating individuals, they present their own choice of method. In both instances they often ignore cultural constraints, including the definition of the profession and the desire for academic prestige and power that shapes their enterprise.

26. See Sheldon S. Wolin's discussion of "methodism" in "Political Theory as a Vocation," reprinted in *Machiavelli and the Nature of Political Thought*, ed. Martin Fleisher (New York: Atheneum, 1972), pp. 23–75.

27. In *Reading the Post-Modern Polity*, Shapiro is sharply critical of Elster's transformation of mythic art into rationalistic time (in the latter's *Ulysses and the Sirens*); cf. Segal's discussion of time as an active agent in *Oedipus Tyrannos*. Rather than serving as something Oedipus can find out and know with certainty, time "becomes an active force that finally found him out. . . . Rather than being an aid to human understanding time seems to have a kind of independent power that blocks knowledge" (p. 87).

28. The idea of tragedy as a political institution is explored in my introduction to *Greek Tragedy and Political Theory* and in chapter 2 of *The Tragedy of Political Theory* (Princeton, NJ: Princeton University Press, 1990).

29. See Knox, *Oedipus at Thebes*, and "The Freedom of Oedipus," in *Essays Ancient and Modern* (Baltimore: Johns Hopkins University Press), pp. 45–62. Though I think Knox's argument provocative, there is a danger in turning theater into history; see Froma Zeitlin's "Thebes: Theater of Self and Society in Athenian Drama," in *Greek Tragedy and Political Theory*, ed. Euben, pp. 101–142. This idea of theater should not be wholly alien to us given such works as Arthur Miller's *The Crucible* and Tony Kushner's *Angels in America*.

30. Nussbaum, *Love's Knowledge*, pp. 16–17.

31. Christ Rocco, "Between Modern and Postmodern: Reading the Dialectic of Enlightenment Against the Grain," *Political Theory* 22, 1 (February 1994): 71–94.

32. Arendt introduces the contrast between actor and spectator as a way of understanding philosophy with a parable attributed to Pythagoras. At a festival "some come to compete, others to sell things, but the best come as spectators *(theatai)*, so in life the slavish men go searching for fame and gain while the philosophers search for truth." (See *Thinking*, Volume I of *Life of the Mind* [London: Secker and Warburg, 1978], pp. 129–31.) She develops her notion of representative thinking (which she takes from Aristotle and Kant) in "Truth and Politics," *Between Past and Future: Eight Exercises in Political Thought* (New York: Penguin Books, 1977), pp. 227–64.

33. Men did but women did not. Whatever the official power women had in public life through festival and cult, even with their informal power (as that appears in fourth-century B.C.E. orators), and however powerful in tragedy and comedy, women were excluded from the central political institutions of the culture.

34. See the discussion in Segal, *Oedipus Tyrannos*, pp. 150ff and chapter 4 ("Identity and the Oedipus Tyrannos") in my *The Tragedy of Political Theory*.

35. See for instance his presidential address, "The New Revolution in Political Science," *American Political Science Review* 62, 4 (December 1969): 1051–61, his "Political Science in the United States: Past and Present," in *The Development of Political Science: A Comparative Study*, ed. David Easton, John Gunnell, and Luigi Graziano

(London and New York: Routledge, 1991), and his "Division, Integration and Transfer of Knowledge," in *Divided Knowledge,* ed. David Easton and Corrine S. Schelling (Newbury Park, CA: Sage, 1991).

36. "The New Revolution in Political Science," 1058. One could not make such claims about contemporary political theory as practiced by postmodernists, Habermasians, neo-Marxists, Rawlsians, critical legal theorists, and feminists, all of whom are as alert to the dynamics of late capitalism, the growth of the megastate, and the politics of social movements as conventionally defined political scientists. One could even make the case that the natural law tradition Easton dismisses was not ignorant of the problems of industrial society but saw them differently and in some cases with real insight.

37. I have made this argument at length in chapter 8 in *The Tragedy of Political Theory* (Princeton, NJ: Princeton University Press, 1990).

38. I have explored these continuities in *Corrupting Youth: Political Education and Democratic Culture* (Princeton, NJ: Princeton University Press, 1997).

39. In the chapter on *fortuna* in *The Prince,* Machiavelli argues that we must believe ourselves capable of overcoming *fortuna* because if we don't we will certainly not be able to do so. This counsel comes from a desperation in the face of historical transformations that threaten to leave men helpless and without *virtu.* The same tone is sometimes present in Easton's essays.

40. Easton, "The New Revolution in Political Science," p. 1054. I am denying just that unless we take a very wide view of "technical," and even then I regard it as one component among many. (The whole debate echoes the argument between Socrates and the sophists and rhetoricians in such dialogues and in the *Protagoras* and *Gorgias* over whether politics can be a technē.) What Easton and rational actor theorists share is the commitment to make politics a science and a belief that the failure of political science "to advance" reflects a remediable failure to achieve that goal.

41. Gunnell and Easton, introduction to *The Development of Political Science: A Comparative Study,* p. 1.

42. Easton, "The Division, Integration and Transfer of Knowledge," p. 7, and "Political Science in the United States," pp. 283–84.

43. See p. 1054. Euripides' *Bacchae* is a quite wonderful commentary on "chopping things up into manageable bits," as I have suggested in "Dismemberment in the Bacchae," in *The Tragedy of Political Theory,* chapter 5.

44. On the Humpty Dumpty problem, see Easton, "The Division, Integration and Transfer of Knowledge," pp. 12–13.

45. Of course no one is less a stranger and more at home than Oedipus.

46. Again, no one could be a more legitimate king. Oedipus is a *tyrannos* not so much because he acts tyrannically as because he has come to power through extraordinary means. "Tyranny" was a contested notion until the fourth century, when it came to have most of the connotations we attribute to it today. (The idea that intelligence is the prime condition for ruling is of course central to Plato's idea of the philosopher-king.)

47. See Segal's discussion in *Oedipus Tyrannos,* pp. 6ff.

48. The quote and argument are from Reinhardt in his *Sophocles,* trans. Hazel Harvey and David Harvey (New York: Barnes and Noble, 1979), pp. 111–12. I think

Reinhardt exaggerates, but it is a provocative point nonetheless, especially for a discussion of rational actor theory.

49. The danger of such evolutionary stories is that they slight the degree to which what seems overcome by events or thought remain the ground for everyday life. So in making this point, I do not want to exaggerate or simplify. The old ways did not disappear; in fact, they became more aggressively asserted. Perhaps the best, surely the most amusing, demonstration of this is the contest between the old and new education in Aristophanes' *Clouds*.

50. See Kristen Monroe's summary in *The Economic Approach to Politics*, p. 4, and Herbert Simon's discussion of bounded rationality in his two-volume work with that title (Cambridge, MA: MIT Press, 1982), especially chapter I.

51. See Arendt's discussion in the *Life of the Mind*, Vol. 1, and *The Human Condition* (Chicago: University of Chicago Press, 1958).

52. That her act occurs in the bedroom, in private, has a certain dramatic appropriateness. But that it is also where women were supposed to be in Athenian ideology. In practice, though, women were often out in public either preparing for and leading religious processions, in the *agora* selling with their husbands (or instead of them, when the men were off with the fleet), visiting friends, or jointly doing "woman's work."

53. Cameron, *The Identity of Oedipus the King*, p. 115. I have discussed this theme at length in Chapter 4, "The Identity of Oedipus the King," in *The Tragedy of Political Theory*.

54. See the discussion in Knox, *The Freedom of Oedipus*.

55.

> Aiai, dustanos egō
> poi gas pheromani tlamōnta moi
> phthoa diapōtatai phradēn;
> io diamon in exēllou

> Where am I going? where on earth?
> where does all this agony hurl me?
> where's my voice?—
> winging, swept away on a dark tide
> O dark power of the god, what a leap you made!

> *(1309–11). This is the Fagles translation as modified by Segal.*

56. *Oppression and Liberty*, trans. Arthur Wills and John Petrie (Amherst: University of Massachusetts Press, 1958), p. 96.

57. Reinhardt, *Sophocles*, p. 134.

58. One meaning of *episkēpto* is "to make, lean upon, throw light upon, or impose upon." Another is "to lay a strict charge upon someone or command them to do something." A third is "to prosecute or indict." Given the themes of the play, the word, like the act of self-blinding, brings the parts into a whole.

59. David Johnston, "Human Agency and Rational Action," in Monroe, *The Economic Approach to Politics*, p. 106.

60. See his discussion in *Problems of Dostoevsky's Poetics*, trans. Caryl Emerson (Minneapolis: University of Minnesota Press, 1984) pp. 6–7, 32, 97.

61. Indeed, Frederick Ahl would suggest that this is precisely what I have done. He argues that Oedipus's assumption that he did indeed kill his father and our presumption that he is right is precipitous given that those upon whose testimony he (and we) relies to prove his guilt often have "vague identities and questionable motives" and that the king's conclusions are based on words that are "notoriously elusive and prone to ambiguity." In Sophocles' *Oedipus* (Ithaca and London: Cornell University Press, 1991), p. 28.

62. See John H. Schaar and Sheldon Wolin, *The Berkeley Rebellion and Beyond* (New York: The New York Review of Books, 1970).

63. Stanley Fish, "The Common Touch, or One Size Fits All," in *The Politics of Liberal Education,* ed. Darryl J. Gless and Barbara Herrnstein Smith (Durham and London: Duke University Press, 1992), p. 251.

64. Bernard Williams, *Shame and Necessity,* p. 166–67.

7

Empirical Theory 1997

Who's Kissing Him—or Her—Now?

Catherine Zuckert and Michael Zuckert

1953 saw the inauguration of Dwight Eisenhower for his first term, and it brought the televised Army-McCarthy hearings. 1953 was one of the years the Dodgers and the Yankees duked it out in a Subway Series—the Dodgers were still in Brooklyn. Ike, Roy Cohn, Pee Wee Reese—it seems a long time ago. 1953 was also the year David Easton informed the political science profession that what it most needed was empirical political theory. His book *The Political System* almost instantly became one of the definitive documents of the behavioral revolution, which, in turn, more or less defined the profession during the late 1950s and 1960s, at least up until Easton's American Political Science Association presidential address of 1969.[1] Today, however, empirical political theory as defined by Easton seems to have gone the way of Ebbets Field and brinksmanship.[2] Only rational choice theory seems at all powerful, and its limitations are now quite well known, as most of the other chapters in this volume testify.

No doubt the promise of empirical theory was very great—the ever sought, never found genuine science of politics. Probably this promise was overblown from the start. Easton himself shifted direction in 1969 in a statement that some took as a complete retreat from, even betrayal of, the hopes of 1953.[3] At the very least, Easton's call for a "postbehavioral" revolution was a partial retreat, an open recognition of the political developments of the mid- and late 1960s, which made a theoretical political science seem a luxury for quieter hours. It was also an acknowledgment of the more subdued riots and crises in intellectual orientation among those who thought about theoretical issues in the social sciences. The call for a postbehavioral revolution was, in sum, a halting and partial recognition of the waves of post- and antipositivism that were becoming so powerful.[4]

Where Easton had spoken in 1953 of "the decline of modern political theory" and others at the same time had gone even further to speak of the death of traditional political theory, by 1997 the situation has become quite different. The behavioral movement, in part assimilated into the mainstream, hardly exists as such. Not only does political theory live, but more work that concerns or resembles Plato and Aristotle, Hegel and Nietzsche, is being done than work that resembles systems theory or follows Easton's strictures in *The Political System*.[5] The story of political theory from 1953 to 1997, then, is a story of the announcement, rise, and steep decline of empirical theory.

It is nonetheless not easy to describe in a few words just what has replaced empirical theory. Roughly speaking, there seem to be three large clusters of positions dominant in political theory today. One set of theorists adheres to what we might call "revivalist" doctrines, ones that harken back to very old traditions of political thought and analysis. Typical representatives of revivalist theory are Hannah Arendt, Alasdair McIntyre, and Leo Strauss.[6] Another group of theorists, whom we call "restorationists," have attempted to restore what has all along been a more or less live, more or less dominant system of political thought, modern liberal political philosophy. The towering name in this enterprise is John Rawls, but there are others as well—Ronald Dworkin, William Galston, and Robert Nozick, to name a few.[7] The third group of theorists are the overturners, the radical innovators, the enfants terribles of the academic world: the postmodernists, the feminists, and related practitioners of new modes of theorizing. Here some of the familiar names are Michel Foucault, Jacques Derrida, Richard Rorty, and Iris Young.[8]

The practitioners of these three broad types of political theory disagree with each other over quite a range of issues; indeed, they frequently see the positions taken by one of the others as the chief enemy to be overcome. Yet they are remarkably at one in rejecting the chief tenets of the Eastonian program for empirical theory. We can indeed derive a pretty fair idea of the course of political theory in the nearly half-century since *The Political System* if we consider how our three current types of theorists respond to the three chief claims raised by Easton on behalf of empirical theory: first, the conception of theory contained in his call for theory; second, his rejection of traditional theory via his acceptance of a positivist approach to the problem of facts and values; and, finally, his call for a reconceptualization of politics as "the authoritative allocation of values for society as a whole."

THE EASTONIAN PROGRAM

The call for empirical theory came among what Easton believed were signs of declining faith in reason and science in the West.[9] One such sign was "the present concerted attack against the use of scientific method in the social sciences."[10] This "concerted attack" was fed by a growing skepticism about the effectiveness of scientific method in social research,[11] a skepticism based in large part on the failure of thirty years of the scientific study of politics to produce much by way of results. "In spite of undeniable accomplishments . . . the condition of American political science is disturbing and disappointing."[12]

Easton shared this feeling of disappointment but differed in his diagnosis of the causes for political science's poor showing. He called not for a retreat but for a more sophisticated version of science. Political science was failing because it had an immature and grossly imperfect idea of what a scientific approach truly requires. Political scientists had become "captive of a view of science as the objective collection and classification of facts and the relating of them into singular generalizations."[13] Easton called such a position "hyperfactualism" and noted that its adherents tended to see theory of all sorts as the antithesis of the genuinely scientific—that is, empirical and unspeculative—enterprise in which they were engaged.[14]

Contrary to the skeptics about theory, Easton held that the presence of theory "is an index of the stage of development of any science, social or physical."[15] He thought it was neither possible nor desirable to dispense with theory. It was impossible because "a fact is a particular ordering of reality in terms of a theoretical interest." As Easton also put it, "There is no such thing as a pure fact." Every fact, he argued, is an aspect of reality extracted and described by an observer on the basis of some "prior interest," some "frame of reference that fixes the order and relevance of the facts." A given event may be described in an infinite number of ways, and only the observer's prior interest gives shape to the particular set of "facts" that appear. When the observer's frame of reference is "raised to the level of consciousness," then we have what Easton calls "theory."[16] But whether raised to that level or not, such frames of reference, or preobservational commitments and interests, are inescapable.

Although this line of thought had many echoes of postpositivism in it, Easton tended to interpret it in terms that made it compatible with positivism's instrumental notion of theory. He insisted that theory is important because it is useful in social science as a "device for improving the dependability of our knowledge." This latter task, quite different from making explicit our pretheoretical understanding, is accomplished by theory, because "knowledge becomes critical and reliable as it increases in generality and internally consistent organization, when, in short, it is cast in the form of systematic generalized statements applicable to large numbers of particular cases."[17] Easton understood this view of theory to be identical with that prevalent in the natural sciences. The goal is the formulation of very general theories from which can be deduced very specific propositions, in the form of predictions, which can then be empirically tested.[18] Theory thus is a way to make empirical research coherent, additive, and fecund. That is to say, it is ultimately instrumental.[19] Theory thus serves in the first instance as a sieve; it helps select the facts of interest. The empirical theorists did not doubt, however, that there are facts prior to and independent of the application of theory.[20] Theory also helps generate new hypotheses about further facts and causal relations in the world, which are thereby already connected to other established facts and causal relations in the theory. This notion of theory, then, did not challenge science as understood in the positivist mode but merely reinforced that understanding.[21]

Easton was very careful to distinguish the theory for which he was calling from traditional theory—he was as set against the latter as he was against hyperfactualism. He was particularly opposed to the form in which traditional theory showed itself in the decades before he wrote. Traditional political theory had undergone a serious decline into "historicism"—that is, into the merely historical study of past political theories.[22] Easton also insistently distinguished the empirical or causal theory he advocated from the nonhistoricist form of traditional political theory in political science—"discussion of political values or the philosophy of politics," or "value theory."[23] Although Easton did not entirely dismiss "value theory," he approached it very much in a positivistic and relativistic spirit. He accepted as a valid starting point for reflection the so-called fact-value distinction: "facts and values are logically heterogeneous."[24] "The factual aspect of a proposition refers to a part of reality; hence it can be tested by reference to the facts." Moral propositions are entirely different, however; they "express only the emotional response of an individual to a state of real or presumed facts."[25] Because science deals with reality, Easton argued, value theory can be no essential part of it.

Yet, just as Easton gave far more weight than his fellow political scientists did to the (relatively) nonempirical dimensions of theory, so he differed in denying the possibility of a value-free political science. Human beings are necessarily valuing beings; nonetheless, the values of the scientist need not compromise the validity of his or her research and theory. Although values are unavoidable, the point of proper method is, in effect, to neutralize them by raising them to transparent self-consciousness and subjecting oneself to the strictest standards of scientific logic and empirical verification.[26] Easton was thus not entirely an orthodox positivist as that was understood in 1953. One suspects that his deep acquaintance with Max Weber—and, through Weber, with Nietzsche and other harbingers of antipositivist currents of thought—was responsible for his deviationism. Yet in the final analysis Easton's thought turns on the same set of distinctions that positivism does—the distinctions between facts and theory and between facts and values. Despite a few subtleties and complexities, despite some confusion, the positivistic roots of his position seem quite clear.

The third feature of Easton's call for empirical theory was his new conceptualization of politics as "the authoritative allocation of values for a society." This conceptualization provided the basis for the identification of "the political system" and thus supplied the central idea both for his early programmatic statement and for his later, more detailed forays into substantive empirical theory. *The Political System* was in large part a response to the suspicion voiced by some social scientists that "the study of political life can never reach the level of the other social sciences because it does not constitute a distinctive theoretical field such as economics or psychology."[27] Easton understood the challenge posed in that judgment to go very deep. "The question of the existence of a political system . . . is . . . vital to the development of political research."[28] If the political system does not exist as a separate and specifiable sphere, then political science as such must disappear for want of a subject matter.

In his discussion of alternative conceptualizations of the political, Easton explored the reasons his fellow social scientists doubted the ontological status of politics as a sphere of reality fit for scientific study. First, these social scientists frequently identified the political sphere with the state. Easton countered that the state is underinclusive, by no means coterminous with political life. For example, he noted, tribal societies have politics, but they do not have states.[29] Perhaps most significant to Easton, however, was the following problem: definitions of the state always refer to some set of "value-concepts." Even Weber's effort to define the state in a relatively neutral manner ended up containing a reference to the normative notion of a monopoly of "legitimate" coercion. Thus, even the Weberian definition, to say nothing of the Lockean or Hegelian efforts, enshrined a value idea at the very center of political science. Given Easton's views on the scientific nonstatus of such value notions, the state simply would not do.

Ostensibly more value-neutral, and thus prima facie more promising, was the chief alternative to the state as a way of defining the political: power, "the effort to influence others."[30] Easton found the problem here to be more or less the obverse of the problem with the state. Politics as power is overinclusive. Power exists in all spheres of social life, and if politics is nothing but power, then the worst fears voiced by the social scientists are realized—there is no sufficiently separate political sphere to warrant or sustain a separate political science. Thus, Easton's new definition of the political stood at the point of intersection between his two other central themes. It bore the marks of the instrumental role of theoretical concepts in identifying and constituting as a unity an aspect of "reality" for scientific investigation, yet it did so in a way that respected Easton's value-skepticism. His conceptualization of the political itself bore the brand, then, of the two dichotomies that are constitutive of the notion of empirical theory as such: the fact-theory and the fact-value distinctions.[31]

It also should be obvious that the application of these two dichotomies to the question of what constitutes the political could not produce as determinate an answer as Easton gave. Easton considered the political a sphere for the "allocation of values," a clear reference to the parallel characterization of the economic sphere. Both sciences study allocation of values, but political science studies "authoritative" allocations—that is, allocations that occur via authority relations rather than via exchange relations. Thus, Easton's grasp of the political took its bearings substantively from economics and proceeded by way of distinguishing politics from economics. The prior identification of the economic was the prerequisite for the identification of the political. Whether Easton's grasp of the political was as universal or as novel as he claimed is open to question: *The Political System* reproduced as the very definition of the political a certain conception of politics that came to dominance in the United States with the New Deal—namely, that the economic sphere is not the sole adequate allocator of values but is and needs to be supplemented by political allocations.[32]

For a while it looked as though the scientific revolutionaries might succeed in routing the traditional theorists and hyperfactualists along with merely "common sense" political scientists. One hostile critic in 1963 spoke of behavioralism as the new orthodoxy of the profession, and in the mid-1960s political scientists were finding traditional theory the least valuable subfield in the discipline.[33] Yet the Eastonian program never went unopposed. On the contrary, the three clusters of theorists who predominate in the field today emerged in a succession of waves, each of which was marked by sharp opposition to the underlying assumptions of the agenda for empirical theory. Each of them emphasized a different one of Easton's three chief themes, but together they constituted quite a devastating critique.

REVIVALISTS

From its inception the "behavioral revolution" was accompanied by a theoretical critique. In the years following World War II the most outspoken critics of the movement to make the study of politics scientific were often emigrés—Hannah Arendt, Hans Morgenthau, Leo Strauss, and Eric Voegelin.[34] Whereas most Americans still believed, perhaps naively, in the truth as well as the beneficent practical results of scientific inquiry, these German-educated scholars had been schooled in a penetrating philosophical critique. Moreover, the underlying references within empirical theory to parochial American events and themes were evident to these emigrés.

Having studied with Edmund Husserl and Martin Heidegger, both Strauss and Arendt were familiar with the phenomenological critique of empirical science and thus never could accept the conception of theory animating the call for empirical theory.[35] Husserl had pointed out that we do not actually experience ourselves as bombarded with a chaotic mixture of sense impressions or data that we proceed to order according to our own needs and convenience, as the empiricists maintained. "Empiricism" itself is a theoretical construction designed to explain a pretheoretical experience. The extent to which empiricism not only presupposes but is itself founded on and defined by this pretheoretical experience can be seen in the definitions of the various "empirical" sciences by their subject matters— bio-logy, socio-logy, chemistry, even the political as discussed by Easton. In their very definitions, these sciences thus take the existence and intelligibility of their various subject matters for granted. If science is to be firmly founded, it is necessary to go beyond this "naturalistic fallacy," the mere acceptance of kinds of existence or being as given, in order to rigorously examine the foundations of science in a pretheoretical experience of the "world" (*Lebenswelt*). Because both the experience and the understanding of that experience in the modern world are already theoretically formed and shaped, Heidegger added, we must first submit the theoretical ideas we have inherited to a "destructive" historical critique if we are to recapture the original, the pretheoretical experience on which science itself is based. We must, in other words, free ourselves from the traditional, the inherited, the abstract and often, therefore, empty understanding of the concepts we continue to use in our attempts—theoretical as well as nontheoretical—to comprehend the world. We must attempt to recapture the original experience out of which science—and, as it turns out, politics—grew in ancient Greece.

Husserl and Heidegger were concerned primarily with the foundations of human knowledge or science; neither paid much sustained attention to politics. But by the end of World War II it was clear that politics had the capacity to destroy science, if not humanity altogether. It was impossible, both Arendt and Strauss concluded, to understand the world and, even more important, the human beings who somehow comprehend it without taking account of the role politics plays in the ordering of their lives.

In the United States these scholars discovered their colleagues were almost totally unaware of the phenomenological critique of science and the philosophical tradition that underlies it. Heidegger himself had been implicated, moreover, in the horrible politics of the Third Reich. Both Strauss and Arendt found it necessary, therefore, to explain why they thought it necessary to return to a study of ancient Greece for the sake of recapturing a sense of the true character of politics—and, therein, the only possible basis for a science of politics—in terms somewhat different from those that had been used in Europe.

Finding himself surrounded, particularly at the University of Chicago, by advocates of the scientific study of politics, Strauss presented his case for the need to ground the study of politics in a critical, untraditional rereading of the history of political philosophy in the form of a critique of positivism and historicism.[36] What struck many of his colleagues as mere antiquarianism (a concern with history) or naiveté (the demand that "scientists" pay attention to the "common sense" basis of their own categories of thought) was, in fact, an argument intended to clear away the theoretical obstructions that prevented political scientists from getting to the "stuff" they purported to study.

Political action aims either at preservation or change, Strauss observed; preservation of the good, change of the bad. Political action is, therefore, always guided by some notion of the good, not only of the individual but also and preeminently of the community. Because the common good is complex and hence difficult to comprehend, it is almost always a subject of disagreement. People nevertheless want to know what it is. The disagreements characteristic of political life thus lead naturally to an examination of the validity of the different claims about what is good; thus, the inquiry characteristic of political philosophy arises (as in ancient Greece) out of political life itself. By dismissing the possibility of attaining any knowledge of the good on the basis of the fact-value distinction, positivistic political scientists deny themselves the possibility, from the outset, of understanding the guiding concern or principle of political action. They thereby preclude study of the source of political conflict and disagreement. By denying the legitimacy or meaningfulness of any evaluative statement, they make it impossible for political scientists to describe the phenomena they purport to study accurately, because those phenomena are themselves irreducibly evaluative. Political societies are organized around some understanding of "the good life," the life the citizens of that polity hope and strive to achieve. This understanding thus determines what is deemed important in that society; it distinguishes one society from another. Because they reject the pertinence of these different understandings, positivistic political scientists lack any standard of importance or relevance in designing their studies. Facts are facts; they can be collected about virtually anything, certainly any and all forms of human endeavor.

If they rigorously adhered to their own positivistic principles, Strauss observed, the advocates of a strictly empirical or scientific study of politics would become nihilists. Strictly speaking, they could not maintain that anything—including science or truth—has any more value than anything else. In fact, however, most positivists seem to regard the proposition that no one way of life can be proved to be any better than any other as a justification for liberal democracy. If no particular way of life is demonstrably better than another, we should tolerate them all. At the least, democracy is no worse than any other alternative; and, knowing nothing better, we might as well stick with what we have. Because the gathering of facts or opinions characteristic of "empirical" research is possible only in liberal democracies, moreover, the "scientific" studies seeking "laws of human behavior" tend, in fact, to produce studies of the political life of one particular kind of regime.[37]

The most thoughtful advocates of the scientific study of politics, Strauss predicted, would gradually come to see that their own endeavor was the product or reflection of a certain set of values, of a certain time and place, regime, or "culture." (One finds evidence of this view in the chapters by Easton and Almond in this volume.) No nonevaluative study is possible. Is all "knowledge" or "science" then limited by its temporal and spatial origins? Is there such a thing as science as it has traditionally been understood? That is the challenge raised by what Strauss called "historicism" and what is now known as "postmodernism." If the human mind cannot overcome limitations of time and place, the "scientific" collection of "facts" or even formulation of laws neither is any better grounded nor has any more enduring results than the "normative" analysis of competing claims about what is good or right.

Whereas Strauss thought it necessary to revive political philosophy, both as the natural outgrowth and fundamental source of our knowledge of politics, Arendt wanted to restore political practice or action per se. Going back to the original Greek experience, she argued that private life in the *oikos* (household) had been devoted to the acquisition of the necessities of existence, which are common to all. It was only in the public or the political arena that individuals distinguished themselves by trying to have an effect, to make a name for themselves, and so to be remembered by others for doing not merely what was necessary to maintain existence but what was extraordinary, different, and, because not dictated by the requirements of self-preservation, free. The Greeks clearly distinguished the *economic* power of life and death a despot or master exercised over his slaves from the *political* rule of free and equal human beings. In modern times that distinction—and hence the understanding of the distinctive character of political action—has been lost. Thus, according to Arendt, politics can never come to light as a mechanism parallel to the economy for the allocation of values. Politics is about something else altogether.

Strauss argued that political philosophy developed naturally out of practical political controversies; Arendt, by contrast, thought the emergence of political philosophy in Greece constituted the first step in the historical devaluation and subsequent loss of a sense of the political.[38] Socrates had urged young aristocratic Athenians not to go into politics in order to seek transitory goods such as wealth and honor but rather to strive to come to understand and enjoy contemplating the eternal verities. Such theoretical bliss was achievable, if at all, only for a very few, Socrates admitted. But by convincing people that life here on earth is a vale of tears and that people ought to attend to their eternal salvation rather than their merely ephemeral secular concerns, Christianity popularized the Platonic proposition that the eternal life of the other world is much more important than the affairs of this. After Rome fell, political life, properly speaking, almost disappeared in Europe. When a combination of religious wars, scientific discoveries, and explorations of the New World led people in the seventeenth century to become urgently and explicitly concerned about the affairs of *this* world, they were persuaded by philosophers such as Thomas Hobbes and John Locke that political or public action ought to be dedicated, if not strictly limited, to securing the essentially private, bodily requirements of comfortable self-preservation for all. Once political organization was conceived in strictly instrumental terms, appreciation of the distinctively individualistic and free character of political action undertaken for its own sake was lost. No longer understanding the differences among the three kinds of practice—politics, manufacture, and labor—people in modern times have created a new, "social" middle-world that is neither simply public nor private. They have thus produced the conditions under which politics could be misapprehended in the Eastonian manner.

Dedicated to acquiring the same basic necessities for all, Arendt pointed out, modern social life and the study, or science, thereof were necessarily and effectively homogenizing: "[S]ociety expects from each of its members a certain kind of behavior, imposing innumerable and various rules, all of which tend to 'normalize' its members, to make them behave, to exclude spontaneous action or outstanding achievements." Seeking to find regularities or laws of human behavior, the social sciences not only document but also foster this uniformity. The more modern societies succeed in providing the basic necessities of life, the more the population grows, and the less particular differences or individuality stands out. The outcome is what has become known as "mass society." Like Strauss, Arendt suggested that social science is not merely a reflection of but a contributor to this development:

> The unfortunate truth about behaviorism and the validity of its "laws" is that the more people there are, the more likely they are to behave and the less likely to tolerate non-behavior. Statistically, this will be shown in the leveling out of fluctuation. . . . *Statistical uniformity is by no means a harmless scientific ideal; it is the no longer secret political ideal of a society which, entirely submerged in the routine of everyday living, is at peace with the scientific outlook inherent in its very existence* (emphasis added).[39]

Although Strauss and Arendt agreed that the attempt to make the study of politics scientific obscured, if it did not destroy, the purported subject matter, they emphatically disagreed about the distinctive characteristics of politics.[40] Although David Easton tried, the question concerning the definition or particular nature of the subject matter of political science could not be effectively raised in and for the profession as a whole until the pretensions or principles of a positive, empirical science were subjected to further criticism.

THE RESTORATIONISTS

Writing after (for the most part) the first wave of emigré critics of the behavioral/empirical theory agenda for political studies, John Rawls probably had the largest impact of any single author in redirecting the attention of political theorists from empirical to normative questions. One reason for Rawls's great success is that unlike the emigrés and, later, the postmodernists, he was not heir to the kind of radical critique of science and positivism launched on the continent by the likes of Nietzsche and Heidegger. Rather, he began his career in the orbit of the far more modest revisionism going on within Anglo-American analytic philosophy.[41] Rawls's thinking remained closer to the underlying thought animating Easton's call for empirical theory than did that of any of the other theorists under consideration here. The key difference between Rawls (and his followers) and the other critics is evident in their divergent views on the authority of natural science. As Strauss said, for Heidegger and those who followed him modern science loses its "authoritative character" because it "appears as only one form among many of man's thinking orientation in the world."[42] Rawls is quite emphatically different—"scientific knowledge is a model of sound knowledge."[43]

Accepting the authority of science, Rawls nonetheless broke with the positivist conception of what knowledge is available. He rejected the fact-value dichotomy—or, rather, rejected the value noncognitivism pronounced by positivism and carried over into political science by the adherents of behavioral and empirical theory. Near the beginning of Rawls's chief work, *A Theory of Justice*, we find the magisterial pronouncement: "Justice is the first virtue of social institutions, as truth is of systems of thought."[44] He thus completely reversed the position Easton took on the nature of political reality: value notions such as justice are not unreal emotional add-ons to a real world of unevaluative facts, things that must be set aside in order to penetrate political reality, but are constitutive of the political world. Thus, Rawls believed, the project of empirical theory can never produce significant knowledge about politics. Political theory must be normative theory.

Rawls's major innovation, then, was the claim that normative theory—or rather, knowledge of norms—is compatible with the authority of science. His *Theory of Justice* only lightly developed the ontological and epistemological sides of this important claim, however.[45] As he said in *Theory*, on these matters he "followed with some modification the point of view" expressed in an earlier essay—indeed, in his very first published essay, one built upon his doctoral dissertation. Surprisingly, in light of the centrality of the methodological issue, this early essay and Rawls's dissertation have attracted very little attention. We will focus our comments here on these two early statements, because they develop most fully Rawls's argument for a value cognitivist position.

Rawls attempted to show that moral theory is more or less isomorphic with theory in natural science and that moral knowledge stands on ground as solid as that of empirical knowledge. To prove these assertions, he had to modify to some degree both the positivist notion of science and the positivist notion of morality. Writing at almost the same moment as Easton and in a very similar intellectual milieu, Rawls, like Easton, claimed that in the positivist view ethical norms are "simply the expression of settled emotional dispositions, and, being such, they are not the kind of things that can be submitted to rational criticism and reflection. . . . They may not be validated or invalidated by reason."[46] Rawls intentionally set aside the question of the origin of ethical norms as irrelevant to the main issue—whether such norms may or may not be validated by reason. In seeking to show that they may be, he used a strategy in many ways parallel to Easton's dismissal of the value-laden origin of empirical observations and research as irrelevant to the central matter of validity.

In these early works Rawls developed a complex "decision procedure" by which to show that reason can validate or justify ethical norms; only a brief sketch is possible in the space available here. Rawls maintained that ethical theory, like theory in the natural sciences, must begin with data. The data for science are empirical observations, whereas the data for ethical theory are moral judgments. There is nothing mysterious about these judgments—their status is little different from, for example, votes people cast in presidential elections.

However, the raw data of moral theory, like that of natural science, requires some purification. Only observations that meet certain criteria of methodological adequacy are relevant in science; so Rawls sought moral judgments that adequately reveal the nature of moral phenomena. He specified that only certain classes of moral agents and certain classes of moral judgments should count for the purposes of theory construction. Although this was a potentially controversial step in his argument, Rawls attempted to define these usable moral judgments in a noncontroversial manner. In particular, he used only formal qualifications, not substantive ones, to distinguish among the different moral judgments.[47]

Rawls then proposed an "explication" of the considered moral judgments people make. The point of the explication was to reveal the principles implicit in those judgments. That is, Rawls maintained that a relatively common core at the level of principle is discernible in the class of considered moral judgments actually made: "The attempt to discover a comprehensive explication may be thought of as the attempt to express the invariant in the considered judgments of competent judges in the sense that, given the wide variety of cases on which considered judgments are made at different times and places, the principles of the explication are such that the conscious and systematic application of them could have been a common factor in the determination of the multiplicity of considered judgments as made in the wide variety of cases" (*sic*).[48] Rawls did not consider the explication of the principles somehow implicit in our acts of moral judgment the final step of an adequate moral theory, however. He was not interested in merely displaying the law of operation of our moral faculty (he was agnostic as to whether that is what they are) but rather held that the "principal aim of ethics is the formulation of justifiable principles."[49] Justification is thus a distinct step beyond explication.

Rawls developed a complex four-part test for justifiability, the most important element of which is that "some principles will exhibit a capacity to win free and willing allegiance and be able to implement a gradual convergence of uncoerced opinion."[50] The principles can win allegiance because they are recognized as reasonable and perspicuous explanations of the "moral sense," and it is this power to gain such allegiance that renders them justified, genuinely normative, or capable of articulating "oughts" or "duties."

Rawls pointed out that moral theory thus shares all the appropriate characteristics of scientific theory, properly understood. First, his decision procedure satisfies the positivist demand that the meaningfulness of any proposition be determined in terms of that proposition's "method of verification." The decision procedure is precisely such a method of verification. Second, the relationship between ethical theory and the data of moral life is just the same as that within science and between data and empirical theories. Finally, the ability of the moral principles to gain free and willing allegiance of reasonable agents, the ultimate test of justification, is quite parallel to the standing of "veridical perceptions" and the rules of inductive logic in natural science. There is nothing more arbitrary or merely posited in morality than there is in perception or empirical theory.[51] Rawls leaves us with the view that if science can produce knowledge about the world, then ethical theory can produce valid moral knowledge.

The postmodern thinkers who have come to be seen with Rawls as alternatives to empirical theory agree with him that facts and values stand on a similar foundation, but they are less convinced than Rawls that such a foundation can truly be found. Rawls's dual emphasis on the reasonableness and freedom of the acceptance of principles gives way to an emphasis only on the latter—humanity is stretched across an abyss; there is no ground. Accordingly, for the postmodernists the theme of power rises to much greater prominence in construing both science and the political than for any of our previously discussed theorists, including the Eastonian empirical theorists.

OVERTURNERS: TOWARD A POSTMODERN POLITICAL SCIENCE

At first feminism was far more a political movement than a theoretical rival to empirical theory. Marching to protest the U.S. government's failure to protect the rights of its black citizens, women in the civil rights movement came to see that their own rights were not well protected.[52] Those who moved the issue from the streets to the more reflective groves of the academy developed a penetrating critique not merely of the government of the United States and the liberal theory that underlies it but, ultimately, of theory and science per se.

Although modern theorists and practitioners had been proclaiming the essential freedom and equality of all human beings for centuries, feminists observed, women had never actually enjoyed the same political and economic opportunities open to men. One reason for this persistent sexual inequality, these critics suggested, was that the abstract, general terms used to define liberal political institutions and rights covered over a fundamental factual difference, a sexual division of labor that produced a massive difference in power. Although men and women were both officially citizens, women had rarely been able to exercise most of the rights of citizenship in fact. They had not gained universal suffrage until the early twentieth century, and their ability to acquire and manage property was usually severely curtailed by law. They were even more severely curtailed by social custom, which suggested women should marry, bear and raise children, and conduct most of their activities out of the public eye, in the private sphere. The distinction between public and private, which was the hallmark of modern liberalism, carried over into the Eastonian definition of the political, functioning as an insidious (because largely invisible) source of subjection for women.

That subjection was not merely a matter of custom or informal social practice, moreover. Although liberal institutions and rhetoric obscured the fact, the power men exercised over women was, in fact, fully and formally political. Not merely women's daily activities and economic functions but their very bodies were subject to masculine control—backed by the force of government or law.[53] For women, feminists thus concluded, "the personal is the political." From a quite different perspective, then, feminists agreed with other contemporary theorists in rejecting the very principles according to which Easton thought political science should be constituted.

Inquiring into the source of the norms that relegated women to the private sphere, feminists made their critique of modern political theory and practice even more radical. Initially it appeared that the differences between men and women in life paths could be traced to the fundamental sexual or biological difference in reproductive function. Some early feminists thus eagerly embraced modern science, especially the developing technology of birth control, as the primary means whereby women could achieve real freedom.[54] But feminists since have been led to raise some fundamental questions not merely about the potential effects but also about the epistemological and political status of science and thus of empirical theory itself. The difference between the sexes with regard to reproductive function had traditionally been said to be "natural" or "biological." But, according to modern scientific theory, there is no such thing as a "natural order." The categories in terms of which we understand and organize the world are not in what Kant called "the things themselves." According to the original empiricist philosophers (e.g., John Locke, *Essay on Human Understanding*), human beings gather and organize a chaos of sense data into concepts or categories they construct, consciously or unconsciously, socially more than individually, for their own convenience.[55]

If science is based on a set of categories constructed for the convenience of some human beings, the question naturally arises: for *whose* convenience? For what ends or purposes are the categories employed? After surveying the history of Western thought and practice, feminists have concluded that the categories had been formulated exclusively by and for men, who used the categories not merely to organize but also to manipulate and control not only nature but other human beings—first and foremost, women.[56]

Concluding that science and theory represent not the discovery and contemplation of a preexisting order so much as the imposition of order, feminist critics thus concur with the postmodern contention that science does not constitute knowledge so much as power.[57] But where feminists see this power as exercised by men to control women, the most radical postmodern critics deny that it is possible for anyone to rise to an Archimedean point outside and beyond the realm of discourse from which he or she can impose a system of organization on others.[58] On the contrary, the postmodernists argue, the scientist himself—as much as the facts or world he seeks to discover, if not organize—is produced by and subject to the form of discourse he employs.

There are, of course, significantly different versions of the postmodern reinterpretation of the character of science. The most moderate is the "homegrown" American version, articulated by Richard Rorty, who argues that postmodernism is and ought to be understood as an extension of pragmatism. As pragmatists such as William James and Charles Peirce argued, science does not constitute the discovery of eternal truths or laws of behavior; on the contrary, the scientist collects data and organizes it in the way that works best, the way that produces the best results, with the more or less explicit reservation that he is and will be free to change his findings so that he can produce even better effects as he accumulates new data. What "works" is what produces results people find useful.[59]

Some people worry, Rorty recognizes, that if we deny that there is any given, natural order or "objective" truth, power-hungry individuals or groups will regard this insight as an opportunity to impose the order they construct on others. Friedrich Nietzsche argued that they should. But, Rorty urges, the open-ended understanding of science we have inherited from the pragmatists need not lead to such dire results. On the contrary, the more people recognize that no one possesses or can possess truth in the traditional sense, the more they will see that no way of understanding is intrinsically better, truer, or more well founded than any other. There is no justification, therefore, for anyone's imposing his or her understanding on anyone else. Everyone is and ought to be free to formulate his or her own description of the world he or she confronts. There is no external source of meaning; each person must produce it for him or herself by composing a narrative of his or her life. Recognizing that we do not and never can have "science" or knowledge as it was traditionally understood, Rorty urges, can increase support for liberal toleration. New support is needed, inasmuch as the traditional rationale for liberal political institutions (e.g., natural or human rights) has been seriously undermined by the questions raised about the existence of a natural order and, hence, about the status and character of humanity itself.[60]

Feminists and radical postmodernists object to Rorty's liberal pragmatism because it leaves intact the distinction between public and private life that has made invisible the oppression of women by men. If all we have are "vocabularies," the postmodern theorists of "discourse" ask, can we really talk about "private" meanings? Doesn't language presuppose social interaction? These postmodern critics thus raise questions about the viability of the division between public and private characteristic of liberal political theory. And in response to Rorty's defense of liberalism, feminist critics note that those who judge what knowledge is "useful" are those with the public and political power to do so. Rorty's version of postmodernism rather explicitly functions as a new rationale or justification for the liberal status quo. Along with feminists, French postmodern critics of science (e.g., Michel Foucault and Jacques Derrida) emphasize the heretofore mostly invisible controls effected by apparently impersonal systems of discourse and by supposedly progressive, reformist, and/or humanitarian institutions, such as schools.

In *The Order of Things* Foucault challenged earlier, generally progressive accounts of the history of science like those of the American pragmatists.[61] If we review that history, he argued, what we see in fact is a series of abrupt shifts. For example, in the seventeenth-century "classical" period, everything was understood as a reflection of a part of a universal order or cosmos. The goal of the scientist was thus to classify things according to their place in this scheme. But between 1775 and 1825, Foucault pointed out, in three separate developments, the study of life, labor, and language shifted entirely away from the classifications characteristic of, respectively, natural history, the science of acquisition, and grammar and toward the analyses of the functional interrelations of organic structures. This epistemological sea change, or "event," as Heidegger would say, did not occur as the result of the accumulation of new data. The subjects of the new sciences were constituted within the sciences themselves; they did not exist "out there" in some independent, eternal natural order, waiting to be discovered.[62] The new organic understandings of life, labor, and language "systems" did result in the development of a series of new "human sciences" (psychology, sociology, and ethnology). But, Foucault insisted, these new sciences did not consist in an analysis of human nature. Nor were they defined, like the "scientific" study of politics in the United States, as the application of statistical correlations and probabilities to the study of public opinion. Although they sometimes employed mathematics as a tool, the new human sciences did not differ from earlier studies by their use of quantitative methods. On the contrary, the new "sciences" were distinguished from earlier investigations by their focus on the grounds or conditions of the possibility of science itself. As the source, locus, or foundation of such knowledge, "man" was both the subject and the object of the new "human sciences." And in these "sciences" Foucault observed a dynamic interaction. As "man" attempted to make the material, unconscious, or social, interactive sources of his thought evident, he necessarily changed the unthought into something thought. As a result, he never got or could get to the origin or foundation of his own intellectual endeavor. There was *no* foundation, only interactions among essentially chance events.[63] Nevertheless, these events had an effect; by changing his self-understanding, these "sciences" changed the subject—i.e., "man"—himself.

Science did not consist of theoretical contemplation or active discovery of a preexisting reality, Foucault concluded. It was constitutive and productive, both a result and an expression or exercise of power. The abrupt shifts in the understanding of what constitutes knowledge in a particular area, he later explained in "Truth and Power,"

> are only the sign of something else: a modification in the rules of formation of statements which are accepted as scientifically true. Thus it is not a change

of content (refutation of old errors, recovery of old truths) nor is it a change of theoretical form (renewal of a paradigm, modification of systematic ensembles). It is a question of what *governs* statements, and the way in which they *govern* each other so as to constitute a set of propositions which are scientifically acceptable. . . . In short, there is a problem of the regime, the politics of the scientific statement.[64]

What counts as "science" in one time and place does not so qualify in another. In *The Order of Things*, Foucault explained, he had merely tried to identify and describe these different regimes; he had not tried to trace or explain their emergence or genealogy. He had "confused this too much with systematicity, theoretical, form or something like a paradigm."[65] It took him some time to isolate the central problem of power.

Once Foucault perceived that science itself was a form of power, he also saw it as an effect: "[I]n any society, there are manifold relations of power which permeate, characterize and constitute the social body, and these relations of power cannot themselves be established, consolidated nor implemented without the production, accumulation, circulation and functioning of a discourse."[66] This discourse should not be understood merely as a justification or rationalization for other forces—i.e., as ideology. It is genuinely productive of truth. The development of the modern sciences of psychology and sociology, especially the observational and organizational techniques that accompanied them, has led to a material increase in the power some human beings exercise over others. Merely keeping records—life histories, census data, observing and describing repeated behavioral patterns—enables officials, both private and public, to supervise and organize others according to norms. This supervisory power is neither economic nor legal, however; it is to a large extent a product of systematic observation and increased knowledge. The discovery that science constitutes a form of power thus led Foucault to reconceive the nature not just of science but of power itself.

Since the middle ages, he observed, Europeans have understood power, as Thomas Hobbes did in the *Leviathan*, as a matter of sovereignty. Those who have it can exercise it or transfer it to others—as if it were a piece of property or commodity. Having it is a matter of "right," made effective, in the final analysis, by the exercise of physical force. But, Foucault saw, this "juridical" understanding of power does not describe the "domination" analysts and doctors have over their patients, foremen exert over workers, or teachers have over students. The new forms of power that have developed along with industrialization, urbanization, and representative government are less visible than the power of the king, more complex, more indirect, and hence less easy to identify. Requiring the cooperation of the "subject," they are not simply exercised by some over others; they are, rather, essentially interactive.[67] But they are, precisely for that reason, more effective in shaping human behavior than mere orders backed by physical force.

The postmodern critique thus puts into question all the categories empirical theory takes for granted—facts, science, individuals, politics. Above all, perhaps, it challenges the notion of science as an act of knowing a preexisting state of affairs undertaken by a preexisting self—an act that is essentially different from politics. Foucault's version of postmodernism, at once the most political and the most challenging to political life, culminates in the simple identity "knowledge/power." Ever since Bacon such a link had existed, but the postmoderns say not what Bacon or Hobbes said—that we should pursue science for the sake of power—but rather that science is power, and not just in an instrumental sense. For the postmoderns the word "political" in the phrase "political science" is not an adjective designating the subject matter of study but an adjective specifying the essential character and operation of science itself.

CONCLUSION

Our survey of the various critiques of the scientific study of politics thus leads us back to the centrality of the question with which that critique began: what, if anything, *is* distinctively political? If Strauss and Rawls are right, it is impossible to identify or describe political phenomena except in moral terms. If Arendt is correct, political action itself produces individuals and is impossible to understand if the existence and importance of such are denied. Neither the understanding of the political as "the authoritative allocation of values for society," in the mode of empirical theory, nor the feminist/postmodern definition of "politics" in terms of all-pervasive power relations allows theorists to identify what is distinctive about *politics;* in using such overbroad definitions, these theorists lose the phenomena they purport to study.

As many of the essays in this volume attest, "empiricists" are now willing, even anxious to admit the centrality of historical change, particularity, and cultural differences in the organization and definition of human life. Science is no longer thought to be nonnormative or simply universal—in fact or in principle. The question that animates—or should animate—theoretical discussions of the nature and/or possibility of political science is no longer one of the difference between facts and values or between positive and normative approaches. The three critiques of contemporary empirical theory agree on this conclusion. The question now is, rather, whether there are any transhistorical or transcultural categories. Is science merely a reflection or expression of our particular culture and its values? Does the value-laden character of all facts and of all significant political inquiry render groundless the attempt to acquire knowledge about the way in which human beings both do and should organize their common lives groundless? Or can we recapture an understanding of ourselves and what is distinctively political by subjecting our own modern prejudices and theoretical frameworks to a thoroughgoing critique that is both historical and analytic?

NOTES

1. Cf. John G. Gunnell, *Between Philosophy and Politics: The Alienation of Political Theory* (Amherst: University of Massachusetts Press, 1986); James W. Ceaser, *Liberal Democracy and Political Science* (Baltimore: Johns Hopkins University Press, 1990), p. 72.

2. See David Easton, John G. Gunnell, and Michael B. Stein (eds.), *Regime and Discipline* (Ann Arbor: University of Michigan Press, 1995), p. 4; Gabriel Almond, "Clouds, Clocks . . . ," in *A Disicipline Divided* (Newbury Park, CA: Sage, 1990), pp. 32–65.

3. Cf. Eulau and Gunnell chapters in this volume.

4. Cf. Easton, *The Political System: An Inquiry into the State of Political Science* (New York: Alred A. Knopf, 1953), pp. 327–29, reference to Kuhn.

5. These movements have progressed so far and the recognition of their force has become so widespread that one is tempted to ask rational choice theorists and the other (few) remaining more or less orthodox positivists this paraphrase of Nietzsche's famous question: "Haven't you heard—positivism is dead?"

6. Hannah Arendt, *The Human Condition* (Chicago: University of Chicago Press, 1958); Alasdair MacIntyre, *After Virtue* (Notre Dame: University of Notre Dame Press, 1981); Leo Strauss, *What Is Political Philosophy: And Other Studies* (Glencoe, IL: Free Press, 1959).

7. Ronald Dworkin, *Taking Rights Seriously* (Cambridge, Mass.: Harvard University Press, 1978); William Galston, *Liberal Purposes* (New York: Cambridge University Press, 1991); Robert Nozick, *Anarchy, State and Utopia* (New York: Basic Books, 1974).

8. See especially Michel Foucault, *The Order of Things: An Archaeology of the Human Sciences* (New York: Random House, 1970); Jacques Derrida, *Of Grammatology* (Baltimore: Johns Hopkins University Press, 1976); Richard Rorty, *Contingency, Irony, Solidarity* (New York: Cambridge University Press, 1989); Iris Young, *Justice and the Politics of Difference* (Princeton: Princeton University Press, 1990).

9. Easton, *Political System*, chapter 1.

10. Ibid., p. 15.

11. Ibid., p. 23.

12. Ibid., p. 39.

13. Ibid., p. 66.

14. Ibid., pp. 65, 70–78, Gunnell, *Between Philosophy and Politics*, p. 72.

15. Easton, *Political System*, p. 53.

16. Ibid., p. 53.

17. Ibid., p. 55.

18. Gunnell, *Between Philosophy and Politics*, p. 57.

19. Easton, *Political System*, p. 58.

20. "I do not mean to maintain . . . that the ultimate usefulness of a general theory rests upon anything other than its correspondence with political facts" (Easton, *Political System*, p. 315).

21. For a survey of the nature of the challenge, see John G. Gunnell, *Philosophy, Science and Political Inquiry* (Morristown, NJ: General Learning Press, 1975); Eugene Miller, "Positivism, Historicism, and Political Inquiry," *American Political Science Review* 66 (1972): 796–817; Gunnell, *Between Philosophy and Politics*, 67–69, 70, 72, 73, 78, 79, 82, 85.

22. Easton, *Political System*, 234–37. For a fuller discussion, cf. John G. Gunnell, *Political Theory: Tradition and Interpretation* (Cambridge, MA.: Winthrop Publishers, Inc., 1979), pp. 4–8; *Between Philosophy and Politics*, 19–20.

23. Easton, *Political System*, p. 52.

24. Ibid., p. 221.

25. Ibid.

26. Easton, "Reply to Miller," pp. 280, 286; Easton, *Political System*, pp. 225–29; Gunnell, *Political Theory*, p. 7.

27. Easton, *Political System*, p. 60.

28. Ibid., p. 61.

29. Ibid., 110–11.

30. Ibid., pp. 115–16.

31. Cf. Gunnell, *Between Philosophy and Politics*, p. 78; Gunnell, *Political Theory*, p. 7.

32. The point Easton is making in his definition of the political is thus the same as that made by Robert A. Dahl and Charles E. Lindblom in *Politics, Economics and Welfare* (Chicago: University of Chicago Press, 1953). The difference is that they are quite clear in relating their allocative mechanism to recent political developments in the West and make no claim that their categories capture the nature of the political as such. (Cf. Dahl's persistence in commitment to power, *Modern Political Analysis* [Englewood Cliffs, NJ: Prentice-Hall, 1963], chapter 2.) Easton's conceptualization of the political, meant to be universalistic and value-free, is in fact constituted by silent reference not only to a particular politics but also to the particular politics of his own time and place, including the "value" commitments contained in the New Deal order. (For a similar quasi-concealed debt to the American political order, see Gabriel Almond's various formulations of empirical theory in, e. g., Gabriel Almond and James Coleman, eds., *The Politics of Developing Areas* [Princeton: Princeton University Press, 1960].)

33. Leo Strauss, "Epilogue," in Herbert J. Storing, ed., *Essays in the Scientific Study of Politics* (New York: Holt, Rinehart and Winston, Inc., 1962), pp. 306–7.

34. Cf. Hans Morgenthau, *Scientific Man and Power Politics* (Chicago: University of Chicago Press, 1946); Eric Voegelin, *The New Science of Politics* (Chicago: University of Chicago Press, 1953); Gunnell, *Between Philosophy and Politics*, p. 13.

35. On Arendt and Strauss's relations to Husserl and Heidegger, see *Hannah Arendt and Leo Strauss: German Emigres and American Political Thought after World War*

II, ed. Peter Graf Kielmansegg, Horst Mewes, Elizabeth Glaser-Schmidt (New York; Cambridge University Press, 1995). Strauss's own statement is to be found in "A Giving of Accounts," *The College* (April 1970): 1–5. On Arendt, see Elisabeth Young-Bruehl, *Hannah Arendt: For Love of the World* (New Haven: Yale University Press, 1982); *The Hannah Arendt/Karl Jaspers Correspondence,* trans. Robert and Rita Kimber (New York: Harcourt Brace and Jovanovich, 1992); Margaret Canovan, *Hannah Arendt: A Reinterpretation of Her Political Thought* (Cambridge: Cambridge University Press, 1992); Elzbieta Ettinger, *Hannah Arendt, Martin Heidegger* (New Haven: Yale University Press, 1995).

36. Cf. Strauss, *What Is Political Philosophy,* pp. 9–55; Strauss, "Epilogue," pp. 305–27; Thomas L. Pangle and Nathan Tarcov, "Epilogue," in *History of Political Philosophy,* 3rd ed. (Chicago: University of Chicago Press, pp. 907–34.

37. See Easton, et al., *Regime and Discipline.* We use quotation marks because Strauss denies that such studies are actually either empirical or scientific.

38. In this respect, Arendt's history of the political paralleled Heidegger's account of the history of Being, first discovered in Greece but then gradually covered over and forgotten in the subsequent theoretical development. Strauss's account of Greek thought was intended, on the contrary, to be a critique of Heidegger's account of the "origin" and subsequent "destiny" of the West. Cf. Strauss, *Natural Right and History* (Chicago: University of Chicago Press, 1953), pp. 28–34, 81–119, and Strauss, *On Tyranny,* ed. Victor Gourevitch and Michael S. Roth (New York: Free Press, 1991), especially p. 251.

39. Arendt, *Human Condition,* pp. 40–43.

40. The extent and character of that disagreement are indicated by Strauss and Arendt's differing characterizations of the criminal regimes in World War II. Whereas Arendt argued that "totalitarianism" was an altogether new, unparalleled modern development, Strauss suggested that the governments of Hitler and Stalin needed to be understood as modern variations of the ancient phenomenon of tyranny. Cf. Hannah Arendt, *Origins of Totalitarianism* (New York: Meridian Books, 1953); Strauss, *On Tyranny,* pp. 22–28.

41. See John Rawls, *A Study in the Grounds of Ethical Knowledge: Considered with Reference to Judgments on the Moral Worth of Character,* a thesis submitted to the Department of Philosophy of Princeton University, February 1950, p. 249.

42. Strauss, *What Is Political Philosophy,* p. 17.

43. Rawls, *Study,* p. 288. Also see pp. 226, 229–36, 269, 273–75, 286–92; Rawls, *A Theory of Justice* (Cambridge, MA.: Harvard University Press, 1971), section 9; and Rawls, "Outline of a Decision Procedure for Ethics," *Philosophical Review* 60 (1951): 189–90, 195–96.

44. Rawls, *Theory of Justice,* p. 3.

45. See ibid., p. ix.

46. Rawls, *Study,* p. 3.

47. See Rawls, "Outline," pp. 178–83; and *Study,* pp. 30–61.

48. Rawls, "Outline," p. 186.

49. Ibid.

50. Ibid., p. 188.

51. See especially Rawls, *Study,* pp. 186–92.

52. Sara Evans, *Personal Politics: The Roots of Women's Liberation in the Civil Rights Movement and the New Left* (New York: Knopf, 1979).

53. Kate Millett's ground-breaking analysis of *Sexual Politics* was based primarily on literary materials. More recent feminists such as Carole Pateman have applied the analysis more directly to modern political theory and practice. Cf. Pateman, *The Sexual Contract* (Stanford: Stanford University Press, 1988); and *The Disorder of Women* (Stanford: Stanford University Press, 1989).

54. Cf. Shulamith Firestone, *The Dialectic of Sex* (New York: W. Morrow, 1970); Simone de Beauvoir, *The Second Sex*, trans. H. M Parshley (New York: Random House, 1989), 597–628, 716–732.

55. Cf. the ambiguity in Easton on the status of the political system in *The Political System* and *A Framework for Political Analysis* (Englewood Cliffs, NJ: Prentice-Hall, 1967).

56. E. g., Susan Okin, *Women in Western Political Thought* (Princeton: Princeton University Press, 1979); Allison Jaggar, *Feminist Politics and Human Nature* (Totowa, NJ: Rowman & Allanheld, 1983); Carolyn Merchant, *The Death of Nature* (San Francisco: Harper & Row, 1980).

57. Sandra Harding, *The Science Question in Feminism* (Ithaca: Cornell University Press, 1986); *Whose Science? Whose Knowledge?* (Ithaca: Cornell University Press, 1991); Pauline Marie Rosenau, *Post-Modernism and the Social Sciences* (Princeton: Princeton University Press, 1992), p. 86.

58. For this reason, feminists have disagreed about whether they should ally themselves and their political analyses of both theory and practice with the postmodernists. Cf. Susan Hekman, *Gender & Knowledge: Elements of a Postmodern Feminism* (Boston: Northeastern University Press, 1990); Linda Nicholson, ed., *Feminism/Postmodernism* (New York: Routledge, 1990); Rosenau, *Postmodernism*.

59. Richard Rorty, *Objectivity, Relativism, and Truth* (Cambridge: Cambridge University Press, 1991), pp. 21–125; Rorty, "Foucault and Epistemology," in David Couzens Hoy, ed., *Foucault: A Critical Reader* (New York: Blackwell, 1986), pp. 41–50.

60. Rorty, *Contingency, Irony, Solidarity*.

61. Foucault, *The Order of Things*.

62. Ibid., pp. 217–21.

63. Ibid., pp. 344–87.

64. "Truth and Power," in *Power/Knowledge: Selected Interviews and Other Writings 1972–1977*, ed. Colin Gordon (New York: Pantheon Books, 1977), p. 112.

65. Ibid., p. 113.

66. "Two Lectures," in ibid., p. 93.

67. Cf. "Two Lectures," ibid., pp. 78–108; *History of Sexuality*, Volume I (New York: Random House, 1978), pp. 94–95.

8

The Misunderstood Promise of Realist Social Theory

Alexander Wendt and Ian Shapiro

The collapse of the 1960s consensus around positivism and logical empiricism in the philosophy of social science has generated a variety of responses. Of these, the turn to scientific realism is important because its proponents claim to justify the actual research practices of social scientists. Despite postmodern critiques, social scientists continue to search for causal mechanisms and assume that true statements can be made about the world, though they acknowledge many of the epistemological limits on any such inquiry. By seeming to justify existing scientific practice and shedding the pretensions of positivism, realism has moved toward the mainstream of the philosophy of the natural sciences.[1] It has even seduced hard-bitten quantitative social scientists.[2]

At the same time that many social scientists are embracing a realist philosophy of science, however, some also harbor inappropriate expectations of it. In particular, many proponents of neo-Marxism and structuration theory, both of which have played important roles in advancing realism in the social sciences, suggest that realism either entails their social theories or predisposes us to accept the truth of them. The notion that there is such a thing as "realist social theory" reflects a more general point about the nature of philosophy that we wish to reject: that its task is to generate knowledge about the world independent of the practices of science.[3] Although philosophies of science have implications for the social theories one may entertain,[4] even skeptical philosophies of science such as logical positivism do not imply commitment to any particular theories of politics and society.

An earlier version of this chapter was presented at the 1993 Annual Meeting of the American Political Science Association, Chicago, IL. The authors are grateful to David Dessler, Robert Grafstein, Jeffrey Isaac, Richard Miller, and Richard Rorty for their helpful comments.

Forgetting this fact may lead to unwarranted disenchantment with realism, to the extent that it is identified with the fate of its putative progeny. It may also leave neo-Marxism and structuration theory vulnerable to critique, to the extent that their proponents avoid developing substantive justifications for their arguments, opting instead for spurious appeals to realism. Realism is a philosophy of science, not a social theory, and it is important for both that they not be conflated.

We have two objectives in this chapter. The first is to explain part of the appeal of realist philosophy of science by showing how neo-Marxists and structurationists thought it would help them justify claims about unobservable social structures and power relations. Mainstream social scientists had long delegitimated such claims as "metaphysical" via surreptitious appeals to other philosophies of science, especially logical empiricism and interpretivism, and realism offers a useful corrective to these critiques. Our second aim is to show how many neo-Marxists and structurationists expected too much, obscuring the true relationship between scientific realism and social theory. Although from a realist perspective it may be legitimate to accept that unobservable entities and structures exist, realism does not in itself establish the existence of any particular unobservable phenomenon. That must be done through the normal practice of science. Unlike others who have argued for the existence of a disjunction between philosophies of science and social theories, however, we contend that realism's commitment to truth as a regulative ideal can be expected often to have the unmasking effects that radicals expect from social theory. It also has implications for naturalist theories of human interests that have not hitherto been fully appreciated. The promise of realist social theory, therefore, lies in encouraging social scientists to engage in critical social theory, not in privileging such theory a priori.

The chapter is organized into four parts. In the first we differentiate the domain of philosophy of science from that of social theory and within that context briefly define realism. In the next two we examine what neo-Marxists and structurationists, respectively, thought (mistakenly) they would gain from realism. Finally, we answer the question of why, given the limited significance for social theory that we are attaching to realist philosophical commitments, one should be a realist at all.

REALIST PHILOSOPHY OF SCIENCE AND SOCIAL THEORY

At the outset we distinguish philosophy of science from social theory. By the former we mean the interpretation of the content of science with a view toward establishing the warrants for valid claims about the world. Philosophers of science take the practices of scientists as their starting point and ask questions such as: "How should we think about those practices?"; "Do they give us access to the deep structure of reality?"; "By virtue of what are scientific theories true?"; "Should we regard the unobservable entities often posited in scientific theories as real or fictitious?"; "Is science privileged over other forms of knowledge?"; and, above all, "What are the *grounds* for different answers to these questions?" Nowhere in formulating such questions is it assumed that philosophers will themselves make causal claims about the structure of the world. Theirs is a second-order, or metatheoretical, enterprise; they take the claims of scientists as their data and decide how to interpret them.

Social theory is harder to define, but all social theorists are concerned with making first-order claims about the world or its causal structure. Consequently, their questions are quite different. Social theorists characteristically engage in one or both of two kinds of activity. First, they make ontological claims about the nature of society, institutions, and human agency. Here the concern is with such questions as: "Are societies reducible to the properties and interactions of their members?"; "If not, in what do the emergent properties of society consist?"; "To what extent are human beings intentional?"; and so on. Second, social theorists make substantive claims about the structure of specific societies. These may be empirical, normative, or both. Here the concern is with questions such as: "Is the capitalist mode of production the key determinant of other practices in occidental societies?"; "Is that mode of production exploitative?"; "Are there objective human interests, and if so what are they?"; "Is the failure of workers to overthrow capitalism due to false consciousness?"; and so on.

These two classes of questions—the philosophical and social theoretic—are quite different from one another. A proper understanding of realism's implications for social theory depends on recognizing this difference.

Realism, as we understand it, involves a commitment to two propositions, "realism about entities" and "realism about theories."[5] *Realism about entities* says that the entities found in mature scientific theories—electrons, preferences, or modes of production—exist independently of those theories, even if they are not themselves observable. This assumption leads to one of the distinctive marks of realism—namely, a non-Humean view of causation as the production of effects by unobservable causal mechanisms rather than as constant conjunctions.[6] Realism about entities is opposed by idealists and empiricists, who reject claims that unobservables actually exist and instead treat them merely as helpful fictions or intellectual constructs for organizing experience.

Realism about theories "says that scientific theories are either true or false independent of what we know: science at least aims at the truth, and the truth is how the world is. Antirealism says that theories are at best warranted, adequate, good to work on, acceptable but incredible, or what-not."[7] Realists about theories argue that we must assume the approximate truth of mature theories in order to explain the instrumental success of science in controlling the world,[8] although they disagree among themselves about whether this approach requires a correspondence or a causal theory of truth.

We do not defend either proposition here. What matters for our purposes is that neither supplies significant content to social scientific theories. The claim that one may be warranted in ascribing ontological status to deep social structures does not mean that social theories should include such structures, any more than the claim that one may be warranted in ascribing truth to social theories makes them true. Realist social theorists have often forgotten these points, neglecting some more subtle effects of realist commitments in the process.

REALISM AND MARXISM

The revival of realism in the human sciences was driven in part by scholars who saw in it the possibility of rejuvenating Marxist theory, to which realism did in fact contribute during the 1970s and early 1980s.[9] After showing what Marxists hoped to gain from this move, we argue that their hope was misplaced but that realism nevertheless does have a number of implications for the first-order arguments Marxists are interested in advancing.

Realism and the Revitalization of Marxism

In the early 1970s Marxism was on the defensive in Western intellectual circles. Following the events of the Prague Spring, diminishing numbers of Western intellectuals could endorse any variant of "actually existing communism," yet the Eurocommunist parties of Western Europe seemed to abandon much of what made a Marxian politics distinctive. To the extent that Marxism endured, it was more as a theoretical tradition than as a political program; Marxism offered conceptual tools for understanding the dehumanizing dynamics of capitalism but little, if anything, on the subject of transforming them. Yet even this social theory was problematic. Many of its best-known predictions—from the declining rate of profit, to the emergence of a radical and international working class, to the systemic collapse of the capitalist world order—failed to eventuate. By the same token, Marxism could not easily account for important phenomena that had emerged or endured in the century since Marx's death—the persistence of nationalism, the emergence of durable welfare states in the West, and the roles of ethnicity, race, and gender in oppression, exploitation, and conflict.

In addition to these substantive difficulties, Marxism was under episte-mological attack from two philosophical camps. One was that of the logical positivists, who had played an important role in the rise of behavioral social science during the 1950s and 1960s. Positivists found Marxism wanting in two main respects. First, in contrast to the positivists' insistence that causal explanations be based on relations among observed events, Marxists traf-ficked in an opaque language that made frequent reference to false con-sciousness, misunderstood causal mechanisms, and underlying tendencies. Second, despite the failures of some of their central predictions, Marxists seemed congenitally unwilling to reject Marxist theory. They pointed to an apparently endless chain of countervailing factors—war, imperialism, tech-nology, and "repressive tolerance"—to explain away theoretical failures. These problems seemed to mark Marxism as more religion than science, as Bertrand Russell argued in his *History of Western Philosophy*.[10] Positivist-in-spired behavioralists thought of Marxism as either an object of ridicule or as dangerous nonsense from which undergraduates should be protected and graduate students diverted.[11]

Marxism was also under philosophical assault by the proponents of in-terpretivism, or the "hermeneutic turn." Drawing on Wittgenstein's later linguistic philosophy, the speech act theory of J. L. Austin, and the work of Thomas Kuhn and Feyerabend in the philosophy of science, historians and social scientists such as Quentin Skinner, J. G. A. Pocock, Peter Winch, and Clifford Geertz attacked positivism and Marxism alike. In particular, they were skeptical of the Marxian claim that it is possible to develop a causal social theory by reference to which everyday understandings might be ex-plained as epiphenomenal distortions of actual states of affairs, the latter of which could only be understood by reference to Marxism's explanatory categories. In the interpretivists' view, beliefs, language, and expectations "constitute" social reality, and as such there is no deeper, more fundamental reality of which they are a product. The task of social theory must be to "elucidate" these phenomena, a charge implying something more than re-description yet less than causal explanation.[12]

What divided interpretivists from behaviorists was the possibility of a causal social science; what they shared in common against Marxists was hostility toward theories that referred to what was alleged to go on behind the observable realm of everyday life. Whereas positivists thought unob-servables had no place in scientific theories, interpretivists thought there was no basis for a causal theory that went beyond shared understandings. It was this bias toward the phenomenal that Marxists resisted, and it was because realism offered the possibility of escaping it that many of them found so attractive.

Whatever the difficulties with classical Marxism, these did not seem to add up to the proposition that there is no more to oppression in the modern world than what meets the eye. Epistemological prejudices that ruled out the possibility of mistaken beliefs about interests, unconscious intentions, and unobservable power relations seemed to throw the baby out with the proverbial bathwater. Realism was attractive to many Marxists because it spoke to this possibility. On the one hand, it provided a way of talking rigorously about unobservable causal relations; on the other, it could acknowledge that much of social reality is linguistically constructed without conceding the possibility of identifying the causes of relations of exploitation and domination. By creating room for both the explanatory and normative sides of Marxism, it helped fuel the revival of Marxist theory in the 1970s and early 1980s.

On the explanatory side, realism is compatible with the supposition that there may be a realm of causal mechanisms beyond the world of sense data, an unobservable domain of which the visible world is a product. Realists may concede that large parts of social reality are made up of the beliefs and conventional practices of agents, yet they insist there is no philosophical reason that those beliefs and practices cannot be explained in causal terms. Whereas interpretivists and positivists tended to see consensus about the meaning of language games and social practices as the beginning and end of social life, realists were open to the possibility that apparent consensus might mask hegemony and that, where it did exist, hegemony could be explained by reference to underlying conflicts over the production and distribution of goods. Realism seemed compatible with the Marxian idea of a material base, even if this were now conceived of less mechanically than in the classic statement of the theory.

On the normative side, realism is also compatible with the Marxian language of interests. From Aristotle to Hume to the young Habermas, moral naturalists had talked about interests, linking them to objective human purposes.[13] Ethical naturalism is a doctrine of hypothetical imperatives, in which one travels from "is" to "ought" via theories of human psychology or interests. In the naturalist scheme of things, ethics is a science of prudential judgments concerning how interests are best realized. A Marxian theory of human interests that privileges class is one kind of naturalist ethical theory. For realists it is possible that members of economic classes have common interests, defined as the conditions necessary for members' survival, and that these interests might be more basic than the interests individuals share in common qua individuals, qua members of other groups such as families or nations, or qua collections of genes. On the normative as well as explanatory front, then, realism could seem attractive to Marxists looking for a philosophical foundation to respond to the twin assaults of positivism and hermeneutics.

Unrealistic Marxist Expectations

Marxists have often not been as careful as they might at keeping separate the distinct, if compatible, enterprises of revitalizing Marxism and defending realism. This has occurred partly because the same persons have been engaged in both enterprises and partly because, like Marxists in social theory, realists in the philosophy of science defined their enterprise largely in response to the challenges of positivism and hermeneutics. Whatever the causes of this confusion, the result has been that many Marxists have expected too much from an appeal to realism and so have misunderstood its contribution to their project. Again, we take up explanatory and normative issues separately.

A commitment to realism implies that scientists can and do make warranted claims about an often unobservable reality, and in its causal theory of knowledge it supplies an epistemology by reference to which such claims can be evaluated. This relative openness differentiates realism from both positivist and interpretivist assumptions about explanation, both of which tend (for different reasons) to rule out the kinds of explanations Marxists advance, as we have seen. To that extent, a commitment to a realist philosophy of science is a necessary condition for vindicating Marxism. If realism entails that Marxism's basic explanatory arguments may be true, however, it does not entail that they must be true or even that they are probably true. Realism is not a social theory and as such does not entail the truth of any particular hypothesis about the causal structure of society.

This circumspection is lacking in some examples of Marxist social science, however laudable its substantive claims may be. A recent important statement of realist Marxism by John Lovering illustrates this tendency.[14] Lovering uses realism to intervene in the current crisis of socialist theory by attacking both the reformist market socialism of the British Labor Party and the fundamentalist socialism of more orthodox Marxists. He argues, on the one hand, that the Labor Party's analysis of British society neglects deep structures of exploitation and oppression in favor of surface events and forms and as such reflects a "flat," empiricist ontology (what we would call "antirealism about entities"); and, on the other, that the fundamentalist analysis assumes that the capitalist mode of production is the only significant deep structure in British society. Against the former, Lovering argues that:

> [c]ritical realism holds that reality, including society, is made up of deep structures which condition and make possible the "events" we observe in everyday experience and, importantly, in scientific research and reflection. Causal laws and "laws of history" consist in the constraints and enablements which the deep structures of a particular society entail.[15]

Against the latter, he argues that:

> [o]ne of the implications of adopting a critical realist perspective is that we must regard social practice as made up of relatively enduring structures. More than this, we must suppose a *plurality* of structures, which converge in a specific manner. This commits us to a particular kind of anti-dogmatism, not just because we as honest people can never be sure we have got the analysis exactly right, but because we must presume that the *ensemble of structures* in any concrete situation is a matter for investigation.[16]

From these claims, he concludes that:

> [c]ritical realism argues that we cannot construct "sciences of the concrete" without abstractions which identify deep structures (New Realism [reformist socialism]). Equally, it shows that we cannot have any faith in theories of abstract structures which do not specify the concrete conditions in which they are reproduced (Fundamentalism). The task suggested by critical realism is to develop a Marxist-informed social science which recognises the ubiquitous importance of capitalism, but is also sensitive to its relationship to other structures.[17]

His substantive claims may be correct, but they are not entailed by scientific realism.

Some realists with a sympathetic interest in Marxism, such as Jeffrey Isaac and Peter Manicas, acknowledge that a commitment to realism does not entail the truth of any particular social theory.[18] But they go too far in the other direction; they fail to appreciate that realism does have a variety of first-order implications for social theory. Although realism does not entail Marxist explanations, it is more than merely a condition of possibility for their being true. Indeed, one might say that Marxism and realism exhibit an elective affinity that centers on the potential unmasking effects of truth.

Insofar as scientists who practice their craft on realist grounds—that is, unconstrained by the artificial limitations of empiricism and interpretivism—seek to discover what is actually going on, they will seek to unmask any beliefs and practices that obscure the genuine character of social relations. Interpretivism yields no such unmasking agenda, as its proponents reject the possibility of getting at any objective truth beyond the realm of everyday belief. Positivists share with realists a belief that it is possible to get at the truth of things, but because their epistemology limits them to observables and constant conjunctions, social science practiced on positivist grounds will not unmask hidden causal mechanisms that structure the realm of appearances. To search, with the realist, for underlying causal mechanisms is not to establish any particular hypothesis about how and why causal mechanisms become obscured or even that they are often obscure.

For that reason, scientific realism does not entail that a Marxist, or any other, theory of ideology is true. But the commitment to discovering the truth about causal mechanisms means that realist inquiry may have the kinds of unmasking effects that Marxists seek, and to that extent it not only makes their work possible but motivates it as well.

Stronger arguments can be made about the normative side of Marxism. Starting with a parallel negative claim, we can say that realism offers the comparative advantage that it does not load the dice against certain types of claims about human interests, notably those that appeal to false consciousness, whereas the going alternatives do. Hard-boiled positivists resist the possibility of any objective claims about ethics, other than reporting the assertions of agents, and interpretivists resist just as resolutely the view that people can be ignorant of their genuine interests in ways that can be brought to life by scientific inquiry. Realism is open to the Marxian possibility via a naturalist ethics.

But Marxists have expected much more than this from realism for their normative claims. Roy Bhaskar, for example, believes that realism reveals a natural human interest in emancipation.[19] It is less than clear what the basis of this interest is supposed to be; Bhaskar seems to think it flows out of the fact that human beings are emergent from nature, evolving out of a natural world on which they remain dependent. Thus, he says, "[e]mergent phenomena require realist explanations, and realist explanations possess emancipatory implications."[20]

It is possible, however, to accept the emergence thesis without arguing that there is a human interest in emancipation.[21] It is surely not the case that emergent creatures must have an interest in further emergence or, issues of emergence aside, that emancipation from existing constraints is always and everywhere desirable.[22] Whether an actor has an interest in emancipation from a particular (set of) constraint(s) depends on its needs, the purposes served by the constraints in question, the available alternatives, and the costs of pursuing them. Whether or not there is a universal human interest in emancipation—or anything else—is therefore an empirical question having to do with how humans evolve, what forms their conflicts take, and how their circumstances are affected by events. Some interests probably persist over many circumstances and periods (perhaps even all), whereas others are more parochial and changeable. Nothing in realist philosophy of science tells us what these interests are or how alterable they may be, nor should we expect it to do so. Interests are empirical properties of entities, be they organisms, persons, genders, classes, states, or species. They are discoverable in principle via the methods of science, not via philosophical speculation.

Notwithstanding the lack of a direct connection between realism and a Marxian ethics, when we consider realism's commitment to the possibility of discovering objective knowledge, there is room for a more robust claim in the normative realm than in the explanatory domain. In particular, it is possible for a realist to defend the conditional claim that if there are any objective human interests, then there is a human interest in knowing the truth.

Notice, to begin with, that this claim can be interpreted in at least two ways, which we might dub "intrinsic" and "instrumental." The stronger, intrinsic reading might involve commitments to the proposition that authentic action is better than inauthentic action, that people prefer to act on the truth than not to do so. Such claims about human interests may or may not be true; they do not flow from a commitment to realism, any more than does the claim that there is a human interest in emancipation. They are best thought of as hypotheses, subject to the normal scientific constraints on all hypotheses; they have to be evaluated against the going alternatives by reference to the available evidence.[23]

Of more interest here is the instrumental reading of the claim that human beings have an interest in knowing the truth. If there are any objective interests, then it must be the case that people have an interest in genuine knowledge of what those interests are and of how to attain them. This is true whether the objective interest in question is a general human interest in emancipation or a parochial interest in not living in a house made of asbestos or near a carcinogenic electrical plant. Whatever our objective interests, we have an interest in knowing what they are and acting on them. In short, whatever our objective interests, it follows a fortiori that we have an interest in knowing the truth. Because realism holds out the possibility of acquiring ever closer approximations of the truth, it can deliver something of what Marxists once expected from a materialist conception of history, and to that extent it is more than a mere condition of possibility for a Marxian ethics. For this reason, although it is fair to say that Marxists have often expected too much from realism, it is also fair to say that some of their critics have granted too little.

REALISM AND STRUCTURATION THEORY

Structuration theory is concerned with the relationship between individuals and society, or the "agent-structure problem." Its proponents seek to avoid both methodological individualism and holism by treating the relationship between agency and social structure as a duality of irreducible but mutually constitutive and codetermining entities.[24] This argument first appeared in sociology but has since circulated throughout the social sciences, including political science. Its popularity is related to that of neo-Marxism, as Marx is often seen as an early structurationist, and many protagonists in debates about structuration (Bhaskar, Callinicos, Jon Elster, Anthony Giddens, Sayer) are also involved in those about neo-Marxism. But the agent-structure problem goes beyond neo-Marxism; all social scientific research requires some approach to it, and many structurationists are not Marxists. Nevertheless, like Marxists, many structurationists have unrealistic expectations of realism. As a result, they have avoided some hard questions about what counts as evidence for or against their social theory.

The Structurationists' Realist Hope

Structuration theory is an attempt to construct a social ontology that avoids the purported errors of the functionalist or deterministic structuralisms of Durkheim, Talcott Parsons, and Louis Althusser by giving a greater role to human agency without abandoning a role for deep structures in social explanations. As such, it is a claim about the nature of agents and social structures and how they are related (i.e., a social theory), not about the kinds of ontologies that may in principle be legitimate (i.e., a philosophy of science). Structuration theorists usually define their enterprise as an alternative to methodological individualism, so we begin there.

Methodological individualism involves commitment to the view that social explanations should be given microfoundations by being reduced to statements about the properties of individuals or their interactions. After years of marginalization in the social sciences outside economics, it has reemerged since 1970 with a vengeance in the form of social exchange, rational choice, and game theories; today it has a strong presence in sociology and especially in political science. Individualist explanations should be seen as hypotheses about the nature of social reality, and as such they should stand or fall on the basis of their ability to generate theories that can explain events. Instead, individualists have often defended their view by reference to the spurious argument that claims about unobservable deep structures are inherently "metaphysical" and as such should be ruled out of scientific theories.[25] In so doing, they rely on an antirealist philosophy of science to advance a preferred scientific theory.

The objections to individualism fall into roughly two categories. Substantively, it is claimed that the search for microfoundations cannot succeed because there is an inherently relational quality to social life. From cashing a check to getting married, human actions presuppose an institutional context that constitutes actors' identities and interests and the rules for their activity. Individualists will reply that these contexts themselves exist only by virtue of agents and their practices, an insight that structurationists themselves use vis-à-vis more hard-core structuralisms. But structurationists dispute the further individualist claim that this insight implies the possibility of reducing structural theories to observations about individuals or their interactions. Such reduction has not succeeded in any of the sciences and, if pressed to its logical conclusion, would argue against privileging the individual over its constituent subatomic particles. On a structurationist view, social structures are emergent phenomena, at least partly constitutive of rather than reducible to individuals.

Critics have also objected to the implications of individualism for political theory. Insofar as individualists treat the properties of individuals as exogenously given, they perforce ignore the types of power relations involved in their construction. This neglect leads ultimately to a view of politics in which power is reduced to individuals' coercive efforts to realize given interests, obscuring the role of power in forming perceived interests and subject-positions.[26] Indeed, vindicating this view of power has sometimes been an explicit motivation for methodological individualism. Critics do (or should) not deny that the individualist hypothesis about the power structure of society may be true. Rather, they argue that we should treat it as just that, a hypothesis, to be set alongside the rival hypotheses offered by more holistic theories. No theory should be ruled inadmissible merely because it does not conform to an empiricist epistemology, nor should another be defended merely because it does.

Both of these criticisms depend on the legitimacy of ascribing ontological status to unobservable relationships or mechanisms. Critics of individualism found in scientific realism a justification for such ascriptions and thereby undermined a key argument upon which individualists (mistakenly) relied. Individualism might still be true, but this must be established on the basis of an explanatory superiority over rival theories, not conformity with a philosophical doctrine.

It is less clear that structurationists saw in realism a way to guard the other flank of their advance—namely, their effort to construct a structural sociology that avoids the claimed pitfalls of structuralism—but realism makes a difference here as well. Critics of structuralism have argued that it reduces agents to mere "bearers" or "puppets" of structure and as such leads to a functionalist view that leaves no room for agency in accounting for social change. Giddens and Bhaskar both want to avoid this result, arguing that because social structures exist only in virtue of their instantiation in actors' knowledgeable practices, the potential for transformative agency exists. Realism contributes to the structuration argument through its requirement that the task of social science is the description of causal mechanisms, which are missing from many functionalist theories.[27] In the case of functionalisms that are structuralist in form (e.g., Althusserian Marxism), realism directs our attention to the purposes and practices of agents through which structures work their effects, thus furthering the structurationist search for a "middle way."

The Problem of Justifying Structuration Theory

Some structurationists, most notably Giddens, have gone about formulating their theory without explicit reference to a realist philosophy of science.[28] This approach is consistent with our argument below, though it does not clarify the relationship of realism to structuration theory. We know of only one scholar in the structurationist tradition, William Outhwaite, who argues that realism does not entail structuration theory.[29] The vast majority of structurationists, in contrast, have argued for or implied a one-to-one correspondence between their social ontology and realism. Some attempt to derive structuration theory from realism, in which case the two remain nominally distinct, but increasingly social theorists are speaking as if realism were a theory of agency and structure, in which case the distinction breaks down entirely. The pervasiveness of this view can be perhaps be seen from the following examples.

> [T]he new heuristic [realism] weds these perspectives [interpretive sociologies and structuralism] by arguing that social structure is simultaneously the relatively enduring product but also the medium of motivated human action. ... Thus, social structures (e.g. language) are reproduced and transformed by action, but they preexist for individuals.[30]

> In this regard the program of social scientific realism developed by Bhaskar is strikingly convergent with the "theory of structuration" developed by Anthony Giddens . . . , which similarly seeks to get beyond the idealism inherent in "interpretive sociology," and to articulate "new rules of sociological method" capable of identifying and explaining the material determinants of social life. Despite some differences of terminology, I believe that this convergence warrants my treating these programs together under the rubric of social scientific realism.[31]

> [R]ealism is a very rich philosophical theory which contains, among other things, an ontology, a theory of science, and a theory of social action.[32]

> The picture which critical realism offers is one in which individuals enter into a world which is not of their choosing, and once there they act in ways which partly reproduce, partly transform the structure of that world. But their understanding and ability to control these structural effects are severely limited, and social entities and structures are often reproduced as unintended effects of individual actions.[33]

> The point of critical realism is, of course, that there are both internal and external relations. However, what is of interest here is the nature of internal relations. How do internal relations as 'ideas' come into being? . . . The crucial theoretical problem is thus: in what way are the constitutive rules and social meanings of action produced, mediated, reproduced and changed?[34]

In further defending the importance of the ideas of realism and truthful correspondence in the social studies two claims need to be upheld and shown to be compatible: people are the agents of the social world; social structures causally condition human action. In order to do that, a theory of social action is needed that does justice to the socially constructing power of persons and the uneven distribution and effectiveness of their power.[35]

These threads are interwoven so that the new social realists are able to treat seriously the Durkheimian power of society over individuals and the Weberian powers of actors in society. To accomplish this, the authors utilize structuralist moves to de-functionalize Durkheimian thought, and interpretivist critiques of structuralism to send them back to the hermeneutic tools of inquiry. This is all undertaken with one eye on theories of human agency and the other on Marxian theories of class and state.[36]

The starting point of the scientific realist approach to international structural theory is therefore the recognition that state action is possible and conceivable only if there exist the instruments through which that action can in fact be carried out. Two sorts of instruments or media of action are necessary. First, nations must have resources. . . . Second, nations must have available rules. . . .[37]

I want to argue that to explain or account for social activity we must recognise that the social relations that provide the contextual conditions of interaction exert a structuring effect on it, and must be brought into the analysis to provide a fuller account. . . . Indeed the model of social activity that lies behind this version of realism is that it is intentional, meaningful, creative and evinces the 'knowledgeability' of the actors concerned.[38]

Many of these authors are drawing on the work of Roy Bhaskar, whose *The Possibility of Naturalism* has become something of a canonical statement of "critical social realism." It may be useful to examine his "transformational model of social action" more fully.

Nowhere does Bhaskar argue explicitly that the transformation model is entailed by realism. His claim is rather a "transcendental" one that tries to establish what must be true of the relationship between individual and society in order for us to have knowledge of them (he previously uses this transcendental method to establish the truth of realism). He begins by dispensing with methodological individualism, arguing that it reduces social life to statements about the properties of individuals and as such precludes social science altogether; because society exists prior to the individual and we do have knowledge about that society, methodological individualism must be wrong. He goes on to make short work (about ten pages) of three alternative resolutions of the agent-structure problem in sociology: Weber's, because of lingering individualism and empiricism; Durkheim's, because it neglects human intentionality and reifies structure; and Berger and Luckmann's, because it ostensibly ignores the fact that social structure is already made when agents engage in activity. The result is Bhaskar's own approach, which contends that agents and social structures presuppose one another and so must be ontologically distinct but mutually irreducible entities.

However much one agrees with the final product of the transformational model—and in general we do agree with it—it is doubtful that Bhaskar has succeeded in establishing its truth on transcendental grounds. His portrayal of methodological individualism is a caricature that ignores the fact that some of this doctrine's most important expressions do not reduce the social to the psychological. Game theorists, for example, aim to reduce society not only to the properties of individuals (as Bhaskar emphasizes) but also to their *interactions* (a fact he ignores), which establishes the possibility of an individualist social science. His portrayals of Weber, Durkheim, and Berger and Luckmann are not much better; in light of Bhaskar's rendition, for example, what is one to make of Berger and Luckmann's repeated emphasis on the extent to which people are born into existing institutional structures? More generally, as Albury, Payne, and Suchting point out, Bhaskar's argument depends on there being "universally recognized features of substantive social life" from which transcendental deductions can then be made, and it is precisely these that are at issue in debates among social ontologists.[39] The transformational model may be the best social ontology around, but it begs the question to deduce it from assumptions about social life that are themselves highly contested.

Whether or not Bhaskar's defense of the transformational model is adequate, however, it does not follow from realism. Bhaskar himself says only that the model is "grounded" in realism,[40] a statement that is consistent with either a necessary or sufficient condition interpretation. As the number of quotations above suggests, however, his followers have clearly concluded the latter—perhaps because of the conceptual nature of Bhaskar's argument, which seems to establish that the transformational model is the *only* social ontology that makes sense (although this would still not establish that realism entails structuration theory). Whatever Bhaskar's own intent, the conflation of philosophy and social theory here is virtually complete.

Realist philosophy of science does not entail structuration theory or any other solution to the agent-structure problem. One could imagine a realist argument for methodological individualism: social scientists should follow their natural science colleagues in trying to uncover causal mechanisms at ever more microscopic levels. Indeed, some individualist theories make more sense when interpreted in realist terms than when interpreted in empiricist terms. Do economists really believe that preferences are not real, even though they cannot be observed except as revealed in behavior? Conversely, one could imagine a realist argument for holism: the important mechanisms in social life—e.g., Durkheim's collective representations—exist entirely at the structural level. Or one could imagine a realist argument for interactionism: only this ontology satisfactorily analyzes the mechanisms or social processes by which both agents and structures are reproduced and transformed.

There is perhaps no better indication of the many feasible possibilities here than the diversity of social theories that self-proclaimed realist social theorists have themselves come up with: Harre's model tending toward psychologism, Layder's toward structuralism, Giddens's toward Harre's, Bhaskar's toward Layder's, and so on.[41] The differences among these "realist" models of agency and structure—and among them and their individualist and holist rivals—are differences about where the important causal mechanisms lie in social life. As such, we can settle them only by wrestling with the empirical merits of their claims about human agency and social structure. "How much of agency is in fact socially constructed?"; "How much of social structure is in fact reducible to individuals?"; "What determines the specific historical balance between the reproductive and transformative moments of social activity?";[42] and so on. These are in substantial part empirical questions.[43] They cannot be settled by armchair reflection.

The role of realism in these debates is twofold. First, a commitment to realism is a possibility condition for arguments about unobservable social structures; it protects their proponents against efforts by empiricists and interpretivists to delegitimate those arguments on epistemological grounds alone. This kind of philosophical inoculation is no small contribution in view of the corrosive effects of empiricist philosophy of science on social theory in the past. Natural scientists typically go about their business without any thought about philosophical concerns, and as such philosophers of natural science can treat scientific practices as independently existing data for their own inquiries. The situation is different in the social sciences, where practitioners, insecure about their epistemological status, have looked to philosophers for a model of how to "do science." In the past most of these philosophers have been empiricists rather than realists, and as a result social scientific practice has been heavily influenced by the "dos" and, especially, "don'ts" of their epistemological skepticism—even though empiricism in the philosophy of natural science has been concerned with interpreting rather than legislating scientific practices. A commitment to realism, then, "creates an analytically level playing field"[44] that gives social scientists the same freedom to think about unobservable structures that natural scientists have had all along in trying to explain events. Realism will have served its purpose in this regard when it does not need to be invoked at all—that is, when philosophy of science no longer contaminates social theory. Social theory should be left to sociologists, not philosophers.

Second, realism raises a serious challenge to structuration theory and its rivals. Students of social life who see themselves as realists—as opposed to interpretivists or postmodernists—are committed to the process of discovering the truth about the world, a process governed by an external reality constraint. If agents and social structures are in fact mutually constituting, codetermining entities, then a realist will want to know this. Being a realist, in other words, should encourage theorists to go beyond philosophical polemics and to develop theories about how the relationship between agents and social structures really works. By the same token, however, these theories must be evaluated against the going alternatives in light of available evidence. The advocates of individualism, structuralism, and structuration theory have all done a poor job of specifying the conditions under which their claims about the relationship of agency and social structure would be falsified. If individualists are unable to account for certain properties of agents, or structuralists for social change, these failures might be due to an inadequate conceptualization of the agent-structure relationship and as such might encourage the structurationist. But structuration theory, too, is only a hypothesis that must be falsifiable under certain conditions. "Transcendental" arguments for structuration theory might avoid (and be designed to avoid!) this problem, but for that reason they will not convince skeptics. In short, realism's commitment to the possibility of discovering truth cuts both ways: it allows structuration theorists to place their theory on the table, but it also subjects that theory to the same standards of scientific inference to which they would subject their rivals.

This is not to suggest that rational adjudication among social theories is easy. After all, ontological commitments are often a precondition for any empirical research project and as such are located in the "hard cores" of competing research programs, which are very hard to subject to decisive tests. Moreover, there may even be fundamental incommensurabilities among research programs that defy decisive adjudication. For a realist, these are empirical issues that can be settled only after attempts have been made to compare the explanatory merits of competing theories by reference to some common standpoint or question. We are not optimistic that this can be done, as part of the disagreement between rival social theories seems to center on which questions to ask, but conceiving of these theories as implying hypotheses about the constitution of the social world does reveal whether they provide substantive justifications—either by reference to comparative explanatory power or, at least, with respect to the evolution of their research programs over time. To the extent that a commitment to realism exposes spurious philosophical defenses of social theories, it may provide a positive incentive for proponents to develop better defenses. Philosophical scaffolding alone cannot support a social theory architecture.

THE HEURISTIC ADVANTAGES OF REALISM

Why, then, be a realist? One way to answer this question would be to supply a philosophical defense of realism from the ground up, to make the case that ultimately it is the most coherent view. We think this has been done.[45] Yet every philosophical defense has its vulnerabilities. There is no watertight epistemology, and some of realism's assumptions might be challenged, like those of any other view. Perhaps realists can answer every conceivable challenge and in the end prevail over the going alternatives. At a minimum we know this has not happened; there have been realists and antirealists for centuries, if not millennia. This fact suggests that realists will never "win," will never prove once and for all that they have it all right, will never vanquish the philosophical opposition.

In that case, why not take Richard Rorty's advice and stop talking about epistemological commitments altogether?[46] Rorty's central claim is that thinking of knowledge as a "problem" about which we ought to have a "theory" is a misconception based on the seventeenth-century predisposition toward viewing knowledge as an assemblage of representations. In making this argument Rorty distinguishes "systematic" from "edifying" philosophy. The former operates within a paradigm according to the rules of truth and reference it dictates. The latter, by contrast, rejects such rules and is not in fact concerned with truth at all. For edifying philosophers—and in the present century these include Wittgenstein, Heidegger, and Dewey—the point of philosophy "is to keep the conversation going rather than to find objective truth. Such truth . . . is the normal result of normal discourse."[47] His point is that once we recognize the dominant mode of post-seventeenth-century thinking, with its commitment to the search for apodictic certainty, as a "normal" discourse in this sense, we can give it up. Once we understand the Cartesian and Lockean confusions that generated it, we realize that this way of thinking is "optional"—and so is epistemology, "and so is philosophy as it has understood itself since the middle of the last century."[48]

Realists are not obviously vulnerable to the brunt of this argument because they are not preoccupied with the search for foundational certainty. For them all knowledge claims are corrigible, subject to revision as new knowledge accumulates and mistakes are discovered in existing scientific orthodoxy. Science advances by producing more knowledge, not by making knowledge more certain. The commitment to the existence of truth functions only as a regulative ideal in the conduct of science, a heuristic assumption that gives science its point. Realism is an interpretation of what scientists actually do, not a reconstruction of the logic of scientific inquiry. Realists point out that it is a condition for the conduct of all science that the scientist assumes that there are causal mechanisms "out there" in the world and that the task of science is to discover what they are. Scientists do not seek to offer philosophical proofs of the existence of an independent causal reality, but they nonetheless never doubt that this reality exists.

Still, the question remains: why be a realist? Social scientists should be realists because if they work within a framework of realist assumptions they are more likely to discover what is actually going on in the social world than if they do not. Marxists and structuration theorists, who have been troubled by the different limiting assumptions of positivism and interpretivism, have been right to think that a heuristic commitment to realism is more epistemologically open and less prejudicial of social inquiry than the alternatives., Realism makes possible and motivates the Marxian explanatory project of demystifying power relations, and it makes sense of the Marxian normative project of discovering and pursuing objective human interests. Realism also makes possible the structurationist project of finding unobservable social structures that constitute agents and their practices, though it also pushes that project to identify what would count against its claims.

Critics of Marxism and structuration theory have been right that defenders of these theories sometimes expect too much from realism. Marxists expect too much insofar as they hope that their explanatory categories will be vindicated by a commitment to realism. They also err in thinking that normative claims about emancipatory interests, let alone class-based emancipatory interests, follow from such a commitment. However, as our discussion of the unmasking potential of social science conducted from a realist standpoint reveals, it would be a mistake to conclude that a commitment to realism has no implications for first-order social theory. Furthermore, in the case of naturalist theories of ethics such as Marxism, a realist commitment makes possible an argument that human beings have an instrumental interest in the truth. Admittedly, this is a far cry from establishing the truth of Marx's evaluative prognostications, but neither is it trivial. For their part, structuration theorists also mistakenly think that realism somehow justifies their particular solution to the agent-structure problem. In both domains, realism's value lies in how it contributes to the task of producing plausible theories about how the world works, not in enabling social scientists to avoid having to develop and test their theories through the practices of science.

NOTES

1. See especially Richard Miller, *Fact and Method* (Princeton: Princeton University Press, 1984).

2. See, for example, Thomas Cook and Donald Campbell, "The Causal Assumptions of Quasi-Experimental Practice," *Synthese* 68 (1986): 141–80.

3. See R. Albury, G. Payne, and W. Suchting, "Naturalism and the Human Sciences," *Economy and Society* 10 (1981): 370.

4. As we argued in Shapiro and Wendt, "The Difference that Realism Makes: Social Science and the Politics of Consent," *Politics and Society* 20 (1992): 197–223.

5. The distinction is Ian Hacking's in *Representing and Intervening* (Cambridge: Cambridge University Press, 1983), p. 27. (Note that this is not parallel to the distinction above between philosophy of science and social theory.) The two propositions can be held independently of each other and, indeed, some realists argue that we should only hold one or the other. See Geoffrey Hellman, "Realist Principles," *Philosophy of Science* 50 (1983): 227–49, and Michael Devitt, "Aberrations of the Realist Debate," *Philosophical Studies* 61 (1991): 43–63.

6. For good contrasts of the two approaches to causal explanation see Russell Keat and John Urry, *Social Theory as Science,* 2nd ed. (London: RKP, 1982), Ernan McMullin, "Two Ideals of Explanation in Natural Science," in P. French, et al., eds., *Midwest Studies in Philosophy*, vol. 9 (Minneapolis: University of Minnesota Press, 1984), pp. 205–20, and Miller, *Fact and Method.*

7. Hacking, *Representing and Intervening*, pp. 27–8.

8. This argument has been most fully defended by Richard Boyd; see, for example, "The Current Status of Scientific Realism," in Jarrett Leplin, ed., *Scientific Realism* (Berkeley: University of California Press, 1984), pp. 41–82, and "What Realism Implies and What it Does Not," *Dialectica* 43 (1989): 5–29.

9. See, for example, David-Hillel Ruben, *Marxism and Materialism* (Atlantic Highlands: Humanities Press, 1977); Derek Sayer, *Marx's Method* (Atlantic Highlands: Humanities Press, 1979); Gregor McLennan, *Marxism and the Methodologies of History* (London: Verso, 1981); Keat and Urry, *Social Theory as Science;* Roy Bhaskar, *Scientific Realism and Human Emancipation* (London: Verso, 1986); and Andrew Collier, *Scientific Realism and Socialist Thought* (Boulder: Lynne Rienner, 1989).

10. Bertrand Russell, *A History of Western Philosophy* (London: Allen and Unwin, 1963), pp. 748–54.

11. For a characteristic example of ridicule, see Nelson Polsby, *Community Power and Political Theory*, 2nd ed. (New Haven: Yale University Press, 1983), pp. ix–xviii, 228–32.

12. The term is taken by Quentin Skinner from J. L. Austin.

13. This should not be confused with moral realism, which involves the claim that there are categorical imperatives that have the status of being facts and as such are true or false. A scientific realist can be opposed to or agnostic about this doctrine, and certainly one would expect most Marxists to resist it on the grounds that no propositions have the force of categorical imperatives. On moral realism see Geoffrey Sayre-McCord, ed., *Moral Realism* (Ithaca: Cornell University Press, 1988), especially the chapter by J. L. Mackie.

14. John Lovering, "Neither Fundamentalism nor 'New Realism': A Critical Realist Perspective on Current Divisions in Socialist Theory," *Capital and Class* 42 (1990): 30–54.

15. Ibid., p. 39.

16. Ibid., p. 41, emphases in the original.

17. Ibid., p. 48.

18. Jeffrey Isaac, *Power and Marxist Theory* (Ithaca: Cornell University Press, 1987); Peter Manicas, *A History and Philosophy of Social Science* (Oxford: Blackwell, 1987).

19. Bhaskar, *Scientific Realism and Human Emancipation*.

20. Ibid., p. 104.

21. See Shapiro, *Political Criticism* (Berkeley: University of California Press, 1990), pp. 230–63.

22. For illustration of the quixotic implications of the thesis that emancipation from existing constraints is always and everywhere desirable, see Roberto Unger, *Politics*, 3 vols. (Cambridge: Cambridge University Press, 1987). For criticism see Shapiro, "Constructing Politics," *Political Theory* 17 (1989), pp. 475–82.

23. For a speculative attempt to make the case that there is an intrinsic human interest in knowing and acting on the truth see Shapiro, *Political Criticism,* pp. 266–74.

24. The structurationist label and this particular wording of its claims are Anthony Giddens's; see *Central Problems in Social Theory* (Berkeley: University of California Press, 1979), and *The Constitution of Society* (Berkeley: University of California Press, 1984). Bhaskar's "transformational model of social action" is similar in structure, however, and as such we treat the two labels together. See *The Possibility of Naturalism* (Atlantic Highlands: Humanities Press, 1979) and *Scientific Realism and Human Emancipation*. For an overview of structuration theory in relation to its rivals, see Wendt, "The Agent-Structure Problem in International Relations Theory," *International Organization* 41 (1987): 335–70.

25. The classic articulation of this argument is by Karl Popper in *The Poverty of Historicism* (London: RKP, 1957); for a more recent example see Jon Elster, *Making Sense of Marx* (Cambridge: Cambridge University Press, 1985). For a nice discussion of how an empiricist philosophy of science underlies many calls for methodological individualism, see Jutta Weldes, "Marxism and Methodological Individualism," *Theory and Society* 18 (1989): 353–86.

26. For critical discussion see Steven Lukes, *Power: A Radical View* (London: MacMillan, 1974), and Jeffrey Isaac, "Beyond the Three Faces of Power: A Realist Critique," *Polity* 20 (1987): 4–31.

27. On this point see Jon Elster, *Explaining Technical Change* (Cambridge: Cambridge University Press, 1983).

28. Indeed, this has been quite self-conscious on Giddens's part; see Christopher Bryant, "Sociology Without Philosophy? The Case of Giddens' Structuration Theory," *Sociological Theory* 10 (1992): 137–49.

29. William Outhwaite, *New Philosophies of Science* (London: MacMillan, 1987).

30. Peter Manicas and Paul Secord, "Implications for Psychology of the New Philosophy of Science," *American Psychologist* 38 (1983): 408.

31. Jeffrey Isaac, "Realism and Reality: Some Realistic Reconsiderations," *Journal for the Theory of Social Behaviour* 20 (1990): 5.

32. Brian Fay, "Critical Realism?" *Journal for the Theory of Social Behaviour* 20 (1990): 34.

33. Lovering, "Neither Fundamentalism nor 'New Realism,'" p. 39.

THE MISUNDERSTOOD PROMISE   *187*

34. Heikki Patomaki, "Concepts of 'Action,' 'Structure' and 'Power' in 'Critical Social Realism': A Positive and Reconstructive Critique," *Journal for the Theory of Social Behaviour* 21 (1991): 226.

35. Christopher Lloyd, "Realism, Structurism, and History," *Theory and Society* 18 (1989): 471.

36. David Sylvan and Barry Glassner, *A Rationalist Methodology for the Social Sciences* (Oxford: Blackwell, 1985), p. 83.

37. David Dessler, "What's at Stake in the Agent-Structure Debate?" *International Organization* 43 (1989): 453.

38. Derek Layder, *The Realist Image in Social Science* (London: MacMillan, 1990), p. 163.

39. Albury et al., "Naturalism and the Human Sciences," p. 371.

40. See Bhaskar, *Scientific Realism and Human Emancipation,* p. 103.

41. For more on comparisons among structurationists, see Outhwaite, *New Philosophies of Social Science,* pp. 45–60.

42. Albury, et al., "Naturalism and the Human Sciences," p. 373.

43. See Harold Kincaid, "The Empirical Nature of the Individualism-Holism Dispute," *Synthese* 97 (1993): 229–47, and Wendt, *Social Theory of International Politics* (Cambridge: Cambridge University Press, forthcoming), chapter 4.

44. Robert Grafstein, *Institutional Realism* (New Haven: Yale University Press, 1992), p. 16.

45. See especially Miller, *Fact and Method.*

46. Richard Rorty, *Philosophy and the Mirror of Nature* (Princeton: Princeton University Press, 1979).

47. Ibid., pp. 5, 10–11, 376–89.

48. Ibid., pp. 33, 136.

PART IV

Contributions of Recent Theories

9

The Ferment of the 1950s
and the Development
of Rational Choice Theory

William H. Riker

The 1950s were a period of intense search for new directions in political science. World War II served, in my opinion, as a sharp dividing line between the old and the new. Immediately after the war a huge number of students entered the field. Many people in this cohort were motivated by reformist goals and a practical interest in public affairs. But as they studied traditional political science, they gradually became aware that neither basic theory nor its method, if such existed, was adequate for the simplest prescriptions for reform. In the absence of a discipline they could not diagnose institutional or constitutional problems, and so, of course, they could not prescribe. Consequently, this large new generation provided the impetus for the search for a new kind of political science.

Perhaps the neatest example of the problem was *Toward a More Responsible Two-Party System* (1950), the report of the Committee on Political Parties of the American Political Science Association (APSA). This report, published with the association's imprimatur, presumably displayed the best political science of the immediate postwar period. It was clearly in the tradition of Woodrow Wilson, one of the founders of our profession. Its intellectual parent, E. E. Schattschneider, was without question one of the very best political scientists of the era. Yet the report was thoroughly unsatisfactory. On the descriptive level, it failed to explain why the presumably irresponsible system existed, so it was difficult to see how it might be replaced, except by waving a magic wand. Certainly, there was no hint that convergence to the median voter's preference might create an equilibrium that could not be displaced short of an extremely complicated reordering of politicians' incentives. Indeed, there was practically no discussion of politicians' incentives. Bad as the report was as description, it was vastly worse from a moral point of view. Its implicit purpose was to sharpen the partisan division as it then existed and thus to ensure that the winners kept on winning. As the status quo was then in favor of Democrats, the report should be regarded as a plan for a political system in which Democrats would always win and Republican always lose. Had the report been written in another era, it might not have had such an egregiously partisan effect, but there could be no doubt in 1950 that it was a proposal to elect Democrats forever. Perhaps most shocking, however, was the fact that, although some people saw that the report was bad description, almost no one saw that it was profoundly immoral—a sad commentary on the state of the profession.

At the same time that this large new cohort entered the profession, the field itself lost several of its main resources for reorientation, resources that, given a chance, might have speeded up the development of a discipline. For example, the University of Chicago School of Political Science, which Charles Merriam developed in the 1920s and 1930s, promised leadership for innovation; but under what I consider the almost Satanic influence of Robert Hutchins, for many years the president of Chicago, this brilliant school scattered to the winds. Hutchins made no effort to replace its brightest stars, he drove out its creative young talent, and he made no place for its finest products, half a dozen of whom were subsequently presidents of the ASPA, one a Nobel Prize winner. Hutchins did bring David Easton on board in the late 1940s. Easton's great contribution, quite in the spirit of Merriam's department, was to analyze the defects of the existing political science—precisely the political science that Merriam's department had been trying to replace. But while Easton pointed to new directions, Hutchins, acting with his arrogant and pretentious humanism, replaced this great department's faculty with his pet philosophers, who cared nothing about political science as a descriptive discipline and did not even perceive that philosophy in the absence of science is mere wordplay and cannot be used even for its intended purposes.[1]

Some of the products of that great department survived to contribute to the ferment of the 1950s. But with the core gone, the individuals dispersed—with surprising regularity to locales where they could not influence political science very much—and the best tradition of the 1920s and 1930s was lost.

Harvard was another department that might have served as an intellectual bridge between the 1930s and the 1950s, especially if it had been in competition with the Chicago tradition. But Harvard devoured itself with internecine warfare between two inferior scholars.[2] As a result, some potential bridge builders were driven out, and no intellectual innovation survived.

The net effect of this sharp intellectual and generational break was that scholars coming of age in the 1950s were cut off from tradition and so were forced to experiment with a variety of disciplinary approaches for political science. Perhaps the experimentation was itself useful. But I think it might have been more focused if it had been tied in with an existing intellectual tradition. Let me give an example in the use of statistics. There is, of course, no reason to glorify statistical versatility for its own sake. Nevertheless, statistical devices are useful for systematic testing of generalizations, and they do allow one to escape from the trap of anecdotal evidence. In the 1960s, as survey research became commonplace in our field, many graduate students learned elementary statistics, if not at their home universities, then at the summer program run by the InterUniversity Consortium for Political Research at the University of Michigan. Yet that type of study, which seemed so new in the 1960s, was practiced at Chicago in the 1930s. In 1935 Harold Gosnell published a paper in the *American Political Science Review* that used both regression analysis and factor analysis. In the mid-1950s his student, V. O. Key, published a simple textbook on the subject, intending to make statistics palatable to arithmetically uninstructed graduate students. That device didn't work, however, because users of statistics need to know much more about what they are doing than what Key offered. Herbert Simon made important contributions to the study of regression analysis, but this work primarily affected the development of econometrics. Real usage in our field did not develop until some graduate students began to study econometrics at a much more complicated level, about thirty years after Gosnell published his fine essay. Had the sharp intellectual break not occurred, I suspect, many departments would have been teaching statistics on a regular basis by 1950. As it is, plenty of students still come out of graduate school wholly incapable of judging the quality of an argument when the hypothesis is supported by statistical evidence. That is unfortunate, because they are cut off from many of the exciting developments in the field.

The main attempts to establish a political science discipline in the 1950s were pluralism, behaviorism, and rational choice.[3] Pluralism in the Chicago tradition was carried over at Columbia by a Chicago product, David Truman, whose main work, *The Governmental Process,* echoed the title of Chicago pioneer Arthur Bentley's *The Process of Government,* the first work in the pluralist tradition (1907). Truman became an administrator, but the pluralist tradition was developed and carried forward by Robert Dahl at Yale, where it flourished in a somewhat different form. Behaviorism swept the profession in the 1950s, emanating mainly from social psychologist Angus Campbell and his political science protégés Philip Converse, Warren Miller, and Donald Stokes. Other leaders of the behaviorist movement were

Heinz Eulau and Karl Deutsch. Finally, the rational choice movement was initially led by Herbert Simon. It was nourished by several economists, most notably Duncan Black, Mancur Olson, James Buchanan, and Gordon Tullock, but I believe our group at Rochester, though not formed until the 1960s, was the core of the political science part of the movement.

I do not intend to discuss the relative merits of these approaches except to point out the features that made two of them unacceptable to me.

Pluralism assumes social outcomes are a vector of the interests relevant to some social choice. This is, I think, a valuable insight relative to the older political science, for it emphasizes the importance of variations in tastes and values. Nevertheless, the paradigm offers only the scholar's intuition to explain how these tastes are amalgamated—that is, to state the direction and force of the vector. Indeed, pluralism does not even offer a good way to identify what tastes are. Thus, pluralism allows us to explain outcomes in terms of some assumed tastes, but it does not allow us to test our assumptions about tastes or to factor in the significance of rules or institutions for amalgamation. Yet rules and institutions are significant because we cannot judge the vector of tastes unless we know how the rules for calculating it work. An example from our sister discipline of economics is revealing: the outcome from the amalgamation of tastes under one set of rules—say, an auction market—is quite different from the amalgamation of tastes under another set of rules—say, oligopoly. The lesson to be learned from these merits and defects of pluralism is, then, that political science ought to concern itself with the careful identification and interpretation of both tastes and institutions.

Behaviorism, which was initially developed by comparative psychologists to study the actions of creatures whose thought processes are different from those of humans, has the great merit of avoiding anthropomorphism because it describes only externally observable action, not thoughts or motives. Its great attraction for political scientists probably was that it was supposedly value-free. Thus, it helped keep the scientist from unconsciously attributing his or her own tastes and his or her own interpretation of values to the subjects observed. At the same time it suffered from two serious defects. First, by describing only external action, it omitted a huge portion of known human behavior—namely, the internal, unobservable behavior of choosing between courses of action. Second, it offered no way to interpret alternative institutions, because these are, of course, the product of internal choice. The lesson to be learned from the merits and defects of behaviorism is that the analyst ought to be careful to avoid the casual, causal attribution of the meaning of actions to the actors observed. Rather, the analyst ought always to test his or her interpretation of meanings against possible alternatives. It is also important to relate actions to intentions and to test out this relationship.

The rational choice model has all the advantages and none of the defects of the two previous approaches. Its two main sources developed during the 1950s both derived from economic analysis. Anthony Downs's *An Economic Theory of Democracy* (1957) introduced political scientists to expected utility theory; Duncan Black's *The Theory of Committees and Elections* (1958, though based on papers written in 1946 and 1947) introduced political scientists to notions of preference, transitivity, and equilibrium outcomes. Especially important, I think, was Black's conclusion that the same tastes resulted in different equilibria when amalgamated by different rules. Farquharson's *Theory of Voting*, which introduced the idea of strategic voting, was written in 1957, though not published until 1969. Herbert Simon's *Models of Man* (1958) introduced notions of bounded rationality and demonstrated various applications of the rational choice paradigm. Game theory was first introduced, in a special application, by Shapley and Shubik (1954), made readily accessible by Luce and Raiffa (1957), and applied politically in my *The Theory of Political Coalitions*, Thomas Schelling's *The Strategy of Conflict*, Mancur Olson's *The Logic of Collective Action*, and James Buchanan and Gordon Tullock's *The Calculus of Consent*. Though it took a decade or so for these books to be absorbed by the profession, it was possible in 1973 to write a textbook about the rational choice paradigm (Riker and Ordeshook, *An Introduction to Positive Political Theory*). Since then applications have proliferated.

The main features of the paradigm are as follows:

1. There is an identifiable set of possible outcomes and an identifiable set of possible actions leading to these outcomes.
2. Participants are able to order their preferences over these outcomes transitively.
3. Actors choose among alternative actions so as to maximize expected utility over outcomes.

There are a number of technical controversies about these assumptions, but for political research they can usually be resolved satisfactorily.

About the assumption concerning sets, one dispute concerns whether they include all conceivable outcomes and alternatives or only some humanly manageable number. This is the dispute over bounded rationality, hotly argued but in practice easily resolved. The analyst need only assume that the sets comprise the alternatives and outcomes that participants know about. Of course, clever people often expand this set, but that means simply that reanalysis is in order. The assumption about utility maximization is also hotly disputed, mainly on the basis of Maurice Allais's paradox. Whether the criticism is justified seems to me to be an empirical question to be resolved on a case-by-case basis. The most obvious alternative to utility maximization is to assume that actors minimize regret. If so, then the assumption probably ought to be restated: "Actors choose among alternatives so as to maximize according to some principle of utility over outcomes." The problem then is to ascertain what principle actors appear to be using. On the whole, however, these issues seem trivial alongside the potential achievement of the paradigm.

In order to illustrate the potential of this approach, I will summarize two recent studies: Keith Krehbiel, *Information and Legislative Organization* (1991), and Bruce Bueno de Mesquita and David Lalman, *War and Reason* (1992). In the first book, the problem is: what intentions must be attributed to legislators for them to produce the legislative organization we observe? In the second, the problem is: given various assumptions about tastes, what equilibria follow, and are those equilibria in accordance with observation? Behavioralists cannot answer such questions because they cannot investigate intentions and motives. (For example, behaviorists do well when attributing votes to party identification in a two-party system; but, because the existence of multiple parties allows for sophisticated voting, behaviorists cannot capture complicated intentions of that sort.) Similarly, pluralists cannot deal with these questions because they have no systematic way of investigating how intentions come together to produce equilibrium outcomes.

Rational choice models can deal with these questions because they use the standard method of scientific investigation. In the rational choice model, there is first of all a theory. The analyst infers theorems or hypotheses from the theory, then tests the theorems against observations of nature. If the observations do not falsify the theorems, then the analyst has some confidence that the deduced theorems are correct and that the theory is also. If the tests do not work out, then it's back to the drawing board.

To begin with Krehbiel's work, he notes the existence of two theories of organization of legislatures, which are based on two different assumptions about legislators' intentions in structuring the organization. The dominant assumption is distributive in the sense that legislative organization (e.g., rules, committees, etc.) is said to maximize the interest-group benefits that individual legislators are able to get from them. Scholars as diverse as Lowi, McConnell, Brady, Mayhew, Weingast, and Shepsle use this assumption. An entirely different theory is that legislatures set up committees for the sake of learning about policy from specialists and establish rules to facilitate the incorporation of information into alternatives that produce the hoped-for outcome. Scholars in this tradition are Luce, Cooper, Fenno, and Austen-Smith.

Krehbiel attempts to choose between these assumptions, perhaps not so much to say one is right and the other wrong as to say how they should be used and combined. For this purpose Krehbiel makes two even more fundamental assumptions: 1) the majoritarian postulate—that objects of legislative choice in both the procedural and policy domains must be chosen by a majority of the legislature; and 2) the uncertainty postulate—that legislators are often uncertain about the relationship between alternatives and outcomes. That is, they do not know what a particular legislative action will produce in the way of effects. The main question, then, is whether theories embodying these two postulates yield empirical expectations different from those yielded by theories in which these postulates are contradicted. Because the two postulates initially appear acceptable, if theories embodying them are empirically supported, then we can have some confidence that such theories are better descriptions than those that contradict them.

Distributive theories do in one respect deny majoritarianism because they assume that committees and rules are designed to facilitate gains from trade (i.e., logrolling, etc.). Predictions from such theories include: committee assignments are governed by self-selection, and committees are composed of homogenous high demanders (i.e., members who seek a lot of the benefits the committee can assign) or preference outliers (i.e., members whose interests are far from those of the median member of the legislature on the subject of the committee's jurisdiction); also, to ensure gains from trade, committees (especially those whose jurisdictions cover highly particularistic policies) will be granted favored procedural status (e.g., closed rules).

Informational theories, by contrast, assume a legislature that does not know what public reaction to alternative policies will be. It collects information through committees and engages in debate to inform the members what the effect of their actions will be. Under this theory committee members will not predominantly be preference outliers or high demanders but instead will be distributed over the range of the policy spectrum. (When outliers are on a committee, they are presumably individuals who can specialize on the committee's subject at low cost.) Furthermore, restrictive rules will be granted most often to nonoutlying heterogeneous committees.

So far I have recounted alternative theories according to Krehbiel and mentioned several hypotheses derived from them (derived, of course, in a much more careful way than I have space to set forth). Now for the evidence. At least for the single Congress that Krehbiel studied in detail, only two committees comprise homogenous high demanders and preference outliers. As for restrictive rules, he found that the greater a bill's distributive content, the less likely it was to be granted a restrictive rule; the more outliers on a committee, the less likely a restrictive rule; the more heterogeneous the committee, the more likely a restrictive rule; and the more Republican (i.e., minority) co-sponsors (i.e., the more heterogeneous the support), the more restrictive the rule. Altogether, the evidence is substantial that the need for information is an important feature of legislative organization.

Krehbiel studied only one Congress; it is, of course, necessary to repeat his work on other Congresses, on other legislatures, and in other ways. Nevertheless, by this work he has demonstrated that there is something wrong with the ruling theory. The ultimate outcome may well differ from his statement about information and organization, but there can be no doubt that this research has increased knowledge in a way that would not have been possible with either the pluralist or behaviorist assumptions. For example, the leading pluralist writer, Theodore Lowi, simply lists ways in which interests supposedly dominate distributive policies. But such a listing does not yield a theory that leads to inferences about how this influence provides for domination. Though rational choice writers (e.g., Ken Shepsle and Barry Weingast) have made the same distributive assumption, they have done so within the rational choice model, which is why Krehbiel was able to set up a dialogue on the whole subject.

I turn now to the work by Bueno de Mesquita and Lalman. It is especially interesting for this discussion because it was intended to be an exemplar of the rational choice procedure in the study of politics.

These authors start with what they call "the international interaction game." It is a two-sided, sequential choice game in which the first move requires side A to demand something—or not to demand anything—from the other side, B. If A demands, B has the choice of making a counterdemand or acquiescing. If A does not demand, B has the choice of making its own demand or not. If neither demands, the game is over at the status quo. If B acquiesces, the game is over. But if either side counterdemands or demands, the game continues, through the use of force or not, as the case may be. The possible outcomes, besides the status quo and acquiescence by one side or the other, are: capitulation by one side to force by the other; war; or negotiation. Both sides have preference orders over these outcomes. Some preference orders are universal: for example, A always prefers the status quo over acquiescence to B. Other preference orders are specific to types of players. Thus, if A is a true "dove," it prefers capitulation to B over engaging in a war initiated by B.

The solution to this game consists of backward induction up the game tree. Suppose at node *k* the choices for the true dove, A, are to capitulate or to fight a war initiated by B. Because A's preference between these alternatives is capitulation, we know, even without A's actual choice, that if node *k* is reached, the outcome of the game will be A's capitulation. Given a full set of preferences, it is possible to arrive at a subgame perfect equilibrium—that is, the equilibrium such that at each node *k* the choice made by the participant who chooses at that node is one that leads to the highest expected value that the participant can reach from the node.

The theorems inferred from this game are of the form: "Given the tastes of the participants, a particular equilibrium occurs or one of several possible equilibria occur." Bueno de Mesquita and Lalman use this game to resolve some extremely important issues in the study of international relations.

Probably the most important is the clash between the theory of realpolitik and the theory that nations are driven in international affairs by their domestic concerns as well as their international ones. In the theory of realism or neorealism, it is asserted that makers of foreign policy are motivated by concerns of their international security—that is, they wish to get the most favorable possible outcome in a world of constant threats. But in the domestic concerns theory, a foreign policy maker may be concerned about, for example, the potential political cost domestically of fighting or losing a war.

To choose between these theories, the authors first assume that both sides practice realpolitik and have the appropriate preference orders for that orientation. They also initially assume that both sides have complete information about their own and the other side's abilities and preferences. In such a game, it turns out that war is impossible. If, however, the same game is played by foreign policy makers with various domestic concerns, it turns out that war is possible, even when the players have full information about each other's tastes. Because war is often observed in nature, the fact that it cannot occur under the realist theory but can occur under the domestic concerns theory casts some doubt on the realpolitik version of international interaction.

But, of course, the participants may not have perfect information. What then? In the incomplete information form of the realist version of the international interaction game, participants never acquiesce to another's demand. The databases the authors use to test out their theories are the several bases (collected by other scholars) about wars and violence since, typically, 1815. And in this data set the authors find more than 100 cases of acquiescence out of about 700 cases of demands. So the observation of nature does not support the realpolitik version of the game but does support the domestic concern version because acquiescence is an equilibrium outcome in many cases.

This seems to me a remarkable result. For one thing, it settles a philosophical dispute that is at least as old as Thucydides. Even more important, it settles a practical issue about how to study international politics today. There is much more in this book, as in Krehbiel's, than I have the space to summarize, but I hope I have conveyed the flavor of the analyses.

The books by Krehbiel and Bueno de Mesquita and Lalman demonstrate that, in a pair of contrasting but plausible assumptions about human intentions, empirically one of the pair is quite doubtful. The fact that these are assumptions means that they structure the investigator's theory; they go to the very heart of the research enterprise. They affect—indeed, often dictate—what hypotheses to infer, what facts to gather to test hypotheses, and what applications are indicated and possible. The fact that these assumptions are contradictory means that previous work that uses either one or the other of a pair is suspect, because there has been no good evidence on or testing of the rival assumptions about actor's intentions. Consequently, a large amount of scholarly energy has been dissipated in dispute rather than directed toward discovery.

Such dispute is particularly frustrating because until now, at least, the only basis for defending assumptions about intentions has been the analyst's intuition. "My particular assumption about actors' intentions is valid," says investigator A, "because that's the way people are." Investigator B responds: "Well, your evidence is your intuition and for some reason—bad education, intellectual aridity, poor observation—your intuition is wrong. In fact, people are quite otherwise, and I know it because my superior intuition tells me so." When scholars in the dispute set hypotheses from their intuition, gather data, and then test the data for statistical association, it doesn't make intuitions believable, no matter how strong the statistical association, if neither analyst can offer a good reason for the association's being what it is.

This is just another way of saying that it takes a theory to beat a theory. And that is just what the rational choice paradigm provides: a way to study intentions fruitfully. The trick is to construct a theory into which alternative assumptions about intentions can be inserted. Using the theory allows the analyst to infer what human actions, constitutional structures, or outcomes of conflict ought to be expected if one or the other of the assumptions is probably valid and the theory is probably true. If the expectations differ from each other, from then on it is a matter of collecting evidence about which expectation is best realized in nature. The collection of evidence is the most time-consuming and labor-intensive part of the job. But the evidence is useful only when there is something to test. The purpose of rational choice theory is to make possible tests about intentions in conflict.

It might be thought that other schools could also make such tests on behavior without making any assumptions at all about intentions or about how people relate their intentions internally. But these tests would be reliable only for the behavior tested in the particular case. With no knowledge of intentions or how they might be calculated, it would be impossible to extrapolate from the tested case. One could identify the interests in a particular situation and show how they in fact combine. But without some theory of combination, which is just what the rational choice model is, then the application of the combination to the next situation would be inappropriate.

Of the three main approaches that developed in the 1950s, when it became evident that a new approach was desperately necessary, it seems clear from these examples of recent work that only the rational choice model is capable of satisfying the requirements for a scientific political science.

I conclude with a small memoir. In 1953 I published a teaching book about U.S. government. It wasn't a bad book for the era. Indeed, about ten years later Ted Lowi wrote a review of teaching books in the previous thirty years and, had you not read his critique carefully, you would probably have concluded that he said mine was the best. I won't dispute with him about that. Indeed, his review kept the book alive and producing income for another fifteen years. But I can say that I felt a deep sense of failure when the book was finished. I asked myself: is there a sentence in it that is true, true in the sense that it derives from a theory and has survived attempts at falsification? I had to conclude that there were very few, if any. I began a search for another path and discovered Kenneth Arrow and Duncan Black and social choice theory. About the same time Easton's great book on systems theory was published, I learned of game theory. Then I came across the work that Herbert Simon was doing. All this started me out on a new path and, considering where it has led me and the profession, I am glad I took it.

NOTES

1. Editor's note: I believe Riker refers here to the Straussian philosophers.

2. Editor's note: I believe Riker refers here to the disputes between William Yandall Elliot and Carl Joachim Friedrich.

3. I suppose I ought to include Marxism in this list, but I can't take seriously any wholly deterministic system. Deterministic philosophies are inhumane in that they deny human decision. Since the purpose of a social science is to describe how people do make choices, I ignore Marxism as a trivial sideshow of that era.

10

Theory on the Prowl

Russell Hardin

THE FALLACY OF COMPOSITION

The principal theoretical move in modern microeconomics is the explanation of collective results by reference to individual incentives for choice—the explanation of macro results from micro behavior. For example, prices are macro phenomena that follow from micro choices of consumers and producers. Much of political reasoning historically has been at the collective or aggregate level. It has often been assumed that values at the aggregate level merely reflect values of individuals, as though there were no complications in aggregation. For example, the traditional group theory of politics from Arthur Bentley to David Truman assumed that what the individual members of a group want is what the group, acting in the aggregate, will attempt to provide. This is a very old assumption, going back at least to Aristotle. In the case of traditional group theory, the inference is wrong. Indeed, it may be the most pervasive and destructive mistake in all of social theory.

Rational choice theory is the use of argument from individual incentives to collective outcomes, of micro motives to explain macro behavior.[1] Economic reasoning has been with us for a very long time in many contexts,

This chapter expands on remarks made for the Midwest Political Science Association, Plenary Session: "The Interdisciplinary Foundations of Political Science," Chicago, April 18, 1991, and on part of my paper, "Modern Political Economy: Individualist and Structuralist," presented on the discussion panel, "New Directions in Political Economy," American Political Science Association meeting, Washington, D.C., August 29–September 1, 1991. A companion, expanding on other parts of the earlier efforts, is "The Normative Core of Rational Choice Theory," in Uskali Maki, ed., *The Economic Realm: Studies in the Ontology of Economics* (forthcoming). I wish to thank Kristen Monroe and an anonymous referee for their suggestions on the paper and participants in the 1991 panels for comments. I also thank Paul Beck and Stephen Elkin for organizing the panels and the Andrew W. Mellon and Russell Sage Foundations for generous general support.

but the first big, compelling rational choice theory of politics was, perhaps, that of Thomas Hobbes.[2] Hobbes argued that all would be better off with government than without. Hobbes was self-consciously a master at rational choice theory, and he may have had no peers in self-conscious commitment to it until the past several decades. Still, there were many others between Hobbes and our time. Among others who soon followed were Bernard Mandeville, who explained how public virtues come about as the unintended consequences of the private vices of self-interest, and David Hume and Adam Smith, who gave us philosophical histories of the stages of development of states.[3] Many commentators, from Thrasymachus to Machiavelli and on to contemporary campaign advisers, have argued for the elevation of self-interest—the self- interest of leaders only—above all other concerns. But they have generally not been rational choice theorists in the explanatory sense in which Hobbes, Mandeville, Anthony Downs, Mancur Olson, and, arguably, such practitioners as James Madison have been.

The dramatic and direct influence of economists on the foundations of contemporary political science may reasonably be said to have begun with the work of Joseph Schumpeter on democracy, John von Neumann and Oskar Morgenstern on game theory, Kenneth Arrow and Duncan Black on social choice, Downs on electoral politics, and Olson on interest group theory. As it happens, with the partial exception of game theory, all of these contributions were essentially destructive or negative. They explained why things may be hard or impossible. In particular, they all undercut certain hopes for democratic theory, both as a positive theory and as a normative theory. There have since been many other results that are positive rather than negative, but the tenor of the individualist analysis of politics in what has come to be called rational choice or public choice theory remains pessimistic. The worst results suggest there is little connection between aggregate patterns of individual-level motivations and public choices. Many results, however, explain seemingly odd public choices and institutional devices from individual-level motivations.

Though rational choice is inherently addressed to the individual level, it reaches conclusions at the collective level. In this it is not different from the bulk of traditional political argument. The usual difference is that rational choice analysis connects individual-level actions to collective-level results by focusing on strategic interactions among the individuals, whereas traditional arguments much more commonly infer collective-level results by direct analogy from individual-level intentions or interests. The typical conclusion of a rational choice analysis of politics is against such easy analogical inference from the individual level to the collective level. Indeed, many of the most important conclusions of rational choice analysis are, at least implicitly, against fallacies of composition. We commit a fallacy of composition when, for example, from the premise that every individual can decide how to act, we conclude that the human race or a nation or a group can decide how it will act. Our assumption may be true of *some* inferences from individual to group characteristics, but this must be shown, not merely assumed.

Consider one of the most cited and most influential fallacies of composition in political theory. Aristotle's wonderful *Politics* opens with an extraordinary inference:

> Observation shows us, first, that every polis (or state) is a species of association, and, secondly, that all associations are instituted for the purpose of attaining some good—for *all men do all their acts with a view to achieving something which is, in their view, a good. We may therefore hold* [on the basis of what we actually observe] *that all associations aim at some good;* and we may also hold that the particular association which is the most sovereign of all, and includes all the rest, will pursue this aim most, and will thus be directed to the most sovereign of all goods. This most sovereign and inclusive association is the polis, as it is called, or the political association.[4]

Against this sanguine and simplistic vision, we know that societies are typically torn by deep conflicts, as was Aristotle's Athens. Hence, the form of government that emerges in our society may result from a morass of many conflicting considerations rather than from what any one person—let alone any large percentage of us—would have wanted. It is merely a fallacy of composition that a polis will seek what individuals would seek.

There are two ways to avoid the fallacy of composition in social reasoning. One is to ground all aggregate-level phenomena in individual-level actions and choices. The second is to develop a separate aggregate-level theory that is neither fallaciously inferred from individual-level analogies nor grounded in individual-level actions and choices. The latter approach has been at the center of the program of systems theory (as—preeminently in political science—in the work of David Easton) and of the program of structuralist theory that abstracts from intentions. The former is central to the program of economic reasoning in the social sciences, such as in rational choice theory. It is also often central to the program of much of psychology, especially social psychology. Much of the work of systems theorists is behaviorist in the strong sense that it makes no use of inferences from intentions or reasons. People are as much black boxes as are many system elements. Rational choice theory is inherently intentionalist in large part, although some intentions and preferences may seem virtually objective and may be inferred without being checked against what any subject's mind says. Structuralist theories are often ambivalent on this difference. They invoke both systemic and individual explanations. Unfortunately, they are not generally very clear about how these two articulate with each other.

THE RANGE OF RATIONAL CHOICE THEORY

Economic and strategic reasoning in the rational choice school of political economy have led to dramatic and novel insights, some of which have swept aside past understandings of politics. The grandest result has been the varied and repeated demonstration that the fallacy of composition can vitiate arguments in sociopolitical contexts. In his hotly debated theorem, Arrow attempted to show that principles of rationality that apply to individuals also apply to groups of individuals. He discovered, on the contrary, that they generally cannot, although under certain conditions of shared or patterned interests or preferences they might.[5] Downs showed that the individual voter may have no interest in actually voting or in knowing enough to vote well even though she may have a clear interest in the outcome of the election.[6] Similarly, Olson showed that the individual member of a group of people who share some interest may have no interest in contributing to the group's securing its interest, so that the group may fail and the individual members may lose.[7] In a period of about fifteen years, these three economists took much of the heart out of traditional political theory. They severely undercut democratic theory, and they demolished traditional group theory and the so-called theories of the responsible electorate and responsible parties.

Note that the forms of the fallacies of composition that Arrow faced differ from those that Downs and Olson faced.[8] Arrow's problem is strictly conceptual: is collective preference an analog of individual preference? His answer is generally no, as implied in the title of his original paper on the topic: "A Difficulty in the Concept of Social Welfare."[9] That title essentially states that it is a fallacy of composition to suppose that social welfare and individual welfare are analogous terms. The problem of Downs and Olson is not merely conceptual but is motivational: can a group's interest motivate group action in a manner analogous with the way an individual's interest motivates individual action? Again, the answer is generally no. In this second case, there is also a conceptual problem of whether group motivation makes sense the way individual motivation does. There may be no more natural task for a methodologically individualist theory than to show that individuals and aggregates of individuals are different, that we cannot trivially compose the latter from the former.

Each fallacy was recognized long before the rise of rational choice theory. For example, there has long been debate over the plausible meaning of the "public interest." Collectivities, such as states, were often proclaimed to have interests that could not easily be seen as the interests of individual citizens. E. E. Schattschneider tried to salvage the notion of the public interest by noting that some so-called public interest groups addressed problems, such as capital punishment or vivisection, that were not the direct interest of the group contributors, whose contributions must have been stimulated by public interestedness or moral or other non-self-regarding motivations.[10] Brian Barry, citing older literature, notes that many policies are public in the sense of being generally applicable, whereas others—for example, punishment for a particular crime—are personal.[11] On this view, for example, we may all share an interest in having government or police protection. Barry argues that such an interest is not merely the aggregation or generalization of individual interests. In a somewhat odd sense, he is right. Even the thief has an interest in there being a reasonably good system of law and order because, if there were no such system, there would be such disorder that society would be unproductive and there would be little to steal. However, the interest we share is a grand one because it aggregates over so many of us. It is not merely an aggregation of the interests each of us has in specific instances of police protection but rather, as in Hobbes's theory, the aggregation of the interests all have in a stable order. If such public interests are merely generalizations of individual interests, they might seem immune to the cycling of preferences that leads to Arrow's theorem. But Arrow's theorem applies to whole states of the world, not to piecemeal bits of it, and preferences over whole states are likely to cycle even if we all seemingly share interests in some details, even large details.

Much of the continuation of work on the Arrow, Downs, and Olson problems has been very technical. It is often incisive, but it is also typically very narrowly focused. Other work, such as the microeconomic analyses of more or less every bit of human behavior by Gary Becker[12] and the game theoretic analyses of an increasing number of scholars, now seems broader and more broadly interesting. Moreover, in a pleasing return to the manner of Hume and Smith, there is increasingly common use of rational choice arguments at a discursive rather than technical level to address central problems in politics and in political philosophy.[13] This literature typically brings normative and positive concerns together and sometimes rejects the behaviorist dictum that the positive and the normative can and even must be kept separate. In part, the impossibility of separating the two comes from the very value theory that stands behind the rational choice school. Contrary to common assertions that the value theory is formally neutral or empty, results derived from such theory very often depend on substantive content in it.[14]

In some ways the best current model of this kind of political economy, as articulated in a relatively large body of work, is no longer the Arrow, Downs, and Olson literatures but rather work in law and economics. Much of this work is too narrowly focused on issues of very minor importance to political theorists, such as the effects of particular minor rules of trial procedure and evidence. But much of it is central to the effort to understand political institutions, some of the most important of which are those that promulgate, enforce, and adjudicate law. And, in its usual focus on efficiency, which is sometimes substantively equivalent to welfare and is otherwise a good skeptic's proxy for welfare, law and economics is inherently a rational choice theory with a strong substantive value.[15] Of greatest interest in this work, however, are the actual arguments over, for example, value theory and institutional structures, the level to which justificatory analysis should be directed, and the essentially strategic understanding of laws and legal rights. Arguably, a major reason for the success of law and economics is that it escapes the definitionalist tradition of legal theory—the tradition that focuses on such issues as what law is, on the concept of law, rather than on how it works.

In the massive literature that has responded to John Rawls's theory of justice, the central problems are also the general value theory and the structure of institutions that protect and generate the values. Unfortunately, however, this literature is much less focused on real problems than is work in law and economics, and therefore it is typically much more glib and vague.[16] It seems too easy to think problems can be resolved when they are not being directly confronted. Just when the argument might begin to develop in application to a real issue, scholars too often invoke Thomas Scanlon's formally empty claim that we should accept that result which is a matter of reasonable agreement.[17] In the face of this persuasive definition, a theorist may be reluctant to counter with unreasonable disagreement, although the larger world out there does just that. Alas, the prior questions are whether there is a result that follows from reasonable agreement and what are the principles of "reasonableness" that bring us agreeably to it.

Apart from debate over the quality and relevance of data, internal debate over results in individualist political economy typically focuses on one of two issues: value theoretic assumptions or the internal coherence of deductions from these. The value theory is actually a class of theories.[18] These have grown out of extraordinary debate and criticism over a couple of centuries. Almost uniquely in the social sciences, economics and individualist political economy therefore have very well-articulated value theories. One might object to these theories in many ways, but in raising an objection one has the advantage of a relatively clear and cogent target rather than an amorphous mass of vague generalizations and too firm and specific, but ungrounded, intuitions. Hence, there is a natural tendency for theory in individualist political economy to seem monolithic and coherent—although it may also tend toward the technically tedious and uninteresting, with baroque and rococo encrustations.

Of course, many political scientists think the individualist focus of the economic approach is morally corrosive or descriptively wrong. The latter criticisms are of many kinds. Some argue that people are not like the supposed *homo economicus* of rational choice theory, that people act not from interests but from response to symbols or from moral commitments. Some argue that social outcomes are explained not by individual motives for action at all but by large social structures or general systems.

NORMATIVE FALLACIES

The most conspicuous failing in the fallacy of composition at the base of much of social theory is that it contributes to incorrect explanations and understandings of government and politics. It also, as shown in Aristotle's opening paragraph, contributes to bad normative claims. In part this follows simply from the fact that normative rightness depends on what is possible—as philosophers say, "ought" implies "can." For example, because I cannot possibly rescue someone from drowning in Bangladesh in the next hour, it is false to say that I ought to do so. Bad explanations that mislead us about what is possible can distort our understanding of what is right. Almost the whole of modern political theory is misled in this way. Much of this theory argues from what we want government to be to determine what it ought to be. What we require are devices for composing individual into collective or institutional choices that match our normative expectations and demands.

Consider demands we can place on citizens' knowledge of politics. Downs argues that citizens cannot be motivated to know very much about politics because having such knowledge will make little difference to them politically. For example, as a resident of a large city in a large state in the massive United States, I cannot expect to influence electoral outcomes with my own votes. But then I cannot have great interest in knowing much about the candidates before me. If I do not know much, I may not know how to vote my interests.[19] I can generally expect to gain more from using my time and energy in other pursuits than in following and participating in politics.

One might say it is nevertheless morally incumbent on me to learn about politics and to participate because my doing so contributes to a good outcome that benefits others as well as myself. Even if it is rational or self-interested for me to be ignorant and to participate very little, it may still be wrong. Or is it? Without becoming a full-time politician, I cannot expect to have significant effect on politics no matter how much I strive to learn about it. And, if I learn about politics from reading and participating, I necessarily have to do less of something else. Would I have a better impact on the world or be better off or be a better person for that change in my behavior? Plausibly not. Moreover, I would not want most others to spend too much time learning about politics, because I depend on how well they do other things, all of which would suffer if knowing politics took much of their time. Therefore, it may be neither irrational nor immoral for me—and most other people as well—to be relatively ignorant about politics. This is a moral analog of Downs's critical vision of rationality in politics.

What, then, will I know about politics? I will tend to learn things to the extent that coming to know them is itself rewarding—for example, by being entertaining. But this means that journalists may find that their success in gaining readers depends more on making political news entertaining than on making it informative. They may focus too much on sexual indiscretions and not enough on gross incompetence, too much on third-rate catch-phrases that degrade the language and corrode debate rather than on ideas of governance or policy.

Critics may chastise both the electorate and the press for trivializing the issues. But then the critics are speaking past the rationality of all concerned. An Eric Sevareid might admonish us for not harking to the central issues. But he was not morally in a stronger position—unlike most of us, he was paid specifically to take an interest in the central issues of politics. Most of us are not paid to attend to public interests. We do so, inasmuch as we do, on our own time. And the competition for that bit of time may be stiff, too stiff for anyone to say we morally should have put more of it into learning about a politics over which we can have little influence.[20] We surely must prefer not to pay very many Eric Sevareids to be professionally concerned with our political life, to egg us on to better political behavior. There are other, sometimes better things to do with our money. Analogously, it is not in our interest to invest more directly in political knowledge.

It follows from this view that sometimes it might be wrong to be politically ignorant or to fail to participate. If my government is doing grievous harm to someone, such as Third World peasants in a war zone or an impoverished racial minority in a ghetto, I may be virtually unable to fail to notice. But that means I cannot be rationally ignorant. Hence, if I were to participate, I might reasonably think I could participate intelligently. Moreover, my participation now would be on behalf of a large group, not on my own behalf, and I might readily suppose the costs of my participation would be outweighed by the potential benefits of my participation to the relevant group.

Still, much of the time, my coming to know enough to participate intelligently and my participating might fail to be either rationally or morally required. Admonitions at the level of the polity that we ought to participate for our own collective well-being are a cavalier fallacy of composition. The form of that fallacy is often a blending of the conceptual fallacy identified by Arrow and the motivational fallacy identified by Downs and Olson. It is twice fallacious. At this late date, it is also increasingly contemptible.

INDIVIDUALIST VERSUS
STRUCTURALIST POLITICAL ECONOMY

A full judgment of rational choice theory must turn on comparisons with alternative approaches. The most natural alternative with which to compare it is one that uses much of the same vocabulary and addresses many of the same problems. There are two main branches of modern political economy. One of these, rational choice theory, is, again, essentially an economic version of methodological individualism put to the task of explaining social outcomes, virtually any and all outcomes. Its progenitors include Hobbes, Hume, Smith, and many nineteenth-century economists. The other branch of contemporary political economy is structuralist. It focuses on such social structures as institutions, classes, and movements without trying to unpack them in individualist terms. Its most important progenitor is probably Karl Marx, who wrote in part in reaction to the individualist branch of political economy,[21] and its most important philosopher is probably G. W. F. Hegel.

The common element that gives both these theories claim to the title "political economy" is their focus on interests. The individualist theory is usually, although not strictly always, based on individual self-interest. Structuralist theory is commonly based on claims of aggregate interests, especially the interests of a class. One might immediately dismiss the latter as a likely fallacy of composition. But it need not be if the members of a class share general characteristics that give each of the members of the class more or less the same interest in some collective achievement or provision. For example, the class of workers may have an interest in higher wages if the increase in wages comes merely from reducing the gains of capitalists.

It is only for want of more perspicuous labels that I will refer to individualist and structuralist variants of political economy. Structuralists are less readily identifiable than rational choice theorists or systems theorists, and their views are seemingly more varied. It is ironic that the individualist approach is now commonly thought of as the economic approach to behavior. This view prevails only because the combination of the use of methodological individualism and the assumption of self-interest have been so fruitful that one branch of political economy has spawned the Anglo-Saxon discipline of economics. It is historically wrong to say that economic methods have simply been imported into social theorizing and explanation: economic methods are the *product* of social theorizing. It is true, however, that individualist political economy has enjoyed a remarkable renaissance under the stimulus of many contributions from economists in the past half-century.

Much of political theory, both normative and positive, has been driven by the social-political phenomena of interest. For example, contemporary structuralist theory is driven by concern with the phenomena of revolution, class conflict, and state formation. Individualist political economy is much more driven by theory, almost by theory on the prowl for whatever problems it can take on. Theory in the field seems to be almost self-generating. That it is individualist has given it the advantage of being able to draw on and accommodate itself to individualist value theory as articulated in utilitarianism and economics. (This is a source of criticism for the theory, but it might sooner be seen as one of the theory's great strengths.)

In trying to compare alternative theories as practiced now, one may be struck by how little they actually speak to each other even when they focus on explaining apparently the same phenomenon. It is not merely that different schools do not take each other on—they do a little of that.[22] The greater problem is that they formulate their analyses so differently that they often address quite different aspects of the phenomenon at issue. For example, rational choice and systems theory do not speak to each other virtually as a matter of theoretical principle. Structuralist theorists have been much more ready to attack rational choice theory for what they suppose are its descriptively wrong assumptions.

Among those who think rational choice descriptively wrong is Theda Skocpol. She rejects rational choice and even individual motivational explanations of revolutions because, she claims, "no successful revolution has ever been 'made' by a mass-mobilizing, avowedly revolutionary movement."[23] But it is merely a fallacy of composition to suppose that the outcome of group choices must represent the intentions of the group. It sounds trivial to say it, but we can explain what a group does from the motivations and actions of the individuals who make up the group without supposing that the group has the motivations of any of the individuals—indeed, without supposing that the group has "motivations" in the same way that its individual members have. Yet, as trivial and obvious as this truism is, it is often disregarded in social theory.

Ironically, Skocpol's complaint is similar to that which Adam Ferguson and Friedrich Hayek made against, respectively, social contract visions of organizing society and the Abbé de Sieyès's vision of the deliberate redesign of French society.[24] We cannot design society, Ferguson and Hayek insisted, because too much of it is the product of unintended consequences. But they attempted to understand the development of social institutions by building it up from individual actions that make rational sense on the individual level, and they would surely have attempted to understand a revolutionary change in the same way. Like Skocpol, they were hostile to arguments from social design, but unlike her they were committed to arguments from individual intention.

Theory becomes compelling only if it accounts for phenomena and if it stands up against other theories. To show that a theory is defective, one must show that it is internally inconsistent or put up an alternative theory

that handles its problems better. Among the greatest successes of rational
choice theory have been its demonstrations of the fallacies of composition
inherent in many theories and explanations. Structuralists and systems
theorists do not challenge the internal consistency of rational choice theory. Rather they challenge its assumptions and its applicability. Unfortunately, however, it appears that structuralists, systems theorists, and rational
choice theorists typically focus on different problems. With the exception
of revolution and elections, which interest both structuralists and rational
choice theorists, there is remarkably little overlap in work from these diverse perspectives. Hence, we have few genuine comparative tests among
them. Even when the same apparent phenomenon is addressed by two of
these theories, each is likely to have a very different focus.

The structuralist Barrington Moore asserts that his effort to understand
revolution will address only certain, nameable, major revolutions.[25] The
theory is not intended to address other revolutions nor class or group actions more generally. The theorizing seems grossly ad hoc even if often
brilliant. It is hard to extract from it general principles or arguments that
can be applied to more numerous and plausibly analogous phenomena—
there are no analogous phenomena. Such work is a bit like having a theory
of Richard Nixon or Joseph Stalin rather than a theory of political leadership or paranoid personality. At another extreme is a style of theorizing
that Moore eschews, the style that both Max Weber and Talcott Parsons fell
into in their later years. That style is arid and definitional, seldom if ever
touching ground in real phenomena. It too readily allows for triviality,
looseness, and vacuity—the mind can shift into idle and still churn out
sentences without the disciplining constraint of attention to reality. Both
Weber and Parsons may have owed their styles to the peculiar tradition of
especially German legal theory that is almost entirely definitional.

Between the entirely ahistorical kind of theorizing Moore eschews and
the kind he prefers, which reduces to history, there is theory that touches
ground frequently and at different points on the map rather than a rarefied
few times. Rational choice theory, which is quite general, and some specialized theories (e.g., much of contemporary feminist theory and some traditional legal theory) fall between Weber's sometime wasteland of definition
in *Economy and Society* and Moore's nearly unique historical cases. A scholar
new to the field can apply these theories or the principles that constitute
them to cases or classes of cases and expect to achieve valid results.

WHITHER RATIONAL CHOICE THEORY?

The analytical core of rational choice theory is its individualist focus on
incentives and strategic interactions. Among its compelling implications

are insightful accounts of unintended consequences and the exposure of fallacies of composition, both definitionally and causally. It also provides for a remarkably fertile combination of normative and explanatory concerns. Indeed, in recent decades, rational choice theory has contributed to a renaissance of normative political philosophy.

Why is the understanding of politics apparently such a fruitful field for the application of economic reasoning? The individualist focus of economic reasoning seems especially relevant to the understanding of liberal and democratic politics and of the politics of those with plural ties and commitments. Enough of these commitments can be characterized in welfarist terms, and explicitly in own welfare, to bring them under the rational choice rubric. Rational choice is therefore, perhaps rightly, called bourgeois political theory. It is often asserted that it is less relevant for the politics of close traditional communities. However, James Scott gives us an account of a peasant society that seems to fit the economic approach even as he argues against that approach.[26] Most of us may be less various than Scott. But we may be just as ambivalent about the reach of either school of political economy.

Return for a final moment to the explanation of revolution in individualist and structuralist political economy. Although they may not be resolutely consistent in holding that view, such structuralists as Marx and Skocpol seem to have individuals acting not from will or intent but from structural necessity. Marx supposed class consciousness would develop from individuals' understanding of their common interests. Such understanding was more likely to happen in the factory setting than on scattered subsistence farms. Perhaps achievement of this understanding is one of the structural conditions necessary for revolution. But such a claim finesses the supposition that action follows not from intention but from structural necessity. It is intentional understanding that makes the action plausible. If a working class with class consciousness attempts to seize control of government, its members face all of the usual incentives and—mostly—disincentives for collective action. Class consciousness does not overcome this problem.

Still, structuralist theorists are obviously right in their insistence that structural conditions matter. Such conditions matter for an individualist rational choice account in that they affect costs and benefits of particular actions and they affect the knowledge and understanding of relevant actors. A theorist might not be able to give a rational choice account of all the individual actions that go into a successful collective action. But the theorist might be able to judge accurately when conditions for such an action are more or less prohibitive merely from an account of variations in costs. The rich historical knowledge of a good structuralist account is complementary to the usual analysis of rational choice. Part of what is sometimes counted as structure in such accounts is the pattern of knowledge or motivation of particular people or a class of people.

One might conclude that systems, structuralist, and individualist political theory should somehow be brought together. For the moment, what may be most productive is not merger of the different perspectives but, rather, further development of these and various other theories or perspectives on their own. The great value of a particular, well-developed approach is that it heightens attention to certain aspects of the phenomenon under study. Structuralists may be better prepared to find certain results and rational choice theorists to find others. Rational choice theorists must all agree that real competition in theory should have good effects. Perhaps the same conclusion follows from structuralist, systems, and other perspectives.

It is sometimes argued that modernity in political thought begins with Machiavelli's focus on individual interests. But Socrates earlier focused on individual interests, albeit with the claim that the individual's true interest is to be just. He argued against the Sophists, who seemed to hold that the individual's true interest is to be self-serving, as Machiavelli supposed. The fundamental turn, however, is with Hobbes and his recognition of the need to avoid the fallacy of composition that arises from the focus on individuals.[27] Hobbes's program was about how to found a government on individuals, and in that program he rigorously avoided arguments by analogy from the individual to the societal level. This was a very difficult understanding, especially in an era when there was not yet a standard vocabulary for dealing with it. It is perhaps therefore not surprising that Hobbes's recognition and articulation of the problem are not always grasped by later thinkers.

What might be in the near future for rational choice theory? Much of the theory is not so much nonfalsifiable as it is beyond the capacity of available measures. The equations are pristine and exact, but the apparent data are mushy and vague. Perhaps what is called for is better measurement. But perhaps the more appropriate move is to craft theories that start from the mushy and the vague, theories that accommodate ordinary humans (including rational choice theorists in those moments when they are humans rather than merely theorists).

The best future of rational choice is likely to follow its best past. That has been in two general areas, conceptual and explanatory. First, Arrow's theorem and many other results probe the meanings of our social choice terminology and help to clarify what we can fruitfully talk about. Though further clarification is likely to come, there may not often again, if ever, be so dramatic a result as Arrow's own. The second general area is in explaining various aggregate-level phenomena. Clearly, the best explanations have been those that restricted the value theory and gave it relatively specific substantive content, usually in the form of own welfare. Work that starts from a value theory to give explanatory results likely will continue to be the most successful, satisfying, and productive. Work that assumes an open-ended value theory likely will continue to produce unsatisfying, open-ended results. A large part of what will be compelling in testing rational choice results, therefore, will be tests of specific individual-level value assumptions.[28]

Suppose we agree that the rational choice approach has demolished important but long-entrenched and mistaken views of politics. Still, one may suppose, it faces a much harder and ultimately more interesting task: the construction of accounts of aggregate behavior. Yet at this point, Neil Smelser argues, rational choice theory is in decline. Smelser's general thesis is that, in response to critics, rational choice theorists tend to adjust their theory in ways that make it tautological and nonfalsifiable.[29] There may be such tendencies, as there probably are in all theories. Worse, a drift toward arid tautology and nonfalsifiable claims may occur independently of any effort to fit the facts, as in many of the theorems that extend Arrow's impossibility theorem or the depiction of the theoretical possibilities of voting patterns.

Against Smelser's general claim that the theory is in decline, there are countertendencies that suggest the theory is increasingly ascendant, that it is applied to more and more diverse actual problems. Indeed, currently the most richly successful endeavor in rational choice theory has been law and economics.[30] Other legal theorists must think they are awash in rational choice accounts of everything legal. They may disagree with such accounts, but they often feel they have to take them on, because the economic model is clearly the model to follow or to beat. Rational choice and game theory have also become central to reasoning in normative political philosophy, especially in democratic theory but even in moral theory more broadly.[31] And they have spawned a large and novel literature on norms.[32] Again, other moral and political philosophers increasingly feel bound to take on the rational choice arguments. More generally, throughout rational choice, theorists work backwards from standard assumptions to pose foundational issues in the theory, issues that often come from the effort to make common sense of choices and values (as in the current quest to understand the extent of the endogeneity of preferences and the way endogeneity works in a rational choice account).

It is common to suppose that established theories are succeeded by new theories and fade from consideration. In the social sciences, this may well happen eventually, but in any given era radically different schools of theory may coexist, sometimes in application to quite different phenomena, sometimes with overlapping and hence competing applications. In our era, the most pervasive and most protean school of social theory is rational choice theory, which is applied to virtually everything that involves human choice and even to biological developments. In some of its conceptual clarifications and some of its empirical results, it is so forceful that it sets the terms for debate with other schools of thought. It has made some traditional ways of talking about social action and order untenable. Systems theory is thought by its proponents to offer a grand unification of theory across radically different disciplines. Rational choice theory is less grand, but it is far more profligate with results and with explanatory arguments.

NOTES

1. This is the felicitous phrase of Thomas C. Schelling, *Micromotives and Macrobehavior* (New York: Norton, 1978).

2. Thomas Hobbes, *Leviathan* (1651), any edition, chapters 13–15.

3. Bernard Mandeville, *The Fable of the Bees, or Private Vices, Publick Benefits* (Oxford: Oxford University Press, 1924 [1714], reprinted by Liberty Press, 1988); David Hume, *A Treatise of Human Nature* (1739–40), ed. L. A. Selby-Bigge and P. H. Nidditch (Oxford: Oxford University Press, 1978, 2nd edition), book 3, part 2, sect. 8, pp. 539–49; Adam Smith, *An Inquiry into the Nature and Causes of the Wealth of Nations* (any standard edition [1776]), book 5, chap. 1, part 2, "Of the Expence of Justice."

4. Aristotle, *Politics* (New York: Oxford University Press, 1958), Ernest Barker trans., opening paragraph, emphasis added.

5. Kenneth J. Arrow, *Social Choice and Individual Values* (New Haven, CT: Yale University Press, 1951; 2nd edition, 1963). For Arrow's account of his discovery, see Arrow, *Social Choice and Justice* (*Collected Papers*, vol. 1) (Cambridge, MA: Harvard University Press, 1983), pp. 1–4.

6. Anthony Downs, *An Economic Theory of Democracy* (New York: Harper and Brothers, 1957).

7. Mancur Olson, Jr., *The Logic of Collective Action* (Cambridge, MA: Harvard University Press, 1965).

8. See further Russell Hardin, "Public Choice vs. Democracy," in John W. Chapman, ed., NOMOS 32: *Majorities and Minorities* (New York: New York University Press, 1990), pp. 184–203.

9. Reprinted in Arrow, *Social Choice and Justice,* pp. 4–29 (essay first published 1950).

10. E. E. Schattschneider, *The Semi-Sovereign People* (New York: Holt, Rinehart and Winston, 1960), pp. 20–46.

11. Brian Barry, *Political Argument* (London: Routledge and Kegan Paul, 1965), pp. 190–202.

12. Gary S. Becker, *The Economic Approach to Human Behavior* (Chicago: University of Chicago Press, 1976).

13. Consider the following diverse works: Brian Barry, *Theories of Justice* (Berkeley, CA: University of California Press, 1989); Geoffrey Brennan and James M. Buchanan, *The Reason of Rules: Constitutional Political Economy* (Cambridge: Cambridge University Press, 1985); Albert O. Hirschman, *Exit, Voice, and Loyalty: Responses to Declines in Firms, Organizations, and States* (Cambridge, MA: Harvard University Press, 1970); Margaret Levi, *Of Rule and Revenue* (Berkeley, CA: University of California Press, 1988); William H. Riker, *Liberalism Against Populism: A Confrontation Between the Theory of Democracy and the Theory of Social Choice* (Prospect Heights,

IL: Waveland, 1982); Michael Taylor, *Anarchy and Cooperation* (London: Wiley, 1976).

14. See further Russell Hardin, "The Normative Core of Rational Choice Theory," in Uskali Maki, ed., *The Economic Realm: Studies in the Ontology of Economics* (forthcoming).

15. Russell Hardin, "The Morality of Law and Economics," *Law and Philosophy* 11 (November 1992): 331–84.

16. A rare exception is Charles Beitz, *Political Equality* (Princeton: Princeton University Press, 1989).

17. Thomas Scanlon, "Contractualism and Utilitarianism," in Amartya Sen and Bernard Williams, eds., *Utilitarianism and Beyond* (Cambridge: Cambridge University Press, 1982), pp. 103–128, at pp. 115n, 128.

18. See further Russell Hardin, "Rational Choice Theories," in Terence Ball, ed., *Idioms of Inquiry: Critique and Renewal in Political Science* (Albany, NY: State University of New York Press, 1987), pp. 67–91; "The Normative Core of Rational Choice Theory."

19. Downs, *An Economic Theory of Democracy*, p. 236.

20. Russell Hardin, "To Rule in No Matters, To Obey in All: Democracy and Autonomy," *Contemporary Philosophy* 13, 12 (November–December 1991): 1–7; *Liberalism, Constitutionalism, and Democracy* (New York: Oxford University Press, forthcoming), chapter 4.

21. Marx also occasionally gave individualist accounts of some problems, such as in his explanation of the political cupidity of the French peasants in voting for the second Bonaparte in 1848. See Karl Marx, *The 18th Brumaire of Louis Napoleon Bonaparte* (New York: International Publishers, 1963 [1852]), pp. 123–24. See further Russell Hardin, "Acting Together, Contributing Together," *Rationality and Society* 3 (July 1991): 365–80.

22. See Michael Taylor, "Rationality and Revolutionary Collective Action," in Taylor, ed., *Rationality and Revolution* (Cambridge: Cambridge University Press, 1988), pp. 63–97.

23. Quoted in Taylor, "Rationality and Revolutionary Collective Action," at pp. 76–77.

24. Adam Ferguson, *An Essay on the History of Civil Society* (New Brunswick, NJ: Transaction, 1980 [1767]), part 3, sect. 2, pp. 121–28; Friedrich A. Hayek, *The Constitution of Liberty* (Chicago: University of Chicago Press, 1960), p. 57.

25. Barrington Moore, Jr., *Social Origins of Dictatorship and Democracy* (Boston: Beacon, 1966).

26. James C. Scott, *The Moral Economy of the Peasant: Rebellion and Subsistence in Southeast Asia* (New Haven, CT: Yale University Press, 1976). See further Hardin, "The Normative Core of Rational Choice Theory."

27. Thomas Hobbes, *Leviathan*, chapters 18 and 13–15 passim; *De Cive* [1651; Latin 1642], any edition, 6.1.

28. See further Hardin, "The Normative Core of Rational Choice."

29. Neil J. Smelser, "The Rational Choice Perspective: A Theoretical Assessment," *Rationality and Society* 4 (October 1992): 381–410. More generally, see Donald P. Green and Ian Shapiro, *Pathologies of Rational Choice Theory: A Critique of Applications in Political Science* (New Haven, CT: Yale University Press, 1994).

30. Normative issues in this literature are surveyed in Hardin, "The Morality of Law and Economics."

31. Even the exegesis of past theorists is often done in rational choice terms. For Hobbes, see Gregory S. Kavka, *Hobbesian Moral and Political Theory* (Princeton: Princeton University Press, 1986); for Hume, see Russell Hardin, *Morality within the Limits of Reason* (Chicago: University of Chicago Press, 1988) chapter 2.

32. See for example Edna Ullmann-Margalit, *The Emergence of Norms* (Oxford: Oxford University Press, 1977), and Russell Hardin, *One for All: The Logic of Group Conflict* (Princeton: Princeton University Press, 1995), chapters 4 and 5. Jon Elster both joins and criticizes this endeavor in *The Cement of Society* (Cambridge: Cambridge University Press, 1989).

11

The Political System
and Comparative Politics

The Contribution of David Easton

Gabriel A. Almond

Since David Easton first appeared in print, in his early articles in the years immediately following World War II, and in his remarkable first book, *The Political System: An Inquiry into the State of Political Science* (1953), he has consistently concerned himself with a "general theory of politics." This task, which he set in his professional youth and has pursued from major book to major book until his latest, *The Analysis of Political Structure* (1990), has involved 1) the elaboration and testing of a framework for the logical ordering of empirical political theories and 2) the formulation of a conceptual vocabulary that might serve to unify political study and impart meaning to its various parts by placing them in a coherent theoretical scheme.

Easton's appeal for a general theory to impart sense to our special empirical theories has largely fallen on deaf ears. Indeed, the legitimacy of the effort to formulate such theories has been widely challenged, and the argument has been advanced that if we are to pursue theory at all it must be through propositions of the "middle range." At some point in this exercise in theoretical self-restraint, according to some, a valid general theory will spring into being. Easton appreciated from the beginning that it was essential to create such a theory (or theories) but that this could only occur as a result of sustained intellectual effort at the most general level of political analysis. As he put it in his most recent book, "[W]e cannot expect a full understanding of any major part of the structure of a political system without taking into account the relationship of such a part to what I shall call the overarching or higher-order political structure itself" (1990, p. 5).

Easton's faithful pursuit of this goal is an exemplary episode in the intellectual history of political science, one that deserves far greater appreciation than it has received. His contributions to the development of such a theory are contained in five books written over the last forty-odd years. The first four appeared between 1953 and 1969. The recent history of the political science discipline is suggested by the long interval between the fourth and fifth publications in this series, an interval of more than twenty years. Easton's pursuit of general empirical theory, like much of the rest of mainstream political science, fell afoul of two very powerful disciplinary perturbations in the 1960s, 1970s, and early 1980s: the radicalization of American political science, particularly of comparative and Third World studies, as a consequence of Vietnam, the civil rights movement, and the rise of the counterculture; and the invasion of political science by hard-science, mathematico-deductive models from economics. Each of these perturbations had its own power, that of moral indignation in the case of the first, that of deductive- inductive scientific rigor in the case of the second. Together they shook the foundations and drained the legitimacy of ordinary social and political science scholarship during the 1970s and 1980s. The neo-Marxist and dependency theorists of this period reduced political institutions to the basic economic structure or mode of production. Hence Easton's concern with the political system was set aside as of peripheral importance, or as diverting attention from the normatively correct tasks of theory as facilitating the attainment of socialism. The public choice theorists reduced political structure and institutions to the level of individual choices. As James Buchanan put it in his chapter in a book edited by Easton: "The political structure is conceived as something that emerges from the choice processes of individual participants." (1966, p.26) From this perspective, empirical general theory was viewed as the prescientific construction of frameworks, which the hard science, deductive-inductive approach of rational choice theory would somehow replace.

Two decades later these movements are themselves in retreat. Neo-Marxism and the related dependency and world system theories have been seriously compromised by the collapse of communism and embarrassed by the failures and demoralization of social democracy. Rational choice theorists are in the process of discovering that although political structure may be factored down to individual choices, any particular set of individual choices is made in the context of institutions that, although they are the products of past choices, cannot be described in simple rational choice terms. The norms and behavior patterns of politics occur in systems in which structures perform functions and which need to be described and analyzed in structural and cultural terms if the choices and their policy consequences are to be explained. Much recent rational choice writing describes itself as being "in search of institutions" or as having "rediscovered institutions." Like the "naughty kittens," it was the rational choice people who lost them in the first place.

In the cacophony created by this rejection of scholarly objectivity, on the one hand, and this psychological, economistic, and ahistorical reductionism, on the other, Easton's plea for general theory was "marginalized," to use the language of the postmodernists. In the quieter morning of the 1990s, it is possible to respond to the challenge he issued in the 1950s and 1960s and reaffirmed in 1990. Easton's early articles and first book made explicit, elaborated, and codified a conceptual trend that had begun to manifest itself as early as the publication of Woodrow Wilson's *Congressional Government* (1882), Frank Goodnow's *Politics and Administration* (1900), and Arthur Bentley's *The Process of Government* (1908). Merriam, Lasswell, Gosnell, Key, Truman, other members of the Chicago school, Peter Odegard, Pendleton Herring, Elmer Schattschneider, and other venturesome political scientists had been implementing this empirical processual approach in the decades prior to World War II.

As Easton points out in *The Political System* (pp. 82, 162), Woodrow Wilson was the first American political scientist to make a significant break from the legal institutional format, treating the Congress, political parties, and the executive in processual terms. He was followed by Frank Goodnow, who similarly challenged separation-of-powers legalism with the argument that political reality is a continual process, divisible into politics as constitution-making and legislation performed by a variety of institutions, including nonlegal ones such as political parties; and administration at the point of less discretional implementation and enforcement. Goodnow was the first explicit functional theorist, stressing the multifunctionalism of political structure. Arthur Bentley presented a fully processual model in which politics was reduced, ultimately, to the interaction and equilibrium among interest groups.

The members of the Chicago school, particularly Merriam, Lasswell, and Truman, were moving in the direction of Easton's system analysis. Merriam, in *The Role of Politics in Social Change* (1936), frequently uses the metaphor of a "moving equilibrium" in dealing with the role of politics in society. Lasswell, in his early *Psychopathology and Politics* (1930), used the phrase "the state as a manifold of events" as a rough approximation of the system concept. In the immediate aftermath of Easton's work, Lasswell presented his own version of system functionalism in *The Decision Process* (1956).

In *Group Representation Before Congress* (1929) and *The Politics of Democracy* (1940), Pendleton Herring uses the language of process, equilibrium, and disequilibrium. "In this book," he states in the preface to the latter, "I attempt to evaluate our political process as a method for reconciling change with stability" (pp. viii, ix). In his 1953 presidential address to the American Political Science Association, Herring stated the philosophy of this new political science in these terms: "The systematic analysis of political behavior and political processes is a significant growing edge of knowledge for our field . . . better approached with an air of curiosity about politics than a desire to improve" (December 1953, p. 969). In *The Governmental Process* (1951), David Truman describes the interaction of American interest groups, political parties, Congress, the executive, the judiciary, and the administration in realistic, processual, system and subsystem terms.

These developments occurred largely, though not entirely, in American political studies at the turn of the nineteenth century and the first four decades of the twentieth. In the comparative field, Carl Friedrich's *Constitutional Government and Democracy* (1950) and Herman Finer's *Theory and Practice of Modern Government* (1949) were on the whole dominated by the earlier historical, legal-institutional, and philosophical approaches. They tended to reify governmental institutions and treat political parties and the rest of the political infrastructure briefly and peripherally. They treated modern government in an historicist mode. These scholars saw an inevitable historical trend toward constitutionalism, in the sense of limited government and the rule of law, and representative and deliberative democracy. Friedrich's focus is unmistakable, as formulated in his first chapter: "[T]here can be no more important study than the study of the conditions of the rise of constitutionalism in general and constitutional democracy in particular" (p. 6). Finer concludes his thousand-page text with the comment, "It can hardly have escaped notice that the present work has devotedly avowed the tenet that democracy is the 'right' form of government for mankind" (p. 937). They would not have agreed with Pendleton Herring that the study of politics would be better pursued in a spirit of curiosity rather than a desire to improve. It was this impulse toward scholarly separation of fact and value, the description and explanation of the empirical world, and its improvement, and the development of distancing and ordering concepts that suffused Easton's early work.

My first encounter with Easton's writings took place at a time when I had become involved with the committee work of the Social Science Research Council. In the early 1950s Pendleton Herring, as president of the Social Science Research Council, and David Truman, as chairman of the Committee on Political Behavior along with the members of that committee, decided to establish a separate Committee on Comparative Politics, designating me as its chairman. I accepted this appointment with mixed feelings. I was content to be a member of the Committee on Political Behavior and honored to be associated with Herring, Key, Truman, Leiserson, Garceau, Angus Campbell, and Brewster Smith in exploring interesting and challenging research agendas. This committee blended the intellectual traditions of the Chicago school with the social psychological and survey research traditions of the University of Michigan. There was a remarkable civility and chemistry in that committee. Pendleton Herring was not only a proven scholar of great originality but also a humanist, poet, and host of great charm. The comparative government field was backward, fixed in its ways, and dominated by patriarchal figures who still tended to view America as a cultural colony. I accepted the chairmanship of the committee and embarked on what turned out to be a two-decade-long program of conferences and research projects in the company of Herring, Bryce Wood (who served as committee staff), Lucian Pye (who succeeded me as chairman in 1964), and a group of political scientists who were open to intellectual adventure and who created an atmosphere similar to that of the Committee on Political Behavior.

Easton's and my careers in the 1950s intersected and diverged in interesting ways. I read *The Political System* at the very time that the Committee on Comparative Politics was being formed. I later came to regret that my University of Chicago–bred empiricism made me a little impatient with Easton's careful, theoretically sophisticated and erudite evaluation of the state of political science. In subsequent years, when I have been drawn into intellectual history as a way of refuting some of the barbarisms of my younger colleagues, I have benefited greatly from what is still, in my opinion, the best treatment of the history of political science, written on the eve of the "behavioral revolution." But note that although he entitled his book *The Political System*, Easton did not elaborate the system concept very much in this book. He introduced the concept of "equilibrium" as the central and most general concept of politics, and he did not relate equilibrium to system. I cite these discussions in Easton's first book as one of the two sources of my early version of the political system concept, which I defined in my "Comparative Political Systems" *Journal of Politics* article as follows: "In contrast to process, the concept of system implies a totality of relevant units, an interdependence between the interactions of units, and a certain stability in the interaction of these units, perhaps best described as a changing equilibrium" (1970, pp. 3–29). At this stage of my thinking I drew more heavily on the system definitions found in Parsons and Shils, *Toward a Theory of Action* (1952), in particular their conception of orientation to action, which was the basis for my concept of political culture.

Easton's major impact on my own work came a few years after the appearance of his first book, through an article titled "An Approach to the Analysis of Political Systems" which he submitted to *World Politics* at a time when I was one of its editors (1957, pp. 383–400). This article was a prefiguring of his *A Framework for Political Analysis* (1965) and *A Systems Analysis of Political Life* (1965). It was all there in skeletal form—inputs of demands and supports, conversion, outputs, feedbacks. At the time I was in the early planning stages of *Politics of the Developing Areas* (1960), the first book stemming from work of the Committee on Comparative Politics. I can recall reading the article at my desk and immediately recognizing its importance. Somehow the infrastructure of democratic politics—which had been in process of discovery in the decades immediately before, during, and after, my apprenticeship in Merriam's Department of Political Science at the University of Chicago—fell into place in a systemic conceptual scheme.

Talcott Parsons's formulation, coming out of a mix of sociological, psychological, and anthropological theory, stressed culture and personality, psychological orientation, and socialization processes. It was very influential in the development of my research designs in political culture theory. Parsons's social system concept, by contrast, presented a static model of the polity, treating political decision making in the vague terms of "goal attainment." It is this system concept that appeared in my 1956 article. In *Politics of the Developing Areas,* the system concept drew almost entirely on Easton's 1957 *World Politics* article. Though I cited him substantially in that book, I did not fully acknowledge this intellectual debt.

David Easton, as a young assistant professor at the University of Chicago in the early 1950s, was affiliated with that university's Committee on Behavioral Sciences, which for a period of several years devoted itself to a study of the systems approach from the perspective of all of the sciences. On a weekly basis for a three-year period, Easton was exposed to the uses of the system concept in psychology, biology, neurophysiology, economics, physics, and anthropology. It was in this setting that Easton perfected his system framework. It was this system model, much influenced by cybernetics, that I inherited from Easton's work and that enabled me to codify and systematize the findings and conclusions of the five or six preceding decades of empirical research, primarily on American political processes.

As a graduate student and young teacher of American government in the 1930s, I was the intellectual heir of a literature that, proceeding from the processual conception of the separation of governmental powers, had uncovered a set of nonlegal, or paralegal, infrastructural institutions and processes (including the family and social institutions) of great importance for the functioning of political institutions yet unprovided for in the theoretical vocabulary of political science.

This literature was waiting to be codified. Mead, Benedict, Kardiner, Linton, Inkeles, and a host of psychoanalytically informed anthropologists and sociologists—as well as Merriam, Lasswell, and Leites, among the political scientists—had written about child development and personality and their relation to politics and political leadership. Ostrogorski, Michels, Merriam, Gosnell, Herring, Schattschneider, Key, and others had written about the organization and functioning of political parties. Merriam, Odegard, Herring, Key, Truman, and others had written about interest groups. Norman Angell, Walter Lippman, Harold Lasswell, Paul Lazarsfeld, Karl Deutsch, and others had written about public opinion and the media of communication. David Easton's political system concept made it possible to draw from these substantial literatures in an orderly way an empirically grounded and systemically related set of political functions—political socialization and recruitment, interest articulation and aggregation, policy making and implementation. This is the order that Easton's input-conversion-output model created in my mind, sorting out the stored information I had accumulated from the psychoanthropological literature, the political parties and pressure group literature, the processual literature on legislatures and parliaments, and the literature on the courts as political institutions.

In a 1969 lecture, I described my reaction to David Easton's 1957 article:

> I experienced one of those moments of intellectual liberation in which a concept comes along that gives one's thoughts an ordered structure. My early years as a practicing political scientist were in the great days of "separation of powers iconoclasm" when the "in" term for the empirically oriented political scientists, who were studying "invisible government," or the informal aspects of politics, was the political process.
>
> The notion of political process, as it was expressed in the writings of such men as Pendleton Herring, Elmer Schattschneider, and Peter Odegard, implied interaction and interdependence among the institutions and structures of politics, but the interdependence was treated bilaterally. One examined the relations between pressure groups and Congress, the bureaucracy, political parties, and legislatures, or one might look at the relations between the judiciary, and the legislative and executive processes. Process implied relationship and interaction, but not the full notions of multidirectional interaction and of equilibrium and disequilibrium which are implied in the concept of system. (1970, pp. 275–76).

The dynamic, interactive, input-output model presented by Easton in 1957 enabled me to explicate the functional categories that have played such an important part in my work and to impute meaning to them by arranging them according to his systemic scheme. With Easton's system concept and the early version of my functional categories, I had a model that—even in its primitive form back in the late 1950s and early 1960s—could "travel," could extend the range of comparative politics. With the functions analytically separated from the structures, and with a conception of politics as an input-conversion-output system, scholars not only could compare Britain and the United States in more comprehensive and systematic terms than had been previously possible but also could compare a Britain with a Tanzania or a Nigeria with a Brazil. All political systems could be compared according to a common set of functional categories, with the functions being performed similarly or differently, by similar or different structures, in a systemic, interactive set of relations, constrained by the social structural and cultural environments on the input side and having distinctive consequences for these environments on the output or policy side.

Thus, Easton's work had a major part in *The Politics of the Developing Areas* and in my subsequent work in comparative politics. Though it is true that Lucian Pye in his chapter on Southeast Asia, Dankwart Rustow on the Middle East, Myron Weiner on South Asia, George Blanksten on Latin America, and James Coleman on sub-Saharan Africa twisted and turned on their procrustean beds, *The Politics of the Developing Areas* nevertheless conveyed the message, and some effective empirical proof of its validity, that systematic comparison could be made across nations and cultures, and hence enhanced understanding of all political systems was possible.

Easton's work has diverged from mine over the years. I have continued to benefit from his theoretical work, usually with some delay. For example, his breakdown of the system concept into its three major components—the political community, the regime, and the authorities—was first elaborated in Easton's 1957 article and then fully elaborated in *A System Analysis of Political Life* (1965), yet I did not employ this approach until the second edition of the Almond-Powell *Comparative Politics* (1978), in the discussion of political culture and socialization. It was used there with discriminative power in the analysis of Western and Third World political cultures and, within the Western category, of the divided political cultures of countries such as France and Italy (pp. 38 ff.) Why this important classification of political system components was not employed in *The Civic Culture* (1963) or in the first edition of *Comparative Politics* (1966) I cannot explain, except to acknowledge carelessness and slippage in my scholarship.

This and other differences in our scholarly output may be explained in terms of differences in our scholarly style and in the problems and challenges we were confronting. I was by disposition and choice an empirically oriented political scientist. For me, political theory was instrumental. I have always believed that any theory the human mind could concoct could at best crudely, and often misleadingly, model reality. For me the appropriate relation between theory and empirical research was a constant back-and-forth movement, with much more time spent in the field than in the study. Easton, by contrast, is one of the purest empirical political theorists to have come out of the political science discipline in the last several decades.

Some future empirical theorist reading and comparing Easton's work with mine may demonstrate how a more careful exploitation of Easton's concepts on my part might have resulted in greater precision and insight in my work. Of this I have no doubt. The post–World War II world, with its flattened old nations and its turbulent new nations, lay in front of us. Future scholars eager to make reputations were bent over at the starting line waiting for the signal. We reached into the work of our theoretical colleagues impatiently looking for theoretical maps, for guidelines. With time and testing, these theoretical maps improved.

Thus, the list of seven functions—the four input functions of political socialization and recruitment, interest articulation, interest aggregation, and political communication and the three output functions of rule making, rule application, and rule adjudication—served as the theoretical framework for the first introduction to the politics of the Third World. By the time the second edition of *Comparative Politics* appeared, in 1978, this had come to be the three-level scheme of system, process, and policy functions. The system functions of socialization, recruitment, and communication maintain and transform the structure and culture of the political system as a whole. The process functions (or input and conversion activities) of interest articulation, interest aggregation, policy making, and implementation respond to the impulses coming from the surrounding domestic and international environments, and produce the policy outputs. The policy functions are the extractive, regulative, distributive, and symbolic impacts on the domestic and international environment. These impacts produce the feedbacks that, combined with other social, economic, and political processes, come full circle and produce Easton's inputs of demand and support.

The differences in Easton's and my intellectual style are reflected in Easton's *Children in the Political System* (1969), and my *The Civic Culture* (1963). The central concern of the Almond-Verba *Civic Culture* study was democratic stability. We compared the political attitudes of population samples in two relatively "stable" countries—the United States and Britain—and those of two relatively "unstable" ones—Germany and Italy. Mexico was included for a Third World contrast. Political socialization in the civic culture study was examined through retrospective evidence—that is, adult respondents' memories of their family, community, school, and workplace "political" experiences. By contrast, the Easton-Hess-Dennis project approached children directly in the primary schools as respondents and employed questionnaire and projective techniques in different cities and at different school levels. Thus, the authors were able to present direct evidence on the gradual emergence of attitudes toward extrafamilial authority and relate it through the concept of legitimacy to Easton's system components of community, regime, authorities. This is exemplary, painstaking scholarship, a first step in a very long-range research program. The *Civic Culture* study produced a great many hypotheses, including one that questioned the importance of early childhood socialization as compared with later experiences with authority, particularly work-group authority, and actual experience in relation to political authorities.

The revolution of the 1960s had significant influence on both Easton's work and mine. I became president of the American Political Science Association in 1966, succeeding my graduate school mate, David Truman. Both Truman and I celebrated the arrival of the "system" concept as the basic organizing unit of the new "behavioral" approach without sufficiently acknowledging Easton's pioneering work, even though Easton's two important books had been published in 1965. By that time Easton's social system concept had become a common professional possession. Easton became president in 1969, at a time when universities and, in particular, political science departments were wracked in agony over the student rebellion. Each one of us encountered this rebellion in a different way—Truman as an embattled university provost; Easton as a pleading association president elaborating a "postbehavioral" political science to calm the wrathful and self-righteous young; and I, similarly shaken, trying to balance scholarship and politics in ways that I later had reason to regret.

Responding to the criticism of the late 1960s and early 1970s that the system-functional approach was static and conservative in its implications, I recommended a return to historical case studies to prevent one-sided structuralism or voluntarism in the analysis of political systems and political development. In *Crisis, Choice, and Change: Historical Studies of Political Development* (1973), a group of colleagues and I demonstrated that making sense of political stability and change required a theoretical synthesis of the system-functional and the social mobilizational approaches on the macrostructural determinist side and the coalition theoretic version of the rational choice approach and leadership approaches on the microvoluntarist side. These were my responses to the dual, whipsaw attack on empirical political theory on the part of neo-Marxism and the reductionist methodological individualism of the rational choice approach.

David Easton's longer-run response is contained in his recent book, *The Analysis of Political Structure* (1990), which was ten years in the making. In it he faces in intellectual and scholarly terms the challenge he confronted and sought to solve in his 1969 presidential address—the relation between knowledge and action, scholarship and politics. His flirtation in that encounter with engagement and relevance in the turgid atmosphere and heat of the countercultural rebellion is now replaced by a plea for "the necessity for a continuing interest in fundamentals. . . . [D]espite the perils that we clearly face as we move into the twenty-first century, there is good reason to devote at least a small part of our intellectual resources as a hedge for the future. . . . There is still room for at least some scholars to continue the pursuit of basic knowledge" (p. 287). Before coming to this conclusion, he offers a powerful refutation of structuralism as reflected in the sophisticated neo-Marxism of Nicos Poulantzas—one of the heroes of the academic left. This argument occupies the middle third of his recent book. The first and last thirds of *The Analysis of Political Structure* are taken up with Easton's own pursuit of a theory of political structure. Here he is basically concerned with the philosophy of science "part-whole" problem as developed in Marxism and neo-Marxism and in the structuralism of Lévi-Strauss and others. Positivist science since Descartes has followed a reductionist course, seeking to explain the performance of the whole by the properties of parts. In political science this has taken the form of the emergence of the various specialties in the last century or so—public opinion, pressure groups, political parties, legislatures, executives, bureaucracies, courts. Easton's preoccupation with the political system as a whole, as a higher-order structure in an open hierarchy, is directed at rectifying this reductionist strategy or complementing it with a "whole-part" explanatory strategy. This argument is made in the most thorough and convincing way. But as though he wishes to keep us in suspense in anticipation of his next book, he gives us no hint as to how he proposes to solve the metamethodological problem he presents.

> [T]o say that the political system as such serves as a determinant of its sub-systems is in itself insufficient. The notion of determination is ambiguous; it conceals a number of possible relationships. We need to clarify the nature of the constraints the higher-order structures impose: whether and to what extent they reduce the variety of options open to lower-level structures to a single type (determination in the narrowest and strictest sense), facilitate the emergence of various structural alternatives, or just set broad limits within which alternative forms are possible, depending upon historical circumstances. In short, we need to know whether what is meant is that the lower order is determined in an obligative or facultative sense by the higher order, or whether the lower-order structures are only limited in their range of variation, as part of a nesting hierarchy (1990, pp. 278–79).

This is the problem with which Easton leaves us, presumably the problem that will be at the center of his next book. Fate must surely accede to his request that he be given time to finish this quest, which he has sustained since his early scholarly years.

REFERENCES

Almond, Gabriel A. 1970. *Political Development*. Boston: Little Brown & Co.

———. 1956. "Comparative Political Systems." *Journal of Politics* 18 (August).

Almond, Gabriel A., and James Coleman. 1960. *The Politics of the Developing Areas*. Princeton: Princeton University Press.

Almond, Gabriel A., Scott Flanagan, and Robert Mundt. 1973. *Crisis, Choice, and Change: Historical Studies of Political Development*. Boston: Little Brown & Co.

Almond, Gabriel A., and G. Bingham Powell. 1966. *Comparative Politics: A Developmental Approach*. Boston: Little Brown & Co.

———. 1978. *Comparative Politics; System, Process and Policy*. Boston: Little Brown & Co.

Almond, Gabriel A., and Sidney Verba. 1963. *The Civic Culture*. Princeton: Princeton University Press.

Bentley, Arthur. 1949. *The Process of Government*. Bloomington, IN: Principia Press.

Easton, David. 1953. *The Political System: An Inquiry into the State of Political Science*. New York: Alfred Knopf.

————. 1957. "An Approach to the Analysis of Political Systems." *World Politics* 9: 383–400.

————. 1965. A *Framework for Political Analysis*. Englewood Cliffs, NJ: Prentice Hall.

————. 1965. A *Systems Analysis of Political Life*. New York: Wiley.

———— (ed.). 1966. *Varieties of Political Theory*. Englewood Cliffs, NJ: Prentice-Hall.

————. 1990. *The Analysis of Political Structure*. New York: Routledge.

Easton, David, and Jack Dennis. 1969. *Children in the Political System*. New York: McGraw-Hill.

Finer, Herman. 1949. *Theory and Practice of Modern Government*. New York: Henry Holt.

Friedrich, Carl. 1950. *Constitutional Government and Democracy*. Boston: Ginn & Co.

Goodnow, Frank. 1900. *Politics and Administration*. Baltimore: Johns Hopkins University Press.

Herring, Pendleton. 1929. *Group Representation Before Congress*. Washington, D.C.: Brookings Institution.

————. 1940. *The Politics of Democracy*. New York: W. W. Norton.

————. 1953. "On the Study of Government." *American Political Science Review* 47, 4 (December).

Lasswell, Harold. 1930. *Psychopathology and Politics*. Chicago: University of Chicago Press.

————. 1956. *The Decision Process, Bureau of Governmental Research*. University of Maryland.

Merriam, Charles E. 1936. *The Role of Politics in Social Change*. New York: McGraw-Hill.

Parsons, Talcott, and Edward Shils. 1952. *Toward a Theory of Action*. Cambridge, MA: Harvard University Press.

Truman, David. 1951. *The Governmental Process*. New York: Alfred Knopf.

12

How Feminist Scholarship Could Change Political Science

Nancy C. M. Hartsock

Historically, political science has not been receptive to feminist concerns or, for that matter, to women in general. Women either are invisible as political actors or they are seen to be political actors of a peculiar—often deviant—sort. The response to scholarly work on women and politics has been characterized (accurately in my view) by one commentator as a kind of "radical deafness" in political science (Ferguson, 1987, 211), a failure to engage. Thus, only men appear on the stage as real political actors, and other political actors remain invisible. As a result, a great deal of politics and political activity has remained outside the purview of political science as a discipline. Much of what has been written presents a distorted account because of what has remained excluded, hidden behind a one-way mirror in which the masculine political actors see only themselves reflected back, remaining unable to see what—or rather, who—was concealed behind the "veil of ignorance."[1] Much the same could be said of many other fields in the social sciences.

The absence of a realistic portrayal of women as political actors has necessitated two feminist strategies/reworkings. First, feminist scholars have engaged in re-visioning and revaluing of activities in which women traditionally participate. Second, they have done research on how women participate in politics traditionally defined and have examined the ways women are disadvantaged by certain political institutions and advantaged by others. These efforts have made the discipline a more hospitable place for women and scholarship on women[2] and have raised new and fruitful questions for the discipline to address.

This pattern has been followed in discipline after discipline, as feminist scholars have challenged traditional assumptions and argued for transformation. Judith Stacey and Barrie Thorne (1985) argue that some progress has been made in fields such as history (in terms of the effects of social history) and anthropology (in terms of rethinking the category of kinship). They also attribute the differential progress feminist scholarship has made across different disciplines to the variances in subject matter, underlying epistemologies, and status and nature of theory across disciplines. Any of these factors may facilitate or impede a feminist transformation in a given discipline.

I suggest here that political science's resistance to feminist scholarship is distinct among the social sciences. Some have argued that there is a need for resocialization of political scientists themselves, and this may well ameliorate the problem (Evans, 1986, in Jonasdottir, 1988). It is certainly true that political science, like other social sciences, has represented a tacitly masculine, class privileged, and racially privileged universe as the universe worth studying. Certainly the canon of political theory—what the winners have thought worthy of preservation over a several-thousand-year history— fits that model. It is important to emphasize, however, that the situation in political science is not a matter of prejudice or ill- will among political scientists (although that certainly exists in some cases and has had an impact). Rather, political science as a discipline poses some unique problems for the inclusion of women.[3]

One of the most succinct definitions of the field of political science comes from a 1974 article by Susan Bourque and Jean Grossholtz. They argue that "politics is defined as masculine activity. . . . Those characteristics and enthusiasms which supposedly sway men (war, controversy, electoral manipulation) are defined as specifically political, while those characteristics and enthusiasms which supposedly sway women (human needs for food, clothing and shelter, adherence to consistent moral principles, the preemption of national by human concerns, a rejection of war as rational) are simply not considered political" (cited in Ferguson, 1987, 218). Nannerl Keohane (1981, 423) agrees: "The public realm, across cultures and over the centuries, has been male-centered to an extent unparalleled in other parts of human social life." She goes on to ask why the radical asymmetry between public and private has not become a research question for the discipline. Why has it been taken for granted that men but not women exist in the public sphere?[4]

Politics, war, and diplomacy have been men's work since the ancient Greeks defined much of what we still consider to be the proper concerns of public life. In those definitions, civic personality, masculinity, and military capacity have historically been coextensive (e.g., Hartsock, 1984; Pocock, 1975).[5] Thus, the recent interest in women's relation to and participation in politics has resulted in more than the correction of distortions in scholarly interpretations of women's activities; it has also raised a number of interesting and wide-ranging intellectual questions about the discipline.

What is to be included in definitions of politics? What ought to be required of the good citizen? How should theories of justice be reworked to include concerns traditionally located in the private sphere? How has the development (and current decline) of the welfare state in Western industrial states both included and excluded women as citizens? These are just a few examples of the kinds of questions beginning to be asked. In this chapter I suggest that the new scholarship on women opens questions about the proper subject matter of political science.[6]

TRADITIONAL SCHOLARSHIP ON WOMEN

I began this chapter with the claim that political science has historically been unreceptive to scholarship on women. This lack of interest is evidenced by the failure of many political science journals to publish feminist scholarship and by the failure of many "male-stream" scholars to engage with feminist work.[7] Thus, despite the increasingly rapid growth of feminist scholarship in political science, it remains vastly underrepresented—at times, even absent—in the mainstream of the discipline.[8] Political theory might seem likely to be more receptive than other parts of the discipline to feminist work because that field is less tied to positivist epistemological commitments that stress objectivity in the form of value-neutrality and searches for universal or general laws. In fact, however, feminist scholarship is not prominent in political theory. When the journal *Political Theory* printed an issue on theory for the 1980s, there was no treatment of feminism. And the book *What Should Political Theory Be Now?* published in 1984, contained sixteen essays authored by men, with a single footnote in which the absence of feminist theory was noted (Ferguson, 1987, 213).

Kelly and Fisher have more systematically documented the invisibility of women in political science and of scholarly work on women and politics.[9] They examined the fifteen journals judged to have the highest quality and impact in the profession to search for articles related to women. In all these journals, there have been a total of 433 articles related to women since the journals were founded—1906, in one case. By contrast, since its founding in 1980 the journal *Women and Politics* has published 209 articles related to women. If one looks simply at the *American Political Science Review* from 1949 to 1969, the work of 15 women was published, along with the work of 1,000 men. (Kelly and Fisher, 1992, 7).[10]

The issue, however, is not simply the paucity of scholarly writing about women and politics but also the images they project of women as political (or, more accurately, nonpolitical) actors. Carroll and Zerilli present a summary account of prevailing views of women and politics during a period when women were largely invisible. The canonical texts of the 1970s often described women in the following ways: women are apolitical; they lack political knowledge and interest; they vote less often than men, and when they do, they vote according to their husbands' views; they pay more attention to personalities than issues; they are "more conservative in their political preferences and voting (despite the fact that they vote like their husbands) and less tolerant of left wing political groups" (Carroll and Zerilli, 1992, 9, citing Jaquette, 1974; Bourque and Grossholtz, 1974; Goot and Reid, 1975). The authors note that this picture reflected a series of assumptions about women's behavior. Moreover, some important questions were not asked. Political scientists did not ask why women did not show higher levels of engagement with politics but assumed they knew why. Nor were they interested in the absence of women as political officeholders. (Carroll and Zerilli, 1992, 10).[11]

FEMINIST CRITICISM AND THE NEW SCHOLARSHIP ON WOMEN

What has been the role of feminist scholarship in bringing about change? Several empirical and theoretical projects merit our mention. First, there is the necessary effort to recover women's experience as traditionally defined—to show, for example, that the private sphere is worth analyzing. Such analysis is being done with much success in anthropology, psychology, sociology, and especially in history, where social history—the study of the lives of ordinary people—has made great strides. In addition, we now find studies of women as political actors. These often begin with efforts to examine women and the electoral process, particularly the fact that although there are only slight differences between women's and men's participation in such activities as voting, there are great disparities between them in the holding of public office.[12]

Feminist scholars in the 1980s asked why this was so and in the process raised new questions about the discipline. The answers they found were twofold. First, they looked at the political socialization of women as individuals, using surveys and interviews. More interestingly, they began to focus on supposedly gender-neutral issues such as the importance of incumbency in getting elected and the organization of the electoral arrangements. In the latter case, they found that women candidates got better results in systems of proportional representation than in single-member, geographically defined districts (e.g., Marcia Manning Lee, 1976, cited in Carroll and Zerilli, 1992). Research has also taken on more structural issues, such as how state policies influence and organize family life or contribute to the impoverishment of women. (Ackelsberg and Diamond, 1987, 507).

Second, attention to women's experiences has led to efforts to correct biases and to critique many of the assumptions and findings taken for granted in political science. For example, it would be useful to redo Robert Lane's work on political ideology to include women, as his study (like so many others in other disciplines) was based entirely on interviews with men.[13] This research strategy may have been fueled by his own views of the role of women. Writing out of the dominant ideology of the 1950s, he stated that

> working girls and career women and women who insistently serve the com-
> munity, and women with extra-curricular interests of an absorbing kind are
> often borrowing their time and attention and capacity for relaxed play and
> love from their children to whom it rightfully belongs. As Kardiner pointed
> out, the rise in juvenile delinquency (and, he says homosexuality) is partly
> to be attributed to the feminist movement and what it did to the American
> mother (1959, 355, in Lovenduski, 1981, 93).

Who Governs? should also be reevaluated. Virginia Sapiro (1977) argued that Dahl's data distort or conceal important information about women. She cites his discussion of the Parent-Teacher Association as an important example of these faults. Dahl recognizes that the PTA has a large female membership and suggests that for "many women, in fact the PTA is obviously an outlet for social needs"; perhaps "some female Machiavellians even look upon PTA activity as a way of assuring favorable treatment for their own children" (Dahl, 1961, in Sapiro, 1977, 260–61). Sapiro finds this sloppy empirical work: no motives can be "obvious" to the careful social scientist. Moreover, as Dahl's discussion of the organization proceeds, the women vanish.[14] Dahl notes that the PTA is a "channel through which potential leaders may enter into the school system, test themselves, gain experience, and pass into the ranks of the leaders." But when Dahl discusses the motives of the three most recent (male) appointees to the New Haven Board of Education who had been involved in the PTA, he notes, "To be sure, each of these men had already possessed a strong prior interest in education, but it was when the education of their own children was at stake that they became active in their PTA" (Dahl, 157, in Sapiro, 1977, 261.) Sapiro points out that the motivation ascribed to the women and men is described in quite different terms: "female Machiavellians," as opposed to men more legitimately concerned with the education of their children. In addition, Dahl fails to recognize the systematic exclusion of women from most positions of leadership in public life (Sapiro, 1977, 261–63).

NEW QUESTIONS FOR POLITICAL SCIENCE

As feminist scholars developed their critiques of the ways political science is traditionally done, as they attempted to fill in the gaps and add women's experiences, they often discovered that the gaps and distortions were there for important reasons, reasons based on the shape and definition of the discipline. This discovery, in political science as well as in other disciplines, led to a third task for feminist scholars. It became apparent that existing paradigms systematically ignored or erased the significance of women's experiences. Thus, feminist scholars across the disciplines were led to question and to rethink the basic conceptual and theoretical frameworks of their fields.

The paradigms in political science may make it one of the most difficult social sciences to transform because, as noted above, so much of what has been taken to be its proper subject matter is profoundly masculine. American political science has historically centered its substantive concerns on the institutions of formal government and its actors, studying ordinary citizens mainly in their role as voters or in contexts where their activity affects formal government institutions. The focus has been on activities almost always conducted by men. Historically, the actions of governments have been the actions of men; their policies—both foreign and domestic—have been made by men, with effects on other men in mind. War and diplomacy have also been masculine domains. To the extent that these areas constitute the locations where the paradigms central to political action are defined, women can be seen only as peripheral or deviant actors, actors whose political behavior cannot be explained or understood on the models developed on the basis of men's political activity. As a result, political science has missed or misunderstood much of what should be included under the heading of political action.

Concepts such as justice, equality, citizen participation, democracy, political obligation, social contract theory—all were developed in the context of a public sphere populated only by men. These concepts are now being criticized by feminist political scientists, who are in some cases proposing new understandings that could transform the way the discipline understands these concepts (e.g. Hirschmann, 1989; Mackinnon, 1989; Okin, 1989; Pateman, 1988). I want to address three examples of work that critiques the current paradigms in political science and points to alternative ways of understanding the political world—indeed, in some cases, to the redefinition of what is to count as political. One comes from one of my own projects, one from Carole Pateman, and the third from Susan Okin.

Hartsock: Masculinity in the Political Theory Canon

My own work (1989) suggests that many of the classic works of Western political thought present an understanding of politics structured by an overlay of manliness, citizenship, and warrior status. In addition, the "public sphere" was conceptualized as masculine, in opposition to a "private," female sphere. The business of the public sphere is that of men making war and "political decisions." The business of the private sphere is that of care-taking, rearing children, and household-centered activities (though for the Greeks and Roman republicans, it used to include production) and is the domain of women. Interestingly enough, one can begin to see the welfare state as a kind of contradiction in terms—a point to which I will return later to suggest that in the contemporary world there are gaps between ideology and reality. As a discipline, political science has too often been taken in by the view that politics is about masculine and manly citizenship and the business of making war and not about the daily business of man-aging societies and caring for populations.[15]

This important strand of thinking about politics and public life in the West originated with the ancient Greeks and is still with us today. I have characterized it as the "barracks tradition" to mark the conflation of being manly, a warrior, and a citizen. It emerges in the works we retain from ancient Greece and can be followed later through the revival of republican ideals in Western Europe.[16] In *Politics*, Aristotle attempted to resolve the tension between the gendered public and private spheres by putting house-holds in their proper place—subordinate to the public sphere. Thus, the realm of freedom and leisure in which citizens pursue political activity and war depends on a realm of necessity and work populated by women, slaves, and laborers. Aristotle's thought codifies an additional transition: the war-rior-hero, whose power depends on his valor in battle, gives way to the citizen, whose power depends on his valor in the rhetorical battle of politics. As the Roman empire replaced the Greek city-states, the Roman concept of *virtus* took over many of the connotations of the Greek *arete*, the moral excellence essential to the good citizen, and with it the image of the good-ness of the citizen as a capacity for heroic (especially military) action.

The breakdown of the classical world created the theoretical problem of how to understand change and led to a deification of the female figure of Fortuna. It was she who spun the wheel of fortune; her whims could make a man a prince or could destroy him. She represented a female force who operated through the creation of random disorder. Machiavelli held that the collapse of the Roman Empire was due to a loss of its warrior virtue and looked to the classical world for models of citizenship for his own time. His solution to the problem of disorder presented by Fortuna was a reas-sertion of manliness, or virtue. (The Latin root in question is *vir,* "man.") Summarizing the fundamental problem confronting the prince, Machiav-elli states: "[F]ortune is a Woman, and it is necessary, if you wish to master her, to conquer her by force" (Machiavelli, 1978, 161). Thus, politics and political action for Machiavelli are fundamentally structured by a symbolic gender struggle. He reasserts the centrality of military power as the foun-dation of civic society and, as a result of the centrality of gender imagery to his understanding of politics, worries about how some principalities have become "effeminate" by being insufficiently interested in military issues (Pitkin, 1984). Machiavelli's work can be understood as an account of how to subordinate and suppress the female forces of disorder at work in the human community. Success comes through the operation of masculine virtue closely linked to military capacity. Civic/political leadership requires manliness.

By the eighteenth century, the political community—as theorized in the work of Rousseau and others—was threatened less by the random disorder brought by Fortuna and more by the corrupting and effeminizing influence of commerce. For these thinkers, commerce represented irrational change and degeneration, which would result in subjection to the chaotic appetites and passions of both oneself and others. Rousseau makes clear that refinement of manners, civilization, and culture are all enemies of virtue. His admiration for Sparta, his argument that inequality itself grows inevitably from dependence on others, his denunciation of the theater, and, finally, his arguments that women should be restrained from playing a role in public life—all should be understood as part of an effort to recreate in eighteenth- century Europe the virtue, or manliness, he and other thinkers ascribed to the conduct of politics in the ancient republics. The profoundly structuring influence of gender on Rousseau's understanding of politics is evidenced not as much in what he wrote about women as in his concern for what he termed the effeminacy of the political community. That is, despite Rousseau's views about the importance of keeping women out of public life, his central focus was on the effeminacy of *male* political actors.

I am not asserting that gender is the only issue defining conceptions of the political community. Moreover, I acknowledge that throughout the history of Western political thought, there have been a number of challenges to these modes of thinking about politics. Nonetheless, gender clearly has been one of the important structuring factors in the development of ideas about politics as these appear in the works the modern West considers classics of political philosophy, the books we assign in courses on Western civilization.

Pateman: Manhood and Citizenship

The classics of Western political thought, then, present a very problematic picture for feminists. But the issue is not really the past.[17] After all, we no longer take Aristotle's theory of biology seriously. Why not simply include women in the public sphere and assume that his views on the good citizen apply equally well to both male and female citizens? This line of thought brings me to Carole Pateman's work on women and democratic citizenship (1984) and on what she terms the "sexual contract," which is an invisible precondition for the social contract of theorists such as Hobbes, Locke, and Rousseau (1988). She demonstrates that some of these same issues appear in modified form in contemporary discussions about democratic citizenship, in which unexamined assumptions are made about the gender of citizens. Pateman (1984, 1) notes that within the field of democratic theory the situation does not differ from that characteristic of political science as a whole: "It is not clear that feminist criticism today is taken any more seriously than John Stuart Mill's feminist criticism of liberalism over a century ago."

Pateman argues persuasively that the historical liberal arguments assumed—indeed, required—that the citizen be a man and a head of household. She goes on to argue that contemporary democratic theory, whether of the liberal or participatory variety, falls within this patriarchal tradition. There is talk of "the individual" but a failure to recognize that there are in fact two individuals—one male and one female. The question posed for feminists by the model of citizenship we have inherited is whether achieving equality means including women in the existing model or whether it is possible to rethink issues of democracy and citizenship to recognize women as women and not as "reflections of men" (Pateman, 1984, 4).

Pateman concludes that democratic theory must reject a unitary (and therefore masculine) conception of the citizen and recognize the importance of sexual differences (1984, 4). In making this argument, she uses the now widely shared feminist insight that "unmarked categories" always refer to dominant rather than subjected groups. One important consequence of her argument is that arguments about citizenship could no longer ignore the relationship between home and work. However, she argues, feminists must guard against putting all discussions of women and political life under the heading of the home, or private sphere. Women do increasingly participate in public life as traditionally understood.

A second consequence of Pateman's move to include sex differences in discussions of citizenship is to raise the question of whether full citizenship requires that each citizen participate identically in all the benefits and burdens of public life. Once again, the link between citizenship and military capacity represents an important juxtaposition that raises questions about women's citizenship. Some have suggested that if women are to be full citizens they need to be a part of the military in the same way as men. Pateman's strategy is different: she questions the way in which military service has been connected to citizenship. She recognizes that the willingness to fight and perhaps die for the state represents the ultimate duty for the male citizen. Historically, however, for women the ultimate duty to the state has been motherhood—to give birth for the state (1984, 11). But this has been, in part, the basis for women's unequal citizenship. Pateman argues that "if caring for and educating the young were to be seen as part of political rather than private life, not just the work of individual women, then the practice of motherhood and the capacities it requires could begin to transform understandings of citizenship and the meaning of community" (1984, 13). Such a redefinition of citizenship would also change the definition of the public and the private; the world could not be so neatly divided. And the failure of the theoretical division would have important practical applications for thinking about politics.

Okin: Do Theories of Justice Apply to Women?

My third example of feminist theory's potential to transform the discipline of political science comes from Susan Okin's *Justice, Gender, and the Family*. She points out that recent theories of justice have ignored the fact that society is deeply structured by gender. "Since theories of justice are centrally concerned with whether, how, and why persons should be treated differently from one another," she states, "this neglect seems inexplicable" (Okin, 1989, 8). The traditional distinction between public political life and private domestic life is reinforced by the fact that theorists generally ignore the family and its division of labor. Okin argues that these seemingly gender-blind theories in fact contain assumptions that families and their divisions of labor are structured in traditional, gendered ways.

She takes up a number of theories of justice, but her critique of Rawls's canonical text, *A Theory of Justice,* illustrates her point particularly well. Rawls, she argues, puts forward principles that could lead to a thorough challenge to the gender structure of our society, yet Rawls himself fails to recognize this possibility. Instead, the assumption of the existing gender structure appears repeatedly in his work. Though he sometimes uses gender-neutral terms such as "moral person," his concern with relations between generations is put in terms of "fathers and sons." Okin notes the significance of this formulation given the fact that, traditionally, theories of justice have referred only to men. She asks whether Rawls's theory of justice applies to women (1989, 91). Her questions and concerns are made more plausible by the fact that Rawls takes up the issue of military conscription and concludes that it is justifiable in some circumstances, as long as institutions try to "make sure that the risks of suffering from these imposed misfortunes are more or less evenly shared by all members of society over the course of their life" (Rawls, 380–81). Yet Rawls fails even to mention the fact that women have been exempt from the draft and in most countries are prohibited from serving in combat.

Okin points out a second troubling feature of Rawls' theory: the fact that the free and equal persons in the original position, those who formulate the principles of justice, are not simple individuals but heads of families, representing the family as a group. Traditionally, of course, heads of households have been male (indeed, historically this has often been a requirement for citizenship), and Rawls' strategy leads him to ignore the possibility that life within the family is a proper subject matter for theories of justice (Okin, 1989, 92–93). In so doing, he undermines his own project significantly: he holds that justice is a characteristic of institutions whose members could have agreed to their rules without knowing where they would be located in the structure. But the adults who are not the heads of households (in most cases, wives) are unrepresented in the original position, and, given our current gender structures, they will be left in institutional arrangements in a position of inequality, with no opportunity to be heard or to influence the rules (Okin, 1989, 94).

Unlike Pateman, Okin wants to do away with gender in considerations of citizenship and justice. She holds that democratic ideals require moving away from a society structured by gender toward a society that encourages the equal sharing of paid work, unpaid work, and reproductive labor by both women and men. Such changes would have important effects on a number of public policies. It would mean, for example, important changes in the workplace, a recognition of work done by parents rather than the assumption that those in the work force are not importantly involved with their households (Okin, 1989, 175–76). Once again, it is evident that the traditional division between public and private would be vastly restructured, although in ways quite different from those Pateman envisaged. Whereas Pateman argues for a recognition of gender in discussions of politics and in public policy, Okin argues for the abolition of gender divisions of labor by means of public policies. In either case, however, the definition of what is public and what is private would have to shift to recognize women as integral participants in the political world.

CONTEMPORARY CHANGES
IN THE CONCEPT OF THE POLITICAL

Some important changes have been happening in Western industrial societies. It is no accident that the development of feminist scholarship (and the international women's movement) coincides with the movement of women into paid employment and, in part through this medium, greater participation in public life. The structures of the modern welfare state developed in step with these changes; they represent the state's taking on some of the work of caring and education that Pateman points to and the protection of the vulnerable for which Okin argues. It is the bureaucracy that does this work, and feminist scholars such as Kathy Ferguson (1984) and Eva Kreisky (1988) point to some important changes bureaucracies have made in the relation between citizen and state. Kreisky notes that state bureaucracies were initially organized along the inner principles of the military in terms of discipline and hierarchy. But later, as state activities widened, public welfare and "mothering" became part of the work (1988, 6).

Kreisky argues that in the case of Austria—and, one might suspect, other welfare states—there has been a feminization of public administration in two senses. First, women have been allowed to enter public service in part because they are held to have suitable skills: beautiful handwriting and no great intellectual capacities (1988, 13). Second, the expansion of bureaucracy has feminized the public sphere (a point also argued by Ferguson). What was assumed to be a biological category has now become visible as the political category it has in fact been for several thousand years. The clients of the bureaucracy, as well as the bureaucrats themselves (whether male or female), now must cultivate the "feminine" qualities of dependence, submissiveness, and attentiveness. As one begins to study the modern state, Ferguson argues, one may discover that the relations between women and politics are more complicated than previously understood. In contemporary states, it may not be that women are without power because they are female but rather that they are defined as female because they are without power (Ferguson, 1984, 58, in Kreisky 1988, 17; see also MacKinnon, 1989).

The work of scholars such as Barbara Nelson and Michael Brown on the development of the welfare state in the United States is particularly interesting in exposing the gendered (and, in the case of Brown, raced) quality of the development of welfare state policies. Social Security was consciously structured in the 1930s to respond to the needs of white male workers. As Brown points out, at least one observer in the 1930s noted that "the social security bill looks like a sieve with the holes just big enough for the majority of Negroes to fall through" (Charles Houston, cited in Brown, 1992, 201). Nelson has made similar points about the race and gender biases of Social Security legislation and points out that the introduction of benefits for dependents or survivors introduced in 1939 created a bias against working women (citing Martha Derthick, in Nelson, 1986, 230). She also discusses the development of what has become a two- tiered system of government assistance—one aimed at men, the other at women. Thus, notes Nelson (citing 1980 data), 81.1 percent of AFDC guardians are women, whereas women make up only 41.4 percent of unemployment compensation beneficiaries. She, too, wants to change the definition of the political and argues that in the study of politics it is important to include

> not only the recognition of the exclusion of women from what is traditionally political, but also the inclusion in politics of *(sic)* what women have traditionally done. We shall have gone a long way to creating a more inclusive political discourse if we give attention to families, communities, voluntary groups, social movements, and the welfare state, to name a few topics (Nelson, 1989, 21).

FEMINIST SCHOLARSHIP   *243*

Others (e.g., Bookman and Morgan, cited in Carroll and Zerilli, 1992, 38) recast community organizations not as simply voluntary associations but rather as groups of women challenging the power of the state. Nelson suggests that "it would be very instructive to know the extent to which poor women engage in both electoral and client activities and how the two together inform their understanding of and judgments about government and politics" (Nelson, 1986, 225).

Perhaps we are in the midst of seeing some shifts in the definition of citizenship in the modern world. These changes are not all positive. If feminists want an active and participatory democracy that includes women as well as men, along with all classes and all racial groups, then the inclusion of women in bureaucracies is not entirely positive. Some women are now part of oppressive systems of the state, both subject to and enforcers of state control. Feminist demands that the state finance women's projects such as shelters for battered women may be part of the process of turning the state into an arena of gender as well as class struggle. The 1994 "Contract With America" put forward during the Republican campaign and aggressively pushed in the 1995 legislative session represented a recognition of (and revulsion toward) some of the changes of the last decades. In both political theory and electoral politics, the traditional distinction between public and private is being blurred, as are questions of citizenship and democracy and theories of justice. In addition, the Republican legislative agenda has raised important questions about the extent to which the state can and should regulate (and define what is to count as) family life. As these processes proceed, political science cannot fail to take notice of them.

CONCLUSIONS: FEMINIST CONTRIBUTIONS

Over the next twenty-five years, I would like to see the reconstruction of the discipline rather than the simple addition of gender as a variable. But this undertaking would at least to some extent require a reconstruction of the public world that the discipline studies.[18] Political science is a discipline that reflects and reinforces the collective construction of the public world in the West over the last several thousand years. Its fundamental assumptions are deeply masculinist because the fundamental assumptions of political life have historically been deeply masculinist. We cannot have a political science that fully includes women and their concerns without a politics that also does so. The inclusion of women in the political community as full participants would be an important step toward forging more satisfactory practices of politics and thereby a political science more inclusive of women's lives and concerns.

Feminist scholarship itself faces challenges around issues of inclusion, and these challenges represent important future directions for research. Just as feminist scholars criticized work in political science for making falsely universal statements and assumptions about "citizens" and "individuals," so, too, white feminist scholars in the United States have been criticized by women of color for making falsely universal statements about "women." Many feminist scholars are now convinced of the need to pay attention to more historically specific and contextual issues. A major task for the 1990s will be to unpack the category "women" and to see that public policies have differential effects on different groups of women (Carroll and Zerilli, 1992, 57–60). These efforts are particularly important in the context of the Republican attacks on social programs in the 104th Congress. They argue that their budget provides for important tax savings for families in the form of tax credits for each child, reforms of the student loan program, and so on, and they put forward the dollar amounts than an average family can save. But it is worth noting that in order to receive a tax credit, a family must first earn enough income to pay taxes; it is worth asking what kinds of families are likely to benefit from the government's student loan programs; it is worth asking which noncustodial fathers have regular incomes that can be attached for child support payments. Research on these questions that accounts for variations of family circumstance and form could have important consequences for public policies.

The goal should be to create a more inclusive political science, one that more accurately reflects the diversity of ways in which men and women, Euro-Americans and people of color, are inserted into and help to shape the political system. In the process we should expect our definition of politics and the concerns appropriate to public life to shift in important ways.

NOTES

1. I am, of course, referring to Rawls's use of the term in *A Theory of Justice*. These practices are not at all unique to political science.

2. Martin Gruberg's ongoing documentation of women's participation in the annual APSA meetings provided not only information but some important impetus for change. A number of his reports have appeared in *PS: Political Science*, published quarterly by the American Political Science Association.

3. The inclusion of women has been a problem of both subject matter and inclusion as scholars. Though these are related problems, here I will concentrate on the problems posed by the subject matter and leave the reader to speculate on how the subject matter might attract or repel practitioners. It has been of interest to me that whereas political scientists tend to study institutions, sociologists are much more interested in social movements, in which women, workers, people of color, and others who are excluded from the official establishment make up an important part of the subject matter. The field as a whole has a higher percentage of women scholars and (I suspect) "minority" scholars.

4. Many authors have made this point. Several relevant anthologies include Harris and King (1989); Pateman and Grosz (1986); and Stiehm (1984).

5. It is certainly the case that women have historically been involved in politics, diplomacy, and war. Elizabeth, Catherine the Great, Golda Meir, Margaret Thatcher, and Indira Ghandi all proved themselves better "men" than their opponents. But their sex was always an issue. And who can forget George Bush's invoking his military experience in a vice-presidential debate with Geraldine Ferraro to suggest that she would not be tough enough to push the button?

6. I am struck with the extent to which formerly "private" issues currently dominate "public" discussions—abortion, teen pregnancy, "family values," etc. have become central to at least the media's portrayal of political life. It may be that the discourse about politics is changing faster than the discourse of political science.

7. This phrase was introduced by Mary O'Brien in *The Politics of Reproduction* and has since gained wide currency. It is not, of course, a biological designation but rather one that points to intellectual commitments.

8. Kathy Ferguson points to the fact that the 1983 edition of *Political Science: The State of the Discipline,* edited by a woman, mentions women and feminism in only one of its seventeen articles (1987, 212; see slso Steurnagel, 1986) A new volume on the state of the discipline published in 1993 contains at least one lengthy and comprehensive treatment of the literature on women and politics (see Carroll and Zerilli, 1992).

9. Kelly and Fisher also note that in 1970, only 5 percent of political science faculty were women, and they were clustered at the lower ranks and at undergraduate colleges. Though this pattern of employment is still typical, by 1989 20 percent of political science faculty were women (Kelly and Fisher, 1992, 6).

10. I should note that the journal that published the greatest number of articles relating to women was *PS:Political Science,* with a total of eighty pieces. But *PS* is an internal journal of the APSA, with notes about teaching, members news, and so on. And thirty-one of the articles it published were reports from the APSA Committee on the Status of Women. I note with pleasure that *Political Research Quarterly,* the journal of the Western Political Science Association, my regional political science association, ranks first among the fifteen journals studied in publication of articles related to women.

11. But there is some room for optimism about the future importance of issues surrounding women and politics. When one breaks down the publications of articles relating to women by decade, and when one looks at the content of work on women and politics, a different picture emerges. Of the 433 articles ever published in these 15 journals, 121 were published between 1970 and 1979; 201 between 1980 and 1989; and 49 in 1990–1991. There is clearly a rapidly rising number of articles on women and political life. Feminist scholarship is obviously receiving more serious attention from the discipline, but at present, the authors conclude, only 3 of the 15 journals provide much of a comprehensive overview: *Western Political Quarterly* (now the *Political Research Quarterly*), *Journal of Politics,* and the *Public Administration Review* (Fisher and Kelly, 1992, 25–26).

12. A comparison of issues on which there were greater and lesser gender gaps in the 1994 and 1996 elections could be very instructive about the ways women are interacting with the political process.

13. This could be particularly interesting in the light of work on women's as opposed to men's understandings of ethics, relationships, and so on. See, for example, Carol Gilligan's work, *In a Different Voice* (1982), and Belencky et al., *Women's Ways of Knowing* (1986).

14. This is a common move that goes as far back as Plato's Republic. Women are to be a part of the guardian class, but when discussions of possible military conflicts begin, women strangely vanish from the scene. As Okin (1989) demonstrates, this theoretical move remains in use.

15. The current Republican legislative agenda for profound cuts in the welfare state, coupled with their funding of the military at levels higher than even the military requests, could perhaps be read as a revival of the republican tradition I trace in these few pages.

16. These associations emerged even before conceptions of the citizen of the *polis* were in place and can be found in important forms in works such as the Iliad. (See Hartsock, 1984.)

17. We are still greatly influenced by these theories and the images of citizenship they convey. We still read and teach these works. Moreover, one can find instances of how these images affect not only thinking about politics but political action as well. The shape of political discussion in the United States after its invasion of Panama had a great deal to do with masculinity. One could almost hear George Bush repeating the words of Lyndon Johnson during the Vietnam War. Bill Moyers reported that "it was as if . . . he were saying, 'By God I'm not going to let those puny brown people push me around" (Fasteau, 1976,192; see also Halberstam, 1972, 531–532). The sentiments sound strikingly more appropriate to a street-corner confrontation than to a reasoned discussion of foreign policy.

18. It should certainly be recognized that the political world is in the midst of important upheavals and that gender and race issues are central to the kinds of redefinitions taking place. Rather than making the changes I hoped to see, current officeholders seem to be involved in an effort to remasculinize politics and create not simply a separate private sphere but a subordinate one as well.

REFERENCES

Ackelsberg, Martha, and Irene Diamond. 1987. "Gender and Political Life: New Directions in Political Science." In Beth B. Hess and Myra Marx Ferree, *Analyzing Gender: A Handbook of Social Science Research*. Newbury, CA: Sage, pp. 504–525.

Belencky, Sandra, et. al. 1986. *Women's Ways of Knowing*. New York: Basic Books.

Bookman, Ann, and Sandra Morgen. 1988. *Women and the Politics of Empowerment*. Philadelphia: Temple University Press.

Bourque, Susan, and Jean Grossholtz. 1974. "Politics as an Unnatural Practice: Political Science Looks at Female Participation," *Politics and Society* 4: 255–66.

Brown, Michael. 1992. "Divergent Fates: Race, Gender and the Legacy of New Deal Social Policy," *1992 Proceedings of the Third Women's Policy Research Conference*. Washington, D.C.: Institute For Women's Policy Research, pp. 201–204.

Carroll, Susan, and Linda Zerilli. 1983. "Feminist Challenges to the Discipline of

Political Science." In Ada Finifter (ed.), *Political Science: The State of the Discipline*. Washington, D.C.: APSA, 1983.

Dahl, Robert. 1961. *Who Governs?* New Haven, CT: Yale University Press.

Evans, Judith. 1986. *Feminism and Political Theory*. London: Sage.

Fasteau, Mark Feigen. 1976. "Vietnam and the Cult of Toughness in Foreign Policy." In Deborah S. David and Robert Brannon (eds.), *The Forty-nine Percent Majority*. Reading MA: Addison- Wesley, pp. 183–98.

Ferguson, Kathy. 1984. *The Feminist Case Against Bureaucracy*. Philadelphia: Temple University Press.

———. 1987. "Male-Ordered Politics: Feminism and Political Science." In Terrence Ball, *Idioms of Inquiry: Critique and Renewal in Political Science*. Albany, NY: State University of New York Press, pp. 209–30.

Finifter, Ada (ed.). 1983. *Political Science: The State of the Discipline*. Washington, D.C.: APSA.

Gilligan, Carol. 1982. *In a Different Voice*. Cambridge, MA: Harvard University Press.

Goot, Murray, and Elizabeth Reid. 1975. *Women and Voting Studies: Mindless Matrons or Sexist Scientism?* Sage Professional Papers in Contemporary Political Sociology Series. London: Sage.

Halberstam, David. 1972. *The Best and the Brightest*. New York: Random House.

Hartsock, Nancy C. M. 1984. "Prologue to a Feminist Critique of War and Politics." In Judith Stiehm (ed.), *Women's Views of the Political World of Men*. Dobbs Ferry, NY: Transnational, pp. 121–50.

———. 1989. "Masculinity, Heroism, and the Making of War." In Adrienne Harris and Ynestra King (eds.), *Rocking the Ship of State*. Boulder, CO: Westview, pp. 133–52.

Hirschmann, Nancy. 1989. "Freedom, Recognition, and Obligation: A Feminist Approach to Political Theory," *American Political Science Review* 83: 1227–44.

Jaquette, Jane, S. 1974. "Introduction." In *Women in Politics*. New York: Wiley, pp. xiii–xxxvii.

Jonasdottir, Anna. 1988. "Adding Women and Revising the Discipline." 1988 International Political Science Convention. Unpublished paper.

Kelly, Rita, and Kimberly Fisher. 1992. "Women and Politics: An Assessment of Publications in the Top 15 Political Science Journals." Unpublished paper, Arizona State University.

Keohane, Nannerl. 1981. "Speaking from Silence," *Soundings* 64: 423–32.

Kreisky, Eva (1988) "Bureaucracy and Women," (unpublished paper)

Lane, Robert (1959) *Political Life* (Glencoe, IL: Free Press)

Lee, Marcia Manning (1976) "Why Few Women Hold Public Office: Democracy and Sex Roles," *Political Science Quarterly* 91:296–314.

Lovenduski, Joni. 1981. "Toward the Emasculation of Political Science: The Impact of Feminism." In Dale Spender, *Men's Studies Modified: The Impact of Feminism on the Academic Disciplines*. New York: Pergamon Press, pp. 83–98.

Machiavelli, Nicolo. 1978. *The Prince*. New York: Penguin.

Mackinnon, Catherine. 1989. *Toward a Feminist Theory of the State*. Cambridge, MA: Harvard University Press.

Nelson, Barbara. 1989. "Women and Knowledge in Political Science: Texts Histories, and Epistemologies," *Women and Politics* 9:1–25.

———. 1986. "Women's Poverty and Women's Citizenship: Some Political Consequences of Economic Marginality." In Gelpi, Hartsock, Novak, and Strober
(eds.), *Women and Poverty*. Chicago: University of Chicago Press, pp. 209–32.

Nelson, John (ed.). 1983. *What Should Political Theory Be Now?* Albany, NY: State
University of New York Press.

O'Brien, Mary. 1981. *The Politics of Reproduction*. Boston: Routledge and Kegan Paul.

Okin, Susan. 1978. *Women in Western Political Thought*. Princeton, NJ: Princeton University Press.

———. 1989. *Justice, Gender, and the Family*. New York: Basic Books.

Pateman, Carole. 1984. "Feminism and Participatory Democracy: Some Reflections
on Sexual Difference and Citizenship." Unpublished manuscript.

———. 1988. *The Sexual Contract*. Stanford, CA: Stanford University Press.

Pateman, Carole, and Elizabeth Grosz (eds.). 1986. *Feminist Challenges: Social and
Political Theory*. Boston: Northeastern University Press.

Pitkin, Hanna. 1984. *Fortune Is a Woman*. Berkeley, CA: University of California
Press.

Plato. 1968. *The Republic of Plato*. Ed. Alan Bloom. New York: Basic Books.

Pocock, J. G. A. 1975. *The Machiavellian Moment*. Princeton, NJ: Princeton University Press.

Rawls, John. 1971. *A Theory of Justice*. Cambridge, MA: Belknap Press of Harvard
University Press.

Sapiro, Virginia. 1977. "Women's Studies and Political Conflict." In Julia Sherman
and Evelyn Beck, *The Prism of Sex: Essays in the Sociology of Knowledge*. Madison,
WI: University of Wisconsin Press, pp. 253–66.

Spelman, Elizabeth. 1982. "Woman as Body: Ancient and Contemporary Views,"
Feminist Studies 8, 1: 109–32.

Stacey, Judith, and Barrie Thorne. 1985. "The Missing Feminist Revolution in Sociology," *Social Problems* 32, 4 (1985): 301–16.

Steurnagel, Gertrude. 1986. "Is Anyone Listening?" Unpublished paper.

Political Theory and Public Policy

Marx, Weber, and a Republican Theory of the State

Theodore J. Lowi and Edward J. Harpham

Looking backward, we can see more than sixty years of sustained growth of national government in the United States. We recognize radical institutional development, with large agencies engaging in positive government and trained professionals utilizing sophisticated decision-making techniques based upon exhaustive research and data analysis. We find fundamental constitutional change, with federal courts, including the Supreme Court, steadfastly refusing even to review serious questions about the substantive limits of national government power or the limits of its power to raise revenue, spend money, or incur debt. We note a fundamental shift in public philosophy, in which the national government is obliged or expected to play a positive role in the economy and the society. Did the national government merely grow larger, or was it transformed? Do we live in an extended Republic of 1787, or was the First Republic succeeded at some point after 1937 by the Second Republic of the United States?

It is not at all accidental that the first clear answer, coming in roughly the twentieth year of growth, embraced continuity by embracing American exceptionalism. Looking long and hard at the "liberal tradition in America," Louis Hartz concluded that liberalism saved capitalism and more. It also helped to maintain the nation's link with the exceptionalism of its past and to shield it from the threat of Europeanization. Europeanization seems to be what was at stake in any loss of exceptionalism, and Europeanization was almost certainly what the eighteenth-century founders and twentieth-century liberals were trying to ward off. Twentieth-century pluralist theory was itself a kind of adjustment, a softening of radical individualism in the face of the permanent presence of big government. By the early 1950s, groups had come to replace individuals as the machines in the engine room of American democratic theory.

The trouble with pluralism as philosophy or as empirical science was not that it was wrong. Quite the contrary. The trouble was that it did not go far enough. The trouble was that in accepting the denial of the state and, in effect, accepting the Hartzian argument that exceptionalism was not dead, 1950s pluralism did not see beyond the process being described. It took the state, if at all, as a permanent presence within which a genuinely pluralist political process played itself out.

Critics of the pluralist authors emerged from all over the political spectrum, disagreeing with each other even as they mounted their critiques. But on a few points the critics seemed to be in agreement. First, they agreed that pluralists were missing the biases of pluralism itself. They agreed that insufficient attention was being given to the character and impact of the rules and history within which pluralism operated. They agreed also that there was a cruel optimism in the pluralist treatment of the unorganized and the nonparticipatory. However, though they were well grounded, the antipluralist writings did not come to full realization or acceptance of the fact that government in America had grown to such a degree that it had produced a difference in principle.

Somewhere during the 1960s and 1970s, the American system had its crisis and it died. There emerged a new system that had to be confronted. Despite all the wisdom in Almond's 1989 review essay, we believe he is incorrect in contending that the state never moved out of the mainstream of political science, particularly the state as theory or as the source of theory (1988: 860). The state was coming back, and it was coming back in a form superior to its earlier one. The comeback may have gotten its biggest boost with the formation of the Social Science Research Council (SSRC) and its appeal for "bringing the state back in." But it had started well before that time. Note, for example, the theme of the American Political Science Association (APSA) program of 1981, "Restoring the State to Political Science" (see also Lowi 1988: 885). Whenever it happened, and whoever made it happen, the comeback of the state restored to central value in political science all the literature on public policies, political executives and bureaucracies, state agencies, and other institutions that Almond had cited as evidence of the state's always having been in.

But the return of the state is not merely an established fact. It is an opportunity, one that can easily be lost. This chapter takes up the challenge with a search for sources of state theory in the two schools of thought that dominate current discussion of the state: the neo-Marxist school and the neo-Weberian school. Our purpose is not merely to analyze and criticize each of these two major schools but also to explore whether a theory more appropriate to the new American state can be developed out of them. One thing can be said with some confidence at the outset: whatever state theory is or becomes, it will have to be Americanized as a "republican theory of the state." A republican theory of the state will possess contradictions, as all theories possess contradictions, but 1) they will be American contradictions; 2) they will be explicit rather than hidden contradictions; and 3) the theory will have the advantage of providing its own particular method and data for a level of discourse that can handle the contradictions as empirical questions rather than intractable philosophic problems. This part of our review can be called "bringing public policy back in."

This inquiry begins with a search for the definition and purpose of the state in traditional political theory. We then consider neo-Marxist and neo-Weberian contributions to the theory of the state. Neither of these claims to provide a state theory per se; in fact, each treats the state as part of a still more inclusive theoretical perspective. Therefore, we will refer to these schools as *sources of* state theory rather than as state theories. Finally, we draw some conclusions and attempt to tie an alternate theoretical approach to the study of public policy and the state for the purpose of strengthening both.

THE DEATH AND LIFE OF THE STATE
IN POLITICAL SCIENCE

The theory of the state has played a central role in political thought since the seventeenth century (Held 1989, Vincent 1987). Writers as diverse as the mercantilist pamphleteers of the seventeenth century, Adam Smith and James Madison in the eighteenth century, John Stuart Mill and Karl Marx in the nineteenth century, and Max Weber, Woodrow Wilson, and adherents of the Burgess school of political science in the twentieth century built into their inquiries an investigation of the state as a locus of public power and an initiator of policy. It is not too far off the mark to claim that modern political thought is at its core an inquiry into the nature of the modern state, perhaps the greatest and most dangerous social institution invented in the modern era. Not only are its claims to power unique, but its reach into society and the lives of individual citizens is all-embracing.

Modern theories of the state effectively bridge the gap between, on the one hand, moral inquiries into the origin and extent of legitimate government and, on the other, empirical studies of the specific institutional structures and public policies found in the real world. Modern state theory thus focuses attention upon the various linkages between the state and society and offers a wide variety of perspectives from which to view state power, organized group interests, and public policy. As Andrew Vincent reminds us, there is no "right" theory of the state. It is a contestable concept, reflecting the fundamental values and self-image of the theorist as well as the empirical realities of the society in which the theorist lives (1987: 42–43).

One of the first great modern state theorists was Thomas Hobbes. For him, the absolutist state provided the solution to the fundamental problem of modern politics: order. The goal of public policy was to serve the interests of this state and thus the public. Groups ultimately acquired their authority and legitimacy through the state. Other modern theorists looked at the state in a different light. For Adam Smith, the fundamental problem of politics was not so much one of order as the misuse of public authority. According to the father of political economy, the authority of the state was constantly abused by private groups seeking to promote their own economic interests. His solution was a "system of natural liberty" in which the functions of the state were limited to providing for defense, justice, and a few public works. James Madison's solution, by contrast, was a large republic operating under a system of checks and balances that made it impossible for any one interest to conquer the state for its own advantage. For his part, Woodrow Wilson argued that a sharp line had to be drawn between politics and administration. Elected officials should make the important political decisions for a democratic society, but professional administrators acting in the public interest should oversee the day-to-day operations of the state itself. Though much divided these thinkers in their understanding of the state and its relationship to society, all believed that a study of the state lay at the heart of all political inquiry, particularly matters of public policy.

By the middle of the twentieth century, state theory had effectively died in American political science, being replaced by what has now come to be called the pluralist paradigm.[1] Pluralist writers such as Arthur Bentley (1908), V. O. Key (1942), David Truman (1951), and Robert Dahl (1961) cast aside the "formalisms" of a state-centered perspective, supplanting it with a process-oriented political science that focused attention upon the role played by groups in American society.[2] Not satisfied with the "metaphysical" theories of public power or the explanations of public policy developed by earlier, state theorists, pluralist writers sought to explain all political activities, including the making of public policy, in terms of society.

Under the banner of pluralism, numerous traditional political concepts were recast. For example, James Madison's theory of factions was reformulated into a more benign understanding of interest groups, and his theory of checks and balances within the institutions of government was replaced by a process- oriented theory of the checks and balances found in society. Similarly, the sharp distinction drawn by Wilson between politics and administration was blurred into the "more realistic" study of the politics of administration. Crosscutting cleavages, latent groups, and the democratic culture, not the logic of power in public institutions or the actions of narrowly self-interested groups threatening the autonomy of state institutions, came to dominate the concerns, methodology, and rhetoric of American political science. Similarly, traditional concepts such as the public interest, corruption, and the rule of law gave way to such nebulous concepts as "the rules of the game," the "competitive group process," and "discretionary justice."

What accounts for the decline of state theory and the triumph of a process-oriented, society-centered theory of pluralism? One answer might be that, some time in the twentieth century, political science became precisely what it claimed to be: a science of the political. From this perspective, pluralist political science and the behavioral revolution that accompanied it in the 1950s and 1960s represented the triumph of the real over the ideal, the empirical over the metaphysical.[3] Recent histories of the discipline, however, raise serious questions about this line of argument. As the works of Bernard Crick, Raymond Seidelman and Edward J. Harpham, and David Ricci have shown, the development of an American science of politics is as much a response to the current political world as it is a study of it. The concepts, tools, and methods of political science are shaped in large part by the very political order under study. What was the world being studied by pluralist theorists? The New Deal world—one of newly created public institutions such as the Social Security Administration, state unemployment insurance commissions, independent regulatory commissions, the Tennessee Valley Authority, and the Department of Labor, institutions not yet fully understood nor completely accepted by the public at large. This was also a world of public policy making at the national level, where the government assumed new redistributive and regulatory functions.

Pluralist theory helped to solve the constitutional crisis created by the New Deal (see Lowi 1969). By treating as irrelevant, or unscientific, questions or issues central to state theory—such as the existence and control of political power, the rule of law, the concept of constitutional government, and the idea of the public interest—pluralist theory provided an elaborate explanation and defense of the institutional structures of power and policy that emerged out of the New Deal. In their search for a science of politics, American political scientists came to defend as normal and proper the very institutions and policies that were transforming the American political landscape.

All in all, political science's rejection of the theory of the state is not surprising. Prior to the twentieth century, the United States appeared to be for the most part a "stateless" society—that is, one dominated by state and local governments infused with special interests and tied together by a nation-state of "courts and parties" (see Skowronek, 1982). At best, traditional state theory seemed unable to explain the facts of American political life, undervaluing the democratic culture percolating through its institutions. At worst, it misinterpreted American political life, mistaking democratic participation in public affairs for the intrusion of special interests into the public arena. The national institutions built during the Progressive era and the New Deal, with their amalgamation of private interest

254   THEODORE J. LOWI AND EDWARD J. HARPHAM

and public power, only accentuated the tensions between state theory and the reality of twentieth century political life in America. Political scientists were left with a choice: either accept the theory and use it critically to assess reality or use the reality to build a new theory. For leading political scientists the choice was clear: abandon state theory and replace it with an empirically grounded theory of American political life, one that explained why, despite all the changes that had taken place during the Progressive era and the New Deal, the United States continued to be a democratic society.

Although the pluralist interpretation of American political life dominated political science throughout the 1950s and early 1960s, there were occasional rumblings of discontent. In 1956, sociologist C. Wright Mills argued that pluralism only explained the "middle levels of power," missing entirely the power elite that had coalesced atop American political, military, and corporate institutions. In 1960, E. E. Schattsschneitter spoke of how the pluralist chorus sang with a distinctly upper-class accent. And in 1961, Henry Kariel claimed that American pluralism had actually gone into decline. These rumblings intensified throughout the 1960s, building into a wholesale critique of the pluralist paradigm by the end of the decade. Two concerns lay at the heart of this dissenting view. First, critics maintained that pluralism failed to account for how power was structured in American society or how private power was transformed into public power through political institutions. Questions that had been central to state theory—such as the problems of institutional structure, the relationship between private power and public authority, the nature of political power, the idea of the public interest, and the rule of law—returned to play pivotal roles in the work of pluralist critics (see McConnell 1966 and Lowi 1969). Such themes made it legitimate—indeed, essential—for political scientists once again to consider the state as a theoretical and an empirical problem. Second, it was argued that pluralist theories failed to account for how public policies were actually conceived, passed, and implemented or to identify the crucial variables at the various stages of the policy-making process. Such concerns gave rise to a renewed interest in the study of public policy and helped stimulate the growth of an entire new subfield in the discipline.

The origins of contemporary state theory lie in the critique of the pluralist model of American politics and its defense of the New Deal order. But as there are many critiques of pluralism, so there are numerous contemporary theories of the state. Contemporary state theory must be seen as a river fed by two tributaries, each drawing upon a different source. One tributary has as its source the class-based analysis of Marxism. A second draws upon the institutional analysis of Weberian sociology. Understanding contemporary state theory ultimately means grasping how each of these schools moves beyond the society-based explanations of pluralism and seeks to provide an alternative perspective from which political scientists can view political institutions and structures as well as the making of public policy.

THE NEO-MARXIST THEORY OF THE STATE

One move outside the pluralist paradigm followed directly from the rediscovery of Marx in the 1960s. Stimulated by the dissemination in English of many of Marx's earlier writings, such as *The Economic and Philosophic Manuscripts of 1844* and *Critique of Hegel's "Philosophy of Right,"* as well as later writings such as the *Grundrisse,* younger scholars saw a revitalized Marxism as an alternative to mainstream political science. Attracted by Marxism's placement of class struggle at the heart of capitalist politics, these scholars sought to forge a theory of the state that would show how politics in a democratic society is ultimately shaped by larger social and economic forces.

The starting point for the neo-Marxist theory of the state is Marx's analysis of class relations and the forms of exploitation found in history. According to Marx, human history is a history of class struggle. Class struggles are largely the product of developments in society's material forces of production. Tools, technologies, and productive capacities are thus the driving forces behind history. Changes in these productive forces give rise to corresponding changes in a society's class relations.

Marxism challenges one of the fundamental assumptions of pluralist theory: that modern democratic societies have escaped the economic struggles that defined earlier societies. Pluralist theorists tend to accept the teachings of classical and neoclassical economics that the free exchange of labor and capital in an open market represents an important step forward for the history of freedom. From the Marxist class perspective, however, the capitalist market is simply another arena in which the exploitation of one class by another takes place. Indeed, the underlying dynamic of capitalism, the dynamic that Marx felt spelled capitalism's doom, is the bourgeoisie's ongoing need to accumulate more capital by extracting more value from the productive workers, the proletariat. From this perspective, the unceasing need to accumulate capital, no matter the human cost, ultimately spells doom for the capitalist economic system.

Marx and Engels offer two distinct theories of class struggle. The first, a simple two-class model pitting the bourgeoisie against the proletariat, is developed in *The Communist Manifesto* and *Capital.* Marx sets forth a second, much more sophisticated theory of class struggle in such works as *The Eighteenth Brumaire of Louis Bonaparte, The Civil War in France,* and *Class Struggles in France, 1848–1850.* This model focuses attention not only upon other precapitalist classes but also upon the existence of "class factions" within the bourgeoisie and the proletariat. This richer theory of class conflict is the linchpin for much neo-Marxist theorizing about the state. In addition to recognizing the complexity of the conflicts both across and within classes, it upholds Marxism's basic methodological challenge to pluralist thinking—that class conflict, not group conflict, is the key cleavage that explains the underlying movement of politics in a capitalist society.

Neo-Marxist theories of the state are built directly upon the class view of society. The state is not an impartial umpire balancing the demands of the various groups in society but the vehicle by which one class maintains its rule over another. It thus is understood in terms of the demands placed upon it by the economic structure of society, what Marx referred to as the mode of production. The economic structure of society is "the real foundation" on which a legal and political superstructure—the state—rises and out of which develop definite forms of social consciousness.

The theory of the state found in the writings of Marx and Engels is, like the theory of class struggle, but a starting point for neo-Marxist thinking about the relationship between politics and economics. Arguing that the mode of production is "the real foundation" upon which the state arose and that class struggle conditions the development of the state ultimately raises many important questions about the state itself. What exactly does it mean to say that "the real foundation" of the state is the mode of production? Are Marx and Engels saying that the state must be seen solely in terms of the economic structure of society? If not, to what degree is it not? Can the state ever be viewed as a social or political force independent of the economy itself? To use the language of modern political science, are Marx and Engels arguing that the state is a dependent variable and that the economic structure of society and class struggle are the independent variables?

Marx and Engels themselves suggest a number of intriguing answers to these questions.[4] Attempts to work out a coherent theory of the state from Marx and Engels are suggestive, but incomplete speculations lie at the heart of much twentieth-century Marxist thought. Sharp differences of opinion about the exact nature of the relationship between the economic structure and the political superstructure separate the work of Bernstein from that of Kautsky, Lenin from Luxemburg, and Trotsky from Bukharin (see Howard and King, 1989, 1992). Many of the issues that divide classical Marxists reappear in the ongoing debates among the neo-Marxists as to how best to conceptualize the state from a Marxian perspective. The best reviews of these ongoing debates are Carnoy (1984), Jessop (1982, 1990), Block (1987), and Alfred and Friedland (1985).

One of the fundamental problems neo-Marxists address is the degree to which the state should be viewed instrumentally—that is, as an instrument of the ruling class. The instrumentalist position is most clearly laid out in Ralph Miliband's highly influential *The State in Capitalist Society* (1969). Miliband calls for a rethinking of the role that the state, particularly the bourgeois democratic state, plays in advanced capitalist Western countries. According to Miliband, the "state" is not a thing as such but a symbol for "a number of particular institutions which, together, constitute its reality, and which interact as parts of what may be called the state system" (1969: 49). The "state elite," comprising people who hold positions of authority in the state system, must be seen as a "distinct and separate entity" from the group that holds power in society through control over the means of production. One question that follows is: what is the relationship between, on the one hand, the political power found in the state and wielded by the state elite and, on the other, the economic power of the dominant class in capitalist society, the bourgeoisie? For Miliband, the relationship is an instrumental one. The bourgeoisie effectively channels its class power through state institutions and into public policy by staffing the state apparatus and exerting its influence in the political process. From the instrumentalist perspective, class consciousness is an important prerequisite for class action as well as for an understanding of what the state is and how it acts. For the state to be seen as the instrument of the ruling class, class actors must have a clear understanding of their interests and how the state might be mobilized to serve them (see also Miliband 1972a, 1972b, 1983, 1989).

The instrumentalist theory of the state resembles in many ways the ruling elite tradition of C. Wright Mills (see 1956). Indeed, the ruling elite/business dominance arguments of G. William Domhoff (1970, 1976, 1978) have significantly influenced neo-Marxist theories of the state. Like the instrumentalist Miliband, Domhoff empirically identifies a ruling elite that governs American society through political institutions. Though there are cleavages in this elite, he argues, it acts to maintain and reproduce itself, much as a class in the Marxian sense would. Interestingly, Domhoff rejects being labeled an "instrumentalist," arguing instead that the ruling elite maintains its dominant position without restricting entry to or completely controlling the state (see Domhoff, 1976; Mintz and Swartz, 1985; and Ferguson and Rogers (1986).

Instrumentalist theories of the state have been challenged by a growing group of structuralist theories that reject "economic reductionism." According to structuralist theories, the state serves the needs of the capitalist class not because it is staffed or influenced by members of that class but because it performs certain functions in a particular social formation. For structuralists, class consciousness is a complex problem that has important implications for our understanding of what the state is and how it functions. Many capitalist interests do not understand what their long-term political interests are. Indeed, one of the primary responsibilities of state institutions in a capitalist society, structuralists argue, is to identify those long-term interests and determine how they might best be met through state action and which might be greeted with hostility by various segments, or factions, of the ruling class. Whereas instrumentalists view the state as a set of mediating institutions transforming class consciousness into public policy, structuralists see the state as a "relatively autonomous" institution whose function is not simply to serve the changing whims of the dominant class or sections of it but to identify objectively what its long-term interests are and to develop policies serving these interests.

Structuralist theories of the state are heavily indebted to the work of two European Marxists whose works became available in English in the 1960s and 1970s: Antonio Gramsci and Louis Althusser. Gramsci, an Italian Marxist who originally wrote in the 1920s and 1930s, focused attention upon the role of the state in maintaining the ideological hegemony of the dominant classes in civil society. Althusser (1971), a French Marxist influenced by Claude Levi-Strauss, brought a structural perspective to Marxism, granting considerable autonomy from economics to both politics and ideology in any particular social formation.

The ideas of Gramsci and Althusser are formulated into a critique of the instrumentalist perspective by Nicos Poulantzas, whose early work (1969, 1973) offered a largely structuralist account of the state. The organization and functions of the state, he argued, are shaped by the structure of class relations. The state reproduces class structure because it articulates economic structures into the political realm. Though the state has relative autonomy, it exists to serve the hegemonic purposes of a capitalist class that is divided into conflicting factions. In his later work (1978, 1979, 1980), Poulantzas moved away from a largely structuralist account of the state to one focusing upon the nature of the class struggle, specifically how the state is shaped by the class struggle and helps to shape it through public policy. Poulantzas's work has enormous importance for contemporary neo-Marxist theories of the state. It is the subject of much critical commentary (see in particular Jessop [1982], Carnoy [1984], and Easton [1981, 1990]) and the starting point for many other theorists' works.[5]

Seeking to move beyond the functionalism built into so many neo-Marxist theories of the state, other accounts emphasize the contradictory roles given the state under conditions of advanced capitalist development and the various crises that develop out of such contradiction. For example, Bob Jessop (1982, 1990) notes that accumulation not only can take multiple forms under capitalism but also can be disrupted by the state through public policy. James O'Connor (1973, 1984) focuses upon the fiscal crisis confronting the state, a crisis brought on by the growing demands placed upon it by monopoly capitalist development. Along a slightly different line of thought, Alan Wolfe (1977, 1981) argues that the state's crisis of legitimacy has its origins in the structural process of capitalist development, specifically the state's growing inability to balance the demands of capitalist development with the democratic demands of liberal democracy.

In sorting out many conceptual problems regarding the theory of the state, neo-Marxists often find themselves trapped in a dialectic web of their own making. Carefully trying to distinguish their own theories of the state from other scholars', these writers often become caught up in a sort of newspeak that makes it difficult for outsiders to understand exactly what is being said or what it means. Occasionally it appears as if the formalisms of state theory have overwhelmed the world being studied.

Nevertheless, neo-Marxist state theorists present some of the most intriguing discussions of public policy found in the recent political science literature. Among the most important are analyses of welfare policy (Piven and Cloward, 1968, 1987), old-age policy and the Social Security Act (Quadagno, 1984, 1988, 1985; see also Domhoff, 1986, 1986–87), labor policy, regulatory policy (see Noble 1982, 1986), and educational policy (Bowles and Gintis, 1976). What distinguishes these public policy studies from run of the mill studies is that they are constantly tuned into larger questions. What role does state-sponsored welfare play in stabilizing and maintaining a capitalist society? Whose interests are served by old-age pension policies? To what degree is labor policy (e.g., the Wagner Act) a reflection of the class structure of American society and to what degree does it reshape this structure? Can the state be used to promote "progressive" policies in the interests of the subordinate classes, or is public policy forever trapped in the logic of capitalistic development? Dissatisfaction with the reigning pluralist paradigm in political science may have stimulated the development of neo-Marxist theories of the state, but it may be the grand theoretical perspective such theories provide for the study of public policy that continues to fuel it today and into the future.

THE RETURN TO WEBER

A second tributary feeding contemporary state theory is a revitalized Weberian tradition in political science. Like the neo-Marxists, the neo-Weberian state theorists believe pluralist theory has lost sight of the state as a political institution that evolves over time or as a significant variable in policy analysis. But they are dissatisfied with the overly deterministic nature of most instrumental or structuralist theories offered by neo-Marxists. By reviving concepts, initially developed by Max Weber, such as "state and society" and "politics and markets," these neo-Weberians articulate a more contingent state-centered theory of politics than that found in neo-Marxism, viewing the state as a potentially autonomous institution in society capable of acting in its own interests.

In contrast to neo-Marxian theories of the state, which ultimately depend upon an understanding of the nature of class conflict (in particular economic systems), neo-Weberian theories begin by defining the state in purely political terms. According to Weber, the state refers to that political organization which claims a monopoly over the legitimate use of force in a particular territory. In formal terms, the "modern state"

> is a system of administration and law which is modified by statute and which guides the collective actions of the executive staff: the executive is regulated by statute likewise, and claims authority over members of the association (those who necessarily belong to the association by birth) but within a broader scope over all activity taking place in the territory over which it exercises domination (1978: 41).

Following Weber, neo-Weberians argue that the state is best seen as a distinct public organization that claims control over a certain territory and formulates and pursues policies that cannot simply be explained in terms of the interests of the various organizations, groups, or classes in the society (see Skocpol, 1980; Stepan, 1978; Migdal, 1988).

State-based explanations of public policy from a neo-Weberian perspective thus are sharply differentiated from the societal explanations found in traditional pluralist thought. The state is treated as an independent variable capable of acting in its own interest. This means that a state not only is able to have its own set of preferences but also is capable of acting on those preferences in the policy process. One of the most intriguing conclusions to emerge from the neo-Weberian perspective is that states can act autonomously in a variety of ways, depending on the relationship that exists between their preferences and those of other key political actors in society (see Nordlinger 1981, 1987).

Theoretical questions about the autonomy of the state are closely related to other, more empirically grounded questions addressed in the work of many neo-Weberians—questions about "stateness" (that is, the strength or weakness of a state) (see Nettl 1968). But rather than assuming, as neo-Marxists do, that some a priori relationship exists between the state and society neo-Weberians view the linkage in the real world as something contingent and amenable to change given particular historical occurrences.

This desire to understand the contingent real-world relationships between the state and society lies at the heart of neo-Weberians' attempts to develop ways to measure empirically and to study comparatively the autonomy of the state. What makes a state strong and capable of acting autonomously from or even in opposition to the interests of major groups or classes in a society? Why are some states comparatively weak and easily penetrated by social interests? Why are some states strong and capable of resisting such penetration? How does the weakness or strength of a particular state affect its ability to influence the organization of society itself, or to pursue public policies in both the international and domestic arenas?

(See Krasner, 1978; Skocpol, 1980; Skocpol and Finegold, 1982, 1990; Skowronek, 1982; Migdal, 1988; and Bensel 1984, 1987, 1990.) Such state-based questions distinguish the neo-Weberian approach to the study of politics from both pluralism and neo-Marxism.

Focusing upon stateness has led neo-Weberian scholars along a variety of research agendas, each with his or her own set of issues and themes. Three agendas stand out in the Neo-Weberian literature on the state: one focusing on regime analysis, a second on the question of state building, and the third on public policy.

In many ways, regime analysis follows in the footsteps of Charles Lindblom, whose *Politics and Markets* developed an analytical framework highly reminiscent of Weber's *Economy and Society* (see Elkin 1985; Stone 1989; Katzenstein 1978, 1985; Samuels 1987; Eisner 1991, 1992, 1993). Regime theorists recognize that a division of labor between state and society or state and economy exists in every regime. They seek to identify the basic organizing principles in a regime and to consider the consequences of this regime for both social and political structure and for the making of public policy. Liberal democratic regimes, for example, are characterized by market-based production and distribution and popular control of the state through democratic processes. By studying the structural linkages between democratic state institutions and the market economy at particular points in time, regime theorists argue, we can understand why state officials beholden to a citizenry and concerned about their own career interests at the same time become concerned over the performance of the national economy. Though often critical of existing regime structures, the portrait of business-government relations that emerges out of this form of inquiry differs significantly from that sketched by the neo-Marxists. Certain social groups, such as leading sectors of business, may occupy a privileged positions in the regime, but such a position is by no means guaranteed, nor is it expected to exist forever.[6]

A second research agenda to emerge in the writing of neo-Weberian state theorists centers around questions of state building. How are modern state institutions built? Why are state institutions built at different points in time in different countries? Are there different paths to state building, and, if so, do they carry separate consequences for the making of public policy? What social, political, and economic factors account for the building of weak or strong states in different societies?

Not surprisingly, such questions attract comparative political scientists to the neo-Weberian theory of the state (see Bendix 1964, 1978; Tilly 1975; Skocpol 1980; Stepan 1978; Migdal 1988). But they also spark interest in neo-Weberian thought among students of American politics, who for much of the twentieth century focused on exceptionalism. Not satisfied with looking at the United States as a special case having little or nothing in common with other nations, neo-Weberians seek to understand how the imperative of state building in the modern world was translated into twentieth-century institutions. They have focused attention upon a variety of questions largely understudied by American political scientists, including the nature of the "stateless" society in the nineteenth century (Skowronek 1982; Hattam 1990; Orloff and Skocpol 1984; Sterett 1990; James 1992), the role played by national institutions in mediating regional economic conflicts (Bensel 1987, 1990), and the importance of urban machines to state building in the late nineteenth and early twentieth centuries (Bridges 1986; Shefter 1975, 1979, 1983, 1986; Katznelson 1989; McDonald 1989).

A third agenda found in the work of the neo-Weberians centers around questions of public policy. Because they regard representatives of the state as potentially independent actors, neo-Weberians examine the policy process differently than mainstream scholars or neo-Marxists do. Focusing upon the structural relations among state institutions, political parties, and major social and economic groups at a particular point in time enables neo-Weberians to make broad-ranging historical comparisons across countries. A number of state-centered comparative studies of policy assess the leading role state representatives have played in policy formation under different historical circumstances in different countries (see Heclo 1974, Skocpol and Ritter 1991, Wilsford 1991).

The most important contributions of neo-Weberians to the study of public policy may be those that place American public policies in a broader context. By contrasting the strong state institutions found in European countries with the weaker ones found in the United States and by analyzing how U.S. institutions are freed from or dependent upon other key groups in society, neo-Weberians are able to address questions about public policy that have confounded American political scientists for decades. Why is there no socialism in the United States? Why does state ownership of industry play such a small role in public policy in the United States? Why was the United States one of the last countries in the West to develop national welfare state institutions? Why is there some form of national health insurance in all Western industrial countries except the United States? Why do economic regulation and industrial policy in the United States differ so much from similar programs in other industrialized countries? How does a particular state's place in the international system affect its ability to make policy in a variety of areas?

Much of the policy-oriented work about the United States published by neo-Weberians centers around the policies and institutions that emerged out of the New Deal. They offer alternative explanations of the meaning of American exceptionalism in the nineteenth century and the role played by the New Deal and state initiatives in creating new institutions in the twentieth century.[7] As with neo-Marxist policy literature, neo-Weberian studies continually raise questions about the large picture, both across policy areas and across different economic and political systems.

There is, however, an important difference between the two. Lacking the certainty provided by the Marxian theory of history, neo-Weberian policy studies can be attached to a variety of political perspectives and values. Neo-Weberians must supply a coherent political perspective from which to view policy debates. Sadly, although many are willing to provide the perspective, the coherence is all too often lacking.

IS THERE A REPUBLICAN THEORY OF THE STATE?

The preceding review of the neo-Marxist and neo-Weberian schools of state theory leads to a sense of meaningful convergence. The state becomes necessary if observers of political life are to make the leap from experience to purpose. In other words, the role of the state in political theory, as in political practice, is ideological. The state is a system of ethics, a sense of a higher and more cumulative goal, a basis for distinguishing good politics from bad. The state is not really a quantity to be measured. It is a term of art. It is not, in the end, to be defined solely by its legitimate coercive powers, its comprehensive reach, or its autonomy. It is not a unitary independent variable shaping all that it surveys. The state's role in theory is to provide a discourse that links empirical reality with collective purpose. The state integrates normative inquiry with empirical study, focusing attention upon the ethical significance of various linkages in society that are established and sustained by political means.

There is a value dimension to neo-Marxist analysis that directly intrudes upon its empirical investigation of the state. After the revolution, when the proletariat becomes the dominant class, the state may serve it as well as it served the bourgeoisie. The revolution will not lead to capitalist turnover; quite the contrary, the capitalist industrial structure will be kept in place to serve a different interest. In effect, capitalism becomes the state; without classes, the old state will wither away, leaving the former capitalist system itself, rendered benevolent in the absence of the predatory entrepreneurs, bosses, rentiers, rent seekers, and coupon clippers. Individuals in the classless society become benevolent, contributing to the collective according to their ability and in turn achieving some identity with their product and some association, absent the cash nexus, with genuine equals in a genuine community. In brief, like most religions, which are oblivious to the state (as in "render unto Caesar . . . "), Marxism after the revolution, within a benevolent and then perhaps an irrelevant state, seeks the perfectibility of human beings—and assumes it is possible. This essential assumption is the great leap of faith in the ideological domain of Marxist state theory.

Perfectibility of individuals is a convergent feature of another school of thought that has not been considered in this essay: the neoclassical, or public choice, approach. Like neo-Marxism, public choice theory provides an approach to the state grounded in a vision of man's place in society. However, the starting point for understanding state and society in neoclassicism is not class relations but rather the individual choice of rational utility maximizers. The state thus emerges as a political institution with a logic of its own out of the collective action of individuals pursuing their self-interest over time.[8] There is a bit of irony in this formulation. Whereas neo-Marxism moderates the radical perfectibility of individuals that is so important in classical Marxism, public choice neoclassicism actually radicalizes its classical model. Perfectibility is written all through the neoclassical, public choice view of the state. What is more perfect than a rational, self-seeking, competing individual? Indeed, these individuals have to be doubly rational, in that they are willing to play the game by the rules and also to abide by the outcome. Take a favorite neoclassical parable, the Prisoners Dilemma. Two prisoners, prisoners indeed, play for an eternity their game, always (as in tic tac toe) making the same predictable, inexorable decision. What happens to the game if we add a rule—imposed by the liberal state, let us say—that prisoners cannot be held incommunicado, or that each prisoner can consult a lawyer before answering? Such a rule represents a state's choosing to suboptimize by displacing or moderating individual rationality. Neoclassicism can make a place for the state, but with the exception of a few public goods the neoclassical state could shrink, if not wither away, just as the neo-Marxist state can. And, as in the Marxist example, the small and irrelevant state in the neoclassical ideal is brought to us courtesy of the perfectible individual.

Although Weberian state theory does not rely on human perfectibility, it has come close to an ideology of institutional perfectibility. The Weberian state is in fact a *source* of rationality rather than dependent upon or incidental to it. Although all institutions and collectivities are coercive, the state is distinguished from all others because its coercion is legitimate. Legitimacy can come from many sources. Some authors identify four sources, others three. But for any classification, only the divine, or charismatic, source is totally nonrational. Once established, by whatever means, legitimacy has its own reason, which functions in two ways: 1) through laws and rules or tradition, whose purpose is to make conduct more predictable and calculable; and 2) through bureaucracy, the purpose of which is to give society a higher element of rationality and efficiency.

These observations are meant not to denigrate existing approaches but rather to establish just what kind of a resource base each state theory provides for a more satisfactory state theory. We must grasp not only the substance of current theories of the state but also the limits of their applicability, their contradictions, and the myths they develop to smooth them over. No state theory can avoid contradiction. Nor can any state theory separate facts from values, whether covered by myths or not. It is clearer now than ever that the whole point and purpose of the state is precisely to combine facts and values. Weber's effort to separate the two has been widely misunderstood.

It is our belief that the return of the state in political science is genuine—neither accidental nor a product of borrowing from comparative politics. New concern for state theory is a genuine and appropriate reaction to the end of exceptionalism, to the virtual certainty that the United States has been Europeanized sufficiently to have lost its uniqueness and to have taken on most if not all of the attributes of statehood. We feel Birnbaum is too rigid in his insistence that there is no American state (Birnbaum, 1982), but we can agree that American state theory will not and cannot be identical to European state theory. However, it also will not be a specialized theory of the American state. Its contradictions will be generalizable at least to all countries attempting democratization, and it will be superior to other state theories in that it will have a more solid empirical grounding. This is where public policy is brought back in.

This construction begins at the point where Madisonian theory failed. Madison's Constitution failed because it did not prevent, in our opinion, the coming of the Second Republic—which is precisely what the Constitution was designed to prevent. It is hard to say a constitutional theory failed when its constitution persisted 150 years and survived probably the most devastating civil war ever fought. But, given the near-universal assumption that we are still operating under the Republic of 1787 (to call it the "First Republic" would be to admit its impermanence), it is both timely and fair to count Madison out at last.

Yet he did not go down without a struggle. The Supreme Court threw in the towel after only a few rounds, validating the new state's regulatory dimensions as well as its welfare, or redistributive, dimensions. All of this happened in 1937 (*NLRB v. Jones and Laughlin Steel*, and *Steward Machine v. Davis*). Since 1937, it would have been a waste of time to appeal a federal regulatory or welfare statute to the Supreme Court on grounds of unconstitutionality.

However, other players in the defense of Madisonian theory did not give up so easily. These other players were political scientists. The pluralist theory of the 1950s (to be distinguished from the pluralist philosophy of the first quarter of the century, as referred to by Truman) sought to salvage America's unique antistate state by updating the Madisonian process and applying it to post–New Deal politics. There is no need to go into the details of pluralist theory here; the bottom line is that, like the theories outlined above, this pluralist theory depended upon perfectibility. The pluralists tried to save the old republic by discovering the underlying perfectibility of the process. Facts and values were neatly combined and smoothly articulated. Competition by self-interested groups oblivious to larger consequences or public needs produced felicity as well as equilibrium. And all of this was made possible by the all-pervasive acceptance of the Lockean consensus and the "rules of the game." This was the classical economic analysis, with the group taking the place of the individual or the firm; but the pluralists discovered in all of this a benevolent process that would at one and the same time tame the citizen and save the citizen from irresponsible elites.

But pluralist theory explained only half of Madison's program, because competition among factions was only half of his analysis, if that. The other half appeared in the Constitution, in which groups (or factions) were not the main competitors but were in fact constituencies for the real competitors, the constitutionally created branches of government. The purpose of Madison's proposition to "extend the sphere" to continental size was to "take in a greater variety of parties and interests [to] make it less probable that a majority of the whole will have a common motive to invade the rights of other citizens." Why? "The regulation of these various and interfering interests forms the principal task of modern legislation" and "involves the spirit of party and faction in the necessary and ordinary operations of government" (*Federalist, No. 10*). Quite clearly, the objective implied in Madisonian theory was *to keep groups out of direct competition* while giving each group the incentive to support the Constitution out of fear that some other group may come to dominate it.

Madisonian theory is actually superior to contemporary pluralist theory *because it makes more of a place for the formally constituted institutions of government.* The modern pluralist, by making groups the main players and by allowing them theoretically to provide the solution to the political game, combined the worst of the old system of government with the new. The most important feature of the new system is, in fact, the size and political vitality of the formal institutions of government. Making groups part of the process weakened the theory of pluralism and contributed to the delegitimizing of the newly emerging state.

But Madisonian theory, superior though it may be to contemporary pluralism, is still a failure because it is predicated upon a balance of power and accountability through competition at the top and upon a dynamic whose successful outcome was to be measured largely by governmental inactivity, or an inability to act—by stalemate. Madisonian theory leaves out the one truly modern element: *administration*. We prefer this term to "bureaucracy" because "administration" more strongly implies process as well as structure and because it is not limited to the executive branch. In addition to more than 2.5 million civilian administrators in the executive branch, there are more than 30,000 in the legislative branch, and the federal judiciary, though much smaller, spends most of its time interpreting the statutes and overseeing the process of administrative implementation in the executive branch.

Thus, the restoration of Madison in a new state theory is predicated upon the one element whose presence Madisonian theory sought to avoid and whose size and power could not have been imagined by eighteenth- or nineteenth-century state builders. The modern state also required of its theorists a stronger dose of administrative awareness than Madisonians possessed. Furthermore, the new theory is predicated upon the use of history; Madisonian and neo-Madisonian pluralism are both too cross-sectional. Madison and his contemporaries used history and comparative politics to an impressive extent, but both of these elements were surprisingly absent in the articulation of the dynamics of their theory. A new state theory, what we are calling a republican theory of the state, will have to be grounded in historical development—specifically, in institutional history, which includes the development of institutional structures and institutional products. Republican theory is not simply a theory of governmental development but a theory of a government of laws. Therefore, a political science of the state must embrace history and jurisprudence. Jurisprudence entails an exploration of the uses to which states can be put as well as the historical sequences and consequences of each particular use. It is to us very significant that "law" and "policy" are virtually synonymous in English and that in the last couple of decades policy replaced law as the preferred reference. This probably happened because a more inclusive and reciprocal term was needed to soften the unilateral and rigid connotations of law. But for whatever reasons policy became the preferred term, it is ironic that no one seemed to notice the peculiar appropriateness of this exchange. Policy shares its etymological roots with "police," and both terms come from *polis*. Thus, it seems to us obvious that the best and first way to study the *polis* is to study policy.

We believe public policy is the appropriate method for state theory and that it will make our republican state theory superior to other sources of theory. Public policy as a source of empirical data has two great advantages. First, public policy *is* the state in sustained, repetitive, and purposive action. Public policy, properly classified, puts us in the presence of the state. No one has ever *seen* the state; it is a construct, just as "systems" and "power" are constructs. Public policy, when classified according to known and accepted dimensions of jurisprudence—for example, the coerciveness of states and the use of rules by states to articulate their intentions—provides a rough metric for most of the characteristics of states that all political scientists want to address: autonomy, strength, permeability, elitism or pluralism, predictability, accountability, even rationality.

Second, public policy as a source of data is superior to attitudes, voting patterns, election results, budgets, expenditures, and aggregate economic data because public policy already exists at a level of discourse appropriate to the state or to those institutions defined as constituting the state. Most political data with which we work are at such a micro level that they require a whole series of interlocking statements before they bear upon a state-oriented discourse. To put this the other way around, the more state-oriented the discourse, the more valuable are the case studies of policy making and the analyses of laws that have been faithfully produced by scholars, albeit for different purposes, for generations. And the more state-oriented the discourse, the better our chances of escaping the uniqueness of each case study and of developing a basis for generalizing from cases. The biggest problem with policy case studies is how to define what the case is a case *of*. This problem points to the symbiotic relationship between policy studies and state theory.

It also points to a big problem with the existing sources of state theory. As we see it, existing theories employ data that tend to be too remote from the theoretical discourse to which they are addressed. The data on "class interests" required by a Marxist analysis may create a presumption that state and prevailing class interests are, in the long run, highly consonant. But those same data cannot move analysis very far beyond proof of that presumption. And the presumption is true: can anyone imagine any state systematically *opposed* to its own society's sources of goods and services? The data and method required by Weberian analysis tend to encourage reification of the state and its institutions. "Ideal-typical" organizations can limit as much as enhance exploration of the nuances and varieties of state experience or the political values that underlie them.

Thus, by integrating public policy with state discourse, new state theory may have found a way to produce a superior, more interesting political science, even if no synthetic and highly consensual state theory per se can be developed. It is in this sense and for this purpose that we view "state theory and public policy" as not just another subdiscipline but, modestly, a metadiscipline—or, arrogantly, the new political science.

Until now, we have envisioned the new state theory as a consequence of the Europeanization of America and the loss of American uniqueness. We conclude on a slightly different note: the Americanization of Europe and, probably, other places. Liberalization of European states and democratization of previously authoritarian states involves the superimposition of accountability and of lawlike restraints on the absolute values of order, equality, or rationality upon which the more orthodox states tried to build themselves. Through this development, an American state theory, a republican theory of the state, could actually become a truly comparative world theory of the state. And what a healthy development this would be—America again the model. But not American institutions—they are not appropriate for imitation. It is America's peculiar contradictions and how we deal with them that will—justifiably, we think—make us once again the envy of the world.

NOTES

1. For extended discussions of the rise of pluralism in political science, see Seidelman and Harpham (1985), Ricci (1984), Lowi (1969/1979), and Crick (1959).

2. The work of Arthur Bentley was largely ignored when originally published. After being rediscovered in the early 1950s by leading political scientists such as David Truman, Bentley and his work *The Process of Government* became commonly cited in the discipline. Interestingly, pluralist analysis was only one way station on the road toward the sort of interactional analysis upon which Bentley ultimately sought to base a theory of politics. But whether one reads Bentley as an interactional theorist or as a pluralist, he is clearly an antistate theorist. Mid-century political scientists' attraction to his work might have been due as much to his antistatism as to his protopluralism.

3. For more detailed discussions of these issues see Seidelman and Harpham (1985), chapter 5, and Ricci (1984).

4. One answer found in the introduction to *Contribution to a Critique of Political Economy* is that economic variables seem to determine political variables. At other times, however, Marx and Engels argue that the state is capable of escaping the class struggle and acting on behalf of capitalist interests whether or nor these interests are consciously understood (see *Eighteenth Brumaire of Louis Bonaparte*). Here neither politics nor the actions of the state are explained solely by economic variables. Engels's final attempt to sort out the relationship between economic factors (such as changes in the forces of production and class relations) and political variables (such as the state) muddies as many waters as it clears (Marx and Engels, 640–41).

5. Fred Block (1987), for example, specifically rejects the idea that capitalist interests know how to preserve a capitalist order, seeing the contours of contemporary capitalist society defined by a three-sided conflict between capitalists, state managers, and the working class. Erik Olin Wright, by contrast, views the state structurally in terms of changing forces and relations of production that occur as a result of class struggle and capitalist competition. Adam Przeworski and Michael Wallerstein (1982), meanwhile, suggest that the state should be viewed from a broader perspective than is often found in structuralist accounts. Under the proper conditions, they argue, the state can be a vehicle for making, maintaining, and coordinating class compromises between elements of the bourgeoisie and the working class, the sort of compromises fostered by the American state during the New Deal.

Claus Offe (1975) develops an interesting variation of the structuralist argument in his work. Heavily influenced by the Frankfurt school, Offe views the state as being independent of either instrumental or structural capitalist control, constrained by the need to maintain its own legitimacy by mediating the demands of workers. In the end, the state is limited by the conflicting demands of capital accumulation and legitimacy.

6. Eldon Eisenach (1990) puts an interesting twist on regime theory by using it as an organizing perspective for viewing the evolution of American political thought.

7. Weir and Skocpol (1985), Katzenstein (1985), Hall (1985), Lange and Regini (1989), Gourevitch (1986), and Zysman (1978, 1983) offer leading state-centered perspectives on comparative economic policy. Some of the most important social policy studies from a neo-Weberian perspective are Amenta and Skocpol (1986, 1988, 1989); Weir, Orloff, and Skocpol (1988); and Skocpol (1994). Influential neo-Weberian studies of economic and regulatory policy in the United States include Skocpol and Finegold (1982, 1990) and Eisner (1991, 1992, 1993).

8. The literature on the neoclassical or public choice school of thought is enormous. Good introductions to the assumptions underlying the approach are Mueller (1989), Johnson (1991), Riker (1982), Dunleavy (1991), Riker and Ordeshook (1973), Aranson and Ordeshook (1985), Arrow (1963), and Ordeshook (1990). Excellent critical commentaries on the use of rational actors models are Almond (1991) and Monroe (1991). Buchanan and Tullock's *The Calculus of Consent* (1965) and Mancur Olson's *Logic of Collective Action* (1965) and *The Rise and Decline of Nations* (1982) have had major impacts in the public choice literature as well as in the pluralist literature in political science.

REFERENCES

Alford, Robert R., and Roger Friedland. 1985. *Powers of Theory: Capitalism, the State, and Democracy*. Cambridge: Cambridge University Press.

Almond, Gabriel. 1988. "The Return of the State." *American Political Science Review* 82 (September): 853–74.

———. 1991. "Rational Choice Theory and the Social Sciences." In *The Economic Approach to Politics: A Critical Reassessment of the Theory of Rational Action*. Edited by Kristen Renwick Monroe. New York: Harper Collins, pp. 32–52.

Althusser, Louis. 1971. *Lenin and Philosophy and Other Essays*. New York: Monthly Review Press.

Amenta, Edwin, and Theda Skocpol. 1986. "States and Social Policies." *Annual Review of Sociology* 12: 131–57.

———. 1988. "Redefining the New Deal: World War II and the Development of Social Provision in the United States." In *The Politics of Social Policy in the United States*. Edited by Margaret Weir, Ann Shola Orloff, and Theda Skocpol. Princeton: Princeton University Press, pp. 81–122.

———. 1989. "Taking Exception: Explaining the Distinctiveness of American Public Policies in the Last Century." In *The Comparative History of Public Policy*. Edited by Francis G. Castles. London: Polity, pp. 292–333.

Aranson, Peter, and Peter C. Ordeshook. 1985. "Public Interest, Private Interest, and the Democratic Polity." In *The Democratic State*. Edited by R. Benjamin and S. Elkin. Lawrence, KS: University Press of Kansas, pp. 87–178.

Arrow, Kenneth. 1963. *Social Choice and Individual Values*. 2nd ed. New Haven: Yale University Press.
Bendix, Reinhard. 1960. *Max Weber: An Intellectual Portrait*. Garden City, NJ: Doubleday.
———. 1964. *Nation-Building and Citizenship: Studies of Our Changing Social Order*. New York: Wiley.
———. 1978. *Kings or People: Power and the Mandate to Rule*. Berkeley: University of California Press.
Benjamin, R., and S. Elkin (eds.). 1985. *The Democratic State*. Lawrence, KS: University Press of Kansas.
Bensel, Richard. 1984. *Sectionalism and American Political Development, 1880–1980*. Madison: University of Wisconsin Press.
———. 1987. "Southern Leviathan: The Development of Central State Authority in the Confederate States of America." *Studies in American Political Development* 2: 68–136.
———. 1990. *Yankee Leviathan: The Origins of Central State Authority in America, 1859–1877*. New York: Cambridge University Press.
Bentley, Arthur. 1908/1967. *The Process of Government*. Cambridge MA: Harvard University Press.
Birnbaum, Pierre. 1982. "The State Versus Corporatism." *Politics and Society* 11, 4: 477–501.
———. 1988. *States and Collective Action: The European Experience*. Cambridge: Cambridge University Press.
Block, Fred. 1987. *Revising State Theory*. Philadelphia: Temple University Press.
Bowles, Samuel, and Herbert Gintis. 1976. *Schooling in Capitalist America: Educational Reform and the Contradictions of Econonic Life*. New York: Basic Books.
Bridges, Amy. 1984. *A City in the Republic: Antebellum New York and the Origins of Machine Politics*. New York: Cambridge University Press.
———. 1986. "Becoming American: The Working Class in theUnited States before the Civil War." In *Working Class Formation: Nineteenth Century Patterns in Western Europe and the United States*. Edited by Ira Katznelson and Aristide Zolberg. Princeton: Princeton University Press, pp. 157–96.
Brinkley, Alan. 1984. "Writing the History of Contemporary America: Dilemmas and Challenges." *Daedalus* 113: 121–41.
Buchanan, James. 1975. *The Limits of Liberty: Between Anarchy and Leviathan*. Chicago: University of Chicago Press.
Buchanan, James, and Gordon Tullock. 1965. *The Calculus of Consent*. Ann Arbor: University of Michigan Press.
Cammack, Paul. 1988. Review of "Bringing the State Back In." *British Journal of Political Science* 19: 261–90.
Carnoy, Martin. 1984. *The State and Political Theory*. Princeton: Princeton University Press.
Cawson, Alan. 1989. "Is There a Corporatist Theory of the State?" In *Democracy and the Capitalist State*. Edited by Graeme Duncan. Cambridge: Cambridge University Press, pp. 233–52.
Clark, Gordon L., and Michael. 1984. *State Apparatus: Structures and Language of Legitimacy*. Boston: Allen and Uniwin.

Crick, Bernard. 1959. *The American Science of Politics*. Berkeley: University of California Press.

Dahl, Robert. 1956. *A Preface to Democracy*. New Haven: Yale University Press.

——. 1961. *Who Governs?* New Haven: Yale University Press.

Deutsch, Karl W. 1981. "The Crisis of the State." *Government and Opposition*. 16: 331–43.

Domhoff, G. William. 1970. *The Higher Circles: The Governing Class in America*. New York: Random House.

——. 1976. "I Am Not an Instrumentalist." *Kapitalstate* 4: 221–24.

——. 1978. *The Powers that Be: Processes of Ruling Class Domination in America*. New York: Random House.

——. 1986. "On Welfare Capitalism and the Social Security Act of 1935." *American Sociological Review* 51: 445–46.

——. 1986–87. "Corporate Liberal Theory and the Social Security Act: A Chapter in the Sociology of Knowledge." *Politics and Society* 15: 297–330.

——. 1987. "The Wagner Act and Theories of the State." *Political Power and Social Theory* 6: 159–85.

Duncan, Graeme (ed.). 1989a. *Democracy and the Capitalist State*. Cambridge: Cambridge University Press.

——. 1989b. "Mill, Marx, and the State." In *Democracy and the Capitalist State*. Edited by Graeme Duncan. Cambridge: Cambridge University Press, pp. 105–21.

Dunleavy, Patrick. 1991. *Democracy, Bureaucracy, and Public Choice: Economic Explanations in Political Science*. New York: Prentice-Hall.

Dunleavy, Patrick., and B. O'Leary. *Theories of the State: The Politics of Liberal Democracy*. London: Macmillan.

Easton, David. 1981. "The Political System Besieged by the State." *Political Theory* 9: 303–25.

——. 1990. *The Analysis of Political Structure*. New York: Routledge.

Eckstein, Harry. 1979. "On the 'Science' of the State." In *The State*. Edited by Stephen R. Graubard. New York: Norton, pp. 1–20.

Eisenach, Eldon J. 1990. "Reconstituting the Study of American Political Thought in a Regime-Change Perspective." *Studies in American Political Development* 4: 169–230.

Eisner, Marc Allen. 1991. *Antitrust and the Triumph of Economics: Institutions, Expertise, and Policy Change*. Chapel Hill: University of North Carolina Press.

——. 1992. "Institutional Evolution and Regulatory Change During the New Deal: The Origins of the Associational Regime." Paper presented at the 1992 Meetings of the American Political Science Association, Chicago, September 3–6.

——. 1993. *Regulation in Transition*. Baltimore: Johns Hopkins University Press.

Elkin, Stephen L. 1985. "Pluralism and Its Place: State and Regime in Liberal Democracy." *The Democratic State*. Edited by R. Benjamin and S. Elkin. Lawrence, KS: University Press of Kansas, pp.179–211.

Evans, Peter B., Dietrich Rueschemeyer, and Theda Skocpol (eds.). 1985. *Bringing the State Back In*. Cambridge: Cambridge University Press.

Ferguson, Thomas. 1984. "From Normalcy to New Deal: Industrial Structural, Party

Competition, and American Public Policy in the Great Depression." *International Organization* 38: 41–94.

Ferguson, Thomas, and Joel Rogers. 1986. *Right Turn: The Decline of the Democrats and the Future of American Politics*. New York: Hill and Wang.

Finegold, Kenneth. 1988. "Agriculture and the Politics of U.S. Provision: Social Insurance and Foodstamps." In *The Politics of Social Policy in the United States*. Edited by Margaret Weir, Ann Shola Orloff, and Theda Skocpol. Princeton: Princeton University Press, pp. 81–122.

Finegold, Kenneth, and Theda Skocpol. 1984. "State, Party, and Industry: From Business Recovery to the Wagner Act in America's New Deal." *Statemaking and Social Movements: Essays in History and Theory*. Edited by Charles C. Bright and Susan F. Harding. Ann Arbor: University of Michigan Press.

Galambos, Louis (ed.). 1987. *The New American State: Bureaucracies and Policies Since World War II*. Baltimore: John Hopkins University Press.

Goldfield, Michael. 1989. "Worker Insurgency, Radical Organization, and New Deal Labor Legislation." *American Political Science Review* 83 (December): 1257–82.

Gourevitch, Peter. 1986. *Politics in Hard Times: Comparative Responses to International Economic Crises*. Ithaca: Cornell University Press.

Graubard, Stephen R. 1979. *The State*. New York: Norton.

Greenberg, Edward S., and Thomas F. Mayer. *Changes in the State: Causes and Consequences*. Newbury Park, CA.: Sage.

Hall, Peter A. 1986. *Governing the Economy: The Politics of State Intervention in Britain and France*. New York: Oxford University Press.

Hartz, Louis. 1955. *Liberal Tradition in America*. New York: Harcourt, Brace, and World.

Hattam, Victoria. 1990. "Economic Visions and Political Strategies: American Labor and the State, 1865–1896." *Studies in American Political Development* 4: 82–129.

Heclo, Hugh. 1974. *Modern Social Policies in Britain and Sweden*. New Haven: Yale University Press.

Held, David. 1989. *Political Theory and the Modern State: Essays on State, Power, and Democracy*. Stanford: Stanford University Press.

Holloway, John, and Sol Picciotto. 1978. *State and Capital: A Marxist Debate*. Austin: University of Texas Press.

Howard, M. C., and J. E. King. 1989. *A History of Marxian Economics: Volume I, 1883–1929*. Princeton: Princeton University Press.

———. 1992. *A History of Marxian Economics: Volume II, 1929–1990*. Princeton: Princeton University Press.

Ikenberry, G. John. 1986. "The Irony of State Strengths: Comparative Responses to the Oil Shocks in the 1970s." *International Organization* 40, 1: 105–38.

Ikenberry, G. John, David A. Lake, and Michael Mastanduno (eds.). 1988. *The State and American Foreign Economic Policy*. Ithaca: Cornell University Press.

James, Scott C. 1992. "A Party System Perspective on the Interstate Commerce Act of 1887: The Democracy, Electoral College Competition, and the Politics of Coalition Maintenance." *Studies in American Political Development*. 6, 1: 163–200.

Jessop, Bob. 1982. *The Capitalist State: Marxist Theory and Methods*. New York: New York University Press.

———. 1990. *State Theory: Putting the State in Its Place*. University Park: Penn State University Press.

Johnson, David B. 1991. *Public Choice: An Introduction to the New Political Economy*. Mountain View, CA: Mayfield Publishing Company.

Jordan, A. G. 1981. "Iron Triangles, Wolly Corporatism and Elastic Nets: Images of the Policy Process." *Journal of Public Policy* 1: 95–123.

Kantor, Paul. "The Political Economy of Business Politics in U.S. Cities: A Developmental Perspective." *Studies in American Political Development* 4: 248–68.

Kariel, Henry. *The Decline of Pluralism*. Stanford: Stanford University Press.

Katzenstein, Peter J. ed. 1978. *Between Power and Plenty: Foreign Economic Policies of Advanced Industrial States*. Madison: University of Wisconsin Press.

———. 1985. *Small States in World Markets*. Ithaca: Cornell University Press.

Katznelson, Ira. 1986. "Rethinking the Silences of Social and Economic Policy." *Political Science Quarterly* 101 (Summer): 307–25.

———. 1989. " 'The Burdens of Urban History': Comment." *Studies in American Political Development* 3: 30–50.

Katznelson, Ira, and Bruce Pietrykowski. 1991. "Rebuilding the American State: Evidence from the 1940s." *Studies in American Political Development* 5: 301–39.

Kesselman, Mark. 1982. "The Conflictual Evolution of American Political Science: From Apologetic Pluralism to Trilateralism and Marxism." In *Political Values and Private Power in American Politics*. Edited by J. David Greenstone. Chicago: University of Chicago Press.

Key, V. O. 1942/1947/1952/1958/1954. *Parties, Politics, and Pressure Groups*. 5th. ed. New York: Thomas Crowell.

Krasner, Stephen. 1978. *Defending the National Interest: Raw Material Investments and U.S. Foreign Policy*. Princeton: Princeton University Press.

———. 1984. "Review Article: Approaches to the State: Alternative Conceptions and Historical Dynamics." *Comparative Politics* 16, 2 (January): 223–46.

Lange, Peter, and Marino Regini. 1989. *State, Market, and Social Regulations: New Perspectives on Italy*. Cambridge: Cambridge University Press.

Laski, Harold. 1919. *Authority in the Modern State*. New Haven: Yale University Press.

———. 1935. *The State in Theory and Practice*. London: George Allen and Unwin.

Lindblom, Charles. 1977. *Politics and Markets: The World's Political Economic Systems*. New York: Basic Books.

Lowi, Theodore J. 1964. "American Business, Public Policy, Case Studies, and Political Theory." *World Politics* 16 (July): 677–715.

———. 1969/1979. *The End of Liberalism*. 2nd ed. New York: Norton.

———. 1978. "Public Policy and Bureaucracy in the United States and France." *Comparing Public Policies: New Concepts and Methods*. Edited by Douglas E. Ashford. Vol.4 of Sage Yearbooks in Politics and Public Policy. Beverly Hills, CA: Sage, pp 177–96.

———. 1988. "Return to the State: Critique." *American Political Science Review* 82, 3: 885–91.

McDonald, Terrence J. 1989. "The Burdens of Urban History: The Theory of the State in Recent Social History." *Studies in American Political Development* 3: 3–29.

Macpherson, C. B. 1989. "Do We Need a Theory of the State?" In *Democracy and the Capitalist State*. Edited by Graeme Duncan. Cambridge: Cambridge University Press, pp. 15–32.

March, James, and Johan Olsen. 1984. "The New Institutionalism: Organizational Factors in Political Life." *American Political Science Review* 78: 734–49.

Marx, Karl, and Friedrich Engels. 1972. *The Marx-Engels Reader*. New York: W. W. Norton.

McConnell, Grant. 1966. *Private Power and American Democracy*. New York: Atheneum.

Migdal, Joel S. 1988. *Strong Societies and Weak States: State-Society Relations and State Capabilities in the Third World*. Princeton: Princeton University Press.

Miliband, Ralph. 1969. *The State in Capitalist Society*. New York: Basic Books.

———. 1972a. *Marxism and Politics*. Oxford: Oxford University Press.

———. 1972b. "The Capitalist State: A Reply to Nicolas Poulantzas." In *Ideology in the Social Sciences*. Edited by Robin Blackburn. London: Collins.

———. 1983. "State Power and Class Interests." *New Left Review* 138: 57–68.

———. 1989. "Marx and the State." In *Democracy and the Capitalist State*. Edited by Graeme Duncan. Cambridge: Cambridge University Press, pp. 33–55.

Mills, C. Wright. 1956. *The Power Elite*. London: Oxford University Press.

Minz, Beth, and Michael Schwartz. 1985. *The Power Structure of American Business*. Chicago: University of Chicago Press.

Monroe, Kristen Renwick. 1991. "The Theory of Rational Action: Its Origins and Usefulness for Political Science." In *The Economic Approach to Politics: A Critical Reassessment of the Theory of Rational Action*. Edited by Kristen Renwick Monroe. New York: Harper Collins, pp. 1–31.

Mueller, Dennis C. 1989. *Public Choice II: A Revised Edition of* Public Choice. Cambridge: Cambridge University Press.

Nettl, J. 1968. "The State as a Conceptual Variable." *World Politics* 20: 559–92.

Noble, Charles. 1982. "The Regulation of Social Regulation: Class Conflict and OSHA." In *The Political Economy of Public Policy*. Edited by Alan Stone and Edward J. Harpham. Beverley Hills: Sage, pp.73–92.

———. 1986. *Liberalism at Work: Work and the Rise and Fall of OSHA*. Philadelphia: Temple University Press.

Nordlinger, Eric A. 1981. *On the Autonomy of the Democratic State*. Cambridge: Harvard University Press.

———. 1987. "Taking the State Seriously." In *Understanding Political Development*. Edited by Myron Weiner and Samuel Huntington. Boston: Little, Brown, pp. 353–90.

O'Connor, Robert, 1973. *The Fiscal Crisis of the State*. New York: St. Martin's.

———. 1984. *Accumulation Crisis*. New York: Blackwell.

Offe, Claus. 1975. "The Theory of the Capitalist State and the Problem of Policy Formation. *Stress and Contradiction in Modern Capitalism*. Edited by Leon Lindberg, Robert Alford, Colin Crouch, and Claus Offe. Lexington MA.: Lexington Books, pp. 125–44.

Offe, Claus, and Volker Ronge. 1975. "Theses on the Theory of the State." *New German Critique* 6: 139–47.

Olson, Mancur. 1965. *The Logic of Collective Action: Public Goods and the Theory of Groups*. Cambridge: Harvard University Press.

————. 1982. *The Rise and Decline of Nations: Economic Growth, Stagflation, and Social Rigidities*. New Haven: Yale University Press.

Ordeshook, Peter C. 1990. "The Emerging Discipline of Political Economy." *Perspectives on Positive Political Economy*. Edited by James E. Alt and Kenneth A. Shepsle. Cambridge: Cambridge Univesity Press, pp. 9–30.

Orloff, Ann Shola. 1988. "The Political Origins of America's Beloved Welfare State." In *The Politics of Social Policy in the United States*. Edited by Margaret Weir, Ann Shola Orloff, and Theda Skocpol. Princeton: Princeton University Press, pp. 3–36.

Orloff, Ann Shola, and Theda Skocpol. 1989. "Why Not Equal Protection? Explaining the Politics of Public Social Spending in Britain, 1900–1911, and the United States, 1880s–1920." *American Sociological Review* 49: 726–50.

Piven, Frances Fox, and Richard A. Cloward. 1971. *Regulating the Poor: The Functions of Public Welfare*. New York: Pantheon.

Plotke, David. 1989. "The Wagner Act, Again: Politics and Labor, 1935–37." *Studies in American Political Development* 3: 105–56.

Poggi, G. 1978. *The Development of the Modern State*. Stanford: Stanford University Press.

Poulantzas, Nicholas. 1969. "The Problem of the Capitalist State." *New Left Review* 58 (November/December): 67–78.

————. 1973. *Political Power and Social Classes*. Translated by Timothy O'Hagen. London: Verso.

————. 1978. *Classes in Contemporary Capitalism*. Translated by David Fernbach. London: Verso.

————. 1979. *Fascism and Dictatorship*. Translated by Judith White. London: Verso.

————. 1980. *State Power Socialism*. Translated by Patriock Camiller. London: Verso.

Prezworski, Adam, and Michael Wallerstein. 1982. "The Structure of Class Conflict in Democratic Capitalist Socieites." *American Political Science Review* 76, 2: 215–38.

Quadagno, Jill S. 1984. " Welfare Capitalism and the Social Security Act of 1935." *American Sociological Review* 49: 532–47.

————. 1985. "Two Models of Welfare State Development: Reply to Skopcol and Amenta." *American Sociological Review* 50: 575–78.

————. 1988. *The Transformation of Old Age Security: Class and Politics in the American Welfare State*. Chicago: University of Chicago Press.

Ricci, David M. 1984. *The Tragedy of Political Science: Politics, Scholarship and Democracy*. New Haven: Yale University Press.

Riker, William H. 1982. *Liberalism Against Populism: A Confrontation Between the Theory of Democracy and the Theory of Public Choice*. San Francisco: W. H. Freeman.

Riker, William H., and Peter C. Ordeshook. 1973. *An Introduction to Positive Political Theory*. Englewood Cliffs, NJ: Prentice-Hall.

Sabine, George. 1934. "The State." *Encyclopedia of the Social Sciences*. New York: McMillan.

Samuels, Richard J. 1987. *The Business of the Japanese State: Energy Markets in Comparative and Historical Perspective*. Ithaca: Cornell University Press.

Sanders, Elizabeth. 1986. "Industrial Concentration, Sectional Competition, and

Antitrust Politics in America, 1880–1980." *Studies in American Political Development* 1: 142–214.

———. 1992. "Response to Scott James 'A Party System Perspective on the Interstate Commerce Act of 1887.' " *Studies in American Political Development* 6, 1: 201–05.

Schattsschneitter, E. E. 1960. *The Semi-Sovereign People*. New York: Holt, Rinehart, and Winston.

Seidelman, Raymond, with the assistance of Edward J. Harpham. 1985. *Disenchanted Realists: Political Science and the American Crisis, 1884–1984*. Albany: State University of New York Press.

Sharkansky, Ira. 1979. *Whither the State?* Chatham, NJ: Chatham House.

Shefter, Martin. 1986a. "Trade Unions and Political Machines: The Organization and Diorganization of the American Working Class in the Late Nineteenth Century." In *Working Class Formation: Nineteenth Century Patterns in Western Europe and the United States*. Edited by Ira Katznelson and Aristide Zolberg. Princeton: Princeton University Press, pp. 197–276.

———. 1986b. "Political Incorporation and the Exclusion of the Left: Party Politics and Social Forces in New York City." *Studies in American Political Development* 1: 50–90.

Shonfield, Andrew. 1965. *Modern Capitalism: The Changing Face of Public and Private Power*. New York: Oxford University Press.

Skocpol, Theda. 1979. *States and Social Revolutions: A Comparative Analysis of France, Russia, and China*. Cambridge: Cambridge University Press.

———. 1980. "Political Response to Capitalist Crises: Neo-Marxist Theories of the State and the Case of the New Deal." *Politics and Society* 10: 155–201.

———. 1992. *Protecting Soldiers and Mothers: The Political Origins of Social Policy in the United States*. Cambridge: The Belknap Press of Harvard University Press.

Skocpol, Theda, and Edwin Amenta. 1985. "Did Capitalists Shape Social Security?" *American Sociological Review*. 50: 572–75.

Skocpol, Theda, and Kenneth Finegold. 1982. "State Capacity and Economic Intervention in the Early New Deal." *Political Science Quarterly* 97 (Summer): 255–78.

———. 1990. "Explaining New Deal Labor Policy." *American Political Science Review* 84 (December): 1297–1304.

Skocpol, Theda, and G. John Ikenberry. 1983. "The Political Formation of the American Welfare State in Historical and Comparative Perspective." *Comparative Social Research* 6: 87–148.

Skocpol, Theda, and Gretchen Ritter. 1991. "Gender and the Origins of Modern Social Policies in Britain and the United States." *Studies in American Political Development* 5: 36–93.

Skowronek, Stephen. 1982. *Building a New American State: The Expansion of National Administrative Capacities, 1877–1920*. Cambridge: Cambridge University Press.

Solo, Robert A. 1982. *The Positive State*. Cincinnati: Southwestern Publishing Company.

Stepan, Alfred. *The State and Society: Peru in Comparative Perspective*. Princeton: Princeton University Press.

Sterett, Susan. 1990. "Constitutionalism and Social Spending: Pennsylvania's Old Age Pensions in the 1920s." *Studies in American Political Development* 4: 231–47.

Stone, Clarence. 1989. *Regime Politics: Governing Atlanta*. Lawrence, KS: University Press of Kansas.

Therborn, G. 1980. *What Does the Ruling Class Do When It Rules?* London: Verso.

Tilly, Charles (ed.). 1975. *The Formation of National States in Western Europe*. Princeton: Princeton University Press.

Truman, David. 1951/1971. *The Governmental Process*. 2nd. ed. New York: Alfred A. Knopf.

Vincent, Andrew. 1987. *Theories of the State*. New York: Basil Blackwell.

Weber, Max. 1964. *The Theory of Social and Economic Organization*. New York: Free Press.

———. 1968. *Economy and Society*. 3 vols. Edited by G. Roth and C. Wittich. New York: Bedminster.

———. 1978. *Weber: Selections in Translation*. Edited by E. G. Runciman. Translated by Eric Matthews. Cambridge: Cambridge University Press.

Weir, Margaret. 1988. "The Federal Government and Unemployment: The Frustration of Policy Innovation from the New Deal to the Great Society." In *The Politics of Social Policy in the United States*. Edited by Margaret Weir, Ann Shola Orloff, and Theda Skocpol. Princeton: Princeton University Press, pp. 149–197.

Weir, Margaret, Shola Orloff, and Theda Skocpol (eds.). 1988. *The Politics of Social Policy in the United States*. Princeton: Princeton University Press.

Weir, Margaret, and Theda Skocpol. 1985. "State Structures and the Possibilities for 'Keynesian' Responses to the Great Depression in Sweden, Britain, and the United States." In *Bringing the State Back In*. Edited by Peter B. Evans, Dietrich Rueschemeyer, and Theda Skocpol. Cambridge: Cambridge University Press, pp. 107–63.

Wilsford, David. 1991. *Doctors and the State: The Politics of Health Care in France and the United States*. Durham: Duke University Press.

Wilson, Woodrow. 1887. "The Study of Administration." *Political Science Quarterly* 2 (June): 202–17.

Wolfe, Alan. 1977. *The Limits of Legitimacy: Political Contradictions of Late Capitalism*. New York: Free Press.

———. 1981. *America's Impasse*. New York: Pantheon.

Wright, Erik Olin. 1979. *Class, Crisis and the State*. London: Verso.

Zeitlin, Maurice (ed.). 1980. *Classes, Class Conflict, and the State*. Cambridge, MA: Winthrop.

Zysman, John. 1978. "The French State in the International Economy." In *Between Power and Plenty*. Edited by Peter Katzenstein. Madison: University of Wisconsin Press, pp. 255–93.

———. 1983. *Governments, Markets and Growth: Finance and the Politics of Industrial Change*. Ithaca: Cornell University Press.

Human Nature, Identity, and the Search for a General Theory of Politics

Kristen Renwick Monroe

In the 1986 film *The Mission,* the Indians and Catholic priests in a humane and enlightened Indian mission in colonial Brazil become pawns in a game of power politics involving Spain, Portugal, local political authorities, and the Catholic Church. As the film ends, the mission is destroyed and its inhabitants massacred. The local authorities bring word of the atrocity to the Catholic bishop, who, although responsible for the mission, authorized the action for reasons of state. The bishop reads the report and asks the two local political leaders, with some dismay, "And you have the effrontery to tell me that this slaughter was necessary?"

"I did what I had to do," replies the first official, rather casually. "Given the legitimate purpose which," he reminds the bishop, "you sanctioned, I would have to say, yes, in truth, yes."

The second official expresses some semblance of regret. "You had no alternative, Your Eminence. We must work in the world. The world is thus."

"No, Señor," the bishop replies. "Thus have we made the world." He crosses to the window and then, speaking to himself, says, "Thus have I made it."[1]

I intend this exchange to focus attention on a set of central concerns for social science and political philosophy: the existence of a human nature and the role of human identity and agency, especially through culture and political institutions, in shaping and defining that nature. Is there an immutable human nature, a political reality based on an inborn disposition that we must recognize and accept, much as we accept the constraints of

This chapter has benefited greatly from comments by David Easton, Mark Petracca, and Catherine Zuckert, as well as from discussions with James Hankin, Matthew Levy, and Mark Sellick.

the biological and the physical world? If so, what role do human beings, acting through cultural and political institutions, play in shaping that nature?

The assumption that there is a human nature, and that this nature can be discovered and analyzed, lies at the heart of social science. It distinguishes modern political thought from ancient and forms the foundation for the kinds of empirical political theory discussed in this volume. If there is no basic human nature, then there can be no behavior that occurs with such regularity, regardless of cultural and historical constraints, that we can speak meaningfully of laws of social science. In this case our discipline is not a science in the post-Enlightenment sense, and we must instead adopt another approach, such as the historicism of Marx and Hegel, the interpretive analysis of critical theorists, or the cultural ethnography of anthropologists. If there is an enduring and fundamental human nature, however, then social scientists can and should try to understand its defining characteristics. We should seek to specify the lawlike regularities that flow from this basic nature, for we can build successful political institutions only if they are in harmony with that nature.

It is obvious from the preceding chapters in this book that beliefs about an underlying human nature touch at the foundations of many important intellectual movements—and disagreements—in contemporary political science. Within this volume, Easton, Gunnell, and Riker describe behavioral political scientists' search for regularities in politics as they sought to establish a science of politics. Rational actor theorists—such as Hardin and Riker—assume that this nature exists and that its inherently self-interested or at least goal-directed character forms the basis of political science. A strongly dissenting opinion comes from Euben, whose discussion of Oedipus is intended to illustrate the difficulties in achieving objective self-knowledge. In a similar vein, the Zuckerts describe the postmodern position: there is no constant human nature on which scientific theories can be constructed, and the entire concept of so-called political reality is a product of our own construction, an artifact created by dominant groups as part of their attempt to retain power. Cultural theorists—such as Almond—would fall somewhere in between, suggesting that various social entities help in the creation of human nature.

I address some of these ideas in this chapter. Section 1 suggests how my own intellectual journey reflected important changes in the discipline. Section 2 considers what recent debates in empirical political theory counsel concerning general theory.[2] Section 3 asks which regularities in human behavior might form the building blocks for a general theory of politics. This section, the heart of the chapter, focuses on the following fundamentals: self-interest; desires for respect, affection, and group membership; intentionality and inferentiality; and desires for control and predictability in life.

In Section 4 I sketch the outlines of one theory that may capture some of these critical aspects of human nature.[3] My conclusion suggests that the complex variations on any intrinsic human nature carry two important implications. First, they should encourage humility and encourage us to be more generous with each other as we grope along in our common enterprise. Second, they should encourage us not to search for a universal theory of political life but rather to attempt to understand and specify the conditions under which particular theories will most satisfactorily explain how real human beings behave.

SELF-INTEREST AND HUMAN NATURE

The Attraction of Rational Actor Theory

I found much of the discipline's intellectual action reflected in my own scholarly journey. I arrived at the University of Chicago in 1968 from Smith College, where a traditional government department stressed political history, law, and institutions. Behavioralism had made some inroads, mostly in U.S. voting studies and in the cultural approach to comparative politics. The Straussian approach was widely applied in political theory. There were a few nods to Marxist notions of social class but only passing reference to feminist theory, despite the fact that Smith was a women's college. In the main, political life as I knew it in 1968 remained the domain of great men, not of structures or systems.

Arriving at the University of Chicago, I was delighted to discover that what I had been excited by in a few comparative politics courses—cultural analysis à la Almond and Powell—was part of a far-reaching intellectual movement. It represented more than just an attempt to move away from Western bias in the analysis of non-Western political systems, as important as this was. The cultural approach was part of an attempt to construct a more general theory of political life. Easton's systems analysis was the critical work, and Easton's influence pervaded the department at Chicago, as it did the discipline as a whole.[4] I should perhaps add that I did not know David Easton while at Chicago and certainly was not aware of any of the disagreements or feuds that tore at the discipline and enlivened discussion among Easton, the behavioralists, and the Straussians, among others.[5] I learned of such matters much later, as one learns of ancient wars.

If I was initially strongly attracted to what I then knew as cultural theory because of its attempt to speak about politics in more general terminology, I was equally disappointed by the lack of specificity to its analysis. I came to find concepts such as interest articulation and interest aggregation useful starting points for analysis, but they remained meaningless unless supplemented by much historical, factual knowledge of specific countries.[6] The value of old-fashioned historical knowledge was further underlined by the nation's main political foci during my graduate school years: the war in Vietnam and the civil rights movement. On these issues, the scholars who made the most sense to me were the historians, not the behavioralists or the systems theorists.

I was perhaps unfair in asking too much of a method, but my disillusionment made me a willing target for intellectual seduction by a theory that offered rigor, parsimony, successful prediction, and solid scientific foundation in its basic assumption concerning human nature. That theory was rational choice theory, which is founded on the belief that we can best explain human behavior by assuming people pursue perceived self-interest, subject to information and opportunity costs.[7] The critical Enlightenment assumptions underlying this theory were seldom discussed. Indeed, I doubt many of the economists who proselytized so convincingly were even familiar or concerned with these assumptions, viewing economics more as a technical science than an intellectual discipline.[8] Yet even if the economists were unaware of the philosophical foundations of their discipline, I found these assumptions quite attractive, both in a normative and a positive sense. I still do.

What are these assumptions? The heart of the theory remains self-interest. Although I have been one of the most persistent critics of the assumption that humans universally pursue self-interest, I have been surprised at the alacrity with which rational actor theorists in political science have been willing to abandon this assumption. They have retreated far too quickly, it seems to me, to what they find a less controversial position: that rational action is merely consistent goal-directed behavior.[9] This move seems akin to throwing the baby out with the bathwater and reduces the theory to a tautology.

We can concede that self-interest is not a universally valid assumption on which to base explanations of human behavior but still retain it as a good starting place for theories about how people act. Self-interest not only explains much of crude power politics but also relates closely to a philosophical statement—implicit in economics and rational actor theory, as in liberal political thought—that individuals know best what is best for them. This assumption of self-knowledge seems particularly powerful both because it has so much empirical validity and because it carries with it a powerful normative statement in defense of human liberty.[10] No longer should an individual be told—by tradition, the state, the family and kin group, or religious authorities—what is best for him or her to do. Despite well-discussed qualifications to the belief in the possibility of self-knowledge, the normative aspects of this assumption help grant individuals the freedom to shape their own lives.[11]

Similarly, the macrolevel extension of this assumption—Adam Smith's supposition that the common good can and will emerge if every individual pursues his or her own self-interest—may not always be valid; yet it, too, constitutes an important and liberating myth, an ideal to be pursued with some hope of attainment in many political cultures. No matter how tenuous the empirical links, the normative associations among self-interest, self-knowledge, and general welfare constitute one of the appeals of rational actor theory.

As the intellectual child of the Enlightenment, rational actor theory carries with it a similarly powerful argument in favor of resolving human conflict not through physical force, tradition, or religion but through reasoned discourse. Although such resolution is not always possible, we need only look at the wasteful carnage of war to remind ourselves of the value of reasoned discourse as a tool of statecraft and the resolution of individual or group conflict.[12]

Further Enlightenment assumptions infuse rational actor theory with an emphasis on the individual and the concept of human agency. The theory assumes that people have choices and that we understand what happens in the world by understanding the choices made by these rational individuals.[13] Political events are not just random or capricious. They are not dictated by gods, stars, or evil spirits, nor are they determined by historical patterns, social structures, or socioeconomic class. Rational actor theory places human beings at the center of their own lives. People count. They are what cause things to happen. The realm of choice is frequently quite limited, but some choices do exist. The assumption of choice presumes some ability to control one's environment. Whenever I find myself criticizing rational actor theory, I remind myself of the tremendous hopefulness and concern for individual freedom inherent in the theory. These are not assumptions I want to relinquish without overwhelming empirical evidence that they are unrealistic. It is these tacit assumptions underlying rational actor theory that make the theory so powerful, if only as a normative theory.

Limitations of Rational Choice Theory

Not everyone shares my fondness for these Enlightenment assumptions. Several recent schools of thought find them little more than the ideological tools of powerful, white European men.[14] Many normative democratic theorists find rational choice theory of "narrow and dubious applicability," less a science than an ideologically bounded concept of social science (Levy 1996).[15] They join Straussians in pointing to the deleterious moral effects that ensue from conceptualizing citizens as self-interested, autonomous individuals. Insofar as rational actor theory engenders the kind of self-interested behavior it supposedly is merely reporting, it creates a perversion that we might describe—à la Plato—as a kind of ignoble lie.[16] Whatever we call it, if we accept as science what is actually merely an ideology that justifies selfish and competitive behavior, we degrade our public policies and our intellectual discourse.[17]

Deconstructionists move beyond this criticism to argue that the entire enterprise of seeking scientific regularities in social life is futile and represents an attempt by the dominant group to impose its view of reality on others. I know far too little of deconstructionism to comment on it with authority, but I find two of its tenets particularly troubling: its denial of any objective reality and its rejection of what I think of as a scientific method.[18]

I understand that much in life is subject to interpretation and that we all put our own subjective and biased spin on reality. Certainly, my own empirical work on altruism, genocide, and self-interest illustrates the behavioral importance of different perspectives on reality.[19] But none of these considerations challenge my fundamental belief in the existence of some kind of objective reality, however differentially it is interpreted, or my conviction that some representations of this reality will be more accurate than others. This seems such a fundamental part of social science that I am genuinely puzzled about why anyone who denies it wants to be in social science in the first place. A closely related problem concerns empirical verification and the extent to which reasoned discourse can further knowledge and resolve disagreements about the nature of reality. How can I engage in a meaningful dialogue concerning the existence and particulars of political life with someone with whom I share no commonly agreed upon method for resolving intellectual disagreements concerning this political reality?[20]

Other scholars—from feminists to Marxists—reject rational choice theory's emphasis on the individual as the prime actor in politics, arguing that we are not active social agents making free choices and that oppressive social forces create false consciousness.[21] Still other social scientists have challenged rational actor theory on more technical grounds. Psychologists, for example, suggest that the human psyche does not function as rational actor theorists describe it through their goal-directed model of cost-benefit calculus.[22] Much of the important work in cognitive psychology suggests clear limitations on decision-making abilities imposed by human cognition.[23] These works focus on limitations in the mind's computational qualities, qualities that exist apart from any influence from the social environment. They speak directly to the foundation assumption in rational actor theory: that agents pursue goals and make choices in a certain way and that this particular reasoning quality constitutes a universal, even a defining, characteristic of humanity. The psychological literature forges important links to work concerning the cultural influences on the mind, utilizing script or schema theory to explore how the mind's organization of incoming data reflects cultural and historical influences.[24] This critique thus reminds us to consider the limitations imposed on independent agents by social structures and history, limitations that form the core of sociological and Marxist critiques of neoclassical economics.[25]

I accept that rational choice suffers from serious limitations. What are the implications of these limitations for the construction of future empirical theories of politics? Do such limitations preclude us from constructing general theories of politics? I think not. To move discussion in that direction, let me first suggest what general theory can and cannot provide and then discuss the particulars of human nature that I believe may serve as building blocks not for a universal theory but for a general theory that works well within carefully specified domains.

THE PURPOSE OF GENERAL THEORY

Our first task is to distinguish general from universal theory. I think of universal theory as being equally applicable in all areas of social science, from politics and economics to sociology and anthropology.[26] I consider general theory more limited; it explains certain explicitly designated classes or categories of phenomena[27] and works well within these clearly specified domains but not others.[28] The main purpose of general theory is to construct a conceptual framework through which to make sense of disparate phenomena.

Domain Specification

If we limit our theories to certain domains, we can make the theories problem-driven, not method-driven.[29] However, we are still left with a significant obstacle in theory construction: providing a theoretical basis to establish which type of theory is appropriate to which realms of action.[30] Specifying the categories for which particular theories should apply is not easy and constitutes one of the substantial problems of theory construction.

Heuristic Value

"Give me a fruitful error any time, full of seeds, bursting with its own corrections," Pareto said of Kepler.[31] One important function of a theory is to stimulate other work that will correct its errors and omissions. Rational choice has been particularly useful in this regard, and all of us owe it a great debt for the richness of the debate it generated.[32] Any theory developed in the future should be offered in this spirit and hope to stimulate as rich a debate as rational choice has sparked. In constructing empirical tests, we should demand that they point to errors and omissions in the theory and hope they will suggest new ways to examine empirical reality.

Predictability

One frequent test of a theory is its ability to predict. Friedman (1953) made this a hallmark of economic theory, and rational choice theorists have often pointed to predictability as their trump card, arguing that even if their assumptions are questionable, the models constructed on rational choice assumptions fare better than other models in predicting empirical political outcomes.[33]

Most of us prefer being right to being wrong. But should we consign a theory to the scientific dustbin 1) just because its predictions are off or 2) because it does not easily lend itself to tests that will indicate that theory X is right if outcome A occurs and theory Y is right if outcome B occurs? I can think of no theory in political science that has achieved this second, rather stringent criterion of scientific testing. Even the first may be too much to demand of a science of politics.[34] I turn for support in this heretical statement to the recent discoveries that astronomers, in their estimation of the number of galaxies in the universe, were off by approximately 40 billion. Now that's a big number, even for political scientists used to dealing with the federal deficit. And galaxies are not small items. Does an error of this magnitude mean astronomy is not a science? Of course not. It simply demonstrates the limits to scientific predictability in certain disciplines.[35] In this regard, political scientists must harbor modest hopes for what we can achieve and fall back on the covering-law approach to social science, in which the development of a general theory is justified by the realistic aspects of the theory's general assumptions.[36] We can accept the limits of prediction in political science but still offer important forms of scientific explanation and systematic revelation through our theories.

Empirical Tests and Comparisons

In discussing the covering-law approach I assume that 1) political phenomena are to be explained in terms of the underlying factors that give rise to them; 2) at least one of these factors must constitute a law—i.e., be universally true within the specified categories of action; and 3) such explanations produce conclusions that are testable, at least in the crude sense of there being empirical data of some kind against which the law can be checked. The problem for any empirical theorist is that realistic assumptions may lack determinacy or testability and therefore be unfalsifiable.[37] This leaves the theorist in a quandary, because indeterminacy and lack of testability invalidate both the covering-law method and the instrumental method of scientific testing. I find no happy solution to this problem.

Given this constraint, how are we to test our empirical theories? We can divide into two categories the philosophy of science arguments concerning how theories are rejected or accepted. Some scholars argue for testing the theory with relevant empirical evidence; others (Lakatos 1970) argue for explicit comparison with alternative theories. Both tacks seem reasonable.[38]

These are the desiderata in a general theory. Let me now turn to a discussion of the particulars of human nature that I believe form the building blocks of that theory.

BASIC COMPONENTS OF A GENERAL THEORY

I assume, first, that there are enough regularities in human behavior to make possible the specification of a general theory, at least in principle.[39] I assume further that any such theory should build on the assumption that human nature is multifaceted and subject to shaping by political, social and cultural influences.[40] Finally, more immediate situational and contextual factors may serve as important constraints on human behavior. Within these parameters, however, we can discover central tendencies in human behavior. It is these tendencies that should serve as the basic building blocks with which we construct theories of political behavior.

Self-Interest

Self-interest, defined as the desire to further one's perceived well-being, is not a bad point from which to begin the search for foundation assumptions concerning human nature. This explains why the economic theory of rational action, which rests on the assumption of self-interest, has been one of the most successful theories in contemporary social science.[41] Nonetheless, self-interest is not the only constant in human nature; individual proclivities to pursue self-interest are shaped by culture and by political institutions, resulting in a reality far more complex than that posited by economics and rational choice theory.[42] An overemphasis on self-interest as the defining characteristic of humanity limits conceptions of what it means to be human and poses particular difficulties for the theorist once we move into the political realm. Exclusive reliance on self-interest lends a crudity to the intellectual debate over the human nature on which political institutions must build and results in misguided public policies.[43]

Respect, Affection, and Group Membership

Our selfish individual desires are balanced by less self-centered—although certainly still individual—yearnings for respect, affection, and membership in a valued group or social unit.[44] These yearnings, which make us the social beings Aristotle described, exist apart from cultural constraints. Cultural factors are relevant, however, in setting the cognitive salience of group membership.[45] I intend the term "cognitive salience" to imply that the group is held in high regard by the actor and is one the actor understands in a cognitive, affective, and normative sense. The actor understands how others in the group think and reason, not just in the predictive sense but in the normative or affective sense; the actor relates to and respects the way these people are living their lives. It is from individuals in such groups, not from unknown others or from people for whom one has little regard, that one wishes respect and affection. The longing for membership in and respect and affection from such groups constitutes a fundamental of human nature; any theory thus must allow for individual desires for respect, dignity, and social acceptance.[46] These needs limit the selfishness that often accompanies self-interest; they form a crucial link with the concept of self embedded in the assumption of self-interest and should play a critical part in theory construction, as they have for philosophers since Plato.

I assume that self-interest and group needs play such central roles in human nature that we may reasonably think of them as being akin to biological needs (say, for food and sleep) rather than as culturally instilled drives. A different type of building block concerns desires for predictability and control and the concepts of intentionality and inferentiality.

Predictability and Control

People want to feel a sense of control over their lives; they want events in their world to occur with enough consistency to be predictable. We may not always succeed in discerning the underlying patterns in human behavior, but we need to feel that such a pattern exists, that we can eventually gain sufficient insight to impart some modicum of certainty to our lives. Despite the extensive psychological and philosophical literature suggesting the extensive and frequent limitations on choice, people want to feel that choices do exist, for with choice comes the possibility of both prediction *and* control.[47] A theory of politics needs to allow for this desire.

Although I have referred to a sense of control and the ability to predict as desires, they might be so necessary for mental health that we should consider them needs. Psychological work on identity, for example, treats control and predictability as factors critical for emotional health. It is perhaps significant that general discussions on the creation of identity—which focus on factors ranging from mental structures to performance and social discourse[48] and which assume individuals have different degrees of flexibility in their identities[49]—invariably emphasize the importance of cognitive consistency.[50] Indeed, cognitive consistency—the idea that the world is what it seems to be—is said to provide a key source for an individual's psychic comfort and therefore the maintenance of identity.[51] A theory of politics must allow for desires (or needs) for predictability and control.

Intentionality and Inferentiality

Despite obvious difficulties in inferring motivation from acts, people must and do deduce others' intentions from their actions in order to make sense of daily life. The tendency to assign meaning or coherence to disparate phenomena rather than remaining content with literal descriptions does not mean that people believe all actions are the result of conscious forces;[52] we also ascribe intentionality to unconscious intentions and motivations.[53] Nor does it mean that structural factors and institutions—abstract entities such as political systems, states, or class—impose no limits on intentionality.[54]

To say that it is valid to explain behavior through the assumption of agents acting on intentions is not, however, to suggest this is the only way human beings operate.[55] We need to allow for the many permutations of and limitations on choice in our theory construction. To do so, I turn to the concepts of identity and self. These concepts draw on much that is rich in rational actor theory. They allow for cultural influences and some of the problems identified by critics of rational choice theory, from deconstructionists to normative critics to psychologists. Identity and self provide the intellectual mortar with which to bind together the building blocks of human nature into a general theory of politics.

Let me now sketch the essentials of such a theory, one constructed around perceptions of self. I believe this theory might profitably be used in conjunction with, or even in lieu of, rational actor theory to explain political behavior and that it has direct relevance for the way in which identity affects political choice, particularly ethical political action.[56] Because I have discussed this theory elsewhere, I summarize only the central points here.[57]

PERSPECTIVE: A GENERAL THEORY?

Perceptions of Ourselves in Relation to Others

Perspective is an empirical theory, developed as part of my attempt to understand altruism. I thus restrict discussion to ethical political actions, defined here to include acts where there is clear state involvement and where individual ethics are involved.[58] Within this category of action, the essence of the theory can be stated succinctly: certain kinds of political action emanate primarily from one's perception of self in relation to others; this perception effectively sets the domain of choice options perceived as available to an actor, both in an empirical and a moral sense.

Certain situations present choices—we could also call them options or alternative forms of action[59]—that affirm or deny one's perception of self in relation to others.[60] As a general rule, political behavior flows naturally from this perception. To pursue an action that deviates in any significant regard from self-perception necessitates a personal shift in identity that can occur only at great psychological cost and upheaval for the actor. The range of self-images available will be provided, to a large degree, by the deep, tacit cultural assumptions of the society to which the actor belongs, with actors gravitating toward different images according to both internal (genetic propensities)[61] and external (situational and contextual factors) influences.[62]

Ethical Acts Are Instinctual, not Conscious

Ethics arise not from conscious choice but rather from deep-seated instincts,[63] predispositions, and habitual patterns of behavior that are related to our central identity.[64] The factors that produce what Hutcheson (1728/1971) called our "moral sense" range from genetic programming to social roles and culturally inculcated norms; they include (but are not restricted to) values that we consciously know we hold. Our actions in situations that tap on ethical concerns are motivated more by our instinctual sense of self than by any conscious calculus.[65] This emphasis on central identity should not imply that an actor may not have conflicting identities. Indeed, one of the challenges facing my theory of perspective lies in determining how individuals respond when they feel conflicts between the core parts of their identity. (Tension between my identity as a mother and my identity as a scholar exemplifies but one such conflict.) It seems clear that although identity excludes some sets of actions, it also may leave available whole other sets, not just one particular action. We need to construct political theories so they allow for conflicts between, ambivalence concerning, and shifts among critical aspects of core identity.[66]

Identity Supersedes Consciously Held Moral Values

Identity is more basic than conscious adherence to moral values.[67] As a general rule, most people do not sit down and consciously survey, assess, and choose one set of moral values to guide their lives. Rather, adherence to moral values—whether this adherence is loose or rigid—evolves out of one's core identity.[68] This core identity includes our innermost sense of who we are and what ties and obligations we believe we have to others.

Furthermore, the emphasis is on an actor's individual identity, not what social psychologists refer to as social identity, which enters more through the perceptual aspect of the theory and which is more malleable than is individual identity.[69]

Decisions as Recognition, not Choice

One's basic conception of oneself is fundamental and preset for most adults. If an issue touches on this sense of self, then action becomes less a choice among alternatives and more a recognition, akin perhaps to an inner realization, of who one is at the most fundamental level of self-awareness.[70] This self-recognition involves an acceptance that only certain options are available to one because of who one is—more precisely, because of who one perceives oneself to be.[71] The key to action is our perception of self in relation to others rather than "objective," third-party assessments of these relations.

The dominance of recognition over creation may occur because core identity emanates at least in part from genetic factors and early childhood experiences and develops at such an early age that its basic construction cannot be said to result from an individual's own free choice or will.[72] We may modify our core identities later in significant ways, but only at great psychological effort.

Agents Discover Rather than Create Their Identities

Closely related to the above is the idea that core identity is not created by an agent so much as it is revealed to an actor through his or her own acts, through the actor's realization that he or she can't do X but feels compelled to do Y. It therefore seems more appropriate to speak of an agent's recognizing, rather than creating, his or her own master or core identity.[73]

Self-discovery, even of this central core to our identity, can be a continual, ongoing process of filling in the blanks, or it may occur in intermittent and revelatory events. Though the basic contours of our core identities remain relatively constant, minor adjustments to them are probably ongoing. Less critical aspects of identity are seldom immutable and may be continuously more fully honed through the process of living.[74]

The recognition of a certain core identity or character may be as important as the existence of that character or identity. If I believe I have one identity and act in accordance with it, that is more important than whether or not this is, in fact, my central character. (For example, genocidalists frequently see themselves as victims acting to redress a grievance. What the rest of the world recognizes as barbaric acts of murder, the genocidalists view as preemptive strikes necessary to prevent their own murders. See Monroe 1994b.)

Domain Restriction: The Nature of Ethical Political Decisions

Although the above-described theory of perspective may well have broader application, it was developed to explain ethical political decisions. Most ev-

eryday decisions that involve conscious choice neither involve political ethics nor strike at our basic sense of self. These decisions involve most economic acts (e.g., where to eat or which car to buy) and many political acts
(e.g., whom to vote for or whether to donate money to a particular political
campaign). This tendency is only a general rule; it does not mean that some
individuals might not treat economic or political actions as ones that relate to their basic identity; individual core values, after all, vary drastically
from one person to the next. Furthermore, any given individual may vary
the way particular political acts are viewed at certain points in time. (Or-
dinarily, I may view elections in the Downsian sense and perform a traditional rational calculus when deciding whether and how to vote. At other
times, however, I may view an election as a kind of moral referendum,
as many Americans did during the Vietnam War.) The key is to understand when an actor views an action as falling into the ethical political
realm and when the act is subjected to more traditional political or economic calculus.

Once we enter the realm of ethical political acts, our empirical work
should attempt to answer questions such as the following: what is the role
played by situational factors in framing options and in triggering relevant
aspects of identity? Is the function of the choice or the nature of the individual the critical factor in triggering the perspective that then determines
action? How immutable is identity and for what kinds of individuals? These
are but a few of the questions that need to be answered.

Comparison with Rational Choice

Philosophers of science disagree over the best method for accepting or
rejecting theories. Some scholars argue for testing the theory empirically,
and others argue for explicit comparison with alternative theories. In
other work, I have subjected the theory of perspective to empirical testing, utilizing it to examine empirical phenomena as disparate as altruism
(1996), genocide (1995b), and religious fundamentalism (1997). Here,
let me contrast perspective with an alternate theory. Rational choice theory seems the logical contrast, both because it has been so successful in
political science and because it offers itself as both a positive and a normative theory, thus making it particularly applicable to ethical political decisions.

Such comparisons could take many forms, and I mention only two here.
In the first comparison, I suggest that rational choice provides only one
menu of choice, whereas perspective allows for different menus, depending on how our different self-images and perceptions trigger different structures of choice. In the second, I refer to claims that rational choice fails to
explain normative, expressive, and intrinsic motivations and social identifi-

cation and suggest how perspective may allow for such phenomena, thereby explaining them more fully.

EXAMPLE 1. Choice and Conscious Calculus. Consider two separate categories of action: those involving issues that strike at our central sense of self and those that touch at a more superficial level of identity.[75] The theory of perspective suggests that, as a general rule, the more deeply an action touches on our core identity, the less likely it is to be subjected to a rational calculus and the more likely it is to be placed into the kind of perspectival matrix the theory outlines.

Rational actor theory does not divide action into those categories. It assumes agents have preferences and that these preferences can be rank-ordered—consciously or subconsciously—in some rough fashion to provide each actor with a preference structure. The costs and benefits are then calculated, and the actor chooses between alternatives.

Which theory is more realistic? I would argue for perspective. In particular, I submit that there is what we might think of as a deep structure of choice. We might think of people as possessing menus of choice in the same way that we have menus on computers.[76] Rational actor theory delineates one mode. When the actor finds[77] that mode appropriate, he or she plugs into it in much the same way one might select the "edit" menu in a word processor to cut and paste text or the "format" menu to change typefaces.

But the rational mode is not the only mode. There is, for example, what we might call the script mode, when automatic behavior takes over. (An emergency-room surgeon called in for a last-minute operation may be told only that the patient needs to have an appendectomy; this information triggers the script for performing this operation.) There is also compulsive or frustration-instigated behavior.[78] There is a mode for creative genius, a mode for inspiration, and so on.

Each person's menus—to continue the computer metaphor—may differ. Bert's "software" may contain an advanced menu for ambivalence but an elementary menu for rational action and a mid-level menu for fixated behavior. Ernie's may contain an elementary menu for ambivalence but a sophisticated menu for rational action and a highly developed menu for creative genius. And so on. Whether or not an actor is rational is no longer the interesting question, as we now view rational behavior as only one mode of action. Rather, we want to know how the basic menus differ from individual to individual and when particular menus will be selected. How are these basic menus formed? How does a person choose within the menus that exist on his or her cognitive screen? When, how, and why does a person dump a menu? For what reasons does someone add a new one? These are all questions that need to be answered. But none will even be posed if we limit ourselves to thinking only in the rational choice mode.

EXAMPLE 2. Rational Choice and Collective Action. Taylor (1995) argues that rational choice theory may be useful under some conditions but does not help us understand behaviors that cannot be treated as instrumental. He points to collective action and cooperation, in particular, as behaviors that require us to consider "normative, expressive, and intrinsic motivations and social identification, and to the conditions in which they are mobilized" (Taylor 1995:223). Such acts, Taylor argues, are greatly "facilitated by community, by social networks, by repeated interaction in a stable group, by ongoing social relationships" (1995:222).[79]

How do such social relations facilitate cooperation? Rational choice's answer is that these relations serve to make cooperation the most rational option. Or, the theory suggests, the community may offer both negative and positive sanctions that overcome the free-rider difficulties involved in collective action.

Taylor points out, however, that there is an alternate explanation. The community may provide "the conditions in which normative motivation, social identification, and in some cases intrinsic motivation are mobilized" (232). For example, group membership leads to the development of shared norms. Continuing interaction in such groups leads to the creation of social identity. Rational choice theorists ignore the extent to which people

> cooperate because they identify with the group and are disposed to respect its norms (and may even be committed to them). In the case of hierarchy, cooperation . . . might be explained not as the rational conditional cooperation of purely self-interested actors, but in terms of normative (and perhaps expressive) and intrinsic motivations that can be mobilized or activated if (and only if) hierarchical subordinates are treated by their superiors in the right way (Taylor, 1995:233).

Taylor does not contend that people never act as the rational model suggests, but he does claim that there is much behavior that cannot be explained by rational choice. He concludes that cooperation suggests only one instance in which alternative interpretations of the same phenomena may be just as plausible as the rational choice interpretation.[80] I agree. Perspective allows for such considerations by allowing actors to alter their basic view of themselves in relation to others, sometimes seeing themselves as tied to others, at other times seeing themselves as alone and without ties depending on the situation, framing, and so forth.

CONCLUSION

What can we conclude from the foregoing discussion? It seems clear that, although the regularities in human behavior are sufficient to justify a search for patterns that can be developed into theories of political life, it is more difficult to argue that such theories can be universal in nature. Why is this so? The existence of cognitive limitations to observing and understanding different minds and cultures offers one explanation.[81] A second explanation lies in the multifaceted aspect of human nature.[82] This characteristic makes specifying a universal theory of politics extremely difficult and suggests the wisdom of attempting to understand and specify those conditions under which particular theories best apply. The malleability of human nature returns us to further consideration of the role played by culture and by political and social institutions in shaping the basic components of human nature.

These questions are so large and so daunting that one can understand both the tendency to despair and the attraction of postmodernism, which is certainly wise to remind us of our different perceptions of a common reality.[83] But here is where we can take the postmodern challenge to the possibility of creating an objective science of politics and use it to construct better empirical political theories. For example, insofar as the theory of perspective builds on individuals' genuinely different ways of looking at and understanding the same reality, it would seem to answer much of what seems valid in the postmodern critique, without requiring us to accept the more excessive claims of postmodernism.

In arguing for the development of general but not universal theory, I grant that people form subjective views of political reality. But this fact does not mean there is no one reality, no objective facts in political life. It merely suggests that each of us comes to understand the objective political "realities" in our own, often highly idiosyncratic individual way, using the intellectual tools that work best for us.

Let me digress briefly and through a personal example suggest what the problem of different minds dealing with one reality implies for general theory.

My husband once studied physics and still reads physics texts. Occasionally, he gets so excited about an idea that he wants to share it with me. As he talks, he invariably notices that my eyes are glazing over. It's not that I don't believe physics exists as a comprehensive intellectual or physical reality; it's just that at some level it does not mean much to me. I understand, respect, and even incorporate the knowledge of certain laws of physics into my daily life. But that isn't the way my mind works, and I need frames of reference constructed for me before I can converse about advanced concepts in physics.

If some of us need frames of reference to deal with physical reality, the need must be even greater with political reality and with many of the political theories developed to analyze that reality. I, for example, find much to disagree with in rational choice theory and am put off by what often feels like arrogant imperialism among a few rational choice theorists. But I understand the theory because, essentially, it works the way my mind works; at least, it comes close enough that I can find meaning in its terminology and its ways of structuring an argument. I think in terms of people. I see political life in terms of human agents, not structures or classes. This does not mean I never utilize terms such as "political system" or "state" in my own discourse, but at some visceral level I don't really know what a state or a political system looks like apart from the individuals within it. Therefore, theories of the state will have limited meaning *for me*.

Similarly, I understand the postmodernists' argument that there are what Hirschman (1977) called tacit assumptions in a historical time or place whose importance for political life is difficult for others to learn of and comprehend. I recognize, for example, that I have limited insight into ancient people who believed in the divine rights of kings or into contemporary cultures that espouse clitorectomy.[84] But does this mean there was or is no political reality in this murky past or these distant cultures, or that some attempts to understand such reality will not be better than others? I think not. How we go about best understanding these cultures, how we enter into a different mind, is unclear. The problem is an old one.[85] Perhaps we need people who build bridges from one discipline to another, just as we utilize interpreters to translate languages for us. Perhaps work in developmental psychology, on how children develop a theory of other people's minds, will prove helpful. These are routes I hope will be explored in future work.

Now, what does all of this have to do with general theory? For me, it suggests that we should view political science "less as a prizefight between competing theoretical perspectives, only one of which may prevail, and more as a joint venture in which explanations condition and augment one another" (Green and Shapiro, 1994:204). Rather than arguing over the superiority of various theories in political science, we should work to understand and build on a theory's strengths and utilize its failings to point to new directions useful for theory construction. We need not relinquish our search for a general theory of politics, but we should be more generous in our dialogues with each other as we grope along in our common enterprise. We should talk more with each other, listen more carefully, and retreat less into our own intellectual inlets. It is, after all, the search for better understanding of political life that is central, not whether one scholar's understanding is better than another's. By reminding ourselves that we are all students of the political and that we share a common venture, we can minimize divisive contention and encourage intellectual exchange. Certainly this has been my intention in organizing this volume. I believe contemporary political theory could benefit greatly from such a dialogue.

I have moved too far afield and ended by throwing too much into our intellectual mélange. But there is much of great intellectual interest that has excited me in the last twenty-five years, and I would like to see discourse return, with both civility and passion, to discussions of general theory in the future. I offer my ideas in the hope that they will inspire future generations much as David Easton's works inspired me and so many others. Embracing such an intellectual enterprise is the best way to honor Easton's contribution to political science.

NOTES

1. This is a rough quote written after viewing the videotape; it is not taken directly from the screenplay (which is credited to Robert Bolt).

2. Throughout this discussion I use the term "general theory" to cover explanations of a whole domain of phenomena, as opposed to "partial theory," which covers only part of such a domain, or specific theorems, which cover lower-level parts.

3. Because of space constraints, I cannot articulate precise ways in which this theory draws on these fundamentals.

4. Indeed, it now seems ironic that Easton may be denied some of the credit he deserved in the discipline because of the fundamental importance of his work. Like many other great theories, Easton's systems analysis makes so much sense that the ideas seem rather obvious once you are exposed to them. The mere fact that we now speak of a political system as a general term illustrates my point.

5. This reflects the ignorance of a naive graduate student rather than the intensity of the intellectual debates.

6. My interest in cognition and the process by which an individual structures and processes information comes from a desire to return to much that attracted me to cultural analysis.

7. The dominant trend in philosophy since Hobbes has been to assume that there is a human nature and that it is self-interested (Mansbridge 1990, Myers 1983, Monroe 1996). Philosophers such as Cropsey (1977) have argued that this was the point at which philosophy gave up the game to economics, the dismal science founded almost exclusively on the assumption that man is a self-interested, state-of-nature being who grows apart from the direction and guidance from the polity. This general view has dominated recent discussions among political scientists, with the exception of those scholars who adopt a more historical methodology (the Marxists), those who reject the Enlightenment mode of science (the postmodernists), and those few political scientists concerned with identity and its effect on political action.

8. One economist friend carefully explained the economic concept of externalities to me, offering it as a concept useful for political scientists interested in defining when a state should intervene in matters otherwise deemed private. When I suggested that this idea owed an intellectual debt to John Stuart Mill's distinction between self-regarding and other-regarding actions, I was informed that it had been

Milton Friedman's idea first and that Mill must have borrowed it from Friedman. The chronological impossibility of this failed to dampen my friend's belief in the inherent superiority of his discipline.

9. See Myers (1983), Mansbridge (1990) or Monroe (1991, 1995a).

10. The liberal assumption stands in contrast to the older tradition of civic republicanism. This issue is discussed more critically in this volume by Peter Euben and by the Zuckerts.

11. Despite its limitations, a belief in self-knowledge may serve as a useful myth. I leave aside discussion of how self-knowledge can be revealed or made possible. In general, I assume that enabling self-knowledge to occur, as opposed to assuming it as a starting point, constitutes part of liberalism's contribution to social institutions and government. Communitarians would argue that self-knowledge can only be possible through communal interaction. See Euben's chapter in this volume.

12. This assumes people want to reason, which is different from having the capacity to reason.

13. Easton discusses this in his chapter, as does Riker.

14. I must group together diverse and complex works for purposes of exposition and space.

15. Petracca (1991) suggests that structuralists, poststructuralists, and Straussians have made this same argument. See also Digeser 1995.

16. I am indebted to Matthew Levy for suggesting such a possibility to me.

17. See Petracca 1991 for a review.

18. Catherine Zuckert informs me that postmoderns reject both subjectivity and objectivity as concepts, arguing that we cannot think outside of language, which is a social product that changes over time.

19. Monroe (1994b, 1995b and 1996).

20. I have separated these two points, leaving aside discussion of the relationship between postmodernism's arguments against objective reality and its failure to provide a commonly agreed upon method for resolving intellectual disagreements.

21. See Lowi and Harpham, Hardin, or Hartsock in this volume, or Ferber and Nelson (1993) for a review of feminist theory and economics.

22. These critiques are well known. See Kahnemann, Slovic, and Tversky (1982), Rosenberg (1991), Wittman (1991), and Green and Shapiro (1994) for summaries of the literature.

23. See Heider (1958), Festinger (1957), Koffka (1935), and Kahneman and Tversky (1972) inter alia.

24. See inter alia Fiske and Taylor (1984), Kohlberg (1981), Rosenberg (1988), or symbolic interactionists dating from G. H. Mead (1934).

25. Lowi and Harpham touch on some of this in their chapter in this volume.

26. I would argue that much of the hostile criticism of rational actor theory emanates not so much from disagreement with its substantive tenets as from its claims to universalism. Not all rational choice theorists make such claims, but the field as a whole has tended to be associated with such extreme claims because of the enthusiasm of a few advocates, such as Becker (1976). See Green and Shaprio (1994) for a criticism of universalistic claims by rational choice theorists.

27. Easton points out that my usage of the term, though generally accurate, differs from general usage insofar as the domain specified frequently refers, at least in practice, to disciplinary boundaries; hence, we speak of general theories of politics or general theories of economics. In contrast, I would argue that we can specify the domain to refer to inter or intradisciplinary divisions, as Parsons did by specifying his theory as a general theory of social structure.

28. It seems clear to me that rational choice theory, for example, works well as a general theory within clearly specified domains but does not provide the universal theory desired by some. (This is meant not as criticism; developing general theories seems a worthwhile and a more realistic goal for political science.)

29. A major criticism of rational actor theory centers on this, with critics charging that rational choice analysts became so entranced with methodology that they constructed models and applied them willy-nilly, cramming complex empirical data into simple frameworks and thereby distorting political reality. See Monroe (1994a) for a review.

30. I may merely be postponing this problem. Theory specification also needs to address the issue of when one theory will have high explanatory value and another theory will have low value. I try in my theory construction to speak to this issue. See Monroe (1996).

31. I owe this lovely quote to Taylor (1995:225).

32. As I reread the literature in the debate over rational choice, it struck me that much of what looks like backpedaling on the part of rational choice theorists when confronted with evidence contradicting their theory may actually just be the natural response of scientists trying to fill in holes or weak spots in their initial theory. This natural process by which scientific advances are made and solidified can be seen more clearly if we remove the confrontational nature of the debate.

33. Thus, much of the success of rational choice theory rests on its ability to provide verifiable empirical predictions. The validity of this claim has come under attack of late, but it remains a perennial concern of those who want to see a science of politics. See Green and Shapiro (1994) or Brennan and Lomosky (1993).

34. Hope for, yes; demand, no.

35. Flippancy aside, each discipline or area of inquiry probably sets its own acceptable levels of prediction. Meteorologists, for example, are happy if they can predict snowstorms; they do not seek to predict where each snowflake will fall. Space constraints preclude further discussion of the selection of acceptable levels of disciplinary predictions of aggregate versus individual behavior, itself an interesting scientific issue.

36. Rational choice theory has oscillated between the instrumentalist approach and the covering-law approach. The first, associated with Milton Friedman, emphasizes the success of testable predictions regardless of the reality of the assumptions, the second is associated with Hempel (1948/1965).

37. In many theoretical formulations, the empirical validity of the assumption is less important than the theoretical consequences it gives rise to and their testability. I touched on this issue briefly in my remarks about Friedman's positive economics.

38. The theory outlined in Section 4 has been subjected to empirical testing, utilizing phenomena as disparate as altruism (1996), genocide (1995), and religious fundamentalism (1997). In other works (Monroe 1996), I have offered specific contrasts by illustrating how this theory offers different kinds of explanations from those rational choice theory would offer. In doing so, I am responding to what Shepsle colorfully dubbed the First Law of Wing Walking: "Don't let go of something until you have something else to hold on to" (Shepsle 1995:217). I am, in effect, suggesting that the kind of perspectival theory presented below offers scholars something other than rational choice theory onto which they may hold, at least as they deal with the intricacies of ethical political behavior.

39. In this, I am agreeing with modern political scientists.

40. I disagree with state-of-nature theorists, who posit a nature of man outside political institutions, and agree with the ancients, who found a strong role for the *polis* in shaping human beings.

41. See Green and Shapiro 1994 for a dissenting view.

42. Rational actor theorists have identified the self-interested or goal-directed aspect of this human nature, some arguing that it is the very process of ratiocination that distinguishes us as humans. This view is disputed by many, among them psychologists, who challenge this depiction of the human psyche, arguing that the mind does not function at all as rational actor theorists describe it. Communitarians and many normative theorists have further questioned the description of the human nature propounded by rational actor theorists, finding it too ideologically bounded. Postmoderns take an even more extreme position, arguing that any so-called political reality is primarily a product of our own construction.

43. Work by Gary Becker (1976) and his students provides examples of this exclusive emphasis on self-interest.

44. John Harsanyi (1960) argues that human behavior can be explained largely in terms of two dominant interests: economic gain and social acceptance. I am effectively modifying Harsanyi's basic conceptualization.

45. "Salience" may not be the correct word here, so consider the following illustration:

In *Black Lamb, Grey Falcon*, West describes a train trip to the Balkans in the 1930s. As the heroine and her husband travel through Germany, they discover others sitting in their reserved first-class seats. West is embarrassed as the people in her seats leave and is surprised at the extent to which the other passengers in the coach discuss the event in judgmental terms, highly critical of people who take seats to which they were not entitled. As the train crosses the national frontier from Germany, the conductor enters the compartment to examine passports and tickets. It turns out the rest of the people in the compartment also have second-class tickets and that the practice of taking a first-class seat until it is claimed by its rightful owner is widespread, an expected norm. For West, this makes the grumbling and criticism all the more difficult to understand: "I got up and went out into the corridor. It was disconcerting to be rushing through the night with this carriageful of unhappy muddlers, who were so nice and so incomprehensible."

West mulls over this event, trying to understand why it so disturbed her, as the train pulls into the station just outside Zagreb:

I leaned out of the window. Rain was falling heavily, and the mud shone between the railway tracks. An elderly man, his thin body clad in a tight-fitting overcoat, trotted along beside the train, crying softly, "Anna! Anna! Anna!" He held an open umbrella not over himself but at arm's length. He had not brought it for himself, but for the beloved woman he was calling. He did not lose hope when he found her nowhere in all the long train, but turned and trotted all the way back, calling still with anxious sweetness, "Anna! Anna! Anna!" When the train steamed out he was trotting along it for a third time, holding his umbrella still further away from him. A ray of light from an electric standard shone on his white hair, on the dome of his umbrella, which was streaked with several rents, and on the strong spears of the driving rain. I was among people I could understand (West 1941: 38).

West illustrates what I mean by cognitive salience when she describes herself as being among people whom she could understand.

46. These are the needs on which communitarians base their theories. It is perhaps significant that communitarians tend to refer to these as "needs," not as "drives," "passions," or "desires," because the concept of a need denotes a normative aspect. Society could reasonably be argued to have an obligation to fulfill human needs as opposed to desires, which seem more self-imposed demands for which society is not responsible. I am grateful to David Easton for pointing out this distinction to me.

47. This is control by the individual, not by another.

48. For an excellent overview of psychological discussions of social identity, see Hankin (1996).

49. These range from individuals with concrete mental structures to those locked in social roles to those exhibiting more flexible performances and self-narratives.

50. They also emphasize validation and self-esteem, which relate to the second category of needs: respect, affection, and group membership.

51. Validation, the idea that others agree with our performance or presentation of identity, establishes identity as socially recognized. Self-esteem is key in both processes and is said to provide ontological security that we know who we are. All these literatures, which address identity at the individual level, not as group or collective identity, thus seem to emphasize what I have characterized above as the need for consistency.

52. This is why behavioralism eventually dissatisfies.

53. Ferejohn and Satz (1995) assume that intentionality and the tendency to ascribe motives to others' behavior—what Ferejohn and Satz call the charity principle—implies "that universalistic explanation is possible in social science" (1995:81).

54. The human tendency to infer intentions from action accounts, at least in part, for the dissatisfaction with behavioralism. It also explains much of the attraction of rational actor theory. The assumption of intentionality plays a critical role in normative theory, where it is used to assign responsibility and blame in moral philosophy, for example. In arguing that human political behavior is the result of agents with intentions, I—along with economists and moral philosophers—assume that human beings are causal agents who make choices and act on them in the

reasonable expectation that the events that follow will advance the agent's goals. This assumption reveals an intentionalist approach to social theory and reflects the hopefulness of the Enlightenment. This carries both normative and positive value in a theory and needs to be brought into our theory construction.

55. Johnston (1991) has pointed out the extent to which certain behaviors can be understood more fully either by reference to an ambivalence model of human behavior or as programmed sequences imbedded within larger sequences, such as the routinized decisions over where to turn the car on the same old drive to work. Neither model posits the traditional concept of choice assumed by rational actor theory.

56. The individual's relation to the state lies at the heart of political philosophy, be it ancient philosophy (such as Plato's or Aristotle's), liberal political thought (à la Hobbes and Locke), communitarian critics of liberalism (Taylor, Sandel, or MacIntyre), or postmoderns (such as Foucault). See Digeser (1995) for an overview.

57. Monroe (1994b, 1996).

58. This could include a wide array of acts, depending on how broadly one conceives of the realm of state action and ethics. This narrow interpretation would make the theory most applicable for events such as genocide or people who risk their lives to prevent genocide. A broader interpretation of "ethical political behavior" would place more acts into the domain of this theory if we were to assume that all acts involving others are political.

59. I make this distinction because choice often entails the concept of freedom of action.

60. Because of this theory's interdisciplinary nature, I try to describe it using simple language, intelligible to readers who are not necessarily well-versed in the intricacies of particular fields or debates. Within space constraints, I will try to define my terms and make reference to some of the more technical debates in the various literatures, providing references for the reader. (Identity, schema, the self, culture, choice, cognition, and agency are but a few examples of the complex concepts on which much has been written.) See Bruner (1988, 1990), Elster (1979, 1986), Johnston (1990), or Taylor (1989) on agency, intentionality, and the self. See Axelrod (1973) or Johnson-Laird (1983) on schemata and schema theory.

61. It is controversial to speak of personality traits as being genetically determined, but initial research from twin studies seems too important to be ignored.

62. For example, Hirschman (1977) describes how the tacit assumptions of Western European society shifted so that the basic drive for self-preservation became associated with having possessions. (More goods make us less vulnerable and therefore better protected.) This associates self-identification with possessions. Calvinism encouraged this process, so critical for liberal capitalism.

63. Wilson (1993) makes a similar point. See this or my empirical work on altruism (1996) for empirical substantiation of this claim.

64. I believe this is personal, not social identity, although my thinking remains unclear on distinctions at this point.

65. This approach follows an important but not dominant tendency in philosophy. It views morality as emanating from the passions rather than from the intellect.

G. E. Moore, Adam Smith, David Hume, and Hutcheson all stressed the passions as the origin of morality; Plato, Kant, and the utilitarians stressed the intellect.

66. See Johnston (1991) or Elster (1986).

67. Moral values can be viewed as external to the agent, whereas identity cannot.

68. This treatment of moral values owes much to the concept of moral sense theory discussed by Darwin (1859/1936) in his theory of evolution. The closest work in contemporary moral philosophy would be recent work by Williams (1981) or Nussbaum (1986).

69. See Hankin (1996) for a discussion of social identity.

70. Grafstein (1995) suggests that individual agents do not choose to have a certain kind of moral character but can instead learn about their character through the nature of their behavior.

71. In stating this, we must bear in mind the interactive extent of our self-perceptions via processes such as socialization and reinforcement.

72. The literature on identity construction ranges from political culture theory and Foucault's conception of discourse to microsociological perspectives and psychological theories stressing consideration of specific mental structures and processes in cognitive psychology that try to specify the interaction between subjectivity and social context through concepts such as role theory and literatures on the presented self. For a review see Hankin (1996).

73. I use the terms "master" and "core" identity interchangeably.

74. A full discussion of identity lies beyond the scope of this chapter.

75. Though the theory of perspective differs in several important ways from rational choice theory, because of space constraints I can discuss only one difference: the way in which we might draw critical distinctions concerning the cognitive links among perceptions, decision-making, and behavior. Other distinctions of equal importance that I must ignore include fluidity of identity, the extent to which we have multiple or competing identities, and insecurity about our central identity.

76. Petracca alerts me to the extent to which this analogy oversimplifies. I do not mean to suggest that modes are necessarily distinct; in fact, they probably overlap and intermingle in complex ways.

77. I use the vague verb "find" intentionally because I am not sure to what extent actors may be aware that they are making a choice as to "menu" of choice.

78. Eckstein (1991) and Gilani (1995) describe this in work on analgesic cultures, especially cultures of great poverty in which people cannot be said to have goals they can follow.

79. See also Brady, Verba, and Schlozman (1995) or Putnam (1993).

80. Taylor develops these ideas much more completely than I can in a short example. See Taylor (1987, 1995).

81. I think there are linkages between these cognitive limitations and our ability to construct general theories, although I do not yet understand the nature of these linkages and remain frustrated, groping in the dark as I work to comprehend them.

82. One large question, left unanswered here, is how to distinguish core parts of our personalities from less central parts.

83. Indeed, some postmoderns deny any objective reality.

84. The best estimates suggest such genital mutilation has been inflicted on approximately 80–100 million girls and women and that clitorectomies will continue to be performed on 2 million youngsters every year (A. M. Rosenthal, "Fighting Female Mutilation," *The New York Times,* April 12, 1996: A15).

85. Poor Anne Boleyn, who would have fared better had she more fully appreciated the divine rights of kings, may not have known about the law of gravity, but she knew in advance that when the executioner let the axe drop above her head, it would fall.

REFERENCES

Axelrod, Robert M. 1973. *Framework for a General Theory of Cognition and Choice.* Berkeley: Institute of International Studies, University of California.

Becker, Gary. 1976. *The Economic Approach to Human Behavior.* Chicago: University of Chicago Press.

Brady, H. E., S. Verba, and K. L. Schlozman. 1995. "Beyond Ses—A Resource Model of Political Participation." *American Political Science Review* 89, 2: 271–94.

Bruner, Jerome. 1990. *Acts of Meaning.* Cambridge, MA: Harvard University Press.

———. 1988. *Actual Minds, Possible Worlds.* Cambridge, MA: Harvard University Press.

Cropsey, Joseph. 1977. *Political Philosophy and the Issues of Politics.* Chicago: University of Chicago Press.

Darwin, C. 1859/1936. *The Origin of Species by Means of Natural Selection.* New York: Modern Library.

Digeser, Peter. 1995. *Our Politics, Our Selves?: Liberalism, Identity, and Harm.* Princeton: Princeton University Press.

Eckstein, Harry. 1991. "Rationality and Frustration in Political Behavior." In K. R. Monroe (ed.), *The Economic Approach to Politics: A Critical Reassessment of the Theory of Rational Action.* New York: Harper Collins, pp. 74–93.

Elster, Jon. 1986. *The Multiple Self.* Cambridge, New York: Cambridge University Press.

———. 1979. *Ulysses and the Sirens: Studies in Rationality and Irrationality.* New York: Cambridge University Press.

Ferber, Marianne, and Julie Nelson. 1993. *Beyond Economic Man.* Chicago: University of Chicago Press.

Ferejohn, John, and Debra Satz. 1995. "Unification, Universalism, and Rational Choice Theory." *Critical Review* 9,1–2 (Winter–Spring): 71–84.

Festinger, Leon. 1957. *A Theory of Cognitive Dissonance.* Stanford: Stanford University Press.

———. 1954. "A Theory of Social Comparison Processes." *Human Relations* 7: 117–40.

Fiske, Susan T., and Shelly E. Taylor. 1984. *Social Cognition.* Reading, MA: Addison-Wesley.

Friedman, Milton. 1953. *Essays in Positive Economics.* Chicago: University of Chicago Press.

Giddens, Anthony. 1984. *The Constitution of Society.* Berkeley: University of California Press.

Gilani, Bijan. 1995. "Poverty, Education and Democracy." University of California at Irvine, working paper.

Grafstein, Robert. 1995. "Rationality as Conditional Expected Utility Maximization." *Political Psychology* 16, 1: 63–80.

Green, Donald, and Ian Shapiro. 1994. *Pathologies of Rational Choice*. New Haven: Yale University Press.

Hankin, James. 1996. "On the Self and Social Context: A Review of Identity Theory in Political Science." University of California at Irvine, qualifying paper, April 1996.

Harsanyi, John. 1960. "Rational-Choice Models of Political Behavior versus Functionalist and Conformist Theories." *World Politics* 21: 513–38.

Heider, Fritz. 1958. *The Psychology of Interpersonal Relations*. New York: Wiley.

Hempel, Carl G. 1948/1965. *Aspects of Scientific Explanation and Other Essays in the Philosophy of Social Science*. New York: Free Press.

Hirschman, Albert O. 1977. *The Passions and the Interests: Political arguments for Capitalism Before Its Triumph*. Princeton, NJ: Princeton University Press.

Hutcheson, Francis. 1728/1971. *An Essay on the Nature and Conduct of the Passions and Affections*. New York: Garland.

Johnson-Laird, Phillip N. 1983. *Mental Models: Toward a Cognitive Science of Language, Inference, and Consciousness*. Cambridge, MA: Harvard University Press.

Johnston, David. 1991. "Human Agency and Rational Action." In K. R. Monroe (ed.), *The Economic Approach to Politics: A Critical Reassessment of the Theory of Rational Action*. New York: Harper Collins, pp. 94–112.

Kahneman, Daniel, Paul Slovic, and Amos Tversky. 1982. *Judgment under Uncertainty: Heuristics and Biases*. New York: Cambridge University Press.

Kahneman, Daniel, and Amos Tversky. 1972. "A Subjective Probability: A Judgment of Representativeness." *Cognitive Psychology* 3: 430–54.

Koffka, K. 1935. *Principles of Gestalt Psychology*. New York: Harcourt, Brace and World.

Kohlberg, L. 1981. *The Philosophy of Moral Development*. San Francisco: Harper and Row.

Lakatos, I. 1978. *Mathematics, Science, and Epistemology*. Cambridge and New York: Cambridge University Press.

Levy, Matthew. 1996. "Reason and Rationality." University of California at Irvine, working paper.

Mansbridge, Jane (ed.). 1990. *Beyond Self-Interest*. Chicago: University of Chicago Press.

Mead, George H. 1934. *Mind, Self, and Society*. Chicago: University of Chicago Press.

Monroe, Kristen Renwick. 1996. *The Heart of Altruism: Perceptions of a Common Humanity*. Princeton: Princeton University Press.

——. 1995a. "Psychology and Rational Choice Theory." *Political Psychology* 16, 1: 1–22.

——. 1995b. "The Psychology of Genocide." *Ethics and International Affairs* 9: 215–39.

——. 1994a. "A Fat Lady in a Corset: Altruism and Social Theory." *The American Journal of Political Science* 38, 4: 861–93.

——. 1994b. " 'But What Else Could I Do?' A Cognitive-Perceptual Theory of Ethical Political Behavior." *Political Psychology* 15, 2: 201–26.

Monroe, Kristen Renwick, with Lina Haddad Kreidie. 1997. "The Perspective of Islamic Fundamentalists and the Limits of Rational Choice Theory." *Political Psychology* 18, 1: 119–42.

Myers, Milton. 1983. *The Soul of Economic Man*. Chicago: University of Chicago Press.

Nussbaum, Martha C. 1986. *The Fragility of Goodness: Luck and Ethics in Greek Tragedy and Philosophy*. Cambridge, New York: Cambridge University Press.

Petracca, Mark P. 1991. "The Rational Actor Approach to Politics: Science, Self-Interest, and Normative Democratic Theory." In K. R. Monroe (ed.), *The Economic Approach to Politics: A Critical Reassessment of the Theory of Rational Action*. New York: Harper Collins, pp. 171–203.

Putnam, R. 1993. *Making Democracy Work: Civic Traditions in Modern Italy*. Princeton: Princeton University Press.

Rosenberg, Shawn W. 1991. "Rationality, Markets, and Political Analysis: A Social Psychological Critique of Neoclassical Political Economy." In K. R. Monroe (ed.), *The Economic Approach to Politics: A Critical Reassessment of the Theory of Rational Action*. New York: Harper Collins, pp. 386–404.

——. 1988. *Reason, Ideology, and Politics*. Princeton: Princeton University Press.

Shepsle, Kenneth A. 1995. "Statistical Political Philosophy and Positive Political Theory." *Critical Review*, 9, 1–2 (Winter–Spring): 213–22.

Taylor, Charles. 1989. *Sources of the Self: The Making of the Modern Identity*. Cambridge: Harvard University Press.

Taylor, Michael. 1995. "Battering Rams." *Critical Review* 9, 1–2 (Winter–Spring): 223–34.

——. 1987. *The Possibility of Cooperation*. Cambridge: Cambridge University Press.

Tversky, Amos, and Danie Kahneman. 1974. "Judgment Under Uncertainty: Heuristics and Biases." *Science* 185: 1124–31.

West, Rebecca. 1941. *Black Lamb, Grey Falcon: A Journey Through Yugoslavia*. New York: Viking Press.

Williams, B. 1981. *Moral Luck: Philosophical Papers*. Cambridge and New York: Cambridge University Press.

Wilson, James Q. 1993. *The Moral Sense*. New York: The Free Press.

Wittman, Donald. 1991. "Contrasting Rational and Psychological Analyses of Political Choice: An Economist's Perspective on Why Cognitive Psychology Does Not Explain Democratic Politics." In K. R. Monroe (ed.), *The Economic Approach to Politics: A Critical Reassessment of the Theory of Rational Action*. New York: Harper Collins, 405–32.

CONTRIBUTORS

Gabriel A. Almond was educated at the University of Chicago and has taught at Brooklyn College and at Yale, Princeton, and Stanford universities. A fellow of the American Academy of Arts and Sciences, the American Association for the Advancement of Science, the American Philosophical Society, and the National Academy of Science, he was awarded the James Madison Award by the American Political Science Association in 1981. Almond was president of the American Political Science Association and served on the board of directors of the Social Science Research Council. His numerous publications include *A Discipline Divided: Schools and Sects in Political Science; Progress and Its Discontents; Comparative Politics: Systems Process Policy; Crisis, Choice and Change; The Civic Culture; The Politics of the Developing Areas;* and *The American People and Foreign Policy.*

David Easton was educated at the University of Toronto and at Harvard University. He has taught at Harvard University, Queens University in Canada, and the University of Chicago, where he is the Andrew MacLeish Distinguished Service Professor Emeritus. He currently is Distinguished Professor of Political Science in the Department of Politics at the University of California, Irvine. He is a fellow of the American Academy of Arts and Sciences, of which he was vice-president from 1984 to 1989. Among his many honors, he enjoys membership in the Royal Society of Canada, served as chair of the Board of Trustees of the Academy of Independent Scholars from 1979 to 1981, and served as president of the American Political Science association for 1968–1969. His numerous publications include *The Political System: An Inquiry into the State of Political Science; A Framework for Political Analysis; A Systems Analysis of Political Life; Children in the Political System; The Analysis of Political Structure;* and *The Development of Political Science: A Comparative Survey.*

Murray Edelman taught at the University of Illinois and the University of Wisconsin, retiring in 1990. His chief interests are political language and symbolism and empirical theory. His books include *The Symbolic Uses of Politics, Constructing the Political Spectacle,* and *From Art to Politics.*

J. Peter Euben is Professor of Politics at the University of California, Santa Cruz. He is the editor of *Greek Tragedy and Political Theory,* co-editor of *Athenian Political Thought and The Reconstitution of American Democracy,* and the author of *The Tragedy of Political Theory* and *Corrupting Youth: Political Education and Democratic Culture.*

Bernard Grofman is Professor of Political Science and Social Psychology at the University of California, Irvine. He is a specialist in the theory of representation. His major fields of interest are American politics, comparative election systems, and social choice theory. He is the co-editor of *Choosing an Electoral System; Electoral Laws and Their Political Consequences; Information Pooling and Group Decision Making; The Federalist Papers and the New Institutionalism; Controversies in Minority Voting: The Voting Rights Act in Perspective,* and *Quiet Revolution: The Impact of the Voting Rights Act in the South, 1965–1990.* He is the editor of *Information, Participation & Choice: An Economic Theory of Democracy in Perspective; Political Gerrymandering and the Courts,* and *Legislative Term Limits: Public Choice Perspectives.*

John G. Gunnell received his Ph.D. from the University of California at Berkeley. He is currently Professor of Political Science at the Graduate School of Public Affairs, State University of New York at Albany. His areas of scholarship include various aspects of political theory, the history of political science, and the philosophy of social science. His latest book is *The Descent of Political Theory: The Genealogy of an American Vocation.* His other works include *Between Philosophy and Politics: The Alienation of Political Theory; Political Philosophy and Time: Plato and the Origins of Political Vision; Political Theory: Tradition and Interpretation;* and *Philosophy, Science, and Political Inquiry.*

Russell Hardin was educated at the University of Texas in Austin, where he was elected to Phi Beta Kappa. He received his Ph.D. from MIT and was a Rhodes scholar at Oxford, a National Fellow at the Hoover Institute and an Earhart Fellow. He has taught at the University of Chicago, where he was the Andrew Mellon Foundation Professor. He is currently Professor of Politics at New York University. His books include *Morality Within the Limits of Reason; Collective Action; Rational Man and Irrational Society?;* and *One for All: The Logic of Group Conflict.*

Edward J. Harpham is Associate Professor of Government and Political Economy at the University of Texas at Dallas. He received his BA from Pennsylvania State University and his MA and Ph.D. from Cornell University. He has taught at the University of Houston and the University of Texas at Dallas and was vice president of the Southwestern Political Science Association for 1993–1994. Harpham is the author and editor of numerous articles and books in the fields of political theory, public policy, and American government, including, with Anthony Champagne, *Texas at the Crossroads; John Locke's Two Treatises of Government: New Interpretations;* and *Reading in Texas Politics.* He is currently engaged in two research projects: a series of articles on the political economy of Adam Smith and a book on economic and political development in the United States.

Nancy C. M. Hartsock is Professor of Political Science at the University of Washington. She is the author of *Money, Sex, and Power: Toward a Feminist Historical Materialism* and is working on a manuscript entitled *Postmodernism and Political Change.* She is also part of the associate editors group for *Signs: Journal of Women in Culture and Society.*

J. A. Laponce, former president of the International Political Science Association, was educated at the Paris Institut d'Etudes Politiques and UCLA, where he received his Ph.D. His many honors include being a Killam Fellow and a John Simon Guggenheim Fellow. He has taught at the University of Santa Clara, now teaches at the University of Ottawa and at the graduate school of Arizona State University in Nagaoya, Japan, and is on the faculty at the University of British Columbia. His books include *The Protection of Minorities; The Government of France Under the Fifth Republic; People Versus Politics; Left and Right: The Topography of Political Perceptions;* and *Languages and Their Territories.*

Theodore J. Lowi has been the John L. Senior Professor of American Institutions at Cornell University since 1972. He received his Ph.D. at Yale and taught at Cornell and the University of Chicago. Professor Lowi has contributed to the study of politics in a variety of areas, and in a survey of members of the American Political Science Association he was named the political scientist who made the most significant contribution during the 1970s. He has written or edited a dozen books, among them *The Pursuit of Justice* with Robert F. Kennedy and the highly influential *The End of Liberalism. The Personal President—Power Invested, Promise Unfulfilled* won the 1986 Neustadt Award. His most recent book is *The End of the Republican Era.* Lowi is a fellow in the American Academy of Arts and Sciences and was appointed the French-American Foundation's Chair of American Civilization in Paris. Professor Lowi has served as president of the Policy Studies Organization and as first vice president of the International Political Science

Association. He served as vice president of the American Political Science Association for 1985–1986 and president in 1990.

Kristen Renwick Monroe was graduated with honors from Smith College and received her MA and her Ph.D. from the University of Chicago. She is the author of *The Heart of Altruism: Perceptions of a Common Humanity* and *Presidential Popularity and the Economy* and is the editor of *The Economic Approach to Politics: A Critical Reassessment of The Theory of Rational Action* and *The Political Process and Economic Change.* She has taught at the State University of New York at Stony Brook, the University of British Columbia, New York University, and Princeton University. She is Professor of Politics and Associate Director of the Program in Political Psychology at the University of California at Irvine.

William H. Riker, past president of the American Political Science Association, was educated at DePauw University and received his Ph.D. from Harvard. He taught at Lawrence University and at the University of Rochester, where he was the main force behind the development of what became known as the Rochester school. His many honors include honorary degrees from Uppsala University in Sweden, DePauw University, and the State University of New York at Stony Brook and membership in the National Academy of Science and the American Academy of Arts and Sciences. His many works include *The Theory of Political Coalitions; Liberalism Against Populism: A Confrontation Between the Theory of Democracy and the Theory of Social Choice; The Art of Political Manipulation; Federalism: Origin, Operation, Significance;* and *The Development of American Federalism.* Professor Riker died shortly after this piece was written; our thanks to Mrs. Riker for allowing us to publish it.

Ian Shapiro is Professor of Political Science at Yale. He has written extensively on democracy, distributive justice, and the methodology of the social science. His most recent books are *Pathologies of Rational Choice,* with Donald Green, and *Democracy's Place* (Cornell University Press, forthcoming).

Alexander Wendt is Associate Professor of Political Science at Yale. His interests are in international relations theory, social theory, and the philosophy of social science, and he has published a number of articles on the social construction of identity in international politics. He is currently finishing a book, *Social Theory of International Politics,* forthcoming from Cambridge University Press.

Catherine Zuckert is a professor of political science at Carleton College, Northfield, Minnesota. Her writings include *Natural Right and the American*

Imagination and *Postmodern Platos: Nietzsche, Heidegger, Gadamer, Strauss, Derrida*.

Michael Zuckert is the Edward and Dorothy Congdon Professor of political science at Carleton College, Northfield, Minnesota. His works include *Natural Rights and the New Republicanism* and *The Natural Rights Polity*.

INDEX

Gosnell, Harold, 193, 220
Gould, Thomas, 137n.9
Gourevitch, Peter, 270n.7
government: sustained growth in United
    States, 249. *See also* state, the
governmental orientation, versus policy
    orientation, 77–78
graduate curricula, German model for, 49
Grafstein, Robert, 303n.70
Gramsci, Antonio, 258
Grawitz, Madeleine, 90
Greece, ancient: Arendt and Strauss on,
    149, 151, 164n.38; drama as political in-
    stitution, 121; Funeral Oration of Peri-
    cles, 127; politics as men's concern in,
    232, 237; Socrates, 151, 214; Sophists,
    121, 131, 140n.40, 214; Thrasymachus,
    203; Thucydides, 127, 199; women's
    place in, 122, 139n.33. *See also* Aristotle;
    Oedipus Tyrannos; Plato
Green, Donald P., 136n.1, 296, 298nn.22,
    26, 299n.33
Greenstein, F., 90
Grofman, Bernard, 4
Grossholtz, Jean, 232
group membership, 287–88, 294
group theory, 103, 111n.2, 202, 205
Gruberg, Martin, 244n.2
guidance, political, 60
Gunnell, John G., 3–4, 41n.1, 67n.1

Habermas, Jürgen, 121
Hacking, Ian, 185n.5
Hall, Peter A., 270n.7
Hammond, Thomas, 81
Handbook of General Psychology, 95
Handbook of Political Science (Greenstein and
    Polsby), 90
Hankin, James, 301n.48, 303n.72
Hardin, Russell, 7–8
Harpham, Edward J., 8–9, 253
Harre, Rom, 180
Harsanyi, John, 300n.44
Hartsock, Nancy C. M., 8, 236–38
Hartz, Louis, 249
Harvard University, 192
Hattam, Victoria, 262
Hawkesworth, M., 90, 93–95
Hayek, Friedrich, 211
Heclo, Hugh, 262
Hegel, G. W. F., 210, 280
Heidegger, Martin, 148, 149, 153, 159,
    164n.38, 183
Heider, Fritz, 298n.23
Hempel, Carl G., 299n.36
hermeneutics, 109, 170

Herring, Pendleton, 221–23, 224, 225
heuristic value of theories, 285
higher-order political structure, 219, 229
Hirschman, Albert O., 296, 302n.62
historicism, 146, 150, 151, 222, 280
Hobbes, Thomas: and fallacy of composi-
    tion, 214; on interest of all in stable or-
    der, 206; on power as sovereignty, 160; as
    rational choice theorist, 203, 210; read-
    ing seventeenth-century England into na-
    ture, 136n.5; on scope of politics, 152; so-
    cial contract, 239; state in thought of,
    251–52; subfield citations, 94, 95
holism, 39–40, 89, 181
Howard, M. C., 256
human actor: actor-centered approach, 18,
    23; in behavioralism, 15, 18; in postbehav-
    ioral political science, 18–23; in rational
    actor model, 21–23, 27–32; in Weberian
    intentionalism, 20–21; Weber on study
    of, 20. *See also* human agency; rational ac-
    tor models
human agency: agents discovering not creat-
    ing their identities, 291; rational choice
    theory assuming, 283, 284, 301n.54. *See
    also* human actor
human behavior: aggregate behavior, 20;
    altruism, 28, 29, 289, 292; ambivalence
    model of, 302n.55; collective action, 294;
    deducing others' intentions, 289,
    301n.54; economic gain and social accep-
    tance as explaining, 300n.44; ethical
    political acts, 289, 291–92; perspective
    theory of, 289–94; as programmed se-
    quences, 302n.55; reason in, 19; as rela-
    tional, 176; scientific method applied to,
    19, 20; situational and contextual con-
    straints on, 287; as text, 35–36. *See also*
    behavioralism; regularities in human be-
    havior
human nature: as basis of political science,
    9; culture and institutions affecting, 279,
    280, 287, 295; as multifaceted, 287, 295;
    reality of, 279–80; and self-interest, 281–
    85, 297n.7; social science assuming, 280;
    static conceptions of, 136n.5; theories as-
    suming a particular view of, 101, 108–10
human perfectibility, 263–64, 265–66
Hume, David, 94, 203, 206, 210, 303n.65
Humpty Dumpty problem, 37–38, 125
Husserl, Edmund, 148–49
Hutcheson, Francis, 290, 303n.65
Hutchins, Robert Maynard, 10n.12, 46n.62,
    84n.17, 192
Hyneman, Charles, 73
hyperfactualism, 61, 145, 146

identity: conflicting identities, 290; consciously held values superseded by, 290;
and control and predictability, 288; as discovered not created, 291; ethics arising
from, 290, 293; fluidity of, 303n.75; genetic and early childhood factors in, 291;
individual and social, 290; literature on
construction of, 303n.72; perception of
self in relation to others, 289–94
ideology: behavioralists on, 15; conceptual
framework compared with, 110; ideological basis of scientific inquiry, 32–34; instrumentalism underwriting, 67; Lane's
study on excluding women, 235; objectivity claims as, 119; rational choice theory
as, 284, 300n.42; the state as ideological,
263; veiled promotion of, 104–6
indeterminacy, 286
individualism, methodological. *See* methodological individualism
induction: and abstract approach to political science, 88; versus deduction, 76; in
survey and opinion research, 21
inequality, 109, 156, 238
inferentiality, 289, 301n.54
informational theories, 197
Information and Legislative Organization
(Krehbiel), 196–98
Inkeles, Alex, 224
input-conversion-output model, 225,
226–27
institutions: actual behavior of, 31, 45n.42;
and amalgamation of tastes, 194; human
nature shaped by, 279, 280, 287, 295;
Marxism on, 220; public choice theory
on, 220; and rational choice theory, 220;
in republican theory of the state, 267;
rules in, 30–31
instrumentalism: critical literature on,
69n.43; as deconstructing itself, 67; in
economics, 65; and empirical testing,
286, 299n.36; ideology underwritten by,
67; of Lasswell, 56; in rational actor
model, 66; rationality as interpreted by,
27; social science as interpreted by, 53–
54; the state view instrumentally, 256–
57; theory as interpreted by, 64–67,
145–46
intentionalism, Weberian, 20–21
intentionality, 289, 301n.54
intentions: assumptions about, 200; deduc-
ing others', 289, 301n.54; rational choice
theory as intentionalist, 200, 204
interests: the common interest in politics,
30; in distributive policies, 198; empirical theories serving, 104; facts as involv-

ing, 145; in history of political thought,
214; in individualism and structuralism,
210; individual versus group, 205–6; long-
term interest, 28; in Marxism, 6, 104,
171, 174–75; in pluralism, 194; public interest, 205–6, 252; and the state, 260. *See
also* self-interest
*International Bibliography of Political Sci-
ence,* 90
international interaction game, 198–99
International Political Science Abstracts, 90
International Political Science Association, 90
international relations, 36, 95
interpretive analysis, 20, 21, 280
interpretivism: behavioralism distinguished
from, 170; Marxism criticized by, 170;
positivism contrasted with, 170; in postbehavioral phase, 16; realists rejecting, 6;
unmasking as impossible for, 173
InterUniversity Consortium for Political Research, 193
Isaac, Jeffrey, 173

James, Scott C., 262
James, William, 157
Jessop, Bob, 256, 258
Johns Hopkins University, 49, 50
Johnson, David B., 270n.8
Johnson, Lyndon, 246n.17
Johnson-Laird, Phillip N., 302n.60
Johnston, David, 302nn.55, 60
journalism, 78
jurisprudence, 267
justice: compared with truth by Rawls, 153;
Easton on, 153; rational modeling in
Rawls's theory of, 22; social justice, 79,
84n.21; women in theories of, 240–41
Justice, Gender, and the Family (Okin), 240
justification, 155

Kahnemann, Daniel, 298nn.22, 23
Kant, Immanuel, 94, 95, 157, 303n.65
Kaplan, Abraham, 57–58
Kardiner, Abram, 224
Kariel, Henry, 254
Katzenstein, Peter J., 261, 270n.7
Katznelson, Ira, 262
Keat, Russell, 185n.6
Kelly, Rita, 233, 245n.9
Keohane, Nannerl, 232
Key, V. O., 7, 193, 220, 222, 224, 252
King, Dave, 81
King, Gary, 81
King, J. E., 256
knowledge, globalization of, 39–40

McDonald, Terrence J., 262
McIntyre, Alasdair, 144
Mead, G. H., 298n.24
Mead, Margaret, 224
meaning, postmodernism on, 35, 158
men: citizenship and manhood, 238–40;
"man" including women, 137n.8; politics
as concern of, 232, 237, 246n.17
Merriam, Charles, 51–53; Chicago School
under, 192; empirical processual approach of, 221, 224; on empirical theory,
52, 54; on political theory, 52, 54; systems approach in, 221
methodism, 122
methodological individualism: Bhaskar's argument against, 179; in history of political thought, 214; on individuals and aggregates as differing, 205; in rational
choice theory, 176, 212–13; a realist argument for, 180; revolution as explained by,
213; versus structuralist political economy, 210–12; structurationist opposition
to, 176–77
methodology: empathic understanding
method, 19, 20, 32; *Oedipus Tyrannos* illu-
minating, 115; in postbehavioral phase,
16; questions outstanding for postbehavioralists, 20, 27–36; Rice's inventory of
social science, 55–56. *See also* methodological individualism; scientific method
Michels, Robert, 224
microeconomics, 202, 206
middle-range theories, 26, 219
Migdal, Joel S., 260, 261
Miliband, Ralph, 256–57
military service, and citizenship, 239
Mill, John Stuart, 239, 252, 297n.8
Miller, Warren, 193
Millett, Kate, 165n.53
Mills, C. Wright, 254, 257
Mintz, Beth, 257
Mission, The (film), 279
modeling, formal. *See* formal modeling
Monroe, Kristen Renwick, 9, 270n.8,
297n.7, 300n.38
Moore, Barrington, 212
Moore, G. E., 303n.65
moral realism, 185n.13
moral sense, 289, 290, 302n.65
moral theory (ethics): behavioralists making ethical evaluations, 62; ethical acts as
instinctual not conscious, 290; ethical
naturalism, 171, 174; ethical political
acts, 289, 291–92; ethics arising from
our central identity, 290, 293; in Foucault, 137n.13; justification of moral judgments, 155; ought implies can, 208; posi-

tivism on objective ethics, 174; rational
actor model in, 22, 215; and science for
Rawls, 154–55; social science developing
from, 49. *See also* values
Morgenstern, Oskar, 203
Morgenthau, Hans, 148
Morton, Rebecca, 81, 85n.32
Mosca, Gaetano, 59, 90
motherhood, 239–40
motivations, 289
Moyers, Bill, 246n.17
Mueller, Dennis C., 270n.8
multidisciplinary training, 38

Nagel, E., 42n.4
national government, sustained growth in
United States, 249
National Science Foundation, 46n.62
naturalism, ethical, 171, 174
naturalistic fallacy, 149
needs, versus desires, 301n.46
Nelson, Barbara, 242, 243
neobehavioralism, 13, 40–41
neoclassicism, public choice, 264, 270n.8
neo-Marxism. *See* Marxism
neopositivism, 34
neo-Weberian state theory, 259–63; agendas of, 261; and human perfectibility,
264; public policy in, 260, 262–63; regime theory, 261, 270n.6; on state building, 261–62
Nettl, J., 260
New Deal, 148, 163n.32, 253, 262
"New Revolution in Political Science, The"
(Easton), 41n.1, 42n.4
Nietzsche, Friedrich, 119, 146, 153, 158
nihilism, 36, 150
NLRB v. Jones and Laughlin Steel, 265
Nobel Prizes, 91–92
nomothetic (covering law) model of explanation, 32, 65, 286, 299n.36
Nordlinger, Eric A., 260
normative fallacies, 208–9
normative political theory: as compatible
with science for Rawls, 153; and empirical political theory, 47, 75–76; intentionality in, 301n.54; and rational choice theory, 213, 215, 300n.42
norms, social, 45n.40, 81, 218n.32, 220
Nozick, Robert, 144
Nussbaum, Martha, 121, 138n.24, 303n.68

objectivity: aiming to escape ties to place
and people, 119; as APSA goal, 50; and
ideological bias of scientific method, 33,
34; and positivist fact-value distinction,
57; possibility in political science, 8, 109,

303n.65; and rational choice theory, 206, 210; in state theory, 203, 251, 252; subfield citations, 94

Smith, Brewster, 222

Smith College, 281

social action, transformation model of, 179–80, 186n.24

social capital, 81

social change: individual actor in, 20; political science as means of, 53; understanding versus, 78–79

social choice theory: instrumentalist interpretation of, 66; and rational actor/choice theory, 136n.1; Riker's discovery of, 201

social contract, 239

social control: Merriam on, 52; as social science's purpose, 54

socialization theory, and comparative politics, 8

social justice, 79, 84n.21

social norms, 45n.40, 81, 218n.32, 220

social psychological theories, 109

social realism, critical, 179

social science: human nature assumed in, 280; instrumentalist interpretation of, 53–54; mass society fostered by, 152; meeting human needs as purpose of, 60; methodological individualism in, 176; as objective institution, 57; philosophy of science influencing, 82n.11; postmodernism in, 36; realism assumed in, 284; as resting on value assumptions, 63; Rice's inventory of methods in, 55–56; scientific method in attacked, 145; social control as purpose of, 54; sources of American, 49; speculation as suspect in, 53. *See also* economics; political science; psychology; social theory; sociology

Social Science Research Council, 43n.22, 55, 222, 250

Social Security, 242, 253, 259

social solidarity, and self-interest, 30

social theory: critical theory, 109, 280; definition of, 168; empiricism's corrosive effect on, 181; rational adjudication among theories, 182. *See also* political theory

society-centered approach, 18, 23

Society for Experimental Economics, 85n.33

Society for the Advancement of General Systems Research, 107

sociology: articles quoted in political science journals, 92, *93;* core of attention lacking in, 95; interdisciplinary links

with political science, 91, *92;* postmodernism in, 36; power based on techniques of, 160; structural-functionalism derived from, 108; women in, 244n.3

Socrates, 151, 214

solidarity, self-interest and social, 30

Sophists, 121, 131, 140n.40, 214

Sophocles. *See Oedipus Tyrannos*

sovereignty, 160

specialization, 14, 37–38, 44n.27, 46n.62, 125

spectator in the theater, as model for political theory, 116, 122–23

speculation, 51, 53, 63

Sphinx, riddle of the, 5, 116–17, 126–27, 136n.8, 137n.9

Staatslehre, 48, 55

Stacey, Judith, 231–32

state, the: as corporate actor, 23; growth of national government, 249; as ideological, 263; individual's relation to, 302n.56; instrumentalist view of, 256–57; multitude of meanings of, 25; neo-Marxist theory of, 255–59, 263; neo-Weberian theory of, 259–63, 264; nineteenth-century idea of, 54; as not coterminous with politics, 147; as object of inquiry for political science, 48, 52; as orienting concept for political science, 17–18, 25–26, 89, 95, 250, 251–55, 265; and public policy, 8–9, 267–68; as relatively autonomous, 23, 43n.20; republican theory of, 250–51, 263–69; sovereignty, 160; *Staatslehre,* 48, 55; structuralist theories of, 257–58, 269n.5; totalitarianism, 60, 164n.40; tyranny, 140n.46; value-concepts in definitions of, 147; Weber's definition of, 260; welfare state, 237, 241–43, 246n.15, 262

state actor model, 23

state building, 261–62

state-of-nature theory, 297n.7, 300n.40

statistics, 193

Stepan, Alfred, 260, 261

Sterett, Susan, 262

Steward Machine v. Davis, 265

Stokes, Donald, 193

Stone, Clarence, 261

Strauss, Leo, 149–51; ancient Greece as interest of, 149, 164n.38; at Chicago, 149–50; liberalism criticized by, 59; and phenomenology, 148–49, 163n.35; as revivalist, 144, 148; on science for Heidegger, 153; on totalitarianism, 164n.40

Straussians, 281, 283

structural-functionalism: as framework for

Compositor: J. Jarrett Engineering, Inc.
Text: 10/12 Baskerville
Display: Baskerville
Printer and Binder: BookCrafters, Inc.